Stealing the State

Russian Research Center Studies, 89

Published under the auspices of
the Davis Center for Russian Studies
Harvard University

Stealing the State

CONTROL AND COLLAPSE
IN SOVIET INSTITUTIONS

Steven L. Solnick

Harvard University Press

Cambridge, Massachusetts

London, England · 1998

Library of Congress Cataloging-in-Publication Data
Solnick, Steven Lee.
    Stealing the state : control and collapse in Soviet institutions /
Steven L. Solnick.
        p. cm. — (Russian Research Center studies ; 89)
    Includes bibliographical references and index.
    ISBN 0-674-83680-4
1. Institutional economics—Case studies.
2. Organizational change—Soviet Union.
3. Soviet Union—Social conditions—1970–1991.
4. Political culture—Soviet Union.
5. Perestroika.
6. Soviet Union—Politics and government—1985–1991.
I. Title. II. Series.
HB99.5.S64   1998
338.947—dc21   97-13909

For my parents

Acknowledgments

Though they bear no responsibility for the faults of the final product, many individuals have contributed to this work.

This book began as a dissertation, and I must first express my gratitude to my advisers: Timothy Colton, Jorge Dominguez, and Samuel Huntington. At different junctures along the way—during the writing of the dissertation and since—each has offered invaluable encouragement or inspiration. When the collapse of the Soviet Union upset the original research design, their quiet faith that I would sort things out gave me the confidence to strike out into unexplored territory.

The fieldwork for the book was primarily conducted during two lengthy stays in Russia. The first, an exchange with the Soviet Sociological Association, was sponsored by the International Research and Exchanges Board (IREX) and the Social Science Research Council. The second, at Moscow University, was a Fulbright-Hays Fellowship, administered by IREX. The research would have been impossible without this support, and I acknowledge it gratefully. I want to add my special thanks to the IREX program officers who provided both logistical and moral support through some good times and some very bad times, particularly Liz McKeon, Karen Kiesel, Todd Weinberg, Carol Erickson, and Paula Ramalay.

The writing of the dissertation was generously supported by a Kukin/Pew Fellowship at Harvard University. I also owe extensive debts to the officers and staff of both the Russian Research Center (now the Davis Center for Russian Studies) and the Center for International Affairs at Harvard. For several years I loitered happily between these two great communities, and I appreciate the hospitality and the indulgence of all concerned.

While revising the manuscript, I enjoyed the support of both the Harriman Institute at Columbia University and the Kennan Institute for Advanced Russian Studies in Washington. The administrators and researchers of both institutions provided moral and intellectual encouragement beyond the call of duty. I am particularly grateful to Laura Sheahan, Kate Blumenreich, and Leslie Powell for research assistance. I am also grateful to the Hoover Institution at Stanford University for providing support during the final stages of editing.

Despite some of the conclusions of this study, I must confess to having had terrific luck in finding dedicated and sincere officials at several Soviet agencies, libraries, and institutes. The staff at the archives of the Young Communist League (Komsomol) not only provided me with 95 percent of everything I requested to see, but also fed me and offered a daily dose of tea and biscuits. I must also give special thanks to Rein Vöörmann and Jaak Uueküla of the Estonian Academy of Sciences for proving that world-class social science was attainable within the Soviet borders.

Without minimizing the help provided by all the individuals who consented to be interviewed for this study, I must acknowledge several contributions that proved indispensable: Maria Ivanovna Kirbasova supplied her personal files for me to photocopy, while Dzhakhan Pollyeva and Victor Minin were equally helpful opening doors. Marina Kozorezova at the Institute for State and Law clarified murky legal issues, and Mikhail Topalov of the Institute of Sociology guided me through the world of Soviet sociology. Finally, Vladimir and Olga Sloutskii made life in Moscow more bearable and more comprehensible during those long hours when the research was going nowhere.

No thoughts of Moscow are complete without mention of my support network of fellow researchers: Susan Bronson and Joel Hellman offered intellectual stimulus as well as true friendship. So did Scott Bruckner, Mike McFaul, Julie Newton, Rob English, Lisa Tucker, Phoebe Brown, Joe Schull, Jo Andrews, Sarah Mendelson, Scott Parrish, and several others who deserve to remain anonymous. These friends are responsible for many of my best Moscow memories, even those that involved Finnish breakfast cereal.

Finally, I must give special thanks to those individuals who helped shape the written work that follows. Mark Beissinger helped set the ball rolling (though he thought it was heading somewhere else) and Bill Zimmermann helped keep it moving. Brian Silver and Barbara Anderson offered a crash course in survey design and interpretation. Blair Ruble provided insightful advice at several key junctures. Sayres Rudy, Kellee

Tsai, Lisa Anderson, and two anonymous reviewers read the entire manuscript and offered valuable suggestions and advice. In addition to those already named, the following individuals provided helpful comments on drafts of various chapters: Tom Bernstein, Andrew Cortell, Rick Ericson, Thane Gustafson, Bill Jarosz, Bob Jervis, Ira Katznelson, Bob Keohane, Julianne O'Connor, Maeve O'Connor, Ron Rogowski, Ken Shepsle, Regina Smyth, Dorothy Solinger, Debora Spar, Jack Snyder, and Mark von Hagen.

Portions of Chapters 2 and 7 appeared in "The Breakdown of Hierarchies in the Soviet Union and China: A Neoinstitutional Perspective," *World Politics* 48, n. 2 (1996); I am grateful to Johns Hopkins University Press for permission to use that material here.

It is customary to conclude with effusive thanks to friends and family. My debt to them is too great to summarize briefly, however, and I'm sure they'd all prefer I just stopped writing.

Contents

Tables and Figures

Introduction

In the early years of the Stalin regime, a group of editors of the satirical magazine *Krokodil* set out to ridicule the industrial bureaucracy. The conspirators created a mythic organization, dubbed "The All-Union Trust for the Exploitation of Meteoric Metals." The group managed to procure an official seal for the venture and printed official-looking stationery listing a board of directors chosen from Russian comic literature.

Letters were sent out on this stationery to a number of Soviet trusts, offering them metal from meteors that were due to fall in Central Asia on certain dates already known to the All-Union Trust for the Exploitation of Meteoric Metals. The letters stressed the superior quality of the metal on offer, and replies soon began to pour in from all over the country. Zara Witkin, an American engineer who later heard of the episode, recounted the responses in his memoirs:

> In exchange for some of this precious meteoric metal, the Furniture Trust offered complete equipment for the offices of the vast organization of the "Society for the Exploitation of Meteoric Metals." The Automobile Trust offered to exchange cars for metal. The State Phonographic Trust felt that the hardships of the expeditionary parties to be sent by the society to recover the meteors from Central Asia would be so great that they offered phonographs and records.[1]

Armed with these offers, the group was able to secure a large line of credit from the State Bank for the purposes of "expansion of their organization." The scam finally came to a halt when the band imprudently attempted to convince the Deputy Commissar of Heavy Industry to use these bank funds to construct a large factory. Lazar Kaganovich, Stalin's deputy, was reportedly amused by the prank, but he forbade *Krokodil* from ever describing it in print.

Objectives of This Book

The story of the Meteoric Metals Trust illuminates some of the factors that ultimately led to the disintegration of the Soviet system, but it also deepens its mystery. Quite obviously, logic or common sense played little role in routine decision making from the earliest days of the Soviet regime. Procedures and documentation mattered far more than any sort of Weberian rationality in guiding the behavior of policy makers: a seal and some official stationery were adequate proof that a nonsensical ministry actually existed. It seems a marvel, therefore, that a system so complacently accepting of its own artificial reality could have survived decades of inescapably real challenges like war, famine, and crash industrialization. It seems equally puzzling that the altogether less ominous challenge of internal reform—a challenge surmounted several times before in Soviet history—could lead to its fragmentation and ultimate collapse.

This book asks why the reforms of the perestroika era caused Soviet institutional structures to break down rather than to adapt or evolve. It is not the first book since 1991 to offer an explanation of the Soviet collapse, nor is it likely to be the last. It is motivated, however, by two broader goals: to employ insights from the non-Soviet literature on institutions to create a model of Soviet disintegration and to use the Soviet case in turn to enrich and extend general theories of institutional behavior.

Most of the current literature on the demise of the Soviet system proceeds from the macro level, stressing such factors as economic inefficiency, inept leadership, international competition, moral bankruptcy, or institutional rigidity. These analyses look at the Soviet system as a whole, evaluating its strengths and weaknesses against a changing background of domestic and international challenges. From this perspective, however, the Soviet collapse appears overdetermined: any of these factors seems capable of bringing down the *ancien régime*. As Adam Przeworski has noted, "It is easier to explain why communism had to fall than why it did."[2]

Surprisingly few analyses of the Soviet collapse have looked inside the State Furniture Trust or the other vast bureaucracies that came to crowd the Soviet landscape. This is particularly vexing, since these structures began to disintegrate almost as soon as perestroika was launched. This book looks within these institutions to offer and test an alternative theory of the collapse, utilizing insights from neoinstitutional theory. It argues that the Soviet system did not fall victim to stalemate at the top or to a revolution from below (though elements of both were present) but rather to opportunism from within. The decisive blow to the Soviet state and economy came from disintegration of structural controls that kept "the typical soldier or policeman or bureaucrat" loyal to the state.[3] Once the *servants* of the state stopped obeying orders from above, its fate was sealed.

This book is not intended merely as an "application" of neoinstitutional theory to the Soviet case, however. It also has the more ambitious goal of extending the reach of general theories of hierarchy and control in large organizations. Economic theories of institutions were not formulated for cases like the Soviet or post-Soviet reforms. The neoinstitutional paradigm emerged to explain what structural form organizations will take in response to a given set of conditions and how different conditions will produce different organizational structures. These models tend either to be static or to utilize comparative statics; little attention has been devoted to the actual dynamics of organizational creation, collapse, or transformation.

In this book, I describe how standard elements of neoinstitutional analysis like monitoring schemes, information flow, property rights, and authority relations can also interact dynamically, resulting in dramatic shifts in organizational form. The Soviet case demands a new evaluation of some of the fundamental assumptions of neoinstitutional models, propelling them into uncharted territory and offering exciting new directions for the development of theory.

The Approach

As the preceding section suggests, this book departs from traditional elite- or society-centered approaches in attempting to understand why *and how* the Soviet system collapsed between 1986 and 1991. The Soviet state and economy consisted of a vast linked network of hierarchical institutions. Hierarchy is a standard element of any planned system, from capitalist firms to government bureaucracies. However, the pervasiveness of hierarchical organization that accompanied Stalinist central planning became both a hallmark and a defining feature of Soviet-style Communism. This distinctive institutional blueprint was responsible for Samuel Huntington's evaluation of Communist states in his 1968 classic *Political Order in Changing Societies:* "They may not provide liberty, but they do provide authority; they do create governments that can govern."[4]

This study, which might well have been subtitled "Political Change in Ordered Societies," looks within the hierarchies that constituted the Soviet system to explore when and why Soviet bureaucracies lost the capacity to govern. Just as the concept of "authority" stood at the heart of Huntington's notion of governmental robustness, it also features prominently in my account of hierarchical fragility. At first subtly, and then momentously, bonds of authority within Soviet hierarchies were eroded by the reforms launched by Mikhail Gorbachev. Once the links within the hierarchical chain were broken, the hierarchy itself ceased to function as it had for decades. As the case studies in this book suggest, hierarchical breakdown was not a consequence of some broader "collapse" of the Soviet system but rather constituted the systemic collapse itself. Any explanation of the collapse, therefore, must begin with an analysis of the nature of power and authority within Soviet bureaucracies.

To look within Soviet bureaucracies, I employ a framework that focuses on choices made by individual decision makers within a hierarchical setting. This rational choice approach allows empirical testing of modified hypotheses drawn from institutional economics against those derived from more "traditional" analyses of Soviet (and post-Soviet) politics. While the latter theories emphasize the key role of ideology, interest groups, or leadership, the former assign a greater weight to individual opportunism and institutional incentives.

Any actor-centered framework is extremely data-hungry, and for decades the closed Soviet system resisted even the most concerted efforts to look within Party and government institutions. This book utilizes data sources that became available in the late 1980s—demographic data, surveys, interviews, and archival documents—to reexamine the nature of hierarchical authority during periods of stability as well as breakdown. I focus on three distinct policy-making institutions, all of which dealt with the mobilization of the younger generation of Soviet citizens. The common focus on youth enhances comparability among the three cases; as discussed in Chapter 3, it also provides a set of cases that offers strong tests for hypotheses derived from both traditional and neoinstitutional theory.

Though the goals of this analysis are broad, I hope to be clear at the outset about its limitations. This is not a book about "why Gorbachev happened." Nor is it really about why reform happened, though it does help explain why reform *didn't* happen in the wake of earlier initiatives that left institutional incentives largely untouched. Instead, this study discusses why—once Gorbachev initiated reforms that changed the incentive structure facing midlevel and local bureaucrats—the institutions that constituted the Soviet system collapsed instead of adapting.

The Basic Argument

Two elements are central to any description of intraorganizational dynamics in a hierarchical setting. First, we must examine the preferences of individual decision makers. In traditional Sovietological theories, these preferences were either assumed to reflect those of the top political elite (as a consequence either of careful elite recruitment or ideological indoctrination) or to reflect interests of distinct groups in society. These perspectives framed much of the protracted colloquy over totalitarian and pluralist models of the Soviet policy process. This book admits a third perspective, usually confined in Soviet and post-Soviet studies to analyses of the industrial planning system: that individual bureaucrats were primarily self-interested and highly opportunistic in pursuit of that self-interest. Their opportunism was chiefly limited by the authority of their bureaucratic supervisors, whose property rights over organizational assets were clear. When either authority relations or property rights eroded, institutional collapse was unleashed.

The second central element of organizational dynamics is the nature of monitoring and sanctions within the hierarchy. Soviet organizational structure determined not only lines of authority but also the flow of information up and down the bureaucratic hierarchy. Local officials controlled what information reached their supervisors. Just as artificial "Potemkin villages" hid the squalid countryside from traveling tsars, plan fulfillment reports obscured the true state of Soviet economic and social relations from Moscow planners. General Secretaries determined to make their own observations found contemporary versions of Potemkin villages thrown up for their benefit. For instance, when Mikhail Gorbachev, newly selected as Party leader, decided to observe for himself conditions in a local hospital, he found "the beds . . . occupied by healthy, well-fed security officers [from his own security detail] with closely cropped hair, who warmly commended the medical staff and the hospital food, while finding it difficult to be precise about their ailments."[5]

Control over information is a critical factor in understanding the behavior of the bureaucrats who fell for the Meteoric Metals trap. Letters bearing an official seal were accepted as fact because no bureaucratic rules mandated that these facts be verified or even that they make sense. The same uncritical acceptance was applied to data from any "official" source: the editors of *Krokodil* obtained their seal in the first place by planting a bogus advertisement in a local paper seeking a lost seal and then offering the ad to an official at the State Rubber Stamp Trust as proof the stamp needed to be replaced.

Institutional responses—offers of automobiles or furniture or phonographs—emerged automatically from a rational calculation of costs and benefits (the metal was to be of unusually high quality, after all) based on wholly irrational inputs. Perhaps most important, despite the pervasive controls imposed by the planned economy, bureaucrats in the Furniture or Automobile Trusts still had the latitude to redirect resources to an unanticipated folly like the quest for meteoric metals. In other words, outside the rigid domain of the Plan's specific targets, controls were virtually nonexistent.

The case studies at the heart of this book reveal that half a century later individual bureaucrats in the institutions under investigation were still manipulating the formalized system of information flow to pursue private agendas, with little regard for the practical consequences of their actions. In particular, the pervasive system of concrete performance targets offered local and branch managers extensive latitude in running their daily affairs, provided they were able to meet, on paper at least, their regular performance targets. Equally important, local bureaucrats generated the reports on which their own performances were monitored and evaluated by superiors. For much of Soviet history, this arrangement provided the lubricant in the klunky machine of central planning, permitting the economic, political, and social systems somehow to function despite the shortcomings of the central plan.

Ironically, once Gorbachev attempted a limited decentralization, these same institutional attributes promoted institutional collapse. The initially modest fiscal and organizational reforms of 1986–87 made it even easier for bureaucrats to circumvent supervision by higher echelons of the organizational hierarchy. Local bureaucrats receiving new discretionary budgetary authority found themselves able to opportunistically pursue self-interested agendas. Institutional resources were openly employed to generate private gains or to defy threats of sanctions.

When officials at the tops of organizations proved unable to control the activities of their subordinates, they invited doubts about what resources they still controlled. These doubts spread the erosion of authority within the organizational structure, as local officials who were still loyal began to wonder whether their subservience might leave them completely disenfranchised if the center collapsed. Ill-fated attempts to reassert central control—for example, in the Baltic states—only exacerbated the crisis by offering further proof of the center's weakness.

Ultimately, at precisely the juncture where the effectiveness of policy reforms depended upon a coherent institutional response, local officials defected en masse and the pillars of the Soviet system crumbled. In effect, Soviet institutions were victimized by the organizational equivalent of a colossal "bank run," in which local officials rushed to claim their assets before the bureaucratic doors shut for good. As in a bank run, the loss of confidence in the institution makes its demise a self-fulfilling prophecy. Unlike a bank run, the defecting officials were not depositors claiming their rightful assets, but employees of the state appropriating state assets.

From this perspective, the image of a "disintegrating" state can be seen as seriously incomplete. Soviet institutions did not simply atrophy or dissolve but were actively pulled apart by officials at all levels seeking to extract assets that were in any way fungible. Where organizational assets were more specific to their particular use by the state, as in the case of draft boards, for example, hierarchical structures proved more resilient. Where organizational assets were chiefly cash and buildings, hierarchical breakdown was almost total. At both ends of the spectrum, the catalysts of state collapse were the agents of the state itself. Once the bank run was on, these officials were not merely stealing resources *from* the state, they were stealing the state itself.

The dynamics of Soviet institutional decline hold important lessons for cases beyond the Soviet Union and for the broader literature on authority and control in large organizations. For instance, this study refutes the conclusion advanced by many students of the Soviet and Chinese transitions that economic reforms need to precede political reforms; this book argues that political stability cannot be viewed as exogenous to the process of economic transitions. Even more broadly, it suggests how bureaucratic insubordination in one division of any large organization might—under particular conditions of uncertain asset ownership and highly constrained information flow—unleash a chain reaction of defiance or defection. It also suggests why that chain reaction occurs so rarely.

Outline of the Book

The first two chapters of the book present a general framework for analyzing hierarchical organization in Soviet-type systems. Within this framework, I compare and contrast different explanations of the nature of hierarchical authority and control. Chapter 1 examines traditional views of the sources of Soviet control, including the roles of ideology, interest groups, and leadership. Chapter 2 considers perspectives drawn from Western theories of the firm, stressing the importance of opportunism, information, and monitoring. In each chapter, I first discuss how these theories accounted for "normal" Soviet policy processes prior to Gorbachev and how they subsequently account for institutional collapse. For each set of theories, I offer hypotheses that can be used to test the predictions of theory against the empirical data from specific cases.

Chapter 3 discusses why a study of policies affecting youth offers a strong test of these hypotheses. Youth were at the same time a key target of ideological indoctrination, a likely source of social unrest, a high priority for Soviet leaders, and the focus of several dedicated policy-making institutions. Thus, youth-policy case studies offer a strong test of ideological, interest-group, leadership, and neoinstitutional theories. After reviewing the notion of a Soviet "youth program," I also consider the lack of evidence for ideological or social-upheaval explanations in any of the case studies.

Chapters 4 through 6 present these case studies in some detail: Chapter 4 offers an analysis of the crisis and subsequent collapse of the Communist Youth League (Komsomol), an organization which, at its peak, counted over 40 million Soviet youth as members. Chapter 5 discusses the policy of *raspredelenie,* a system of mandatory job placements for all university and institute graduates. In Chapter 6, I discuss the system of universal male conscription; the draft is a particularly interesting case because, unlike the other institutions considered, the military hierarchy survived the transition, though not intact.

Chapter 7 reviews the case studies and considers which of the hypotheses of the earlier chapters are supported by the evidence. I conclude that the degrees of organizational collapse observed in the case studies are best understood as organizational "bank runs" triggered by individual actors seeking security or profit in a period of heightened uncertainty. In the second part of Chapter 7, I suggest how this analysis helps us understand the outcomes of reform in other Soviet institutions and probe why decentralization in China did not trigger a similar organizational bank run.

The concluding chapter investigates some of the broader implications of the theory of hierarchical breakdown developed in earlier chapters. Returning to the broader themes of governance and stability at the heart of this study, I explore potential consequences for theories of imperial breakdown, state strength, corruption, democratic governance, and corporate restructuring. I also consider the implications of this analysis for reforms and reformers in the post-Soviet environment, where information flows and property rights within hierarchies remain ambiguous at best.

1 | Control and Collapse: Reformulating Traditional Approaches

"Obedience is what makes government."

—EDMUND BURKE, *Speech on Conciliation with America*

An effective theory of institutional collapse must begin by explaining how institutions functioned prior to their collapse. What factors determined the behavior of the individuals who populated the massive Soviet bureaucratic machine? How much control did supervisors really have over the decisions of their subordinates and, conversely, how much discretion did bureaucrats enjoy to ignore controls placed on them?

In this chapter, I introduce an actor-centered framework for comparing institutions and employ it to refashion traditional theories of Soviet institutional behavior. For each of these sets of theories, I consider how they might account for the institutional breakdown and suggest hypotheses that can be used to test the validity of these alternative explanations. In the next chapter, I use the same framework to develop a "neoinstitutional" explanation of these same phenomena.

Recasting such different theories in the same analytical framework entails risks but provides important benefits. On the one hand, deconstructing traditional models to reveal the embedded assumptions about actors' preferences and constraints demands a reinterpretation of these models with which the original authors may disagree. The resulting straw men can only approximately represent the scholarship from which they are drawn. On the other hand, such an exercise is essential to achieving comparability of theories. In this manner, theories originally formulated to explain steady-state policy making in the Soviet Union and organizational structure in large, stable corporations can yield testable hypotheses about the ultimate collapse of the Soviet system—which neither set of theories explicitly addressed.

By utilizing a common framework, I hope to achieve two goals of comparative politics often alluded to in the abstract: "portability" of theories beyond their originating cases and theory-testing that discriminates among contending explanations by evaluating which *best* describes observed outcomes. The ultimate goal of this analysis, therefore, is not to find the single "true" explanation of the Soviet collapse but rather to determine which contending model of the collapse does a better job explaining the details described in the case studies.

A Framework for Analyzing Institutional and Policy Change

The framework used in this study might be thought of as a microeconomic (or even, in Arrow's terms, "nanoeconomic") approach to describing complex decision processes. Since it lacks much of the rigor of a conventional microeconomic model, however, this approach will be designated as "microinstitutional."[1] The chief merit of such an approach is that it permits empirical investigation into one of the central puzzles of the Soviet collapse: why did Gorbachev's reforms apparently cause mid- and lower-level Soviet bureaucrats to abandon decades-long patterns of subordination and defy the authority of their institutional bosses?

Within this framework, an organization can be defined as a structure for achieving a collective result in which the actions of each member are constrained by certain decisions made by other members.[2] Institutions comprise one or several organizations sharing a policy domain.[3] The microinstitutional approach makes two principal observations about any institution that formulates or implements policy: decisions are made by individual actors, and organizational structure shapes the decision environment of these actors.

Methodological Individualism and Utility Maximization

The simple statement that decisions are made by individual actors reflects two fundamental principles of any rational choice framework: methodological individualism and utility maximization. In other words, the behavior of an institution can be reduced to the aggregate behavior of individuals at all levels of that institution, each of whom bases specific decisions on the perceived costs and benefits to her of alternative courses of action.[4]

While the principle of methodological individualism is straightforward—policy is made by individuals within institutional settings—the principle of utility maximization requires some scrutiny. As March and Olsen write, our understanding of political outcomes at a system level is formed by our understanding of how individuals, pursuing certain axioms of behavior, interact in the aggregate: "We make assumptions about individual consumers to understand markets, about voters to understand politics, and about bureaucrats to understand bureaucracies."[5]

Individual actors have complex utility functions. They may have certain preferred policy outcomes given their professional assignments, but these may occasionally conflict with preferences concerning their careers (e.g., desire for advancement) or personal lives (e.g., desire for privileges or material benefits). Any analysis of organizational performance (including collapse) must address "the connection between the purposes of members of organizations and the purposes of their organizations."[6] Implicitly or explicitly, therefore, such an analysis would require some theory of individual preference formation.

Furthermore, an individual's perceptions of the likely outcomes of alternate actions are not fixed. Rules set or changed by higher levels of the policy-making bureaucracy can alter the options available to street-level actors, as well as the perceived costs and benefits of these options. Under certain circumstances, individuals may conclude that the benefits of defecting from the organization outweigh the potential costs. Their subsequent behavior may reveal their "true" preferences, hidden until then behind a veil of compliance to organizational authority.[7]

Hierarchy and Authority

As the preceding discussion indicates, organizational outputs result from a process that takes place simultaneously and sequentially on several levels. The case studies in this book will focus not only on the top tiers of organizations but also on the lowest level of policy-making bureaucracies, which we might label the "street level."[8] Only at the street level do decisions directly affect the physical world, for here policy principles are turned into action. Higher levels in the organization can affect decisions at lower levels, but actual interactions with citizens (or clients or customers) occur only at the street level. Street-level actors are most often found within local or branch units of hierarchical organizations, as opposed to the purely policy-making "center."

A bureaucratic organization is characterized by a "hierarchical" structure: lower levels of the organization are *subordinate* to higher levels. The hierarchy therefore defines an authority structure in which actors at lower levels accept the power of actors at higher levels to issue orders.[9] When this power to issue orders is eroded, the hierarchy collapses.

Though the concept of hierarchical authority appears straightforward, it merits careful attention. Higher levels of an organization can never completely determine the actions of lower levels; they can, at most, influence final outcomes by recruiting compatible subordinates and making defiance of authoritative decisions exceedingly costly. In fact, actors at lower levels potentially have great power in hierarchical settings: they have access to more specialized information about their assigned tasks than their managers have, and the process of actually imposing sanctions on subordinates is complex and costly. Since all directives emanating from bureaucratic actors require implementation by lower levels of the hierarchy, we might well call higher-ranked actors "dependent" on their subordinates, at least to some degree.[10]

In most Western firms, hierarchical authority is reinforced by the legal system, which preserves the right of employers to dictate work standards and to fire unsatisfactory employees. In nonfirm hierarchies, the lines of authority become somewhat more convoluted. Public bureaucracies, for instance, control the vast resources of the state, including its instruments of coercion. Actors in any public bureaucracy may therefore receive delegated power that is binding even over their principals. Thus, Attorneys General may investigate Presidents or Congressmen, and KGB officers may undermine Party bosses.

The last example above actually glosses over an important distinction of Communist (and post-Communist) systems. The authority of an Attorney General to investigate public servants is created by the Constitution and enforced—and limited—by the judicial branch of government. In the Communist system, there was no third-party adjudicator of jurisdictional conflicts. The perpetuation of links of authority within organizations depended critically upon lower levels of those organizations continuing to acknowledge that authority. As Oliver Williamson has observed, "Hierarchy is its own court of ultimate appeal."[11]

If we are to understand hierarchical breakdown, therefore, we must understand the bases of authority before the breakdown and why they were eroded. This is a particularly difficult task, since the nature and locus of power in any bilateral relationship is often revealed only in periods of conflict. As Arrow has noted, "When conditions are stable, the role of authority . . . is taken for granted and is little questioned."[12]

Power and Control in Soviet Institutions: "Traditional" Theories

The bases of hierarchical control in Soviet institutions are particularly difficult to analyze because there had been no open challenges to the power of the top Party leadership since Stalin. As noted in the introductory chapter, most studies of the Soviet collapse have neglected the dynamics of power and control at mid- and lower levels of the bureaucratic hierarchy. In fact, though much of traditional "Sovietology" concentrated on explaining policy making within Soviet institutions, even this literature tended to treat institutions themselves essentially as black boxes.[13]

Upon close examination, these traditional approaches to Soviet politics reveal different assumptions about the roots and strength of authority within Soviet hierarchies. For instance, some authors assumed that ideological indoctrination or cultural conditioning led subordinates to accept or even embrace hierarchical patterns of control; other theorists portrayed these bureaucracies as direct channels for interest articulation or policy implementation, implying that hierarchical controls were firm and enforced.

Similar assumptions motivated many accounts of Soviet collapse. Breakdown of institutional control was either neglected or portrayed as a byproduct of macro-level dynamics of crisis or revolution. In 1990, for instance, Mancur Olson observed that "since even the most awesome despotisms often rest on nothing more than a shared perception of their guards and administrators, they are, paradoxically, close to disorder and even anarchy."[14] In response, Eugene Huskey and others attempted to recast the actions of midlevel bureaucrats as consequences of developments elsewhere in the system:

Doesn't your argument rest on the tautology that a government falls because a government ceases to be the government? Isn't the really interesting and important issue how it gets to that point? . . . Revolutions do occur when the government relaxes its controls and becomes more flexible, as de Tocqueville said, but why does it do this? Because nice guys come to power? Because of crises that it perceives? Because of pressure from below? This is where the masses come in.[15]

Huskey's comment points to the main poles of debate that dominated the Sovietological literature for decades: elite politics ("the government relaxes its controls") and social forces ("pressure from below"). In this traditional view, bureaucrats and administrators themselves are not independent agents of change.[16]

In a postmortem on Sovietology, George Breslauer argued that the division of the literature into "top down" or "bottom up" models was inaccurate and oversimplistic.[17] Nevertheless, Breslauer's own typology of "alternative futures" suggested by that literature relied heavily upon theoretical "images" of elite polarization and societal assertiveness.[18] Any role for "differentiation within the apparat" was considered as a corollary of elite polarization.[19]

The minimal independent role assigned by Sovietology to bureaucrats and administrators is striking, and an alternative view will be offered in the next chapter. In the remainder of this chapter, however, I will risk reductionism by grouping traditional theories of Soviet politics into those emphasizing the role of ideology, elite politics, and interest groups. These sets of theories incorporated different assumptions about degrees and mechanisms of control over bureaucrats, and, by extension, how those controls became ineffective. By looking at the real beliefs and behavior of bureaucrats in Chapters 3–6, I intend to put these implied theories of collapse to an empirical test.

Ideological Decay

Several authors have linked the systemic crisis of the Soviet system to ideological decay. Alexander Dallin, for instance, argued that Gorbachev's role as the catalyst of reform was decisive because he "put an end to the claim there was one single truth."[20] Rasma Karklins similarly suggested that when Gorbachev ended the Party's monopoly over media and ideology he unleashed the chain reaction that destroyed the "organizational control by the CPSU."[21]

These and other analyses stress the impact of ideological decay on mass political beliefs and behavior.[22] How does ideology affect actors within institutional settings? How might relaxation of ideological controls lead to an organizational crisis?

As I have already suggested, a microinstitutional framework makes no necessary assumptions about the formation of actors' preferences. Theories contending that ideology (or culture) influences the formation of actors' individual preferences are entirely compatible with the microinstitutional framework and its fundamental assumption that decision making is essentially individualistic.[23]

To argue that ideology provided a source of institutional stability, therefore, is to suggest that actors shared similar preferences as a consequence of screening or ideological indoctrination. This convergence of preferences should produce a coincidence of individual and institutional goals. In most theories, socialization and ideological indoctrination of the Soviet elite were assumed to be more or less uniform across different organizations and presumably more intensive than at the mass level.

If ideological controls limit the individuals' motivation to defy the regime, either at the mass level or within state institutions, then other structural controls become slightly less important. Even the totalitarian model recognized that control over society would be impossible without the mobilizing power of ideology.[24] Though totalitarian analyses placed fundamental emphasis on the Party's channels of monitoring and control, they also emphasized the regime's successful programs of socialization and indoctrination—in other words, their shaping of individual preferences at all levels of the system. Socialization and indoctrination, if successful, lower the cost to the regime of maintaining control. The logic of the argument then suggests that—since indoctrination made structural reforms less critical—the failure of ideological controls left Soviet institutions especially vulnerable to collapse.

Implicit in this argument is that state and Party bureaucracies should have had a higher share of "true believers" than did the mass citizenry.[25] Later studies of Soviet officials, however, including Party *apparatchiks*, have downplayed the role of ideology in determining their policy preferences.[26] If the role of ideology was marginal, though, how could the regime's abandonment of Communist orthodoxy have contributed to the loss of control over its own institutions?

Ultimately, this is an empirical question. If the loss of control over hierarchies stemmed from a crisis of ideology, then ideology should have played an important role for the officials within those hierarchies before political reforms were initiated. We can, therefore, test the validity of the "ideological decay" model of collapse by investigating the following hypothesis:

H1.1: *Mid- and lower-level bureaucrats exhibited significant levels of ideological conformity* prior *to the breakdown of hierarchical control.*

In Chapter 3, this hypothesis is evaluated against data on the beliefs of those officials involved in planning and implementing all components of the Soviet youth program.

Elite Politics

Much of the literature on the Soviet policy process tended to treat policy formulation as subordinate to and instrumental in the competition for power among leadership factions. As Brzezinski and Huntington said, "Policy-making in the Soviet Union is not nearly as distinct and identifiable as it is in the United States. Instead, it is one aspect of the struggle for power and is absorbed into it."[27]

Many analysts followed the lead of Brzezinski and Huntington in describing Soviet policy initiation as "trickle down."[28] Policy initiatives were formulated by the Party's Central Committee, resources were then mobilized by the Party, and the Party monitored compliance. This scheme was implicit in many of the earliest studies of the Soviet policy process: even if Party leadership was not portrayed as monolithic, changes in policy, and ultimately institutional performance itself, were seen as the result of factional struggles played out among the top leadership. In Carl Linden's phrase, Soviet leadership politics was "the terrain of battle."[29]

This preoccupation with the influence of the top leadership was also present throughout the lengthy controversy over whether the Soviet system under Brezhnev or Khrushchev could be described as "pluralist." At the center of this debate was the role of certain elite groups (like policy experts) or quasi-autonomous administrative entities (like specific Ministries) in the making of policy.[30] The chief conclusion of most of these analyses was that "outside" (i.e., non-Party) actors may have played some role in debates over policy formation but that final decisions over policy were still reserved for Party leadership. Equally important from the microinstitutional perspective, these analyses assumed that, whatever the nature of the preceding policy debate, actions of bureaucrats at the street level were chiefly guided by the authoritative decisions taken at higher levels.[31]

I will cite just a few examples: Schwartz and Keech described the opposition of educators and parents to Khrushchev's 1958 education reform proposals, but they noted that "insofar as groups influenced the outcome of this issue it was through the communication of their expert judgments to people at the top of the hierarchy who *were* in a position to influence outcomes."[32] In the same vein, Thane Gustafson's discussion of the role of specialists in resource management policy also concluded that ultimate decision-making authority was reserved by the leadership, and "the Soviet expert . . . is clearly on tap, not on top, however much he may be useful or necessary."[33]

While most analyses of the Soviet policy process left the story at the stage of policy pronouncement, at least two mechanisms (beyond ideological conformity, discussed above) were implied as explanations of why actors at the street level implemented leadership policy. The first of these assigned the Party, with its extensive network extending deep into the social structure, the task of enforcing compliance. It was assisted in this task by the two oft-cited "transmission belts": the trade unions and the Communist Youth League. These networks, it was hypothesized, monitored policy implementation and guaranteed that leadership policy was followed. In other words, they effectively constrained the alternative courses of action available to individual bureaucrats at the street level of organizations.

A complementary mechanism for ensuring leadership power relied on purging bureaucrats who lacked explicit bonds of loyalty to the leadership; this was the "personnel weapon." Soviet politics was notoriously clientelistic, and systems of personnel management like the *nomenklatura* and the "circular flow of power" guaranteed that a new General Secretary of the Party could replace Party cadres at lower levels with loyal protégés. These officials, in turn, would have control over all significant personnel appointments in their bureaucratic neighborhood. Rather than manipulating bureaucrats' available options, the leadership could manipulate the bureaucrats themselves.

If leaders did indeed control the policy process down to the street level at least into the Brezhnev period, we should expect to see this reflected in the behavior of actors at the street level. Decisions by the top leadership should produce results and should decisively resolve policy disputes among subordinates. In addition, actors at the policy-making and street levels of analysis should show signs of responding to leadership signals about desired policy outcomes. Conversely, actors at these levels should not be observed acting "spontaneously," independent of any change in directives emanating from higher organizational levels. In other words, if "elite-led" models of Soviet politics are valid, the following hypothesis should hold:

H1.2: Actions of mid- and lower-level bureaucrats prior to the breakdown were determined by, or at least consistent with, instructions from higher levels of the bureaucracy. Commands from above were implemented, at least in large part.

A preoccupation with elite politics at the expense of attention to destabilizing forces from within state institutions has influenced much analysis of the Soviet collapse and, more broadly, of regime transitions. Tom Remington, in a sympathetic review of Sovietology, acknowledges a "theoretical bias in the direction of stability" in accounts of prereform and even reform politics.[34] The more general literature on "transition to democracy" has almost exclusively focused on pacts and coalitions among the top elite, though these players are occasionally portrayed acting on behalf of social constituencies or in response to social unrest.[35]

Even Phil Roeder's explicitly "new institutionalist" theory of the Soviet collapse pays only limited attention to actors below the Central Committee level.[36] Though Roeder claims to "stand apart from the biographical approach,"[37] his account of the Gorbachev era focuses almost entirely on Politburo politics, albeit with some Politburo members linked to broader constituencies. He offers a theory of coalitional politics at the level of the top leadership, a shift in essence from a "great man" approach to a "great men" approach.[38] Disintegration of institutional hierarchies finds no explicit place in this theory.

If elite institutional breakdown was ultimately just a manifestation of coalitional struggles among the elite, we should be able to see evidence of this even at the street level. This can be formulated as a separate hypothesis, related to H1.2 above:

H1.2a: Once breakdown began, divisions within the administrative bureaucracy mirrored divisions among the elite.

Since theories that focused on elite conflict left little room for improvisation by lower-level officials, their preferences are rarely considered by many of the theorists referred to above.

Societal Interests

When autonomous preferences were attributed to street-level actors in the Soviet Union, they were often the preferences of societal interests. Some authors trace the disintegration of the state order to the growing power of these interests, either through the activity of autonomous groups ("civil society") or as represented by actors within the bureaucratic hierarchy ("societal capture").[39] This perspective on the collapse is also captured in Martin Malia's comment: "The attack on the Union came in a vast movement from below in 1990–91."[40]

A well-established Sovietological approach linked actors' policy preferences to the influence of certain sets of societal interests. Applied to the early post-Stalin system, for instance, modernization theory suggested that "rational" politics could replace the "charismatic" rule of the Communist Party and its all-powerful dictator.[41] A similar logic has been applied to the Gorbachev transition, portraying Gorbachev the Reformer as a straightforward response to the pent-up demands of an urbanizing, industrializing, better-educated, increasingly cosmopolitan Soviet populace.[42]

Modernization analyses suffered from a functionalist flaw, however: while a correlation was shown between putative social demands and initial policy responses, the causal link between the two was often implied rather than proven. As suggested in the previous section, one well-documented means of affecting policy was to affect the decisions of the top leadership. Societal interests could either be articulated by proxy or directly.

Most often, interests were represented by policy "experts" who participated in the policy process. Moshe Lewin, for instance, argued that social scientists provided Gorbachev and his advisers with data on the growing degree of modernization in Soviet society and the need for policy adjustment to respond to this development.[43] Direct interest articulation was fairly rare in the Soviet state. One notable exception is discussed in Chapter 6: the lobbying effort by mothers of draftees to widen the availability of draft exemptions under Gorbachev. Other examples include parents' groups lobbying for educational reform under Khrushchev, the rise of environmental activism in the wake of glasnost', and the coal miners' strikes of the late 1980s.[44]

Social groups could also directly affect street-level policy—without necessarily forcing a reply from top leadership—by the simple act of noncompliance. Since the Soviet system relied heavily on mobilization for the implementation of most policy initiatives, bureaucrats at the street level may have found themselves confronted with instructions "from above" to take a certain action and a "constituency" of citizens whose behavior impeded this action. To take an example that will be discussed in Chapter 4, the reluctance of young people to voluntarily join the Komsomol forced local officials to either discard mandatory enrollment targets or disregard the league's policy of selective enrollment. Young people, through their aggregate behavior, could thus change policy without actually engaging in any coordinated collective action.

A comparable feedback loop was at the heart of many explanations linking economic decline and political change. In an elaborate version of this argument, Peter Hauslohner hypothesized that managers and bureaucrats kept the post Stalin welfare structure in place for workers despite its rising cost because they feared worker unrest. Gorbachev's program, he argued, was an effort to create new constituencies more representative of the changing social structure and to motivate them through new structures of benefits and incentives. Thus, according to Hauslohner, certain groups (the Brezhnev constituency of blue-collar workers) affected policy through the implicit threat of unrest, while other groups (white-collar and service-industry workers) affected policy by holding out the prospect of new support.[45]

Yet another mechanism linking policy preferences to societal interests is generational change. As the gerontocratic leadership of the Brezhnev years began to yield power, it was replaced by an elite generation that did not share its historical memory, social origins, or set of priorities.[46] At the very least, the new generation of leaders was expected to be more attuned to the differentiated social structure of Soviet society and to co-opt a new array of managers and bureaucrats at the street level to be responsible for policy implementation. Theories presenting this mechanism for change, however, assumed that generational experience (or social origins) were more decisive in shaping policy preferences than were ideological or political controls.[47]

In sum, then, interest-based theories suggest that mid- and lower-level bureaucrats either aligned their preferences with distinct societal interests or served as conduits for interest articulation to the top leadership. In either case, were these societal interests to be salient, the following hypothesis should be valid:

> *H1.3: Street-level bureaucrats prior to the breakdown monitored the demands of and policy impacts on distinct societal groups.*

Once hierarchical authority began to break down, the underlying loyalties of officials presumably became more significant. If street-level bureaucrats were—or became—aligned with distinct societal interests, competitive forces within the institutional hierarchy would be unleashed. If this theory is valid, then we should expect to observe the following:

> *H1.3a: Once breakdown began, divisions within the administrative bureaucracy mirrored divisions in society.*

Note that this hypothesis may prove incompatible with H1.2a above, offering a discriminating test between top-down and bottom-up theories of collapse. As I have already suggested, neither interpretation is well supported by the details of the case studies in this book.

Summary

In reviewing Sovietological approaches to explaining hierarchical breakdown, I have tried to interpret various images of the Soviet political system through the lens of the individual decision maker. Leaders cannot directly produce desired outcomes in the real world, since these emerge from actions at the street level of the policy process.[48] Our understanding of the causes of the collapse must begin with a clear theory of Soviet politics prior to the arrival of Gorbachev.

If ideology significantly influenced the preferences of street-level actors, then Gorbachev's abandonment of ideological orthodoxy may have contributed to a structural breakdown. If actors at the street level were consistently guided by leadership policies before the Gorbachev reforms, then elite stalemate or coalitional conflicts may have facilitated division or defection at lower levels. If street-level actors either represented or were captured by societal interests, then any weakening of hierarchical controls should have fragmented the institutional structure along these same cleavages.

Though Sovietology often treated its subject matter as *sui generis,* the theoretical perspectives discussed here are echoed in the comparative literature on regime change and nondemocratic systems. The elite-centered approach is dominant in much of the literature on transitions from authoritarianism, for instance, while society-centered approaches dominate theories of revolution and social movements. If these approaches are incomplete in capturing Soviet political dynamics, their dominance in the broader comparative literature may need to be reassessed. At the very least, such a finding would suggest that theories of elite pacts and social movements both would benefit from increased attention to dynamics *within* institutions of state administration.

In Chapters 3–6, I will present data on real decision processes within Soviet hierarchies before and after Gorbachev that allow a test of the hypotheses suggested by these contending views. First, however, I will consider theories that allow for the pursuit by bureaucrats of their *own* interests, which often conflict with those of their superiors or of groups in society.

2 | Control and Collapse: Neoinstitutional Approaches

"Politics: A strife of interests masquerading as principles. The conduct of public affairs for private advantage."

—AMBROSE BIERCE, *The Devil's Dictionary*

The theories discussed in the previous chapter imputed little motive or capacity for autonomy and defiance to lower levels of Soviet bureaucracies; they portrayed hierarchical control as being reasonably firm prior to 1985. In this chapter, I introduce an alternative model of Soviet-type hierarchies, incorporating insights of neoinstitutional economics. This model stresses the limits of hierarchical control in any organizational setting, and especially in a Soviet-type system.

According to this view, actors obeyed directives from higher levels because they were able to do so on their own terms—often in a manner that undermined the very policy goals they were supposed to be promoting. Far from being straight-jacketed by control mechanisms, actors used their control over the information reaching superiors to evade the often-incompatible demands of formal plan targets. Ironically, this formalization of performance measures made management possible in the absence of market signals; simultaneously, it made it possible for lower-level actors to appear to meet the unattainable targets of unrealistic plans without openly challenging their managers.

In this model, hierarchical breakdown results not from the sudden relaxation of comprehensive controls but rather from an incremental increase in the already wide discretion enjoyed by street-level actors. The model suggests that Soviet organizations collapsed not because they were too rigid but rather because they were too flexible.

Neoinstitutional Approaches to Hierarchy

In the neoinstitutional framework, organizations are essentially networks of contractual obligations in which employers attempt to force employees to act in a manner consistent with their (i.e., employers') interests.[1] Organizational structure emerges from the "competition among contracting schemes."[2] In particular, the contractual relationship at the heart of the present analysis is that between manager and employee, since that approximates the relationship between levels of any hierarchy.

In neoinstitutional theories, the roles of manager and employee are generalized as those of principal and agent. An agency relationship is said to arise "when a principal delegates some rights—for example user rights over a resource—to an agent who is bound by a (formal or informal) contract to represent the principal's interest in return for a payment of some kind."[3]

There are two chief determinants of the form and content of principal-agent contracts: the constraints of bounded rationality and the assumption of opportunism by either or both parties. These two elements—opportunism and bounded rationality—represent the chief departures of neoinstitutional theory from the neoclassical paradigm.[4]

Bounded rationality implies that decision makers operate with constraints on their access to information, on their ability to foresee the consequences of their actions, on their knowledge about the present or future actions of others, and on their capacity to fully process and use the data available to them. Consequently, no contract can comprehensively anticipate all potential contingencies; all contracts are to some degree incomplete.

Opportunism is an extension of the utility maximization assumption: individuals may pursue their goals at the expense of others by engaging in concealment, deceit, and other strategic behavior. In other words, actors display more than mere self-interest. They exhibit, in Oliver Williamson's phrase, "self-interest seeking with guile."[5]

In the contractual, or neoinstitutional, paradigm, the problem of opportunism is at the center of the analysis. Organizations are structured to define and enforce contractual constraints on the opportunism of employees.[6] Because of the limitations of bounded rationality, however, it is impossible to write contracts specifying ex ante all possible contingencies that could arise in the employer-employee relationship.[7] This problem is particularly insidious where information or actions known to employees are unknown to supervisors—a common condition in complex, specialized bureaucracies. Under such circumstances, with supervisors unable to predict all potential contingencies in advance and unable to observe all subordinates' activities contemporaneously, employees cheat.

It would be an exaggeration to claim that previous institutional analyses of Soviet politics wholly overlooked the significance of opportunism. Merle Fainsod's account of the Smolensk Party administration, for instance, showed in detail how local Party officials in the 1920s and 1930s pursued personal agendas of consolidating power, selectively embracing Moscow's campaigns as they suited their individual goals.[8] J. Arch Getty, using the same archives, traced the Great Purges to efforts to regain control over provincial Party bureaucracies, which were sliding rapidly into confusion and disarray. Getty portrays a Party that was "inefficient, fragmented, and split several ways by internal factional conflict."[9]

These tales of the opportunism driving local Soviet bureaucrats link their undisciplined behavior to periods of chaos or extreme dysfunction. From a theoretical vantage point, however, constraining opportunism is as critical in stable times as it is in times of crisis. More significantly, under certain circumstances, opportunistic actors may not simply profit from chaos but help to create it themselves.

A Basic Neoinstitutional Model

Any complex hierarchy can be thought of as a chain of linked principal-agent relationships in which "each individual in a hierarchical structure, except at the ultimate levels, is simultaneously a principal and an agent when rights are transferred down the organizational ladder."[10] In all but the most trivial agency relationships, agents know more about their own performance than do principals. The central problem in the theory of principals and agents is: how can managers control subordinates who have information or expertise they lack?[11]

Two types of agency problems arise from this information asymmetry: "hidden action" and "hidden information."[12] These correspond, schematically, to how hard the agent is working (hidden action) and what maximum output level is possible given random factors and the agent's structural constraints (hidden information).

Soviet-type central planning addressed hidden action by specifying precise output targets judged by planners to correspond to maximum effort and optimal utilization of given inputs.[13] Since these outputs (e.g., tons of steel or growth in organizational membership) could in theory be easily observed or verified, agents' overall efforts to pursue these targets could be assumed to be optimal. Though the mandatory planning system had its own high agency costs, these might be thought of as the inevitable price paid to direct and supervise bureaucrats in a system in which information asymmetries were pervasive and extreme.[14]

Meeting these mandatory plan targets, however, naturally became agents' sole objectives; nonmonitored activities were subordinated to plan fulfillment. Perversely, the very mechanisms created to address agency losses thus exacerbated problems of hidden action.[15] As a consequence, Soviet reforms (economic and otherwise) repeatedly redefined the set of target indicators both to minimize the adverse consequences of such goal displacement[16] and to develop a more easily monitored set of performance measures.[17]

The Soviet system also relied upon separate monitoring agencies to combat problems of hidden action. In general, monitoring organizations not only are expensive to set up and operate, but can also provoke costly reactions from agencies being monitored. These can range from the assignment of additional personnel to prepare the paperwork required by monitors to more elaborate schemes of deception or falsifying results. Hierarchies created expressly for monitoring will also suffer from the same problems of hidden information and hidden action as their subjects. The monitors thus also need monitoring, *ad infinitum.*

The Communist Party was often cited as the archetypal monitoring agency, providing performance reports through channels parallel to but supposedly independent of regular administrative hierarchies.[18] Local Party officials, however, often worked in the organizations they were supposed to be monitoring, creating obvious conflicts of interest.[19] More generally, Party officials were not disinterested monitors: their own career advancement most often depended on the successful performance of units in which they served, not on their accurate monitoring of those units. Consequently, Party monitoring often relied upon data supplied by the units under review; unannounced audits were (under Brezhnev, at least) highly unusual.[20]

Even if monitoring mechanisms were more effective, though, use of forcing performance targets still presumes reliable estimates of subordinates' actual performance *potential.* This potential, however, is hidden information, accurately known only by the agents themselves.[21] Furthermore, in any public bureaucracy, target-setting is complicated by the difficulty of measuring organizational outputs.[22] Public bureaucracies must not only develop a mechanism for assessing individual employees but must first devise a system for evaluating the overall output of the organization itself.

One alternative to guessing future performance capacities is to utilize information on the past performance of agents to set output targets. This approach, however, leads to the so-called "ratchet problem," in which principals continuously adjust targets to reflect the performance of the agent in the most recent period. This creates strong disincentives for agents to demonstrate their true productive potential.[23]

This ratchet effect has often been interpreted to mean that agents had little incentive (or faced disincentives) to innovate under central planning, but this is not entirely accurate.[24] Since agents had wide latitude over activities not covered by concrete targets, agents found it in their interest to improvise or innovate extensively to secure a "safety margin," *provided* this innovation did not become known to principals (who would use it to ratchet up performance targets). In fact, the system established powerful incentives for initiative on the part of enterprise managers or local officials, as long as they maintained control over the rate at which the effects of innovations became known.[25]

This manipulation of field-level performance data was possible because the central planning system was used both to set mandatory performance targets and to verify whether these targets were being met. The primary means of monitoring target compliance were reports filed by agents themselves. In practice, the Soviet planning system became the management framework for all economic and political actors (targets were set for *all* bureaucratic tasks, economic or otherwise). As Zaleski noted, "it seems more nearly correct to call the economy 'centrally managed' rather than centrally planned."[26]

Any new information about agents' ability to meet or surpass plan targets would force their renegotiation. This bargaining-like renegotiation went on continuously in all bureaucratic organizations, not just those devoted to industrial production. The tight control of agents over any evidence of surpluses gave rise to the benchmark rule of "planning to the level achieved," a pervasive manifestation of the ratchet problem.[27]

The prevalence of the "ratchet problem" suggests that contracting between principal and agent cannot be modeled as a one-shot operation.[28] If principal-agent relationships are dynamically modeled as a string of short-term agency contracts, subject to ongoing renegotiation, the problem then resembles an iterated game.[29] Within this framework, an effective incentive structure might be based upon agents' *average* performance over time, and repetition of the game can discourage shirking. There are important conditions, however: principals must be capable of committing to a long-term compensation mechanism, agents must neither discount future payoffs nor perceive limits to the duration of the agency relationship, and agents must lack access to external sources of credit.[30] Violation of the first condition gives rise to the ratchet problem; violation of the second and third conditions becomes more significant in times of reorganization or heightened uncertainty.

The discussion thus suggests the following hypothesis:

H2.1: Agents in Soviet hierarchies exploited information asymmetries to evade monitoring by principals.

It is important to note that this hypothesis implicitly contradicts one of the chief hypotheses (H1.2) that emerged in the last chapter: that is, mid- and lower-level bureaucrats were not simply instruments of the top elite but were able to pursue their own agendas.

Adjustments to Standard Neoinstitutional Frameworks

There are three broad areas for which the nature of hierarchical relations in Soviet bureaucracies demand a reconsideration of neoinstitutional propositions. In particular, I wish to reexamine some theoretical assumptions about property rights, risk-sharing, and asset specificity.

Property Rights. As noted in the preceding chapter, all hierarchical systems are authority structures. "An employment contract," according to Arrow, "is precisely a contract on the part of an employee to accept authority."[31] To say the principal has authority is to acknowledge that the agent *accepts* her power to issue orders—at least over a range of activities defined as the agent's "zone of acceptance."[32] As Holmstrom and Tirole have noted, however, "the rights of authority at the firm level are defined by ownership of assets, tangible (machines or money) or intangible (goodwill or reputation)."[33]

An agency relationship is based on the understanding that the principal *owns* and the agent *manages* any resources covered by the contract between them. The agent's ability to exercise temporary property rights over these resources (by convention, use rights, income rights, and transfer rights) depends fundamentally on the delegation of those rights from the principal.[34] Clearly delineated property rights allow the principal to actually transfer control over resources without sacrificing ownership. Thus, property rights determine more than just the distribution of the assets or resources; they frame the issues of power and control central to any hierarchical relationship.

In practice, all rights delegated through institutional hierarchies in Communist systems were based upon the assumption of unchallenged Communist Party hegemony. Top Party leaders could delegate authority for setting planning targets or approving personnel appointments to subordinate organizational levels because their ultimate authority—their ultimate "ownership" of all political and economic resources—remained unchallenged. In the absence of clear legal or procedural norms for third-party resolution of property rights conflicts (and the Soviet system clearly lacked these), the principle of ownership could only be demonstrated by the fact of control.[35] Property rights were rudimentarily defined by the hierarchical organizational structure, rather than the reverse.

In the standard principal-agent model described above, asymmetric property rights define the authority relationship between the two parties: principals can give orders because they own the assets in question. This authority asymmetry balances the information asymmetry favoring agents and permits the hierarchy to function predictably. In the Soviet system, by contrast, the authority of the principal to command the agent could only be confirmed by the agent's willingness to accept that authority. Insubordinate agents could, of course, be removed by force, but most cases of insubordination failed to warrant such a disruptive response.[36] Absent specific countermeasures from superiors, agents could easily begin to use the powers delegated to them *as if* they were their own. Thus, in most hierarchical settings within the Soviet system, we might well regard property rights—and therefore authority—to have been indeterminate.

There has been little attention in the literature on Soviet reform to the nature of property rights and authority relations *within* institutional hierarchies. Property rights reforms were rightly identified as a crucial first step in reducing agency costs, since any reforms that failed to assign market values to outputs would only raise monitoring costs in anticipation of new modes of opportunism.[37] The assumption remained, however, that property rights either were or could easily be made unambiguous, and therefore necessary reforms were essentially redistributive (i.e., the transformation of collective property into private property).[38] The potential impact of such reforms on the integrity of the hierarchical structures received little attention.[39]

Risk-Sharing. Application of principal-agent models to public bureaucracies also demands a reexamination of some of their assumptions concerning risk-sharing. In the standard model of the agency contract, the agent exchanges uncertainty over her compensation in return for making the principal the residual claimant to output from her labors.[40] (Of course, once "insured" against risk, the opportunistic agent loses much of her internal motivation to maximize output. This variation of the hidden action problem, associated originally with the provision of insurance, is known as "moral hazard.")

However, in a public bureaucracy there is no "residual."[41] Furthermore, bureaucracies in command economies generally faced "soft budget constraints": the state covered their operating losses.[42] Taken together, these observations imply that principals in the Soviet hierarchy were neither profit-maximizing nor budget-balancing.[43]

An important consequence of this abrogation of managerial discipline is the nullification of almost all downside risk for principals.[44] Standard agency theory assumes that their claim to the residual gives principals a real stake in uncovering agents' hidden information. This assumption must be questioned in the Soviet context. The lack of interest of even the top leadership in uncovering reliable performance estimates is nicely captured in the following anecdote from a Soviet journalist:

> I vividly remember Khrushchev, in my presence, reprimanding the head of the Central Statistical Department because of his "bourgeois objectivity" and dictating "appropriate" figures to him. Only such "appropriate" figures could create the impression that . . . economic life in the Khrushchev era seemed to be approaching Western standards.[45]

If principals are—or even if they believe themselves to be—insured against the risk of plan failure, they may have few incentives to aggressively develop better solutions to hidden information problems. Even at the top of the hierarchy, officials' *real* self-interest may frequently lie not in maximizing output but rather in preserving their privileged positions by simply appearing to maximize output.

Asset Specificity. Certain types of transactions are more amenable to hierarchic organization than others. According to Williamson, the primary factor driving the emergence of hierarchy is the "asset specificity" of the inputs.[46] This notion may also help explain the survival of hierarchy.

The concept of specificity refers to the availability of alternative uses of particular assets associated with the provision of organizational outputs.[47] Goods or services that can be easily and costlessly redeployed to other uses are more likely to be adequately provided through market-based contracting. Assets with few alternative uses, by contrast, require site- or use-specific investments of greater risk. Potential suppliers and producers are therefore more likely to seek to mitigate this risk through vertical integration. Assets may be specific for a variety of reasons, including immobility, uniqueness of design, or investments in training and even reputation.

Though generally used to account for the origins of vertical integration, a similar logic can be applied to the persistence or even the collapse of hierarchy. Jeffry Frieden, for instance, argues that owners of highly specific assets are more likely to lobby for protectionist policies, because they have the fewest options and therefore the most to lose from a sector-specific slump. A similar logic might be applied to actors within a hierarchy: actors within organizations employing highly specific assets are least likely to challenge hierarchical control because they are least likely to find alternative employment.

Money, for instance, is probably the least specific of all assets. Bureaucrats who shuffle funds could certainly do so in any of dozens of organizational settings. More important, funds can be moved from one organization to another. Property rights can easily become blurred. Bureaucrats who run railroads, on the other hand, have few potential employers to choose from. A railwayman cannot easily divert significant railway assets—or himself—to alternative uses.

Perhaps the most specific assets of all are bureaucratic rents—the appropriatable value associated with the right to regulate other transactions.[48] The right to grant exemptions from the draft, for instance, is extremely valuable in a conscription-based society and is wholly non-transferable in the event the officeholder is transferred to a different agency. Networks of patronage and mutual favors, on the other hand, are transferable.[49] The next section returns to this distinction between specific and nonspecific assets.

These embellishments on the standard assumptions of agency models begin to define a more dynamic variant of the principal-agent relationship, in which environmental characteristics like information asymmetries, property rights, authority claims, and risk-sharing are equally important but more subtly interrelated.[50] They set the stage for considering how the stable relationship of delegated authority depicted by the standard agency model can unravel until the principal can no longer control the agent. The contractual perspective on hierarchy enables us to evaluate how changes in either contract mechanisms or the contracting environment can lead to this unexpected outcome.

Explaining Institutional Change

In the principal-agent model of Soviet-type bureaucracies discussed above, principals' property rights over organizational resources (tangible and intangible) could be understood as ambiguous but unchallenged. This section considers challenges to those rights and potential responses to such challenges.

A Model of Collapse

Principals' property rights depend fundamentally upon agents continuing to abide by the agency contract and managing institutional assets in the principal's interests, rather than in those of the agent. If one agent was revealed to be in violation of this contract, and the principal was unable to remove those assets from her control, we might reasonably conclude that the principal no longer really "owned" the assets in question. The agent's behavior would have gone from shirking to outright appropriation. We might conclude that the principal could no longer exercise her authority over that agent to enforce their contractual arrangement, and other agents under contract to that principal might draw similar conclusions.

The process I am describing is, in many ways, the inverse of a bank run. A bank can be thought of as a single agent with multiple principals. When I place my money in a bank, I retain ownership but temporarily delegate control over those assets to the bankers. If I learn that another investor has been denied access to her account—or even if I believe this is about to happen—this reveals for me some hidden information about the health of the bank. I rush to reclaim my assets, but so does everybody else. The bank fails, leaving all investors poorer, even though the bank might have survived if we had not all panicked.

Now consider the inverse case: I am one of several agents managing different shares of a single principal's assets (call him Andrei). Facing hidden action and hidden information problems, Andrei has designated specific performance targets for us to meet; as long as I successfully meet these targets (or at least convince Andrei that I have met them), my use of my share of his assets is largely unmonitored. I may choose to use Andrei's assets to employ my friends and to rob a store monthly to meet my target, keeping the surplus and including a fictitious report of virtuous investments to keep Andrei happy.

If I now learn that a second agent—call her Zena—has stolen Andrei's money without any reprisals, I face a dilemma. If Andrei goes bankrupt—and Zena's defection has certainly weakened him—all agents will probably lose their access to Andrei's resources. From my perspective, his property rights are suddenly uncertain, making my delegated rights even more precarious.[51] If I defect, Andrei's demise becomes more likely, but I will at least secure control over whatever assets I manage to take with me.[52] Facing this one-shot, n-person Prisoner's Dilemma, my defection is extremely likely. Following the logic of the bank run, I rush to claim my assets before it is too late, even though the assets really "belong" to Andrei.[53]

What in practice might trigger the sudden erosion of principals' authority and begin this organizational breakdown? The critical element in this process is the *perception* that the principal can no longer control his resources. This perception could result from one of two developments: another actor may emerge and claim to own the resources under that agent's control, or agents might find a way to exercise greater autonomy from principals.

The emergence of new or competing principals is rare but not inconceivable. If Andrei's former partner—say, Boris—was suddenly released from jail and claimed to "own" the resources under my management, the conflicting claims would ultimately be resolved in favor of whomever I decide to obey (in the absence of an authoritative third-party conflict-resolution structure). Loyalty, fear of reprisals, or *quid pro quo* might compel me to ignore Boris, but Andrei might be more easily dismissed if I sensed that Boris had a chance of succeeding.[54] The resulting situation, for the case of multiple agents who ultimately are forced to choose sides, is basically the organizational equivalent of "multiple sovereignty" characteristic of revolutionary periods.[55]

Greater autonomy for agents can result from less rigorous monitoring or more flexible performance targets. Either of these modifications to the basic agency contract could be introduced by a principal (perhaps newly selected) who set out to motivate agents to improve real, rather than reported, outcomes. In both the Soviet Union and China, for instance, this was the initial goal of fiscal reforms that granted local officials limited discretionary control over their budgets.

Offering greater autonomy to agents, however, assumes that agents have up to that point been operating well within the "zone of acceptance" recognized by both principal and agent. The motivation for reform, in other words, is the presumption that the plan dictated by the principal has been too restrictive. In the situation presented here agents have already narrowed this "zone of acceptance" considerably, because the fundamental problems of information asymmetry were never adequately resolved. As noted in the previous section, once plan targets were met, agents would divert inputs to building up a safety margin. Additional resources, combined with this accumulated safety margin, could give agents the capacity to resist further exercise of authority from the center. Once all parties recognize this, a process of disintegration is unleashed.

A comparable result emerges from considering similar reforms within the game-theoretic model of organizations as repeated short-term agency contracts. As I noted earlier, the iterated nature of the contracting game reduces the opportunity for agents' shirking, provided (a) the relationship is open-ended or the future is not highly discounted, and (b) agents have limited access to outside credit. The shifts described above undermine precisely these conditions: uncertainty over principals' property rights can cast doubt over the future of the agency relationship and encourage a greater emphasis on near-term payoffs. Greater discretionary control over assets can effectively weaken agents' credit dependence on their superiors. Put more starkly, if employees suspect their boss might soon be replaced and they can afford to lose a bonus or two, the temptation to cheat or even steal will rise dramatically.

This model of collapse suggests two hypotheses about the process of organizational disintegration:

> *H2.2: If reforms exacerbate information asymmetries between principals and agents (for instance, by weakening monitoring mechanisms), opportunism by agents should increase.*
>
> *H2.3: If opportunism by agents escalates to expropriation of organizational assets, principals' authority to enforce other property rights claims (without resorting to force) will be weakened and opportunism will spread until the hierarchy collapses altogether.*

There is an important wrinkle in this picture. Actors in organizations with highly specific assets may find it more difficult to defect in the manner described above. If actors are weighing the potential costs of defection or loyalty against the perceived benefits, as the logic of the preceding model suggests, then asset specificity will affect these cost calculations in important ways. Highly specific assets—for instance, satellites—will be more difficult to appropriate outright during a bank run and will be more costly to redeploy outside the organization. Rubles, by contrast, can be claimed with relative ease and used straightforwardly in other activities. This suggests the following hypothesis:

> *H2.4: Organizations whose assets are less specific are more likely to be susceptible to "bank run" collapses.*

The three case studies in this book involve organizational assets of varying specificity. They should, therefore, serve as a test of this hypothesis and, by extension, the broader claim that actors considering defection from state hierarchies weigh the potential costs of such a decision when considering their options.

Strategies for Arresting Collapse

The preceding account of the organizational bank run described incentives and choices largely from the perspective of the multiple agents who sense that their principal may be weakening. This section briefly considers the principal's perspective.

Consider the situation in which multiple agents contract with a principal in conditions of imperfect information.[56] If the future is discounted or the contract period is finite, the principal must weigh the costs of ignoring individual challenges to his authority (assuming retaliation is costly) against the costs of retaliating forcefully against all challenges to establish his reputation and discourage future challenges.

Analyses of reputational effects have often built upon the model of a chain-store game, in which a monopolist faces potential competitors in a series of discrete markets.[57] The overriding lesson of the chain-store game is that the long-term player (i.e., the monopolist) may choose to sacrifice short-term gains to build up a reputation that will deter some or all future competitors. In other words, he can try to convince risk-averse competitors that he is temperamentally aggressive and will therefore incur the costs of challenging any and all competitors. Absent this reputational effect, regional challengers playing a game in which the future is discounted will expect the monopolist to eventually shift to an end-game strategy and begin acquiescing to limit his losses.[58]

Consider now a variation on the chain-store game in which a single principal controls a large number of agents operating in different regions. In each period, another agent must decide whether to challenge the authority of the principal and appropriate his assets. (This is analogous to saying that the challenge to the monopolist comes not from regional competitors but from his own branch managers, each of whom is considering setting up his own shop and stealing the monopolists' local operating payroll, customer list, employees, etc.) Information flows are highly imperfect: the agent's decision may not be immediately apparent to the principal, nor may the principal's response be unambiguously understood by other agents. Agents with a large accumulated surplus will not be deterred from defecting because they feel they are already beyond the reach of the principal. The question for the principal is how best to minimize defections among other agents.

As I have already implied in discussing the bank run scenario, agents will look at the exchanges between the principal and other agents to assess the likelihood of succeeding at defection. Given the noisiness of the information environment, principals will need to respond to challenges quickly and forcefully to establish a reputation for effective retaliation. Furthermore, they should probably choose weaker agents to punish, since a failed retaliation will lead to an even more rapid erosion of reputation and, by extension, authority.

This analysis suggests two related hypotheses about principals' response to challenges to their authority:

> *H2.5: The likelihood and pace of hierarchical breakdown will be affected by principals' responses to early episodes of open defiance: punishment of offenders will retard disintegration, while acquiescence will accelerate the level of challenges.*
> *H2.5a: Unsuccessful attempts to punish defiant agents will accelerate the processes of hierarchical collapse.*

In the postwar Soviet case, challenges to the leadership's authority were rare and met quickly by a coercive reply. From this perspective, the fixation of the Western media during the 1970s and 1980s on the anemic dissident movement within Russia may have had a mixed effect. Whereas it publicized the existence of dissent, it also amplified the regime's harsh response to this limited challenge. By reporting on this response through authoritative foreign broadcast channels, Western media probably enhanced the regime's domestic reputation for punishing nonconformity.

Such shows of force were inappropriate within structures of state power, however, at least in the post-Stalin era.[59] Corruption by officials was rampant under Brezhnev, and the anticorruption drives of Andropov and Gorbachev were limited in scope. Thus, when local officials began blatantly appropriating the assets of state organizations, few alternatives other than dismissal were open to supervisors. As the case of the Komsomol in Chapter 4 suggests, even dismissal became an empty threat when the assets removed from these organizations were sufficient to underwrite more lucrative future employment.

Behavioral Theories: What's So Neo about Neoinstitutionalism?

The agency model presented above predicts that bureaucrats can and will depart from established rules and norms to further their own self-interest. This prediction largely flows from the assumption that bureaucrats are opportunistic. An alternative view of bureaucracies, which dominated most previous studies of Soviet bureaucratic politics, gives greater weight to the consequences of bounded rationality than to opportunism. According to these "behavioral" theories, most bureaucrats do their best given the unattainability of comprehensive rationality.[60] Bureaucratic insubordination may therefore be a necessary improvisation, given the inherent limitations of the bureaucratic system.

While neoinstitutional theories focus on information asymmetries, behavioral approaches emphasize the general insufficiency of informational inputs to all actors in the decision process.[61] Working with incomplete information, actors must make guesses about the consequences of alternate courses of action (uncertainty) and about future preferences for these possible outcomes (ambiguity).[62]

Institutional rules and routines can be thought of as responses to these problems of uncertainty and ambiguity. Decision makers in complex organizations attempt to minimize the risk introduced by uncertain consequences and rely upon evolved decision rules that are products of historically accumulated institutional experience.[63] Rather than looking for the best possible course of action, which is unknowable to actors at lower levels of the hierarchy, they look only for a good enough solution to their immediate problems. In other words, they "satisfice," and the resulting pattern of action will yield, at best, incremental change.[64]

Pursuing this scenario, we can expect to find bureaucrats hoarding "organizational slack" to enable them to respond to unforeseen circumstances—just as the agents described in the previous section strive to build up safety margins. While most theories present slack as a defensive mechanism akin to bureaucratic overhead, some analyses have shown how forms of bureaucratic insubordination can spur innovation. In his study of "street-level bureaucrats," for instance, Lipsky notes that "different levels of organizations are more appropriately conceived as intrinsically in conflict with each other rather than mutually responsive and supportive."[65]

The success of Lipsky's subjects (local administrators in human services organizations) in circumventing standard operating procedures improves organizational performance (at the street level) and ultimately strengthens the organization. Lipsky's analysis, therefore, tends to treat the rules, and not their circumvention, as the key obstacles to bureaucratic efficiency and responsiveness.

Many discussions of the Soviet bureaucracy have similarly approached sclerotic bureaucratic procedures as an evil to be controlled. Soviet managers or officials who acquired the resources to evade the administrative straightjacket and pursue their own interests were considered to be employing a basic operating technique, a sort of "nonstandard" operating procedure. Their independence from hierarchical controls was often portrayed as a sort of desperate resourcefulness, posing no threat to institutional stability.

For instance, early studies of the Soviet system suggested that "informal adjustive mechanisms" like *blat*, family circles, and informal networks "[kept] things running at times when the formal mechanisms are inadequate."[66] Later, Jerry Hough suggested that "departmentalism and localism" may have represented healthy processes of goal development in the Brezhnevite system.[67] Studies of industrial management, as already noted, portrayed the factory manager resorting to subterfuge in an effort to guard against ever-escalating output targets.[68]

Thus, while information distortion and intraorganizational conflicts were recognized in Soviet bureaucracies without the aid of a neoinstitutional framework, the lingering image was of individuals' struggle to surmount inefficiencies in an environment characterized by pervasive information famine.[69] In Soviet organizations, however, information was not equally distributed (or, rather, maldistributed) and subordinates were not wholly powerless.

These factors become more significant in an environment of rapid change. The opportunistic "contracting agent," I have already suggested, may perceive an opportunity to profit from chaos and might respond by challenging the authority of his supervisors. Under certain circumstances, low-level bureaucrats might become the engines of institutional transformation.

The "satisficing" bureaucrat in a garbage-can hierarchy, on the other hand, should adhere to rules because they reduce uncertainty and offer viable responses to unanticipated challenges. As uncertainty increases, we would expect to see this actor become more conservative and resistant to changes that make her rule-set obsolete. I will use this expectation to frame one final hypothesis, testing the predictions of behavioral theories of organizational behavior and directly contradicting the hypotheses suggested by the contractual model presented earlier in this chapter (especially H2.2 and H2.3):

H2.6: As reforms begin and levels of uncertainty begin to escalate, lower-level bureaucrats should react incrementally. They should not depart radically from established rules.

An extension of this hypothesis might suggest that bureaucrats should not just fail to instigate radical reform, but that they would collectively oppose it. Indeed, the image of "reactionary bureaucrats" was common in the early days of post-Soviet economic reform. Examining the behavior of bureaucrats in times of less radical change may reveal whether they are the enemies of reform predicted by behavioral theories or the potential engines of reform suggested by the agency/bank run model.

Summary

This chapter uses the specifics of the Soviet case to suggest new directions for neoinstitutional analysis.

First, it extends standard theories of the firm to political as well as economic bureaucracies in the Soviet system, asserting that a similar logic governs the behavior of all bureaucrats in analogous hierarchies.

Second, by highlighting the interaction of "opportunism" and bureaucratic structure, the possibility emerges for that structure to weaken and even disintegrate in periods of rapid change. Most standard theories—including area-specific approaches considered in the last chapter and organizational behavior approaches considered at the end of this one—offer few mechanisms for stable institutions to become unstable; by contrast, centrifugal forces emerge naturally from the neoinstitutional model.

Finally, this analysis reconsiders the assumptions of standard neoinstitutional theory and in doing so extends the domain of this theory well beyond its usual focus on Western firms and stable democratic institutions.

3 | Testing Theories of Institutional Change: The Soviet Youth Program

"For fear of losing his job, the schoolteacher teaches things he does not believe; fearing for his future, the pupil repeats them after him; for fear of not being allowed to continue his studies, the young man joins the Youth League and participates in whatever of its activities are necessary."

—VÁCLAV HAVEL, *Letter to Dr. Gustáv Husák*

The preceding chapters have considered alternative explanations of hierarchical breakdown and proposed a set of hypotheses suggested by these contending theories. In this chapter, I consider a strategy for testing these hypotheses in linked case studies, and assess the role of ideology and of social unrest across all of the cases.

A Strategy for Hypothesis Testing

The case studies in this book focus on three institutions that mobilized the younger generation of Soviet citizens: the Young Communist League; the postuniversity job assignments system; and universal military conscription. Four factors make these cases promising candidates for testing the theories developed in Chapters 1 and 2:

1. Soviet youth policies provide a rich lode of material for studying the underlying sources of institutional and policy change. Youth policies affected the lives of every Soviet citizen, structuring citizens' initial contact with official institutions. They also determined how young people organized themselves into groups, spent their summer vacations and free time, found jobs and housing, fulfilled military obligations, and so forth. Youth policies, in other words, were consequential and observable.

2. These policy areas also offer potentially strong tests of the contending models described in earlier chapters. If ideological controls were effective

anywhere, they should have been effective among the officials charged with the upbringing and mobilization of Soviet youth. Youth, after all, played central roles in Communist ideology—New Soviet Man was to begin as New Soviet Child.

Partly as a consequence of their ideological prominence, youth affairs were prominent on the leadership agenda. Therefore, the institutions in charge of the "Soviet Youth Program" were important to the Soviet elite; furthermore, top leaders often derived their only experiences in street-level bureaucracy from their days in the Young Communist League (known universally as the Komsomol).[1] If elite politics determined institutional dynamics anywhere, they should have done so in the realm of youth affairs.

Similarly, if social forces shaped institutional dynamics, they should have had particular salience for the youth program. The younger generation is traditionally a source of pressure for change, particularly in authoritarian regimes. The student movement in Tsarist Russia was an important fountain of opposition to the regime, and the leaders of the Bolshevik Party were themselves so young that a youth wing was formed only as an afterthought. Young people were prominent in the 1968 Prague Spring and in many of the Eastern European democratic revolutions of 1989. If institutions responded to social pressures in general, then youth institutions should have been particularly responsive.

3. The institutional environment for youth policy is easily isolated and investigated. Each major policy area affecting youth was administered by separate hierarchies that left a detailed record of how decisions were made and monitored. In addition, one umbrella organization—the Komsomol—had overall responsibility for supervising the formulation and implementation of all policies affecting youth. All other bureaucratic actors, at some point, interacted with Komsomol representatives. Consequently, the flow of information, at both the policy-formulation and street levels, can be traced as it moved through Komsomol conduits. Much of the data used to construct the case studies in Chapters 4–6 was culled from the archives of the Komsomol, to which I was given essentially unlimited access.

4. Since youth policy was critical to Communism, it acquired a coherence among Soviet political actors and intellectuals which it lacks in the West. As a consequence, Soviet discussions of youth-related problems were more forthright than analogous treatments of, say, workers or Party

members. When empirical sociology gained acceptance in the Soviet Union, some of its earliest (and most accomplished) practitioners studied youth. When journalistic thaws developed in the early 1960s and mid-1980s, they were most evident in the youth press. When local government and Party officials began their exodus to the world of business and commerce, they were following the lead of officials from the Young Communist League. Since discussions of youth policy were richer and more open than debates about other policy areas, they admit a fuller review of the options considered by actors.

Case Studies

In the next three chapters, I consider three specific policy areas, each dominated by different policy-making institutions: political mobilization of youth by the Young Communist League; economic mobilization of youth by the postuniversity job-assignments system; and military mobilization of youth through universal conscription. Each of these chapters will test the set of hypotheses developed in the last two chapters.

The research will look at change over time within each case as well as across cases. By examining longitudinal change, I will be engaging in "process tracing": looking at decision processes within specific institutions effectively breaks each case into a series of steps, with each step offering a potential test of theory.[2] The cases will be organized to facilitate "structured, focused comparison," with the hypotheses from Chapters 1 and 2 providing the structure and focus.

To facilitate this, each case study follows the same pattern. First, I provide some background for the case, placing it in its historical and institutional context. I then examine the institutional dynamics prior to the 1980s, with particular attention to evidence relating to (1) the degree of elite control, particularly over mid- and lower-level officials; (2) the influence of societal interests, both directly and by proxy; and (3) the mechanisms for bureaucratic control within institutions (especially information flow, monitoring schemes, and authority). Finally, I consider the crisis and fragmentation of the relevant institutions, preserving the microlevel focus on the behavior of individual officials.

In presenting the case studies, I try to restrain the natural urge to employ a single theoretical lens to focus the narrative. With the benefit of hindsight it is tempting to present each case as an example of a full or limited institutional bank run, leaving it to the reader to infer the weakness of alternative elite-centered or society-centered theories from what is *not* discussed. The data available from archives and interviews allow a more rigorous approach to hypothesis testing, however, and I therefore use each case study to test the full set of hypotheses from the theories discussed in the preceding chapters. Chapter 7 pulls this material together and considers which of these theories best accounts for the similarities and differences across the three cases. In the remainder of the book, I discuss other cases of institutional collapse or survival—from the Soviet Union, China, and non-Communist systems—in which the bank run model suggests new perspectives. Unlike the detailed case studies, these more cursory treatments are not intended as tests of the model but rather use it as a heuristic.

The rest of this chapter introduces the overall Soviet youth program and addresses two questions common to all three case studies. First, can the outcomes of all cases be explained as responses to the emergence of a rebellious new "Gorbachev generation" (which might support hypothesis H1.3a)? Second, can the outcomes instead be explained as a direct consequence of an ideological crisis afflicting officials in charge of the youth program (supporting hypothesis H1.1)?

Comrades and Sons: Generational Conflict and Soviet Policy

Sensitivity to generational change was a key element of the Russian political tradition.[3] Students played a major role in the radical movements of the nineteenth century that laid the groundwork for the Revolution. Lenin quickly recognized that young people in Russia probably held the key to the success of the Revolution. As early as 1905, he wrote to fellow Bolsheviks Bogdanov and Gusev:

> All we have to do is to recruit young people more widely and boldly . . . without fearing them. This is a time of war. The youth—the students and still more so the young workers—will decide the issue of the whole struggle.[4]

Lenin was concerned about what he called "a sort of idiotic, philistine, Oblomov-like fear of youth" among the Bolsheviks.[5] He feared that these undesirable traits would be passed along to the next generation and urged considerable independence for youth organizations:

> Unless they have complete independence, they will be unable to train good socialists from their midst or prepare themselves to lead socialism forward.[6]

Among Soviet leaders, Leon Trotskii was the most convinced that generational conflict could be harnessed to further the revolution. He called youth "the most reliable barometer of the Party—[which] reacts most sharply against Party bureaucratism."[7] Trotskii's assertion of latent generational conflict incensed Stalin, who accused him of trying to "demagogishly tickle the youth, so as to open and widen the little rift between these fundamental troops of our Party."[8]

Addressing the Third Congress of the Komsomol in 1920, Lenin laid out the rationale for a Soviet youth program that would stress the ideological indoctrination of youth but also offer them the freedom to transcend the class consciousness of their parents:

> Only by radically remolding the teaching, organization, and training of the youth shall we be able to ensure that the efforts of the younger generation will result in the creation of a society that will be unlike the old society, i.e., in the creation of a communist society.[9]

Swept up in the optimism of the Revolution, Lenin assumed that "the generation who are now fifteen" would build Communism over the next ten to twenty years. He told them that "the entire purpose of their lives is to build a communist society."[10]

After Lenin's death, however, the Communist horizon began to recede. It was becoming clear that the young people of the 1920s might have to leave the building of Communism to their children. The goals of the Soviet youth program had to shift as well. If the ultimate heirs to the Communist legacy were still at least a generation off, then the state could justify a far more active role in shaping generational development to ensure steady progress along the road to Communism.

Over the course of the 1920s and early 1930s, the major features of the comprehensive Soviet youth program took shape.[11] Soviet pedagogical policies, after a period of heady experimentation during the "cultural revolution" of 1928–31, abandoned many of their most ambitious social reengineering goals.[12] Soviet education came more fully under Party control, and Soviet schools began offering a more standardized curriculum to a wider range of students. As discussed in Chapter 5, the social origins of students remained a concern in higher education through the 1950s, but efforts to manipulate class distribution of the student body made little headway after the 1930s.

Within the schools, youth were channeled through a series of organizations designed to oversee their political socialization and ideological indoctrination. Young children, aged seven to nine, were enrolled in the Octobrists and then in the Young Pioneers until they reached Komsomol-joining age of fifteen (later fourteen). Both the Octobrists and Pioneers were created in 1922 to extend the reach of the state's official youth program to the youngest children. The Octobrist program was initially intended for preschoolers but was reorganized in 1957 under the auspices of the Pioneers to prepare students in the first three grades for Pioneer membership. The Pioneers, in turn, operated under the supervision of the Komsomol but with far more universal membership.

As I discuss in the next chapter, by the mid-1930s the Komsomol had lost almost all traces of organizational independence and was thoroughly under the control of the Communist Party. After the Second World War, the Komsomol transformed itself into a mass organization, thus creating a unified program of state youth organizations extending from age seven to twenty-eight.

In the late 1930s, as discussed in Chapter 6, military service also became truly universal for Soviet males, and the prior screening of "undesirable" classes was abandoned. The Soviet army became another important instrument of the Soviet youth program, subjecting conscripts to harsh lessons in discipline, patriotism, and ideological training.

Thus, by the outbreak of the Second World War the primary elements of the Soviet youth program were already in place. In the 1950s and 1960s, these programs underwent few significant changes, other than in scale. Virtually all youth programs became more universal and comprehensive under Khrushchev, greatly aided by his universalization of secondary education. All young people would now spend at least eleven years in school (later reduced to ten); during this time they were a captive audience for activists, indoctrinators, and mobilizers. Students were subjected to political education classes in school and through the Pioneers and Komsomol. During vacations, they were organized into labor brigades to work on construction sites or to help in the harvest. Outside classes, all forms of recreational activities were supervised by Pioneer or Komsomol representatives.

As Kassof noted, by the early 1960s the youth program had become essentially conservative—designed to maintain the ideological status quo, ensure adequate discipline among young workers and students, mobilize short-term labor when needed, suppress antisocial conduct, and supervise leisure activities under conditions of growing urbanism and shortages of facilities. It was also supposed to "block the formation of independent youth groups that might challenge the official outlook."[13]

These concerns were of great importance to Party leaders, who watched the performance of youth-related institutions carefully. Under Khrushchev, Soviet officials bemoaned the reemergence of the "fathers and sons" problem. Groups in the youth subculture like *stiliagi* (often translated as "zoot-suiters") or *nibonichos* (from the Russian for "neither God nor the devil") were roundly condemned for exhibiting signs of nihilism or, even worse, worshipping Western music and dance styles.[14] Official press complained about young people trading contraband records on X-ray films and offered increasing reports of "parasites" and "loafers" among the younger generation. Even among the elite students of Moscow University, where Komsomol membership was essentially mandatory, a Western visitor in 1961 observed "the average Russian student is highly apolitical."[15]

The KGB paid particular attention to youth and the youth program. In 1965, for instance, KGB chief Vladimir Semichastnyi addressed a plenum of the Komsomol Central Committee (which he had previously led). He presented a detailed indictment of Komsomol members engaged in such subversive activities as trading with tourists in Minsk or organizing an underground Elvis club in Lvov. All offending individuals were named in the speech, suggesting that KGB files were bulging with detailed reports of similar anti-Soviet activities among the youth. Also singled out for attack was a lecturer at Ternopl' medical institute who had simply advised his students to "worry about pharmacology, not Marxism."[16]

Despite occasional criticisms, the main features of the Soviet youth program changed little after Khrushchev. In the mid-1980s, many Western observers pointed again to warning signs of "generational conflict" among Soviet youth.[17] Groups of *mettalisty* (fans of Western heavy metal music) squared off against iron-pumping *liubery* (named after a working-class Moscow suburb). Soviet press reported with some alarm the mushrooming of thousands of "informal youth associations"—mostly fan clubs of sports teams or rock bands, but all disturbing signs of a youth subculture no longer under state control. Even before many of these trends came into full view, newly selected Party head Iurii Andropov felt compelled to address the generational question directly:

> In our society, there is no conflict between generations—between fathers and sons, as is sometimes said. But this does not mean that all is going smoothly with us . . . The younger generation is no worse than ours—it's just a different, new generation. New generations aren't reproduced like copies on an offset duplicator.[18]

Other Soviet officials, like KGB chief Viktor Chebrikov, insisted that the emergent subcultures among the younger generation were signs of the successful pollution of Soviet culture by Western enemies.[19] And in 1988, the infamous letter by schoolteacher Nina Andreeva, which became a manifesto for conservative reactionaries, centered its anti-perestroika attack on the charge that Soviet reforms were confusing youth and weakening their value structure.[20]

The fears of generational warfare proved highly exaggerated. In his opening address to the Twenty-seventh Communist Party Congress, Mikhail Gorbachev singled out workers, families, women, older people, and non-Russian nationalities as "social groups" in need of special attention, but he made no mention of youth in this context. Despite his calls for a sweeping renewal of society, Gorbachev offered little in the way of a blueprint for restructuring the youth program. In his book *Perestroika*, Gorbachev approvingly quoted a 1987 Party resolution that "called upon party leaders to pay greater attention to the labor, ideological and moral steeling of young people."[21] Beyond this, however, Gorbachev offered no major plan for overhauling the youth program; indeed, he accepted its basic tenet that the state must ensure the proper "formation of the younger generation." The wave of informal groups gradually subsided, provoking no coherent policy response from either the top leadership or lower levels of the hierarchy.

Effectiveness of Indoctrination among Elites and Masses

The preceding discussion implies that Soviet youth in the postwar period did not undergo any dramatic change in their attitudes toward the Communist state or system that confronted the regime with a revolutionary upheaval. Both Soviet and Western attitudinal data on youth confirm this more directly, suggesting that where trends do emerge, they point to increasing passivity and cynicism rather than regime-threatening frustration and foment. Equally important, the data suggest that officials in the youth program were, if anything, even more cynical than the average young person.

These findings emerge forcefully from an analysis of data from the Soviet Interview Project (SIP).[22] Project researchers interviewed nearly 2,800 former Soviet citizens in 1983. The survey sample consisted of emigrés who had left the Soviet Union between 1979 and 1982. This sample is, consequently, predominantly Jewish and, to a lesser extent, drawn from what might be considered the urban intelligentsia. Nevertheless, by investigating relationships *within* this sample, we can illuminate the link between participation in the youth program and ideological indoctrination.[23]

Since this book is concerned with post-Stalin political institutions, I limit the sample to those respondents born after 1941 (1,178 cases). All of the respondents in this subset, therefore, reached Komsomol membership age (fifteen until 1962, fourteen thereafter) after the Twentieth Party Congress. Eliminating respondents born before 1941 produces a subset whose interactions with youth organizations might still have been fresh enough to leave discernible effects at the time of emigration.

Unlike the Communist Party, the Komsomol consisted mostly of "rank-and-file" members. Since the Party was considered a "vanguard" organization, all members were considered "activists" and were expected to carry out tasks for the Party. In the Komsomol, the "activists" were the full-time officials and apparatchiks, as well as the secretaries of primary organizations or group organizers who took on organizational responsibilities without receiving a salary in return. The balance of the membership, which ballooned under Khrushchev and Brezhnev, played far more passive roles, sitting through political education lectures or accepting summer work on construction sites. The sample is composed of Komsomol activists (i.e., officials in some capacity), rank-and-file members (with few responsibilities besides showing up at meetings), and nonmembers (see Table 3.1).

Two questions are relevant here: How did Komsomol members respond

Table 3.1. Soviet Interview Project Subsample:
Komsomol Membership by Year of Birth

Year of Birth	N	Activists (%)	Rank and File (%)	Nonmembers (%)
1941–1945	250	16	55	29
1946–1950	479	18	61	21
1951–1955	291	22	61	17
1956–1960	158	23	57	20
TOTAL	1178	19	59	22

Source: Author's analysis of SIP data.

to the youth program? Were Komsomol activists more likely to be "true believers"? I look at five different measures of direct or diffuse support for the political system: a sense of personal efficacy; levels of cynicism; agreement with official norms of political action; belief in government responsiveness; and degree of personal satisfaction.[24] Since these indicators include normative judgments about the regime after completion of Komsomol contact, they suggest the degree of acceptance of the official ideology.

Table 3.2 shows the outcome of bivariate and multiple regressions of a variety of these measures against previous Komsomol activity. A number of observations can be made from these results.

First, while activism in Komsomol is associated with a significant increase in later self-perceptions of personal influence and privilege, rank-and-file membership in Komsomol is associated with exactly the opposite pattern. As Tables 3.3 and 3.4 indicate, this relationship is not appreciably altered by controlling for education, sex, or interest in politics. Perceptions of personal influence and privilege among nonmembers depend much more on background factors.

This increased sense of personal efficacy[25] for former Komsomol activists does not translate within this sample into a sense of efficacy with respect to participation in public organizations such as unions. The data suggest that respondents became activists in Komsomol in response to a sense of personal ambition. This ambition could lead to achievements in other spheres of activity, which would contribute to a strengthened sense of influence or privilege.[26]

Table 3.2. Political Participation and Measures of Regime Support: Regression Results

Dependent Variables[a]	Komsomol Activists		Komsomol Rank and File		Komsomol Nonmembers	
	r^b	$Beta^b$	r	$Beta$	r	$Beta$
Sense of personal influence	-.181**	-.181**	.137**	.132**	-.025	—
Sense of personal privilege	-.126*	-.126**	.092**	.092*	-.013	—
Sense of having a say in affairs of union	.061	—	-.062	—	.028	—
Perceived honesty of officials: Composite	.001	—	.054	—	-.087*	—
Perceived competence of officials: Composite	-.039	—	.035	—	-.014	—
Perceived honesty of Politburo	-.058	—	.126**	.110**	-.139**	-.112**
Perceived honesty of KGB	-.078	—	.117**	.103**	-.103**	—
Perceived honesty of industry managers	.051	—	-.001	—	-.040	—
Agree with wage norms for Party, KGB	-.042	—	-.285	—	.042	—
Agree with wage norms for worker, farmer	.002	—	-.028	—	.043	—
Attempted to evade the draft (males only)	.009	—	-.002	—	-.004	—
Listened to foreign radio	-.014	—	.082*	—	-.117**	-.095**
Interest in politics	.060	—	.037	—	-.121**	-.072*
View of accessibility of officials	-.025	—	—	—	-.026	—

Source: Author's analysis of SIP data. Komsomol activity is represented by dummy variables for nonmembers, rank and file, and activists, each coded 1-yes, 2-no.

a. Influence and Privilege were self-evaluations based on the five-year period prior to emigration, each coded from 1-low to 10-high. Having a Say in Union Affairs was asked of trade union participants, and coded 1-yes, 2-no. Honesty and Competence of Officials were evaluated from 0-none to 4-all; composite index constructed from averaging responses on eight types of officials. Earning Norms were evaluated as 1-about right, 2-too much, or 3-too little. Interest in Politics was scored 1-little/no, 2-some/much. Other variables were coded 1-yes, 2-no.

b. *r* scores are uncontrolled bivariate correlation coefficients. *Beta* scores represent the standardized regression coefficients for named variables in least-squares regressions that included Parental Class, Educational Achievement, Religious Background, Year of Birth, Sex, and—to control for possible emigré bias on attitudinal questions—Role in the Decision to Emigrate. In both cases:

*-significant at the <.01 level, **-significant at the <.001 level.

Table 3.3. Political Participation and "Efficacy"

Respondents Born after 1941	Percentage Reporting Above-Average Sense of "Personal Influence" [a]		
	Komsomol Activists	Komsomol Rank and File	Komsomol Nonmembers
Entire Sample	47.6	31.8	36.1
Sex			
Male	46.7	33.9	40.9
Female	48.1	30.0	31.3
Education Level			
Higher Education	47.0	32.2	26.6
Less than Higher Education	48.4	31.3	40.3
Interest in Politics			
High	47.3	31.8	35.2
Low	48.2	32.1	37.6

Source: See notes to Table 3.2.

a. Values represent the percentage of respondents in each category of Komsomol activity whose self-evaluations of "personal influence" were above the mean for the entire sample born after 1941.

Among rank and file, the Komsomol experience seems to have undermined perceptions of personal efficacy. This relationship holds for all age cohorts examined here and probably reflects the consequences of the "overbureaucratization" of the Komsomol apparat, which is examined in the next chapter. This alienation of the rank and file is also reflected in their attitudes about the honesty or competence of officials. While there is no significant correlation between Komsomol experience and perceptions of honesty of officials in general, there was a significant link with perceptions of honesty of Party and KGB officials.[2] Specifically, nonmembers of Komsomol tended to view Politburo officials as more honest, while Komsomol rank and file viewed them as somewhat less honest. Komsomol activism was not correlated with perceptions of honesty. A similar relationship, while not shown in Table 3.2, was observed toward local Party and Soviet officials.

This cynicism created by rank-and-file participation is limited, however. There was no correlation, even in bivariate analyses, between Komsomol experience and perceptions of the competence of any group of officials.

Table 3.4. Political Participation and "Privilege"

Respondents Born after 1941	Percentage Reporting Above-Average Sense of "Personal Privilege"[a]		
	Komsomol Activists	Komsomol Rank and File	Komsomol Nonmembers
Entire Sample	53.3	41.9	40.8
Sex			
Male	53.3	39.2	42.5
Female	53.3	44.1	39.1
Education Level			
Higher Education	54.5	44.1	45.6
Less than Higher Education	51.6	39.6	38.6
Interest in Politics			
High	54.4	43.7	39.0
Low	50.0	37.5	45.2

Source: See notes to Table 3.2.

a. Values represent the percentage of respondents in each category of Komsomol activity whose self-evaluations of "personal privilege" were above the mean for the entire sample born after 1941.

Nor was Komsomol experience linked with a sense that Party officials were making too much money or, conversely, that workers were making too little.[28]

If membership in the Komsomol rank and file is associated with decreased personal efficacy and increased cynicism, then it is difficult to say just what is associated with activism in Komsomol. Former Komsomol activists seem no more interested in politics, no more likely to view officials as more or less honest, competent, or accessible, no more satisfied with their standard of living prior to emigration, and no less likely to listen to foreign radio. They are also only slightly less likely to attempt to evade the draft, except for activists with secondary or less education (see Table 3.5). (Draft evasion is a particularly important phenomenon to observe, since it would occur *during* an individual's Komsomol tenure.)

Komsomol activism also seems to have an ambiguous effect at best on the acceptance of basic norms about public versus private rights and responsibilities. As Table 3.6 shows, former activists tend to be slightly more sympathetic toward state control of medicine, agriculture, and in-

Table 3.5. Draft Evasion

Respondents Born after 1941	Percentage of Males Who Attempted to Avoid the Draft[a]		
	Komsomol Activists	Komsomol Rank and File	Komsomol Nonmembers
Entire Sample	25.7	26.1	27.1
Education Level			
Higher Education	33.3	30.9	30.8
Less than Higher Education	3.7	19.2	25.6

Source: See notes to Table 3.2.
a. Based on responses to direct question on whether respondents attempted to avoid military service.

dustry than former rank and file, but nonmembers are even more inclined toward these classical "socialist" goals. Conversely, former rank-and-file youth-league members are consistently less enamored of socialist goals. Once again, while an experience in the rank and file seems to have antagonistic results, service as an activist has little if any lasting impact.

The slightly lower level of cynicism apparent in nonmembers must be seen in light of the diminished interest in politics displayed by this group (the effects on foreign radio listening are shown in Table 3.7, which also shows the slight influence of different roles in the emigration decision). In addition to expressing less interest in politics, the nonmembers also were markedly less likely to participate in unofficial activities, such as attending art shows or study groups, than either former members or activists (these data are not shown). On the whole, while one might expect individuals who had avoided joining Komsomol to be more active and nonconformist overall, especially among emigrés, the nonmembers turn out to be relatively passive and disinterested. Their disinterest may have left them less cynical than their more compliant peers.

These findings would not have greatly surprised Soviet observers, even in the 1960s and 1970s. Youth sociology was one of the first branches of the discipline to receive a firm empirical foundation when Soviet sociology began to find its voice in the mid-1960s.[29] Though rarely couched in the most direct terms, these studies consistently revealed a widespread failure of indoctrination among youth and pointed to unmistakable signs

Table 3.6. Political Participation and Indicators of Political Beliefs: Means Tests

Dependent Variables[a]	Komsomol Activists	Komsomol Rank and File	Komsomol Nonmembers
Satisfaction Index	2.55	2.56**	2.29**
State vs. Private Medical Care	2.81	3.01*	2.50**
State vs. Private Control of Industry	3.66	3.93	3.51
State vs. Private Control of Agriculture	5.45*	5.82**	5.44
Individual/Criminal Rights	4.67	4.57	4.78
Right to Strike	5.27	5.16	5.10
Right to Live without Residence Permits	6.07	6.32	6.12

Source: See notes to Table 3.2. Figures shown are the *mean response* for each group of respondents. Asterisks indicate where t-tests of groups divided by Komsomol activity demonstrated different means significant at the <.01 (*) or <.001 (**) levels.

a. Satisfaction is a composite index based on reported level of satisfaction with housing, goods, medical service, job, and standard of living during the five years prior to applying for emigration. Scale runs from 1 (dissatisfied) to 4 (satisfied). N=964 for this variable. The other six variables measure opinions on state versus individual rights and responsibilities, and have Ns ranging from 1112 to 1165. These answers were coded from 1 (favors state control or social prerogatives) to 7 (favors private control or individual rights).

of passivity or cynicism. As early as 1961, for instance, a survey of 17,000 youth found only 25 percent listing "building Communism" as a prominent goal for their lives.[30] Instead, youth seemed increasingly distracted by music, social activities, and attempts to avoid blue-collar labor.

One persistent theme in Soviet youth sociology was the salience of class differences among the younger generation. The eradication of class-based distinctions was an important tenet of "Communist upbringing." Class cleavages were frequently manifested as differences between students or graduates of general-education secondary schools (ten-year secondary schools) and vocational-technical secondary schools.[31] Despite the higher rate of participation of upper-class youth in sociopolitical work (linked, perhaps, with higher educational ambitions, as the emigré data also suggest), there were clues that they did not take sociopolitical organiza-

Table 3.7. Foreign Radio Listeners

Respondents Born after 1941	Percentage of Respondents Who Listened to Foreign Radio		
	Komsomol Activists	Komsomol Rank and File	Komsomol Nonmembers
Entire Sample	91.6	92.4	83.9
Emigration Decision[a]			
By/For Self	95.3	94.8	87.4
With/For Others	79.6	83.7	74.1

Source: See notes to Table 3.2.

a. 77 percent of the sample indicated that they chose to emigrate either alone or for their own benefit. The remaining 23 percent indicated that the emigration decision was either made by a family member or in the interest of another family member.

tions seriously. A large study of public opinion of youth surrounding the Eighteenth Komsomol Congress in 1979 found that the group least interested in the Congress was "scientific" youth (employees of scientific research institutes), with 25 percent unlikely to discuss the Congress with anybody, followed by university students (16 percent), workers (14 percent), vocational students (11 percent), and rural youth (5 percent).[32]

When researchers attempted to explicitly track the effect of ideological indoctrination, they frequently came up empty. For instance, studies of the effect of Komsomol membership on labor discipline found only slight differences, or none at all, between the performance of Komsomol members and nonmembers of the same age group.[33] Nor were Komsomol members any more likely to initiate contact with officials of local government: a study from the late 1960s and early 1970s in Taganrog found 37 percent of Komsomol members had never contacted a government official, compared with 41 percent for the eighteen to twenty-four age group (and 38 percent for the population at large).[34]

The Western and Soviet findings discussed here suggest that rank-and-file members of youth organizations like Komsomol emerged more cynical and with a lower sense of personal efficacy than nonjoiners. Activists emerged with a higher sense of personal efficacy, though not appreciably reduced cynicism. In other words, well before glasnost', not only was the official youth league ineffective at political socialization, but even the indoctrinators themselves seem to have been inadequately indoctrinated.

The failure of ideological controls among the *aktiv* was generally ac-knowledged as early as the 1950s. Komsomol activists were often labeled "Komsomol radishes"—red on the outside only.[35] The dominant concern of Komsomol activists remained as one critic labeled it in 1957: "to place check-marks in a column of assignments: Done."[36]

Within the organization as well, activists were condemned for cynicism. They were even accused of admonishing rank-and-file members who exhibited excessive enthusiasm. During a 1963 plenum of the Komsomol Central Committee, the First Secretary of the Bielorussian Komsomol, L. G. Maksimov, related the fate of an enthusiastic applicant for Komso-mol membership in Brest. The aspiring Komsomolite wrote a flowery letter to his local committee expressing his heartfelt desire to join the ranks of vanguard youth. In response, he was told to "cut the loud phrases and write it like everyone else."[37] Criticisms like these, made behind the closed doors of the Komsomol Central Committee hall, strongly suggest that Komsomol leaders had no illusions about the problems they faced with their activists.[38]

But while cynicism and apathy are hardly ideal generational traits to be cultivating, they did not necessarily pose a direct threat to the stability of the regime. More specifically, the argument for either an incipient youth revolt or the sudden breakdown of previously effective ideological controls within hierarchies receives little support from the data. The case studies in this book will provide further evidence that Soviet officials were aware of, but not especially alarmed by, the indifference of youth to much of the youth program. One analyst has suggested that the very purpose of the Soviet youth league may have been "socialization into incompe-tence": both activists and rank-and-file members of the league learned that it was far easier to ignore the regime's political rhetoric than to challenge it.[39]

Summary

I will probably not be spoiling much of the suspense in any of the upcoming chapters to reveal that they all recount the demise of the institutions involved. It is tempting, therefore, to dismiss these results as merely consequences of the overarching disintegration of the Soviet Un-ion. The case studies will show, however, that centrifugal forces in these institutions preceded and accelerated the broader systemic collapse rather than the reverse; and they will also reveal important differences among the cases.

This chapter has demonstrated that manifestations of nihilism, apathy, and counterculture among Soviet youth were present for many years; they did not arrive with Gorbachev. Furthermore, actors who served in official organizations seem to have been no less cynical—and were perhaps more so—than their counterparts in the general population. Neither generational conflict nor ideological decay, therefore, can explain the regime's startling loss of control over institutions in the late 1980s. In fact, the case studies that follow suggest that the loss of control over the Soviet "youth program" had little to do with youth at all.

4 | The Communist Youth League

"OK, so they let us break-dance,
OK, so we can be happy sometimes.
But still standing behind the column
Is the man in the thin tie
With cement in his eyes."

—TELEVIZOR, Leningrad rock band, c. 1986

Few organizations in Soviet life touched more people than the All-Union Leninist Communist Youth League (VLKSM), known universally as the Komsomol. Whenever a group of teens or young adults gathered throughout the seventy-three years of Komsomol's existence—on factory floors and on battlefields, in barracks and in dormitories, during wartime and during harvests, at construction sites and on street corners—a Komsomol organizer loomed. Many Soviet leaders, including Mikhail Gorbachev and his foreign minister, Eduard Shevardnadze, had their sole experience with street-level politics in the Komsomol.

Yet by the late 1980s, few organizations were less popular than the Komsomol. Surveys ranking the public image of official and informal institutions invariably ranked the Komsomol near the bottom of the list, below the Communist Party, KGB, Aeroflot, and even the neofascist organization Pamiat'.[1] In 1991, in the wake of the failed Soviet coup, the Communist Youth League dissolved. Its demise, however, was not a consequence of that coup. By the time it finally closed its doors, the Komsomol, unlike the Communist Party, had already been reduced to a mere shell, deserted by its most ambitious leaders and stripped of its most valuable assets.

Before discussing the consequences of perestroika, I introduce the structure and membership of the Komsomol and review some of its key shortcomings and challenges in the postwar period. I then examine the nature of elite, societal, and structural controls over the Komsomol hierarchy from Khrushchev to the early Gorbachev years. Finally, I look at the changes introduced by glasnost' and perestroika and discuss the sudden breakdown of authority within the Komsomol between 1987 and 1991.

Background

History

Prior to 1917, neither the Bolshevik nor Menshevik branches of the Russian social democrats had a separate organization for youth. Many young people already belonged to these revolutionary parties, and the complexities of controlling a clandestine youth league with overlapping goals and membership would have been needlessly risky. In the wake of the revolution of February 1917, however, radical youth groups spontaneously blossomed. Bolsheviks viewed their rapid growth with alarm and responded quickly to infiltrate and undermine these nascent youth organizations. They then began to establish their own youth arm.

At Bolshevik Party meetings in July and August of 1917, delegates debated the character and structure of a proposed Communist youth league.[2] This body would bring together the weak network of Communist youth groups then operating around the country with combined memberships of only 15,000 (two-thirds of which were in the Petrograd youth group). Bolshevik leaders were particularly concerned about the nature and degree of Party control over this new league. They feared a wholly independent organization of energetic and volatile young radicals. At the same time, they recognized that an excessively regimented body would lack the appeal to youth necessary to ensure mass membership and Bolshevik domination over youth culture and activities. There was no point in creating a "vanguard" youth league if its sole function was to siphon the most energetic young revolutionaries out of Party cells and reorganize them as junior Bolsheviks.

The resolution adopted by the Sixth Party Congress in August 1917 shows the delegates' difficulties in resolving the dilemma of autonomy versus discipline. They announced the Party's intention to create "independent organizations, not subordinated to the Party organizationally, but connected with it only in spirit. At the same time, the Party is striving for these organizations to become socialist in character as soon as they are founded."[3]

Despite this declaration, no real progress was made in creating a Bolshevik youth league for over a year. The most important cause of the delay was simply the arrival of the October Revolution: the Party had no organizers to spare. By July of 1918, however, the Party Central Committee deemed the task of consolidating support among youth sufficiently important to convene the founding Congress of its new youth league. On 29 October 1918, 176 delegates assembled in Moscow to form the Russian Communist League of Youth.[4]

The first three Congresses of the Komsomol—held from 1918 to 1920—determined many of its crucial organizational characteristics, most important its future relationship with the Party.[5] Lingering doubts over the degree of permissible autonomy were settled by the immediate need to help the Party prevail in the Civil War and consolidate power in the countryside. For instance, the label "Communist" was left in its title despite objections that the league needed to broaden its membership beyond Communists and appeal to "still uncommitted worker and peasant youth."[6]

More significantly, over the course of these two years, language describing the official relationship of the Komsomol to the Party shifted. Initially, the Komsomol was called "self-standing" and "independent." By the Second Congress, "independent" had been changed in official documents to "autonomous," and the Komsomol Central Committee declared it was "directly subordinated" to the Central Committee of the Party. The Third Congress in 1920, addressed by Lenin himself, approved a new Komsomol Program stipulating that while the league was definitely "autonomous," it nevertheless "subordinates itself to [the Party's] political directives" and operates "under its control."[7]

As the Komsomol's relationship to the Communist Party grew clearer, so too did its immediate functions, as dictated by the Party. In Lenin's address to the Third Congress, he finessed the central question of whether the league was to be an elite "vanguard" of revolutionary youth or to aim for mass membership. On the one hand, he instructed delegates, "You must train yourselves to be Communists." This suggested that the Komsomol, like the Party, was to be a selective recruiter of the most committed activists. On the other hand, he stressed that only the young would succeed in building a Communist society, and therefore the league should "pursue in educating, training, and rousing the entire younger generation."[8]

The Komsomol's earliest relations with rival youth organizations suggested a sweeping interpretation of this latter instruction. As Kenez notes, "one of the main functions of the Komsomol was to prevent the existence of genuinely independent youth organizations."[9] The Party moved quickly through the Komsomol to undermine and dissolve Russian scouting organizations and to forestall the establishment of a Russian Jewish youth organization. The official youth league became the only option open to young people seeking any form of public association. At its Second Congress, the Komsomol declared its opposition even to sports clubs, proposing to integrate such functions within its own structure.

By claiming a monopoly over the organization of youth, the Komsomol forced its own eventual transformation into a mass movement. It did not, however, definitively resolve the inherent contradiction between its roles as elite vanguard and recruitment wing for the Party and as primary "transmission belt" for the indoctrination and mobilization of the young masses. The question was not yet critical at the end of 1920, as the Komsomol included just 2 percent of eligible youth aged fourteen to twenty-three.

During the Civil War and the 1920s, membership grew to over 7 percent of eligible youth, as Komsomol members were pressed into service consolidating Bolshevik power in the countryside and campaigning against religion and illiteracy (see Figure 4.1). While Komsomol group leaders found themselves in conflict with trade union organizers in many factories, in villages they were often the sole representatives of Soviet power. In many of these rural organizations, Komsomol officials had no Party cell to join upon reaching the upper age limit of the youth league and continued to serve well into their thirties or forties. By 1927, over 16 percent of Komsomol members exceeded the upper age limit on membership.[10]

Throughout the 1920s, Party leaders haggled over the appropriate age limits for the organization. In practice the lower limit of fourteen ensured that Komsomol would remain malleable, while the upper bound of twenty-three permitted Komsomol leaders to simultaneously hold

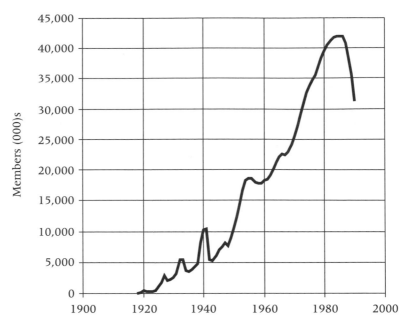

Figure 4.1. Komsomol Membership, 1918–1990 (*Sources: VLKSM: Nagliadnoe Posobie po komsomol'skomu stroitelstvu* [Visual guides on Komsomol membership] [Moscow: Molodaia Gvardia, 1985], 39; Goskomstat, *Molodezh' SSSR* [Youth in the USSR] [Moscow: Goskomstat, TsK VLKSM, and VKSh pri TsK VLKSM, 1990], 151.)

Party cards. The Party began to rely increasingly on Komsomol as a recruitment mechanism, requiring all new members under age twenty to join through their Komsomol organization.

In the late 1920s and early 1930s, the Five Year Plan and rapid industrialization presented the Komsomol with a sweeping challenge to mobilize masses of young people for gargantuan construction projects around the country. Komsomol brigades were dispatched to build the massive power stations in Dnepropetrovsk and new factories in the Urals and Siberia, to work in the coal mines in the Don Basin, and to organize the state farms and machine-tractor stations created by collectivization. They helped build a whole industrial city on the banks of the Amur River, which was named in their honor—Komsomolsk-na-Amur. As the Komsomol shock workers blazed highly publicized trails of glory, the Komsomol came increasingly to be seen as a crucial source of manual labor on a mass scale.

In the mid- to late 1930s, the Komsomol became engulfed in the bloodletting that accompanied Stalin's rise to power; the purges of 1937 decimated Komsomol leadership ranks.[11] The Party ended these purges in 1938 with a condemnation of the "incredible arbitrariness" of the mass expulsions of the previous year.[12] Memberships were restored to many surviving Komsomol activists, and a new membership drive was launched. Many leaders of the Komsomol were elevated to positions in the Party leadership, replacing former supervisors who had fallen victim to the Party purges of the previous years.

The Great Patriotic War (World War II) brought a rapid expansion of Komsomol activities and responsibilities, as Komsomol organizations helped mobilize youth for war and enforce discipline with the armed forces. Most young inductees into the armed forces were simultaneously brought into the ranks of the Komsomol, and millions of young people enrolled in a burst of wartime patriotism. The war, however, took a heavy toll on Komsomol ranks.

Membership grew steadily in the postwar period, especially in the years immediately following Stalin's death. The expansion of secondary and postsecondary education under Khrushchev enabled the Komsomol to increase its membership dramatically in educational institutions. The age limits for membership widened to fourteen to twenty-eight, though officials were exempted from the upper limit. Under Khrushchev and Brezhnev, the Komsomol became an organization with a genuine mass membership. Responding to this flood of new members, it focused increasingly on the two main tasks for which it had assumed responsibility in preceding decades: (1) political and ideological indoctrination of youth and (2) mobilization of large numbers of young people for specific economic or military tasks.

The theme of control emerges clearly from this brief overview of the Komsomol: from the earliest days of the Revolution, the Communist Party feared losing control over a separate organization of young elites, while the Komsomol's responsibilities eventually came to center on ensuring state control over the younger generation. For Komsomol officials, destined to become the leading cadres in the Party, life in the Komsomol was a tense struggle to demonstrate compliance with orders they received and assure compliance with orders they issued. This narrow focus produced an organizational inertia with profound consequences for the league's capacity to control its own personnel.

Structure and Membership

The organizational structure of the Komsomol was closely modeled on that of the Communist Party. At the base of the organizational pyramid were hundreds of thousands of primary organizations based at workplaces, schools and universities, state and collective farms, and army units. The largest of these were subdivided into smaller groups, led by a designated "organizer." Each primary organization "elected" a secretary, who in most cases combined her duties with the normal responsibilities associated with work or school. In practice, secretaries of primary organizations were nominated by district-level committees and often conducted their Komsomol duties while receiving full compensation from their host organizations. In other words, Komsomol activities at the grass roots were subsidized by employers and educational institutions, who both paid the salaries of Komsomol organizers and permitted meetings to take place during working hours.

Moving up the organizational hierarchy, primary organizations were agents of district- or city-level committees (*raikoms* or *gorkoms*), which in turn were subordinated to regional committees (*obkoms* or *kraikoms*) and republican-level central committees. In larger cities, district raikoms reported to the city gorkom, which then reported directly to the republican central committee. The Russian Federation lacked its own central committee and republican organization; Russian obkom officials, along with officials of the other Union-republic organizations, reported directly to the Central Committee of the All-Union Komsomol.

At each level of the hierarchy, governing bodies were, theoretically, elected by and accountable to full membership meetings held at each level of the organization every few years. However, accountability followed the tenets of "democratic centralism," which also governed Party organization. In practice, these elected bodies—central, regional, or district committees—were hand-picked by higher levels of the organization and rubber-stamped by the plenary body. These committees, in turn, named the secretaries, bureaus, and staff that constituted the full-time bureaucracy, or *apparat*, of the Komsomol. This apparat then supervised activities at lower levels of the hierarchy and ensured that delegates selected to attend plenary meetings at each level would faithfully ratify and implement commands issued from the center.

As noted in Chapter 3, the existence of a "rank and file"—dues-paying members not considered to be "activists"—was the primary feature distinguishing Komsomol's structure from that of the Party.[13] Beginning in the 1950s, the gulf between passive rank and file and politically committed activists grew. Though no distinction between these categories was acknowledged in Komsomol rules, the focus of the organization's activities became strangely insular. The league's elite, which was older and heavily dominated by Party members, spent most of its time tending to the political indoctrination and mass mobilization of its general membership. In principle, however, this elite was accountable to the mass membership it was explicitly instructed to socialize and control.

This seeming paradox is linked to the deeper contradictions of a "vanguard" organization striving for universal membership. It calls to mind Allen Kassof's observation that Soviet youth organizations were not really youth movements but rather organizations for youth imposed by adults.[14] By monopolizing all forms of association among young people, the Komsomol was forced to incorporate both the vast majority of Soviet youth who would have preferred no organized activity at all and the smaller cohort that would have formed the core of a genuine youth movement.

The tensions between these groups lie at the heart of the most basic problems that dogged the Komsomol from its earliest days. What were officials supposed to emphasize: training the new generation of Party leaders and functionaries or ensuring that youthful masses were always at the beck and call of the state?

On the one hand, Komsomol statutes specified that it was to be selective: prospective members were required to meet rigorous moral and political standards and pass an examination on the organization's rules and history. Komsomol also had exclusive responsibility for selecting and recommending new members up to age twenty-three to the Communist Party.[15] On the other hand, its missions of indoctrination and economic mobilization required Komsomol to reach out to the broadest possible audience of youth, and the most accessible audience was its membership.

As I discussed in the previous chapter, this dual sense of purpose produced a curious interaction between rank and file and activists: the former were often passive and indifferent, while the latter exhibited distressing signs of careerism and a seeming lack of self-initiative. As a consequence, both organizational goals were subverted: the supposed "indoctrination" of rank-and-file members left them alienated and politically apathetic, while future generations of political leaders learned how to advance up the political hierarchy independent of their actual organizational performance.

Institutional Dynamics within the Komsomol

Both critics of the Komsomol and the organization's own officials often argued that Komsomol was a victim of its own growth. As the ranks swelled, ideological zeal inevitably became diluted. However, in pursuit of their growth targets Komsomol officials showed great initiative, circumventing controls from above and ignoring demands from below. Ultimately, their entrepreneurial zeal was a large part of the Komsomol's undoing.

Elite Controls

Were Komsomol officials both at the top of the hierarchy and at the street level thoroughly subordinated to their Komsomol or Party superiors, as elite-centered theory suggests? The Soviet press and the Komsomol's own archives are filled with evidence of street-level officials acting in open defiance of established league procedures.

In many industrial enterprises or rural settlements, for example, Komsomol organizations languished. In 1975 *Komsomol'skaia pravda* reported on one collective farm *(kolkhoz)* near Tambov where no Komsomol organization had met in over two years and "hooliganism" was widespread. "We aren't the only kolkhoz that's let the Komsomol go," reported the kolkhoz director.[16]

Where Komsomol officials did enforce standards of conduct, they often cited their enforcement as justification for new powers of coercion or compulsion. A 1971 report in *Pravda*, for instance, described "morals clubs" organized in the Oktiabr' district of Leningrad. These units, run largely by Komsomol activists under Party supervision, helped register "troublesome youth" in the district and sought to end their flirtations with delinquency. Remedies apparently included work holidays in the Virgin Lands or early induction into the Army.[17] Less extreme powers were acquired around the same time by Komsomol committees in institutions of higher education, which were tapped to help select the "best" students for receipt of bonus stipends.[18]

Initiatives such as these created a ripe environment for abuse, and a major charge levied against Komsomol officials during the organization's final convulsions was indeed misuse of power and privileges. Just as troublesome, and far more consistently chronicled by Komsomol officials themselves, were the many activists who took no initiatives at all. As unwilling members shuffled into their political-education classes, they were likely to encounter organizers equally unenthusiastic about their responsibilities to the organization.

Even before Stalin's death, "formalism" was a major complaint directed at the work of Komsomol activists. Applied to the work of a Soviet organization, the charge of "formalism" suggested adherence to external appearances accompanied by disregard of the intent or content of specific assignments. It implied an unacceptable lack of contact between officials and rank and file as well. In the case of Komsomol, a primary agent of indoctrination, the charge carried the added suggestion that the indoctrinators themselves were less than pure in their approach to their socialist duties.

The charge of formalism appears often in critiques of Komsomol work at the local or regional level. A 1960 Komsomol Central Committee resolution charged the Cheliabinsk Komsomol with pursuing a "raw numbers approach" that concentrated on paper shuffling. District (i.e., raikom) leaders within the city were charged with having little contact with either members or their own aktiv.[19]

Several years later, a Komsomol Central Committee representative wrote a detailed critique of how local Komsomol meetings were being run. Noting that the average Komsomol member attended over 150 two-hour meetings in the course of a fourteen-year membership, this author complained that virtually all agendas were handed down from higher levels and that meetings themselves amounted to little more than endless repetition of speeches by the same few activists. Organizers' sole concern was to generate warm bodies for these ritual events:

> What happens? As a rule, the same people approach the lectern again and again, as the Komsomolites in the hall openly yawn and drift off. They are merely guests here, and it is boring to be a guest at a meeting.
> . . . Eliminate [the boredom] and there will be no need to "ensure attendance"; the crimson sails of Komsomol romanticism themselves will attract a 100% quorum.[20]

In another example, First Secretary Pavlov, addressing a 1967 Central Committee plenum, attacked the Tomsk Komsomol obkom for "usually remembering about students only when it's necessary to send someone to construction sites, harvest work, or trash collecting."[21]

Shortcomings in Komsomol work did not escape the Party's scrutiny either. Brezhnev, addressing the Twenty-fifth Party Congress, linked the problems of an apathetic membership and a cynical and formalistic aktiv: "They [youth] are prepared to respond sincerely and wholeheartedly to any good undertaking. But confrontations with formalism, with a bureaucratic approach to upbringing work, extinguishes the flame in their hearts."[22]

A Party resolution on ideological upbringing several years later reiterated this concern, attacking both Komsomol and Party activists for permitting a "gap . . . between words and deeds." The resolution was especially pointed in criticizing "formalism," "bureaucratic clichés of all kinds," and "mechanical repetition over and over of general truths instead of the creative comprehension of these truths."[23]

For the most part, the Party attempted to control the Komsomol by controlling its top leadership. Though Komsomol First Secretaries were subordinated to the Party First Secretary, they enjoyed considerable autonomy and authority during the Khrushchev years. According to the two Komsomol chiefs who served under him, Khrushchev encouraged the Komsomol to promote younger individuals to leadership positions and to assert itself independently of the Party. However, Khrushchev's tendency to impose his will by fiat neutralized his progressive attitude toward autonomy.

Vladimir Semichastnyi, for instance, became First Secretary of the All-Union Komsomol in 1958 (for reference, Table 4.1 lists Komsomol leaders

Table 4.1. Komsomol Leaders, 1918–1991

First Secretary	Tenure	Age When Elected	Age When Replaced	Subsequent Career
Efim Tsetlin	Nov.–Dec. 1918	20	20	Komsomol/Party work; shot in 1937
Oskar Ryvkin	1919–1921	20	22	Party work; shot in 1937
Lazar' Shatskin	1921–1922	19	20	Youth International and Party work; shot in 1937
Petr Smorodin	1922–1924	25	27	Party work; shot in 1939
Nikolai Chaplin	1924–1928	22	26	Party work; shot in 1938
Aleksandr Mil'chakov	1928–1929	25	26	Party and Government work; jailed 1938-1954; died in 1973
Aleksandr Kosarev	1929–1938	26	35	Arrested in 1938; shot in 1939
Nikolai Mikhailov	1938–1952	32	46	Secretary, Moscow and Central Committee, CPSU; Minister of Culture; Chmn., State Committee for the Press; retired 1970; died 1982
Aleksandr Shelepin	1952–1958	34	40	Party Secretary; Chairman, KGB; CPSU Politburo, 1966–1975
Vladimir Semichastnyi	1958–1959	34	35	Party Secretary; Chairman, KGB; Dep. Prime Minister, Ukraine; Chmn., "Znanie"; retired 1988
Sergei Pavlov	1959–1968	30	39	Minister for Sports; Ambassador to Mongolia, Burma
Evgenii Tiazhel'nikov	1968–1977	40	49	Party work; Ambassador to Romania
Boris Pastukhov	1977–1982	44	49	Chmn., State Publishing Committee; Ambassador to Denmark
Viktor Mishin	1982–1986	39	43	Secretary, All-Union Trade Unions Council
Viktor Mironenko	1986–1990	33	37	Party work
Vladimir Ziukin	1990–1991	36	n/a	President, "International Cooperation Foundation"

Source: Komsomol'skaia zhizn' no. 20, 1988, 2–17; Ziukin data from material distributed to delegates at Twenty-first Komsomol Congress, Moscow, April 1990.

from 1918–1991). Semichastnyi was thirty-four when elected to replace the forty-year-old Shelepin. He later recalled how Khrushchev would encourage Komsomol leaders to act as aggressive watchdogs, confronting filmmakers guilty of producing too few films for young audiences or other officials guilty of laziness or incompetence: "I don't know, maybe our age played a role here (we weren't yet concerned about securing our post-Komsomol careers), but we never hesitated to take any podium, we were not afraid to criticize."[24]

Khrushchev apparently took pleasure in goading his young protégé even to contradict him, with the supposed aim of underlining the Komsomol's independence.

> Once, when we were still in Ukraine, I came to Khrushchev with some memo (I don't even remember what it concerned). He read it while I waited, and started crossing out one point after another. Then he looked at me and asked,
>
> "Listen, why are you agreeing with everything? Why don't you object?"
>
> "Do you expect me to contradict you?"
>
> "But you presumably met with secretaries of the Central Committee and discussed this before bringing it to me. Didn't you think through these issues already? So, defend them, prove your points!"
>
> This lesson served me well.[25]

Semichastnyi's account, however, suggests not only Khrushchev's desire for a dynamic Komsomol but also the formal subservience of the youth league to the Party in most areas. Khrushchev still needed to approve Komsomol initiatives, with or without discussion. This was true of personnel affairs as well. Semichastnyi recalled his own promotion from Komsomol chief to Party cadres boss:

> I told Khrushchev, "Nikita Sergeevich, I've only been First Secretary [of Komsomol] for one year. And you want to appoint me already to the Central Committee, in charge of Party organizations, no less! In Ukraine, Podgornyi, and in Bielorussia, Mazurov—they'll show up in my office tomorrow, and what am I supposed to say to them?"
>
> "Don't worry," replied Khrushchev, "You'll get used to it, and they'll get used to it. You've been sitting in the Komsomol long enough. How old are you?"

"Thirty-five."

"And Pavlov?" (He was then my second-in-command.)

"Twenty-nine."

"So, it's time to make way for youth."

And so I ended up in the department of Party organizations.[26]

It is implicit in Semichastnyi's account that the leadership of Komsomol—that is, its Central Committee and Biuro—played no role in the selection of his successor. Lists of unopposed nominees were routinely presented to meetings of the Central Committee or Congresses for unanimous ratification. Komsomol archives reveal no substantive discussion of any personnel decisions or changes of leadership at either Congresses or Central Committee plenums prior to the 1990 Komsomol Congress.

Despite keeping Komsomol on a relatively short leash, Khrushchev's affection for the league and its leaders seems to have been genuine. According to Semichastnyi's successor, Sergei Pavlov, Khrushchev's reliance on Komsomol brigades to carry out much of the Virgin Lands campaigns helped breathe new life into the youth league. He also noted the importance Khrushchev attached to Komsomol:

It is difficult to name a single plenum of the Party Central Committee or any ideological conference (and we had quite a few of the latter in those days) at which [Khrushchev] did not address Komsomol directly. I won't deny he had criticisms, but more often his comments took the form of appeals, of hopes he had for the youth.[27]

Khrushchev's public statements reinforce Pavlov's recollections. In 1961, for instance, Khrushchev visited Ukraine and attended a Ukrainian Party plenum on agriculture. He opened his address by upbraiding the Ukrainian leadership for failing to invite the republic's Komsomol leadership to the plenum, despite their critical role in the agricultural life of the republic.[28]

A markedly different relationship existed under Brezhnev, beginning with his very first appearance as General Secretary before a Komsomol audience. Shortly after his ouster of Khrushchev, Brezhnev addressed a special plenum of the Komsomol Central Committee but was offended at not receiving an immediate standing ovation. At a break in the proceedings, according to Pavlov, Brezhnev turned to Party officials present and commented, "There you can see the Komsomol opposition."[29]

This "Komsomol opposition," in Brezhnev's mind, included Pavlov and his two powerful predecessors—the present and former heads of the KGB. According to Pavlov: "Naturally, there was not even a hint of a Komsomol opposition: I saw Semichastnyi and Shelepin less often than I saw the General Secretary himself. Nevertheless, the mutual understanding and single-mindedness of the Khrushchev era was already gone."[30]

Where Khrushchev enjoyed bantering with his young protégés, Brezhnev sought sycophancy and adoration. According to Petr Shelest, the Ukrainian leader who served on the Khrushchev and Brezhnev Politburos, "Brezhnev was particularly frightened of those leaders younger than him."[31] In 1968, he engineered the replacement of Pavlov by Evgenii Tiazhel'nikov, a Party functionary who did not even sit on the Komsomol's Central Committee.

Tiazhel'nikov, at age forty, was the oldest official to take over the leadership of Komsomol in its fifty-year history. His selection demonstrated a reversal of Khrushchev's preference for boosting young leaders—he was a full year *older* than his predecessor. According to the stenographic report of the Komsomol Central Committee plenum, Tiazhel'nikov was nominated by the powerful Party ideology secretary, Mikhail Suslov.[32] Suslov took some time to justify the choice of Tiazhel'nikov, who was then serving as Party ideology secretary in Cheliabinsk. He argued that Tiazhel'nikov's experience with both Party and ideological work would permit the Komsomol to "utilize in [its] further activities the assistance of the Party aktiv." No questions were posed to this unknown nominee by the assembled Komsomol leaders, and he was elected unanimously.

Brezhnev was apparently comfortable with this new Komsomol leader. He was older than the "Komsomol opposition," posed no threat to Brezhnev, and owed his career utterly to the General Secretary. According to Iurii Churbanov, Brezhnev's son-in-law, Brezhnev spoke frequently by telephone with Tiazhel'nikov and often recounted conversations with him to family members at the dacha. "We won't go wrong with him," he would say.[33]

Tiazhel'nikov, for his part, was perfectly cast in the role of bootlick. Addressing the 1971 Party Congress, he praised Brezhnev's speech to the Congress as "a wonderful alloy of wisdom."[34] At the next Party gathering, in 1976, he seized upon a Brezhnev passage calling on the youth league to retain its "youthful energy." With a great flourish, he produced a clipping from a 1935 factory paper featuring a glowing profile of the young Leonid Brezhnev and presented it to Brezhnev at the podium.[35]

Tiazhel'nikov's selection to lead the Komsomol reflected Brezhnev's new conception of its chief role. Khrushchev had wanted an activist Komsomol, nipping at the heels of incompetent bureaucrats and inspiring its membership with heroic missions, but Brezhnev wanted a narrower, more conservative focus. Addressing the Twenty-third Party Congress in 1966, he declared:

It is very fine that Young Communists and other young people are working with such enthusiasm on construction projects and are taking part in the solution of other economic tasks. But at the same time, we cannot forget that the main thing in the work of the Komsomol is the upbringing of youth . . . Some Party and Komsomol organizations at times fail to consider that the present generation of boys and girls has not passed through the harsh school of revolutionary struggle and tempering that fell to the lot of the older generation.[36]

New Party rules approved at this Congress raised to twenty-three (from twenty) the age below which all new Party members must come from the ranks of the Komsomol. At the same time, Brezhnev called for an increased core of Party activists in Komsomol leadership organs. The consequences of both of these policy shifts were striking, and they are shown in Tables 4.2 and 4.3. In effect, Brezhnev was transforming the Komsomol into a more integral component of the propaganda network of the Communist Party. His selection of Tiazhel'nikov—a Party ideology worker—to head the league was a logical extension of this vision.

At every opportunity, Brezhnev emphasized the centrality of indoctrination work to Komsomol's mission. He urged the Sixteenth Komsomol Congress to remind the younger generation of its debt to its forebears and to society. "It is bad if the young are taught to accept life easily," he warned, since "they may involuntarily acquire the dependent's psychology."[37] In 1971, he told the Twenty-fourth Party Congress that Komsomol's central task was "the cultivation . . . of communist ideological conviction and devotion to our Soviet homeland and the spirit of internationalism, as well as the active propaganda of the norms and spiritual values of our society."[38]

By 1974, the need for additional manpower to work in the Non-Black Earth Zone and on the construction of the Baikal-Amur Railroad (BAM)

Table 4.2. Party Members and Candidate Members as a Percentage of Secretaries of Primary Komsomol Organizations

Year	Percent	Year	Percent
1966	14.7	1979	48.1
1967	18.3	1980	48.6
1968	20.6	1981	48.7
1969	26.8	1982	48.8
1970	31.2	1983	48.6
1971	36.9	—	—
—	—	1987	42.3
1974	44.1	—	—
—	—	1990	14.6
1978	47.5		

Source: VLKSM: Nagliadnoe Posobie po komsomol'skomu stroitelstvu [Visual guides on Komsomol membership], 138; 1983, 1987, 1990 figures from *Statisticheskii i spravochnyi material* [Statistical and reference materials] (TsK VLKSM, 1990—distributed to delegates of the Twenty-first Komsomol Congress in Moscow), 108.

reminded Brezhnev of the ideological value of hard work. He lauded Komsomol's contribution of "shock work" brigades to these massive campaigns and told the Seventeenth Komsomol Congress that they were "training a new generation of workers for the scientific-technical revolution."[39] He criticized parents who sought to shelter their offspring from the demanding assignments, warning that such pampering "engenders parasitism and disrespect for work."

By 1978, Komsomol labor brigades were playing a large role in the national economy, but Brezhnev was still concerned about the Komsomol's ideological tasks. He leveled a rare blunt criticism at the Eighteenth Komsomol Congress about formalism in upbringing work: "It is time for all personnel on the ideological front to end the practice of thoughtless and mechanical repetition of truisms that still survives in some places."[40]

In 1981, appearing for the last time at a Party Congress, Brezhnev reiterated his concern about shortcomings in the indoctrination work of Komsomol. He cautioned against merely "increasing the number of 'measures'" but offered little concrete guidance. Instead, he urged Kom-

Table 4.3. New Party Members Recommended by the Komsomol

Year	Accepted on VLKSM Recommendation	As Percentage of All New CPSU Candidates
1968	290,701	44.9
1969	283,309	48.9
1970	312,858	53.8
1971	276,693	56.1
1972	295,242	63.0
1973	351,558	66.2
1974	382,139	68.8
1975	403,925	70.2
1976	435,361	71.4
1977	457,603	72.9
1978	467,143	73.4
1979	477,799	73.9
1980	470,586	73.4
1981	478,178	73.1
—	—	—
1985	468,147	71.6
1986	473,400	71.4
1987	402,293	68.7
1988	268,601	61.2
1989	171,437	54.7

Sources: VLKSM: Nagliadnoe Posobie po komsomol'skomu stroitelstvu [Visual guides on Komsomol membership] (Moscow: Molodaia Gvardia, 1985), 41; 1985–88 data from Goskomstat, *Molodezh' SSSR* [Youth in the USSR] (Moscow: Finansy i statistika, 1990), 156; 1989 data from *Statisticheskii i spravochnyi material* (TsK VLKSM, 1990—distributed to delegates of the Twenty-first Komsomol Congress in Moscow), 104.

somol leaders to "establish a vibrant, creative atmosphere in every Komsomol organization."[41]

Such helpful advice was open to a wide range of interpretations. Apparently some local Komsomol leaders erred on the side of excessive vibrancy, as Konstantin Chernenko, addressing a 1983 Party plenum on ideological work, felt compelled to chide the league for "excessive organizational measures and ostentatious hoopla."[42] Even Mikhail Gorbachev, himself a former Moscow University Komsomol organizer, stressed the ideological tasks confronting Komsomol in one of his first major national speeches, in 1983. Gorbachev, however, included the youth league in a list of other institutions—including the family, school, higher schools, trade unions, soviets, and labor collectives—which *shared* responsibility for socializing new Soviet citizens.[43]

Gorbachev's speech offered a brief hint of the new direction he would give to Party-Komsomol relations after 1986. By freeing the Komsomol from the burden of sole responsibility for the ideological health of the younger generation, he could offer it greater latitude for initiatives in other areas of economic and political life. At the same time, he would break the close subordination of the Komsomol leader to the Party leader.

On the one hand, tight Party control sharply limited the room for independent goal-setting by Komsomol officials.[44] On the other hand, the league's mission of "indoctrination" was vague, and success was difficult to measure. Komsomol heads appear to have been held accountable chiefly for their loyalty to the General Secretary and given few concrete guidelines for assessing their performance. Party leaders, in other words, placed certain boundaries on the Komsomol's performance but did not dictate it. Within the league, the Komsomol's own findings of "formalism" suggested that street-level actors were also adept at exploiting the latitude in the instructions they received.

Societal Interests and Policy-Relevant Data

To determine the responsiveness of Komsomol officials to social pressures and societal interests, we must consider how well Komsomol leaders at different levels understood the consequences of their policies. Early in the Gorbachev years, emigre sociologist Vladimir Shlapentokh argued that it was "difficult to believe" that Soviet leaders were unaware of Soviet youth's rejection of Communist ideology. He was skeptical of the notion, then popular in the West, that leaders were pursuing an "ostrich policy"— ignoring the warning signs of an impending upheaval. He expressed "no doubt" that a policy to contain a generational rebellion was being developed at the highest levels.[45]

Shlapentokh's basic premise is supported by evidence from within the Komsomol, but his conclusions are unwarranted. There is ample evidence that Komsomol officials recognized their failures in inculcating Communist values, but there are few signs that this evaluation played a significant role in determining their behavior. Within Komsomol there were two chief conduits through which attitudes and demands of Komsomol members could have influenced the policy process: sociology and internal networks.

SOCIOLOGY

As discussed in Chapter 3, youth sociology was an important branch of empirical sociology in the Soviet Union in its formative days. The Komsomol was an important early patron of this effort, particularly through its newspaper *Komsomol'skaia pravda*. In May 1960, *Komsomol'skaia pravda* announced the creation of a Public Opinion Institute.[46] The Institute—the first of its kind in the Soviet Union—conducted a total of sixteen polls over seven years, fourteen of which were of the *Komsomol'skaia pravda* readership.

Readership polls are notorious for their problems of selection bias— only newspaper subscribers have the opportunity to respond, and of this sample only the most motivated will actually do so—but many of the questionnaires elicited tens of thousands of responses. Questions were often posed in open-ended format, making analysis more subjective and also giving the newspaper the option of excerpting several provocative results instead of presenting a more scientific analysis. Despite its problems, the polling operation represented a major advance for Soviet public opinion research in general and surveys of the youth population in particular.

While many of the Institute's surveys covered such unobjectionable topics as avoiding war, several polls ventured closer to sensitive areas like the quality of consumer services or use of free time. One survey in particular uncovered the limits of Komsomol's tolerance toward empirical sociology: on 26 April 1966, the Institute published a poll in conjunction with the Fifteenth Komsomol Congress in which readers were asked their opinions about the Komsomol itself. The poll was an abbreviated version of a questionnaire being administered to a scientific sample of 3,000 Komsomol members.[47] According to Boris Grushin, the Institute's research director, readers were so critical of the youth league that publication of the results was barred and the raw data were confiscated and burned.[48] Only two mentions of the results ever appeared. The first, less than a month later, presented brief excerpts from five respondents. The second, in September, commented on the perceived absence of "free and open discussion" (described as *glasnost'*) in Komsomol affairs and particularly the lack of communication (both "upward" and "downward") between Komsomol officials and rank-and-file members.[49]

Despite their prickly response to the *Komsomol'skaia pravda* questionnaire, Komsomol leaders looked to sociology as a potential solution to precisely the problems with communication uncovered by the 1966 survey. In 1965, for instance, Komsomol chief Pavlov called for more "concrete sociological research" to address problems of "a depersonalized, wholesale approach to youth" evident in the work of some Komsomol committees.[50]

Some Komsomol officials seem to have shown particular interest in using empirical sociology to make their data gathering more "scientific." A Komsomol official from Lvov wrote that his obkom had created a special group to coordinate and promote applied sociological research because "the questionnaires that Komsomol committees at plants compile and circulate themselves have nothing in common with sociology."[51]

A similar view was expressed at a 1967 Komsomol Central Committee plenum by Gennadii Ianaev, secretary of the Gorkii oblast Komsomol. Ianaev—who decades later would become Mikhail Gorbachev's vice president[52]—complained about the "amateurishness" with which Komsomol committees had been treating sociological research of student groups. "Groups of sociologists are seriously prepared to help us—practitioners— in our work," he declared. Ianaev cited research conducted in his oblast that found students' selection of "informal leaders" was unrelated to the Komsomol's selection of "formal" leaders. Komsomol officials, consequently, lacked prestige among their members because they were not selected from the pool of "natural" leaders. Sociology, he asserted, could help Komsomol groups identify those students with "genuine authority" and promote them to leadership positions.[53]

Sociological research seems to have received a boost from the 1968 Prague Spring and student revolts in Western Europe. Anxious to avert an explosion from Soviet youth, officials of the Komsomol Central Committee summoned several sociologists to a Moscow meeting.[54] The Central Komsomol School—formerly an administrative training center for regional Komsomol officials—was reorganized as the Higher Komsomol School (VKSh) and given greater responsibility for coordinating research activities.[55] In 1970, a Scientific Research Center (NITs) was created within VKSh; throughout the 1970s and 1980s this center, along with the Institute of Sociological Research of the Soviet Academy of Sciences, produced the vast majority of empirical research on the sociology of Soviet youth.

But this apparent turn to sociology is misleading. A Komsomol Central Committee meeting after the Czech invasion revealed a clear understanding of why Czech youth, and even the Czech youth league, had played a prominent role in the Prague Spring. Iu. Torusev, a Komsomol Secretary recently returned from discussions with the Czech youth league, provided a detailed account of the sources of the crisis—so detailed that league chief Tiazhel'nikov refused requests to distribute copies of it to Central Committee members. "It is obvious," he noted, "that Comrade Torusev's report cannot be distributed in its current form."[56]

In fact, Torusev's report was not even fit to be included in the unpublished stenogram of the plenum. Archival copies of the stenogram reveal that Torusev's comments were edited to lessen the parallels between causes of the Czech upheaval and conditions then prevailing among Soviet youth. For instance, Torusev reported that the Czech youth league missed signs of discontent among youth over social and material conditions (underlined text was excised from the final stenogram, italicized text was inserted):

Youth often failed to perceive progress toward expanding production, resolving housing and communal living issues, there was a drastic shortage of dormitory space, the problem of job assignments, *utilization and prospects* of young specialists after graduation from higher education was unsatisfactorily resolved, so too was the development of facilities for cultural, educational and sporting activity. The Czech youth league was essentially marginal in all these questions, and this could only have affected its prestige.[57]

Clearly, Komsomol Central Committee leaders did not need sociology to tell them that youth were unhappy about shortages that affected their material well-being. Nor were they apparently under any delusions about the overcrowding of dormitories and recreational facilities or about the resentment often felt toward the job-assignments system for university graduates (see Chapter 5 for a detailed discussion of this system). Torusev also warned that the Czech uprising was a consequence of the Czech Komsomol's neglect of their upbringing work but chose not to leave in the record testimony about the speed with which decades of indoctrination could apparently be undone:

> Essentially, from that time [i.e., the 1967 Czech Komsomol Congress, at which voluntary interest-based youth "clubs" were endorsed as primary groups] ideological-upbringing work with youth stopped . . . Czech youth began to change literally before one's eyes. They turned toward the narrow world of vulgar, consumer interests, toward a Western lifestyle and bourgeois ideals of "freedom" and "democracy."[58]

Komsomol officials thus had few illusions about either the irreversibility of indoctrination work or its capacity to marginalize material hardships. The sociological research supported by the Komsomol for the next two decades added little to this instinctive understanding and next to nothing about the effectiveness or shortcomings of Komsomol policies. Standard practice seems to have been to include several questions about Komsomol or Party membership and accompanying "civic assignments" *(obshchestvennaia rabota)* on questionnaires for youth samples.[59] These surveys, however, were often distributed in the field by Komsomol organizers, frequently as part of a Komsomol meeting. Respondents would complete questionnaires individually but could often easily guess (or were sometimes "coached") what the "correct" answers were to any Komsomol-related question.

Analysis of survey responses rarely went beyond simple cross-tabulation of responses according to basic categories (like age or education level). This level of analysis may be useful for providing anecdotal illustrations of social trends, but it cannot support serious analysis of the multiple causes of social outcomes. In part, as several sociologists explained to me, research was hampered by the primitive level of technology for data analysis. One sociologist at the Soviet Academy of Sciences claimed that, as late as 1989, sociologists had access to only one computer center in Moscow with adequate mainframe software for performing multiple regressions—at the Academy of Social Sciences of the Party Central Committee. The software in more common use required each potential response to be coded as a dummy variable and permitted tabular output only.

As a result of these limitations, most sociological research on youth attempted to highlight trends but rarely addressed multiple causality. Most often, Komsomol officials trotted out isolated results of sociological surveys to demonstrate the need for some previously decided policy. Despite calls for "useful" sociology, the research itself was hardly ever policy-relevant.

The lack of concrete recommendations accompanying Komsomol-sponsored sociology was a frequent complaint of Party officials in their evaluations of Komsomol work.[60] Aleksandr Kapto, who had led the Ukrainian Komsomol in the early 1970s, criticized youth sociology for "abstractness" and for limiting itself to the "verification of affirmative tendencies."[61] Years later, Victor Mironenko, Gorbachev's choice to head the Komsomol, would dismiss the entire body of Soviet sociological literature as the "repetition of hackneyed theoretical theses, 'lacquered' statistics, totally out of touch with what is happening . . . among youth."[62]

Sociologists themselves were hardly more charitable toward work done prior to 1986. Several sociologists studying youth told me their work during the 1970s and early 1980s was never explicitly linked to policy formulation. One prominent researcher dismissed most of the data generated by NITs at the Higher Komsomol School as "useless."[63] The director of NITs bitterly complained that "nobody was interested" in his center's research because "knowledge gets in the way."[64]

The true attitude of Komsomol apparatchiks toward research on public opinion might be gauged by a document prepared for a 1976 Komsomol Central Committee plenum that was to consider "moral upbringing." The brief report contained a "review of letters received by the Central Committee" over the past year—an analysis similar to that performed on newspaper readership surveys. According to this study, 4,900 letters concerned "moral upbringing," and 25 percent of these contained recommendations for improving the Komsomol's work in this area. The authors then provided several excerpts of letters meant to illustrate Komsomol workers' indifference to drunkenness, wild appearance, "amoral behavior," the wearing of crosses, "orgies," and homicidal brawling among youth. Close examination of this document, however, reveals that most of the excerpts cited by the Komsomol bureaucrats were authored by the same N. V. Litvinov of Voronezh.[65] Justifying the creation of a new committee on "moral upbringing" apparently took precedence over giving plenum participants a more scientific, or at least representative, portrayal of public opinion.

Direct research on public opinion and social trends was not the sole source of such data for Komsomol policy makers, however. Any good Komsomol secretary was supposed to be aware of his members' opinions from the course of regular meetings with members. In theory, data gathered at the street level was supposed to flow up the Komsomol hierarchy and into the policy process. In practice, this flow was far from smooth.

INFORMATION-GATHERING NETWORKS

The Komsomol's monopoly over the organization of youth at all levels gave it an extensive data-collection network for assessing trends among youth as well as for representing their interests and demands in the policy process. As Jerry Hough noted,

> Komsomol officials inevitably find that the acceptance of regime values by young people . . . depends not only on propaganda activities but also on concrete conditions and policies which are specifically relevant to their lives. As a consequence, Komsomol officials cannot inculcate a Marxist Leninist world view unless they attempt to represent youth interests in the policy process at least to some extent.[66]

Despite having both the motive and the means to represent the interests and demands of its membership, the Komsomol's policy-making process remained oddly insulated from real-world concerns. Both primary representative organs of the youth league—the regular Congresses and the more-frequent Central Committee plenums—proved ineffective as either representative or deliberative bodies.

This fault is perhaps most glaring at the level of the Central Committee, which the organizational scheme of the Komsomol designated as the main policy-making body for the youth league. Central Committee plenums were held two or three times a year, lasting one or two days each (as the Brezhnev years wore on, single-day sessions became the norm). Each plenum was devoted to a particular theme, and its chief product was a resolution on that topic.

Komsomol archives reveal that plenums were carefully choreographed in advance by the Central Committee apparatus, that is, by the permanent Central Committee bureaucracy. Planners meticulously coordinated the schedule of speakers—not merely the main addresses but most of the subsequent speakers as well. Speakers were briefed in advance on points they should make, and some were sent speeches drafted by Central Committee staff. The schedule of events was carefully arranged, including the selection of music that would accompany breaks and exhibits of art or literature to accompany the main theme of the meeting. Resolutions of the Central Committee were drafted in advance of each meeting and circulated to delegates as a typeset booklet. An "editing commission" selected at each plenum would consider comments or criticisms of the draft text received from Central Committee members, but often these amounted to just a few slips of paper suggesting cosmetic changes.

Though there was usually at least a semblance of autonomy attached to the proceedings of the Central Committee, its subservience to the few top officials and their staffs is often apparent even through the filter of stenographic reports. At one 1965 session, for instance, First Secretary Pavlov launched a blistering attack on the poet Evgenyi Evtushenko. As he grew agitated, he ridiculed a regional Komsomol newspaper for serializing a long poem of Evtushenko's. In an exchange later stricken from the official record, he asked the plenum to condemn the newspaper:

> *Pavlov:* Surely in Gorkii oblast' there are young writers in greater need of support . . . than this Evtushenko? But the Gorkii paper thought of this too late. Now he's become so big that even Union papers are below him! Does the plenum of the Komsomol Central Committee agree with this?

Voices from the auditorium: Agreed!

Pavlov: What? You agree they should have reprinted this poem in ten issues?

Voices: No, of course not! (Commotion in the hall)

Pavlov: Well, that's what I was asking you![67]

Such moments of confusion were rare, however, especially as plenums grew more formal and more tedious through the Brezhnev years. Standards for appropriate conduct of plenary sessions became generally accepted, and these standards excluded any meaningful exchange of opinions. The stenographic reports of these plenums grew thinner throughout the 1970s.

Komsomol Congresses, the quadrennial convocations that theoretically represented the ultimate authority within the youth league, were even more carefully choreographed than plenums. Because Congresses brought together nearly 5,000 delegates from around the country, careful deliberation could hardly be expected even under the most receptive circumstances. In practice, however, delegates had little opportunity to offer any substantial input to the making of Komsomol policies. Lists of speakers for all sessions were prepared months in advance of the meeting. Komsomol officials also prepared detailed plans for coverage of the Congress in the press and on radio and television, with schedules for specific articles and proposed authors from within the Komsomol's ranks.[68]

Even the special policy-specific "sections"—organized to permit smaller groups of delegates to discuss topics like education or labor discipline—provided little room for uncontrolled inputs from delegates. These sections lasted no more than a few hours, and speakers included specialists brought in to address the delegates.[69] Planners either prepared or approved texts of speeches in advance, and Komsomol archives show that several texts were on hand for a list of "reserve speakers" in the event time permitted speeches from the floor. These sections concluded by approving "recommendations" prepared by relevant Komsomol Central Committee departments before the Congress even started. Recommendations from all sections were published together and distributed to delegates before the sections even met.

Constraints on open discussion extended to all levels of Komsomol decision making. In 1969, for instance, the Estonian Communist Party complained that the Biuro of the Estonian Komsomol was too fond of discussing questions brought to it for approval:

> Questions considered at meetings of the Biuro . . . are not always agreed to in advance by Secretaries and Central Committee departments. This leads to unnecessary debates during discussions and adversely affects the authority of both Secretaries and workers in the Central Committee apparat.[70]

In Moscow, as well, the Biuro and Secretariat seem to have acted as little more than rubber stamps for actions presented to them. From the vantage point of the Central Committee—to which the Biuro and Secretariat were theoretically accountable—even the responsibilities of these organizations were unclear. Responding to some mild criticisms at a 1975 plenum, First Secretary Tiazhel'nikov acknowledged that the policy process at the highest level was opaque:

> The Biuro and Secretariat is not some abstract concept, not just a group of comrades . . . but concrete people. And each of us must, absolutely, take personal responsibility before the plenum for the results of our work. Perhaps not all members of the Central Committee know how we divide up our responsibilities? Perhaps it would even be useful to explain who deals with what concrete task.[71]

Even allowing for some irony in his tone, it seems remarkable that the head of the Komsomol would suggest that the division of labor among its leading bodies was a mystery to the league's top elected officials. Yet if full-time bureaucrats planned all aspects of Congresses and Central Committee meetings and resolved in advance questions to be considered by its Biuro, it is not surprising that regional officials viewed the center as a black box. The only route by which grass-roots demands could influence Komsomol policy led directly through the Komsomol bureaucracy.

Komsomol bureaucrats did establish elaborate mechanisms for the formal collection and analysis of data from local organizations. The most prominent of these were massive reviews accompanying key events like Komsomol Congresses or an exchange of documents (essentially a membership audit that was ordered every decade or so). During an exchange of documents in 1975–77, Tiazhel'nikov reported that "1.3 *million* critical comments were voiced concerning the Komsomol Central Committee and committees," 20 percent of which included "suggestions . . . for improving their work." A remarkable 75 percent of all "comments and suggestions" were reported to have been implemented.[72]

It is worth pausing to consider these numbers. According to Tiazhel'nikov's statement, the Komsomol bureaucracy, in twenty-one months, received, processed, and acted on several hundred thousand suggestions. While the sheer bureaucratic bravado of this claim is striking, equally striking is the absence of any systematic policy response to, or even analysis of, this flood of street-level input. The resolutions of both the Biuro and Central Committee on the completion of the documents exchange mention that Brezhnev received membership card No. 1, but neither refers to this massive grass-roots feedback. In fact, we must surmise that most of the "suggestions" counted by the Central Committee apparat as "voiced" and "implemented" were merely noted as such in the aggregate by the committees to which they were directed. In other words, much of these data were probably never actually received in Moscow.

Had all these comments been processed in Moscow, of course, the likely outcome would have been gridlock. Such was the result of similar feedback exercises that coincided with the Komsomol Congresses. In the period leading up to each Congress, the Central Committee solicited comments and suggestions on Komsomol work from a wide range of sources. Before the Eighteenth Congress in 1978, for instance, a *doklad* (report) was sent to all regional Komsomol committees to be read at a pre-Congress meeting; secretaries were to summarize comments on it for the Central Committee.[73] In addition, letters were sent to obkoms and raikoms, to Party leaders, government officials, and outside experts requesting advice on improving the work of Komsomol organizations.[74]

These requests produced a torrent of advice and proposals, ranging from brief comments to detailed letters of several pages. These proposals poured into the Central Committee apparat, where they were sorted by category, collated, and farmed out to relevant Central Committee departments for further action.[75] Suggestions from Komsomol officials and outside sources seem to have received equal weight. The same fate awaited comments made at the Congress itself by delegates in public sessions and during the hundreds of meetings arranged for delegates with government and Party officials. Comments were assembled in vast matrices; "action plans" were then prepared according to which a relevant Komsomol apparatchik would investigate each critical assertion, pursue a specific request, or assess a concrete suggestion. Bureaucratic "action," in these cases, consisted not of rectifying the irritating problem but in somehow acknowledging its existence.

The primary result of this massive brainstorming session seems to have been a crushingly long, unprioritized, ad hoc list of initiatives, all of which received roughly equal attention. The compilation of proposals received by the Nineteenth Congress for improving "upbringing work" took up 208 pages in tabular form.[76] These ran from the Minister of Commerce's call for more balanced press coverage of service industries to the Latvian Komsomol Central Committee's proposal to create a journal for students of specialized secondary schools to the comment by the editor of the journal *Avrora* that the consumer industry sector must devote more attention to creating fashionable clothing for youth. Often, contradictory suggestions followed each other on the list, each earmarked for "action" by some Central Committee bureaucrat.

In essence, the Komsomol bureaucracy treated these proposals like any other assignment given to the youth league. Inputs were counted, categorized, and assigned to departments, which then reported on the percentage of items receiving some form of action. By excessively formalizing the procedure for processing advice from the grass roots and from outside experts, Komsomol leaders squandered a rich opportunity to assess social demands and refine institutional priorities. Reading through these hundreds of submissions, it is impossible not to be impressed at both the wealth of data offered by many respondents and the ritualistic rhetoric offered up by the vast majority. No effort seems to have been made by its recipients to separate the wheat from the chaff, to co-opt the more thoughtful contributors into the policy process, or to synthesize any policy recommendations at all from the entire undertaking.

Information, Monitoring, and Authority within the Komsomol Hierarchy

As with all aspects of the centrally planned and administered Soviet system, performance objectives for all officials in the Komsomol hierarchy were translated into more easily monitored quantitative targets. These targets became objectives unto themselves, dictating the range of agents' allowable behavior and limiting superiors' capacity to alter that behavior. Since agents controlled the upward flow of information about their own performances, the reality of Komsomol life at street level was lost behind the mask of voluminous "activity plans" and the blizzard of data reporting plan fulfillment.

The most basic plan feature was a regular schedule of meetings at each level of the Komsomol hierarchy. Secretaries of primary organizations at schools and workplaces were expected to document these meetings, which were to be held at least monthly. They kept records on members' attendance, as well as on the number of speakers and the degree of audience participation in the "discussion" of each meeting's central report. These statistics were then reported to the raikom, which forwarded them up the organizational ladder. In this manner, then, the Central Committee apparat could calculate that 1.3 million members made contributions to the "discussion" over the 1977 exchange of documents.

Meetings of primary and local organizations were as carefully staged as meetings of the Central Committee or Congress. Despite regular attacks on excessive "formalism" in the work of its field organizers, top officials set unambiguous limits on the degree of spontaneity expected at Komsomol meetings. This was quite clear even in 1965, before the Brezhnev torpor had truly set in. During a plenum of the Central Committee devoted to "organizational work in the Komsomol," Sergei Pavlov launched a fierce attack on the activities of local and primary organizations. He complained that most meetings were run entirely by the aktiv. "Consequently," he warned, "Komsomoltsy are already getting used to such a state of affairs, content with the role of audience."[77]

Apparently rising to Pavlov's challenge, several speakers attempted to show their devotion to a spirit of true activism.[78] The secretary of the Ufa gorkom, Iu. Poroikov, complained that the Komsomol's rules had grown out of touch with its membership. He told of one local secretary who grew so tired of chasing members to pay their dues that he simply set up a locked iron box. He then recounted the experiences of another Komsomol organizer at a large enterprise who, rather than surrendering to members' apathy, decided to organize groups by common interests instead of by factory shops: "While this is not according to the rules *(po ustavu)*, we deemed this innovation useful, since it helped bring members together, and revealed significant untapped reserves we could use in our work with youth. It allowed us to conduct this work in conjunction with the interests and demands of the young people."[79]

Rather than receiving the congratulations of his comrades, Poroikov's attempt to introduce real reform ended as a demonstration of the limits of allowable innovation. Pavlov castigated him for showing flagrant disregard for the rules:

Pavlov: Nobody has changed the Komsomol Statutes. How can we sanction such behavior? You're speaking of it at a plenum of the Komsomol Central Committee! You violated the *Ustav* . . . That is not proper. I don't know how else it can be viewed. Don't you agree with me?

Voices: Correct![80]

The lesson of Pavlov's outburst could hardly have been lost on Central Committee members: even though present practices may be ineffective, if you plan to innovate, keep it to yourselves. Local agents easily kept their activities shielded from central scrutiny, because they provided most of the data on activities at their organizational level.

In other parts of his 1965 report, Pavlov touched on several characteristics of Komsomol structure and procedure that made central monitoring of local performance particularly difficult—and afforded agents significant latitude to adapt their behavior to local needs or their own interests. In particular, Pavlov criticized the poor training and excessive turnover of cadres, the poor follow-up on the implementation of decisions, and a purely quantitative approach to the question of membership growth. These symptoms dogged the Komsomol until its final days and can be seen as manifestations of the more general dilemmas of hierarchical control discussed in Chapter 2: property rights, individual incentives, monitoring, and the ratchet problem.

PROPERTY RIGHTS

According to a strict interpretation of league statutes, officials at higher organizational levels were elected by lower-level committees. In practice, candidates for secretary at all levels were selected by the next highest organizational tier and hence could be hand-picked for their loyalty and subservience. This does not wholly explain why these subordinates never took advantage of their formal institutional power to mount even limited challenges from the grass roots.

Local officials were dependent on their superiors for more than just appointment and promotion. Committees at the obkom (regional) or gorkom (city) levels approved all budgetary outlays by primary and raikom (district) Komsomol committee. Local committees lacked the right to establish their own bank accounts; all dues were forwarded directly to supervisory levels, as were all requests for expenditures.[81] Local committees even lacked the right to enroll new members directly.[82] All new memberships were processed at district headquarters in batches that took up increasing chunks of raikom members' days. There could be little dispute over the "ownership" of institutional assets: superiors maintained tight control over organizational resources and delegated only limited powers to subordinates.[83]

The Komsomol Central Committee did offer local officials a set of benefits intended to soften the sting of their subservience. Through the vertical hierarchy, local Komsomol officials could tap the vast resources of the Soviet state and deliver particular benefits to members. In this manner, local leaders could often buy enough goodwill from their nominal "constituents" to last through their often-brief stints with grass-roots politics.

Nowhere was this mechanism more apparent than at Komsomol Congresses. During their stay in Moscow, delegates met in small groups with ministers and Party representatives. These meetings allowed delegates to express local concerns, often presenting detailed demands. These requests, along with other specific "proposals" voiced by delegates from the tribune, were carefully recorded by Central Committee apparatchiks and—just like the massive pre-Congress brainstorming sessions—meticulously tracked and followed up in the months following the Congress. In many cases, these forays into pork-barrel politics yielded tangible results for the provinces—and presumably left field agents marginally more indebted to the Central Committee bureaucrats who had "delivered the goods."[84]

INDIVIDUAL INCENTIVES

In his 1965 report, Pavlov noted that Komsomol group organizers received little or no training for their posts and served chiefly as "dues collectors." Turnover among these part-time officials (who reported to secretaries of primary organizations) approached 100 percent annually.[85] Returning to this topic the following year, Pavlov reported that obkom secretaries had, on the average, two years' experience, while raikom and gorkom secretaries had an average tenure of just one year. Secretaries of primary organizations averaged only seven months' experience.[86]

Several years later, a careful study of the Komsomol aktiv confirmed Pavlov's diagnosis: officials of primary Komsomol organizations received virtually no training and usually served too briefly in their posts to develop any real expertise.[87] A survey of the Kiev Komsomol aktiv revealed that fewer than 40 percent at the gorkom/raikom level had been briefed by their predecessors and nearly 15 percent had received no instructions whatsoever.[88] As a consequence, most secretaries simply preferred to complete organizational assignments themselves rather than to delegate tasks. This reflected an incentive structure that placed its primary emphasis on the fulfillment of concrete assignments.

Not all Komsomol officials were so poorly socialized. The Komsomol aktiv could be divided into three distinct segments: part-time group organizers and secretaries, full-time secretaries of primary, local and regional committees, and full-time department heads (i.e., members of the apparat). Part-time secretaries of primary organizations were four to five times less likely to go on to Party or government work than full-time secretaries (roughly 5 percent of secretaries of the 400–450,000 primary organizations were on Komsomol's payroll).[89] Full-time secretaries and department heads seem to have followed roughly similar career paths, however, and faced similarly high turnover rates.[90]

Thus, while the organizational structure seems to have been split between full-time and part-time employees, no similar division existed between "elected" officials and their administrative staffs. Throughout the regional administration of the Komsomol, great mobility seems to have been the rule, especially below the level of obkom. Even within the bureaucratic structure, officials rarely retained the same post long enough to do more than master the rules. Consequently, planning horizons for officials in both the "representative" (committee) and administrative (apparat) structures must have been quite short indeed. A newly appointed official had few incentives to try to change a rule or assignment that would affect her for only a year or two—particularly if that official aspired to a higher post in state or Party work. It was far simpler to find some way to just "fulfill the plan"—even if that meant, for instance, guaranteeing a 100 percent subscription rate to Komsomol journals by simply paying for them all personally.[91]

Rapid turnover at lower levels of the Komsomol hierarchy also shielded officials from the consequences of their actions; it effectively insured them against the risk of performance failures. In such an environment, principals expecting short tenure in a given post had few incentives to police their agents aggressively. At the street level, officials who quickly learned how to maintain formal compliance with their performance targets were rewarded and thus had few incentives to learn the intricacies of each new assignment.

MONITORING AND INFORMATION ASYMMETRIES

Komsomol administrators faced classic hidden action problems. To evaluate the performance of Komsomol officials in the field, they relied upon reports submitted by these officials themselves. The effectiveness of this mechanism in ensuring that field agents continued to act in the broad interests of their principals—that is, in pursuit of Komsomol goals and objectives—depended crucially on two elements: the designation of plan targets and the reliability of feedback on plan fulfillment.

In his vigorous 1965 critique, Pavlov charged that both of these elements were problematic in Komsomol organizational work. Performance objectives at all organizational levels were often ambiguous, and monitoring of progress toward their achievement was often nonexistent. He criticized Komsomol resolutions for their imprecision, complaining that they often included uplifting phrases like "demand" or "devote attention to" but that monitoring of their fulfillment was treated like some "temporary campaign." He also attacked lower-level organizations for merely repeating the resolutions of higher-level bodies: "Decisions repeat one another without end, and it is impossible to monitor their fulfillment. For instance, why does the Komsomol of the Gosbank in Rostov, with just eight members, need to pass fifty-four resolutions within one year, brandishing the same uplifting slogans, 'broader . . . higher . . . elevate . . . strengthen . . .,' etc."[92]

Pavlov also observed that the "paper blizzard" of resolutions and committee decisions could conceal blatant abuses of power by Komsomol officials. He singled out one Moscow raikom secretary who had allowed fifteen adults, including factory workers aged forty-nine and fifty-three, to use special passes intended for a teenage workers' retreat at a countryside sanatorium.[93]

While there is no shortage of stories about abuses of power, not all violations were venal. There appears to have been considerable confusion at the level of local organizations about how to interpret resolutions or rules emanating from Moscow. Merle Fainsod's portrait of the Smolensk Komsomol in the 1920s and 1930s suggests that Moscow's intentions were often unclear, and this appears to have been a regular feature of center-periphery relations through the years.[94] Komsomol officials traveling through the Far East in the late 1960s, for instance, reported back to Moscow on local officials who felt cut off from their Moscow supervisors. They pleaded for the Central Committee and its publishing house to send them copies of new Komsomol publications, "even if it's just a single copy for us to display in the cabinet."[95] In Estonia, around the same time, a discussion in the press about the merits of raising the Komsomol joining age to sixteen led many local committees to believe the change had been approved; many schools suspended the enrollment of new members for the remainder of the year.[96]

Though Komsomol leaders in Moscow seemed aware that they were producing too many resolutions for any to receive adequate attention, they seemed unable to restrain their proliferation. A historian studying Komsomol activities in the 1970s and 1980s observed that the league's calls for reducing the number of "directives" binding on local organizations from above were actually accompanied by an increase in the number of such dictates. By the mid-1980s, more than fifty separate aspects of organizational work at the local level, including the agendas of group meetings, were dictated by superiors.[97] In 1984, Egor Ligachev scolded the Central Committee for passing over 300 resolutions in three years and organizing over 450 different programs *(meropriiatie)*. Little wonder, he said, that local committees were complaining of overwork, since each of these initiatives created new responsibilities and reporting requirements.[98]

On the one hand, overspecification of local procedures could be viewed as a natural response to problems of information asymmetries. On the other hand, however, local committees ignored many of these formal requirements. When one Central Committee representative observing raikom elections in Moscow objected that candidates had not been discussed prior to the vote—in accordance with Komsomol rules—the raikom secretary bluntly replied, "That's not the way we do it in Moscow."[99]

As a different illustration of this problem, Tiazhel'nikov described to the Central Committee the case of one raikom that was visited by fourteen different obkom representatives in the course of a single year. None of these inspectors "noticed" that only two plenums had been held in the raikom all year or that the number of members paid up in their dues had been systematically inflated.[100] On another occasion, again before the Central Committee, he accused the Komsomol officials in Vladimir and Stavropol of "deceit and windowdressing" in the reporting of their activities.[101]

Central Committee officials periodically dispatched inspection brigades *(brigady)* to provinces to conduct detailed reviews. Judging by the reports of brigady sent to investigate Komsomol's support of the semiannual draft, these auditors relied almost exclusively on data provided to them by local Komsomol officials. No independent verification of these data was apparently sought.[102]

Difficulties in communicating guidelines to agents in the field and the challenges of monitoring compliance with these guidelines naturally led administrators to prefer easily verified measures of performance. The tight control on organizational resources described above, for instance, provided a highly effective system for monitoring activities of local committees. Since raikom officials were forced to submit detailed budgets in order to hold even a minor concert, obkom or gorkom officials could use these budget reports to monitor all activities at the district level. These reports, in turn, were summarized and forwarded to still higher levels, where they buried the central apparat under a mountain of figures describing exhibits mounted or concerts organized. This volume of data was patently unmanageable. Policy makers in Moscow therefore focused on several key indicators as high priority measures of overall job performance.

INDICATOR SELECTION AND THE RATCHET PROBLEM

Komsomol's performance in economic tasks was easily measured by such indicators as the creation and dispatch of shock-work or summer labor brigades. It was considerably more difficult, however, to devise quantitative measures of performance in Komsomol's principal area of responsibility: ideological indoctrination.

Few activities could not be justified under the rubric of indoctrination. Literature, for instance, was an important focus. In 1963, an Army official in charge of Komsomol work dutifully reported to a plenum of the Komsomol Central Committee that ten million of the ninety million books in Army libraries around the country were the works of Marx, Engels, and Lenin.[103] As if counting books were not a sufficient measure of ideological vigilance, officials were also expected to monitor what was being read. Komsomol officials in Kazakhstan in the late 1960s checked the library cards of one hundred draftees and were disturbed to discover most of them exclusively reading foreign literature.[104] In 1972, after a remote radar installation was found to be harboring a nest of Baptists, a military journalist blamed the local Komsomol secretary for conducting poor antireligious propaganda: "The library has just one book on religion, and nobody knows anything about the soldiers' reading habits."[105]

Komsomol officials sometimes went to great lengths to try to grasp (and co-opt) new cultural trends among the younger generation. Komsomol archives, for instance, contain the stenogram of an extraordinary meeting of Komsomol officials from Moscow universities and institutes held in a resort complex outside Moscow. *Easy Rider*—a film banned in the Soviet Union—was shown on the first evening of the weekend gathering and then vigorously discussed by participants.[106]

While it is easy to mock the image of Komsomol's elite watching contraband films in the woods outside Moscow, it is also important to try to understand their unenviable predicament. As Komsomol ranks grew and admissions standards became lax, "indoctrination" became a more difficult and all-encompassing assignment.

Naturally, each new indoctrination campaign introduced the need for new statistics. Detailed statistics were kept on the distribution of civic assignments *(porucheniia)* among Komsomol members.[107] Local officials dutifully organized visits to war memorials or to historical sites associated with Lenin's life and convened reading groups to consider Lenin's works or Brezhnev's war memoirs. An all-Union "military-patriotic exam" was introduced in 1968.[108] Special badges *(znachki)* were authorized and awarded to members displaying various qualifications (detailed guidelines, for instance, accompanied the distribution of fitness medals). For each new program, local officials documented levels of participation and characteristics of participants (or hours spent in readings or lectures, or numbers of badges awarded) and reported these figures to superiors in the Komsomol hierarchy. For all such events, turnout was the chief concern.[109]

By the early 1960s, one indicator had begun to receive top priority from regional and central planners alike: membership. Planners in Moscow carefully examined reports on annual enrollments and on demographics of membership. With Brezhnev's emphasis on ideological training as the primary Komsomol responsibility, it became increasingly important for Komsomol to reach all young Soviet citizens. Consequently, each year Komsomol officials pointed with pride to growth in the Komsomol ranks, and each year maintaining that growth was the prime organizational imperative.

By the late 1960s, and probably earlier, firm enrollment targets were set for each level of the Komsomol hierarchy down to primary organizations.[110] As noted in Chapter 2, annual plan targets were generally derived from previous performance achievements, and Komsomol enrollment targets were no exception. This produced a strong "ratchet" effect.[111] Each year, Komsomol organizers were required to show some growth in membership, if not in absolute terms then as a percentage of eligible youth. Figure 4.2 shows that Komsomol "saturation" continued to grow even after absolute annual enrollment peaked in 1978.

Since enrollment targets were closely monitored and extensively analyzed, local officials spared no effort to meet them. By achieving targets for membership and enrollment, local committees could avoid deeper scrutiny into the details of their unmonitored activity. Excessive effort was apparent even in 1965, in Pavlov's comprehensive critique. He warned Central Committee members, "A purely formal, numerical approach to membership growth is of use to nobody. Not everyone, unfortunately, understands this."[112]

More than a decade later, Tiazhel'nikov warned the Central Committee that enrollment drives still suffered from "formalism and campaigning."[113] Yet another Central Committee report cited numerous letters complaining of "formalism . . . in accepting students into the Komsomol without taking note of their civic activism or academic success."[114]

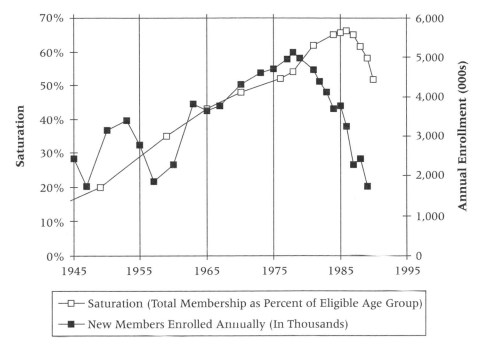

Figure 4.2. Annual Komsomol Enrollment and Saturation of Eligible Komsomol-Age Cohort (*Sources:* For Enrollment—*VLKSM: Nagliadnoe Posobie po komsomol'skomu stroitelstvu* [Visual guides on Komsomol membership] [Moscow: Molodaia Gvardia, 1985], 39; *Molodezh' SSSR* [Youth in the USSR] [Moscow: Goskomstat, TsK VLKSM, and VKSh pri TsK VLKSM, 1990], 154. For Saturation—Kenez, *Birth of the Propaganda State*, 94, 169; Fisher, *Pattern for Soviet Youth*, 140, 190, 280; *Politicheskoe samoobrazovanie*, no. 6, 1974; TsA VLKSM f. 1, op. 2, d. 710; op. 19, d. 271; op. 20, d. 178; *Statisticheskii i spravochnyi material* [Statistical and reference materials] [TsK VLKSM, 1990—distributed to delegates of the Twenty-first Komsomol Congress in Moscow], 95. Saturation figures for 1959 and 1970 are calculated from the census data of those years.)

These warnings—repeated often through the 1960s and 1970s—were contradicted by many other signals sent to local officials. A handbook on Komsomol organizational work, for instance, noted that "constant growth in the Komsomol's ranks is a sign of successful activity, a sign of its fitness and authority among young people."[115] Apparatchiks criticized regions where Komsomol saturation as a percentage of eligible youth fell below the national average.[116] A 1981 report praised the membership drives mounted by local officials, resulting in the enrollment in 1980 of 27 percent of all eligible youth not already holding Komsomol membership (see Table 4.4; the comparable figure for 1977 was 20 percent).[117]

Given these conflicting signals, local officials, not surprisingly, opted for meeting plan targets, even at the cost of excessive "formalism." A Central Committee plenum in 1968, immediately after hearing of the "still untapped reserves for the growth of Komsomol organizations," was warned that many of these organizations were "ignoring work to prepare youth to enter Komsomol."[118] A parallel and even more serious charge added in the 1970s was "violation of the principle of individual selection and inattention to the personality of the young person."[119]

These charges amounted to an indictment of Komsomol organizations for discarding principles of selectivity and voluntarism.[120] Rather than choosing the most able youth, cultivating in them a desire to join Komsomol, and then evaluating their fitness for membership, local organizations had begun enrolling new members en masse to meet growth targets. Large numbers of army conscripts were automatically enrolled in the Komsomol, and membership was mandatory for anyone seeking higher education.[121] Tiazhel'nikov described one mass induction of a group of Pioneers over which Komsomol officials presided with an air of complete indifference. He complained that the admissions were completed without

Table 4.4. Annual Komsomol Enrollment as a Percentage of Eligible Youth Not Already in Komsomol

Year	Percent Overall	Percent Among Students	Year	Percent Overall	Percent Among Students
1977	20	55	1984	26	n.a.
—	—	—	1985	27	55
1980	27	79	1986	23	39
—	—	—	1987	15	25
1982	30	n.a.	1988	14	n.a.
1983	30	n.a.	1989	9	n.a.

Sources: TsA VLKSM, f. 6. op. 19, d. 271, ll. 5-6; "O sostave VLKSM na 1.i.88" (in *Dokumenty TsK VLKSM 1988*, 83); *Komsomol'skaia pravda*, no. 6, 1990.

any trace of ritual or ceremony, and the young Pioneers' initial excitement was quickly deflated.[122]

A Higher Komsomol School study of Komsomol admissions in the 1970s and 1980s concluded that membership growth was achieved by "reliance on unprepared, wholly incidental individuals." The author suggested that the Nineteenth Komsomol Congress had attempted to place renewed emphasis on the quality of new applicants, "but in practice, things remained essentially unchanged." Aggregate, rather than qualitative, indicators determined the behavior of local officials.[123]

Where growth could not be achieved by fiat, it was concocted by guile. At the beginning of the Brezhnev era, Pavlov criticized one gorkom for resubmitting the same eighty membership applications after an interval of just two years to create the illusion of membership growth.[124] At the end of Brezhnev's tenure, Komsomol boss Pastukhov criticized a "perfunctory attitude toward the admission of young men and women," and urged the league to take action against "certain Komsomol officials [who] cover up their inactivity with impressive figures in statistical reports."[125]

Nevertheless, apathetic, or even hostile, youth continued to be swept into the league to pad membership rolls, and careerist activists grew adept at sustaining illusions for superiors that bore little relation to reality. Their superiors, on the whole, accepted the pictures presented to them, if only to placate their own superiors in the Party. Brezhnev's assignment for the Komsomol was "Communist upbringing," and effective indoctrination required near-universal membership.

Crisis and Collapse of the All-Union Komsomol

In the 1980s plan targets became more difficult to meet, and the unconventional "hidden action" necessary to meet them became more difficult to conceal. Confronted with blatant violations of league rules, the center finally granted local officials greater formal autonomy to revive the league's sagging prestige and thus appeal to a new generation of members. As discussed below, this shift had the perverse effect of stimulating many of the unconventional initiatives of local officials, which they ultimately pursued at the expense of Komsomol interests. Rather than unleashing the suppressed initiative of street-level actors, the subsequent cannibalization of Komsomol resources made the league's final disintegration impossible to halt.

The Shrinking Membership Pool

The final crisis of the Komsomol was precipitated neither by a shift in Party youth policy nor by a youth rebellion, but by a demographic slump.

In 1981, a report prepared for the Nineteenth Komsomol Congress warned that the national pool of fourteen- to twenty-three-year-olds had shrunk by over a million since 1979. The State Statistical Office, the report continued, predicted a 6.5 percent contraction of the fourteen to twenty-eight age cohort by 1988. The fourteen to twenty-three age cohort, from which Komsomol drew over 98 percent of all new members, was expected to shrink by 11.5 percent.[126] Even as they were making this forecast, however, Central Committee apparatchiks praised a list of oblasts (mostly in Central Russia, the Urals, and the North Caucasus) where membership *saturation* continued to grow despite the decline in absolute new enrollments.

As Figure 4.2 shows, absolute enrollment figures nationwide began to fall as early as 1978, in response to the first signs of demographic change. However, Komsomol saturation—that is, the number of members as a percentage of all Komsomol-age youth—continued to rise for a full decade. By 1985, nearly 66 percent of all eligible youth belonged to the Komsomol; in some republics, particularly in the Caucasus, Central Asia, and Lithuania, this figure exceeded 70 percent.[127]

Growth in membership saturation, in other words, remained a primary performance target, even as local officials were running out of potential new members. As Table 4.4 shows, the Komsomol in the early 1980s was enrolling annually 30 percent of youth not already in the league. Each year, as the eligible pool of nonenrolled youth shrunk by 30 percent, the cohort of newly eligible fourteen-year-olds became an increasingly fundamental source of new members. As Table 4.5 illustrates, fourteen-year-olds constituted over half of all new Komsomol members by 1984. Youth aged eighteen to twenty-three were another increasingly important source of new members, since this group included students continuing

Table 4.5. Age Distribution of New Komsomol Members

Year	Total[a]	Percent in Each Age Group			
		14	15–17	18–23	>23
1970	4,345	37.0	46.0	16.4	0.6
1974	4,688	37.7	43.8	17.5	1.0
1978	5,130	38.0	42.1	18.5	1.4
—	—	—	—	—	—
1980	4,940	42.1	37.6	18.6	1.7
1982	4,377	47.8	32.9	17.3	2.0
—	—	—	—	—	—
1984	3,700	52.3	32.0	14.0	1.7
1985	3,781	52.2	34.3	12.0	1.5
1987	2,284	49.6	40.5	9.0	0.9
1988	2,421	43.6	48.2	7.7	0.5
1989	1,746	38.7	53.2	7.8	0.3

Sources: VLKSM: Nagliadnoe Posobie po komsomol'skomu stroitel'stvu [Visual guides on Komsomol membership], 28; *Statisticheskii i spravochnyi material* [Statistical and reference materials] (TsK VLKSM, 1990—distributed to delegates of the Twenty-first Komsomol Congress in Moscow), 86; TsA VLKSM f. 1, op. 84, d. 1018a; op. 110, d. 483, 580a.
a. In thousands.

on to higher education who required Komsomol endorsement of their applications.

These enrollment dynamics suggest that local organizations relied increasingly on schools as sources of new members to meet admissions targets. Students were comparatively easy targets for membership drives, since young factory or farm workers were more dispersed and independent and less likely to respond to Komsomol appeals. As Table 4.6 shows, students constituted over 90 percent of all new members by the late 1980s.

Though schoolchildren were easiest to enroll, saturation levels in the schools were already so high as to make growth targets difficult to achieve. Komsomol's own figures showed that enrollment of eligible new members in schools reached nearly 80 percent as early as 1981, up from

Table 4.6. Social Background of New Komsomol Members

| Year | Total[a] | Percent in Each Group | | | |
		Students	Workers	Peasants	Employees
1970	4,345	77.2	11.9	4.1	6.8
1974	4,688	77.4	13.0	3.9	5.7
1978	5,130	77.8	13.5	3.8	4.9
—	—	—	—	—	—
1980	4,940	77.9	14.0	3.6	4.5
1982	4,377	79.3	12.7	3.0	5.0
—	—	—	—	—	—
1984	3,700	83.7	9.1	2.2	5.0
1985	3,781	85.9	7.5	1.8	4.8
1987	2,284	90.1	3.7	1.0	5.1
1988	2,421	92.2	2.9	0.8	4.1
1989	1,746	92.6	2.4	0.8	4.2

Sources: Iurii Marshavin, "Party Supervision of Organizational-Political Strengthening of Primary Komsomol Organizations: Experiences and Problems (1970s and 80s)" (Cand. Hist. Sci. diss., Higher Komsomol School, 1989), 194; *Statisticheskii i spravochnyi material* [Statistical and reference materials] (TsK VLKSM, 1990—distributed to delegates of the Twenty-first Komsomol Congress in Moscow), 86. The "employee" category is represented in Russian as *sluzhashchii.*
    a. In thousands.

55 percent just three years earlier.[128] In their quest to achieve some approximation of universal membership at least among schoolchildren, the enrollment practices of Komsomol committees became increasingly desperate. All efforts focused on the monitored indicator, enrollment; unmonitored ("hidden") activities like ideological indoctrination or cultural activities were neglected. An internal Komsomol report noted as early as 1980:

> Several Komsomol committees have developed the practice of forcing the growth of Komsomol ranks through reliance on students. Komsomol workers concentrate entirely on 14-year-old schoolchildren, without considering qualitative differences among them like personality, scholarly success, or civic activity.[129]

The principle of voluntary membership virtually disappeared. Entire classes of fourteen-year-olds were taken into the organization without so much as a single political lecture. Applicants at group inductions were enrolled without any attention to their supposed qualifications for membership.[130] Many oblasts routinely falsified enrollment figures to meet targets.[131] Others were accused of practicing "enforced" enrollment of seventh graders.[132] Quotas for the enrollment of workers were often met by artificially delaying enrollment of students at vocational schools until their graduation.

Dues went uncollected as long as enrollments or "active" memberships could be reported. Roughly 6 percent of the membership dropped off the rolls annually by not bothering to register with new local organizations after a move or change of jobs.[133] Another 4 percent remained registered with former organizations after they moved—including draftees kept on local lists even after their induction and registration with military Komsomol units—resulting in extensive double-counting of members.[134] Expulsion from the Komsomol was virtually impossible: even convicted felons faced no better than a 40 percent chance of expulsion from this supposed bastion of Communist ideals.[135]

As Komsomol violations grew increasingly flagrant and widespread, the Party Central Committee issued a resolution highly critical of the Komsomol's practices at the local level.[136] In response, the Komsomol Central Committee apparat began drafting a resolution to improve admissions practices. One proposal, raised several times in the past, was to grant local organizations the right to make final admissions decisions themselves, without requiring raikom or gorkom approval.[137] This measure was ultimately approved on an experimental basis.[138] However, a more radical suggestion to "ban the distribution of any sort of plan or control tasks" for admissions was shelved.[139] The final Biuro resolution merely called on officials to fight against "formalism, indifference and red tape" in work with incoming members and to select new members "not merely on the basis of having attained the age of fourteen, but chiefly on the basis of political and moral qualities."[140]

Against this backdrop of increasingly drastic measures to sustain a semblance of membership growth, change finally came to Komsomol's leadership bodies. Less than a month after Brezhnev's death in 1982, forty-nine-year-old Boris Pastukhov was replaced as First Secretary by Viktor Mishin, the thirty-nine-year-old former head of the Moscow Komsomol organization. Mishin had left his Moscow post just four years earlier; it is fair to assume he brought to the job some fresh memories of the growing disdain at the street level for the center's plans and guidelines.

Mishin himself noted that, as Moscow gorkom secretary, he learned how the Brezhnev-era Komsomol had become an important tool for nepotism: "Many influential officials [*chinovniki*] wanted to turn the Komsomol into a means of advancing the careers of their children. They would call often and make demands."[141]

As First Secretary, Mishin found it difficult to set a new course for the youth league. Apparently, Party officials were unsure of the new course they wanted the Komsomol to follow; Mishin later complained of the "oppressiveness . . . [of] dependence on irreconcilable opinions" from above. In his four years in office, Mishin accomplished little reform of the Komsomol, though he noted defensively that many issues were "given some impetus" on his watch and that a "new generation" of Komsomol leaders entered the "political arena" under him.[142] But the Komsomol continued to languish. Even Egor Ligachev, the new Party secretary for ideology, urged the Komsomol Central Committee to focus more on small projects that bring results.[143] Such instruction hardly amounted to an inspirational call to arms.

Mishin did make important changes in one area: public relations. He championed efforts to make the league marginally more responsive to— or at least representative of—the public opinions of its membership. In 1984, for instance, he supported the publication of a novella that painted a dark portrait of life in one Leningrad Komsomol raikom: *Incident at the District Level*.[144] The work, written by a former raikom apparatchik, Iurii Poliakov, lampooned local officials wholly indifferent to supposed norms of admissions and Komsomol discipline. As if to underscore the criticism of local practices, Poliakov was awarded the Lenin Komsomol Prize the following year for the novel.

Mishin also opened important new avenues for the Komsomol press. In February 1984, the Komsomol began publication of *Sobesednik*, a weekly youth feature newspaper. Within a year and a half, *Sobesednik* became one of the most lively publications in the country, often running articles highly critical of Komsomol policies and practices. Together with its parent daily, *Komsomol'skaia pravda*, *Sobesednik* became an interesting paper to read, with a lively writing style and a willingness to confront difficult topics. Despite slumping enrollment figures, subscriptions to *Komsomol'skaia pravda* grew steadily through the 1980s; by 1985 it was one of the most widely read newspapers in the country.

Mikhail Gorbachev's election as General Secretary accelerated the radicalization of the Komsomol press. Encouraged by Gorbachev's call for glasnost', Komsomol newspapers began running extensive interviews, polls, and letters from readers airing, among other things, a wide range of criticisms of the Komsomol itself. Leading the charge were several local Komsomol papers, including *Moskovskii komsomolets* and Leningrad's *Smena*, that hoped to revive interest in the youth league (and thus help attract new members) through sensationalism.

With the introduction of glasnost', street-level antics aimed at sustaining membership growth became the focus of scathing coverage in the press.[145] "Hidden" actions grew difficult to conceal. Newspaper reports openly discussed the artificial inflation of membership figures to meet "targets set on high." A Leningrad Komsomol official admitted that "Up top they demanded good accounts, so we improved upon them." A survey of the Moscow University biology faculty showed that two-thirds of its students would not have joined Komsomol if membership was not compulsory for university admission. A survey in another Moscow institute revealed a majority of members would leave the league if they could. A young worker suggested that restricting membership only to ideologically committed youth would leave the Komsomol with only a fifth of its members.

Pressure mounted in the media and from Party supervisors to find some way to keep the Komsomol from degenerating into an object of ridicule. As these accounts began to fill the media, the Komsomol's public image slumped noticeably. A 1987 film, *Is It Easy to Be Young?* painted a bleak portrait of cynicism and anomie among the younger generation and showed the Komsomol having little if any positive influence. Other films about the younger generation released around the same time, such as *Pliumbum*, *Little Vera*, or *The Burglar*, also assign no obvious role to the Komsomol. Where the Komsomol did appear, as in the 1989 film version of *Incident at the District Level*, its portrayal was unremittingly negative.[146] Surveys of public opinion during this period showed Komsomol's esteem at alarming lows.[147]

In July 1986, Viktor Mironenko was elected First Secretary of the Komsomol. Mironenko, head of the Ukrainian Komsomol, was thirty-three years old. Ten years younger than Mishin, he was the youngest leader of the Komsomol since the Khrushchev years. The timing of Mironenko's appointment suggests that Gorbachev wanted the new leader to be able to orchestrate changes in Komsomol operations at the next Komsomol Congress, which was promptly scheduled for April 1987. Almost immediately, in August 1986, the Komsomol Biuro announced that the upcoming Congress would consider changes in the Komsomol statutes *(ustav)*.

According to Mironenko, he had "a simple personal conversation" with Gorbachev before his confirmation by the Central Committee, but the Party leader set no concrete goals for the Komsomol. While there was some discussion of "the goals of the Party, its objectives for the youth movement," Gorbachev offered the Komsomol considerable latitude to determine its own policies.[148]

Doubtless concerned about the rising tide of negative portrayals of Komsomol activities, Mironenko set out to compensate for its "loss of influence" among youth. In particular, he resolved that the transformation of the Komsomol into a youth wing of the Communist Party had been a "mistake," since it prevented the league from effectively representing the interests of its membership (and therefore undermined a key incentive for youth to support it). He set as one of his primary objectives the "de-politicization" of the Komsomol—a goal that Gorbachev apparently approved explicitly.[149]

Just as the Komsomol had solicited a wide range of suggestions prior to previous Congresses, the Central Committee again issued a call for input to the drafting of new statutes. The appeal generated over 235,000 comments from within the organization during 1986–87, many sent directly to Moscow by individual members.[150] As with previous streams of inputs, these comments were all duly noted by the receiving offices and apparently categorized and tracked by computer.[151] Over one hundred changes were ultimately made in the Komsomol charter in response to these suggestions.

More important than its ultimate impact on the Komsomol statutes was the opening of this feedback cycle to public scrutiny. Komsomol papers routinely carried extensive debates over the league's problems and how they might be addressed in its new statutes. Many of these discussions focused on local officials' preoccupation with achieving membership growth at all costs. A student in Odessa argued that "as long as Komsomol work is judged by the percentage of new members, the Komsomol will have extraneous people."[152]

Mironenko did not wait for the new statutes to address the problem of arbitrary admissions practices. Fielding calls from *Komsomol'skaia pravda* readers barely a month after his election, he announced that the Central Committee had abandoned the use of enrollment targets. Suggesting the decision had actually preceded his own election, he asserted that at recent Central Committee plenums "it has been stated clearly that we must stop for good the practice of sending any sort of control figures for admissions to committees."[153] In an unusual admission that the center's control over local committees was incomplete, however, he admitted that the practice of issuing membership targets was continuing in many areas. He urged local activists to challenge their superiors: "I think, mostly, it's [the fault of] gorkom and raikom secretaries, agreed?"

Several callers denigrated their local Komsomol officials for lording it over their membership. In exchanges that must have struck fear into the hearts of local officials, Mironenko urged them to treat the principles of Komsomol democracy more seriously. In essence, Mironenko sought to augment monitoring from above with monitoring from the grass roots. Working hard to set a new tone for the Komsomol, he responded to one worker who thought it "funny" that his gorkom secretary insisted on using the formal first-name–patronymic form of address:

> *Mironenko:* So why don't you laugh at him if it's funny? Tell him what you think!
> *Caller:* We're already used to it.
> *Mironenko:* You have to get un-used to it, Andrei![154]

Another worker from Gorkii called to complain about the practice of local secretaries and group leaders being designated from above:

> *Mironenko:* The raikom has a right to recommend, don't they? But you have the final say in who is elected.
> *Caller:* It's sometimes difficult to reject their proposals.

Mironenko: You've got to be bold. The raikom has no choice but to ac-
     cept your decision.

As many hundreds of gorkom and raikom secretaries prepared to con-
verge on Moscow in April 1987 for the Twentieth Komsomol Congress,
Mironenko faced the difficult task of convincing them he was serious
about abandoning many of the league's long-standing mechanisms for
controlling activities at lower levels of the hierarchy. For their part, these
regional and local officials were eager to discover what control mechanisms Moscow proposed to put in the place of traditional rule by decree.

Membership Targets and Fiscal Reforms

Even before the delegates for the Twentieth Congress arrived in Moscow,
it was clear that Mironenko was facing agency problems within his own
Central apparatus. Although Mironenko later assured me that top officials
in the league fully expected the "restructuring" process to result in a
natural membership decline of up to 50 percent,[155] his own apparatchiks
seem to have had other intentions.

The Department of Komsomol Organs, which had made the initial
proposal to drop admissions targets in 1984, now seemed unable to adapt
to a world in which voluntary admissions were to be the rule. In a report
prepared before the Twentieth Congress, the department suggested that
68 percent was the "optimal" saturation level for Komsomol organizations
in schools. It further charged that many committees were using the
warning against forcing admissions as an excuse for "inactivity in their
work with non-league youth." Noting that 30,000 primary organizations
annually were admitting no new members at all, the report urged: "Together with the requirement that admissions not be forced, we also
consider it necessary to require Komsomol committees to not permit
baseless restraint in the growth of Komsomol ranks."[156]

The same report also observed that increasing reliance on students as
a source of new members had sharply reduced the percentage of workers
in the Komsomol's ranks. Reminding Komsomol leaders that recent Party
documents called on the Komsomol to raise its influence among youth,
the report added, none too subtly: "reducing membership will lead to a
weakening of this influence."[157]

In the financial control department of the Komsomol's Central Committee, a different group of bureaucrats was considering measures to cope with the economic consequences of falling membership. Since membership dues represented over 80 percent of the budget of Komsomol organizations, declining membership was having serious consequences for the league's finances. The department proposed creating "Komsomol subbotniks" (free labor days) at enterprises and on farms, during which members' salaries would be credited directly to their Komsomol organizations. It also suggested establishing a system of automatic dues payments (i.e., payroll deduction) to improve dues-payment levels.[158]

Automatic dues-payment systems were extremely popular with secretaries of local organizations. A summary of primary organizations' suggestions for revisions in the Komsomol statutes revealed great concern about financial practices. Along with automatic dues credits, many organizations called for the right to have their own accounts for local expenditures and the right to keep a percentage of dues collected from their members.[159] Financial woes were also on the minds of delegates at the Twentieth Congress; according to a Central Committee report, one-eighth of the 1,460 "critical comments" made during the course of the Congress concerned finances of Komsomol organizations.[160]

The Congress itself devoted extensive attention to questions of internal organization and finance. In a break with tradition, the Congress was opened not by Gorbachev but by Mironenko, who reiterated the need for local and primary organizations to assume greater control over their own affairs. In addition to discontinuing admissions targets, new rules gave all primary organizations the right to make final decisions on enrolling new members. Mironenko indicated that all Central Committee guidelines would have to be made more "flexible." He also made good on his promise to promote intra-Komsomol democracy: candidates to the Central Committee were voted on individually rather than as a list.[161]

The most significant changes in Komsomol operations to emerge from the Congress concerned the Komsomol's finances. Mironenko announced a Central Committee decision to permit fifty-six large primary organizations to open their own accounts from which they could run their affairs without seeking approval for each expenditure. These local organizations also received control over their own budgets, dropping the requirement for raikom or gorkom approval.[162] Mironenko promised to extend similar powers to other primary organizations over time.

In the months following the Congress, Komsomol's financial practices

were further restructured.[163] In December 1987, thirty oblasts and republics were given the right to control their own budgets and to keep all
income, including members' dues, derived from sources within their
jurisdiction. Remittances from regional and republican committees to the
Central Committee began to drop off dramatically. New government
regulations sought by the Central Committee removed important restrictions on the permissible uses of Komsomol accounts, allowing funds to be
spent for material or labor expenses. In 1988, the Komsomol Biuro passed
new regulations governing the financial resources of the Komsomol.
These new regulations, in part, extended the perestroika accounting principle of *khozraschet* or "self-financing"—control over all sources of income
and decisions on budgetary expenditures—to all levels of the Komsomol.
By 1989, the budgetary and financial operations of each level of the
Komsomol hierarchy were isolated, and local organizations were keeping
virtually all dues and income from publishing and tourist activities.

Though the Komsomol's budget remained a secret even from its own
Central Committee until at least 1989, the consequences of these moves
are now clear. First, local organizations finally received control over
dues—but precisely as membership was poised to decline. The Central
Committee, on the other hand, was able to use "self-financing" to isolate
its own finances from those of the rest of the league. The Central Committee's liquid assets in 1987 totaled approximately one billion rubles.[164]
By 1989, it had cut its subsidies of local and regional organizations to a
mere 50 million rubles.[165] In 1990, it broke off the Central Committee
budget as a separate account from the rest of the Komsomol's finances.[166]
As one critic of Komsomol finances summarized it, the Central Committee's decision to stop being financed by lower organizational levels
amounted to telling them: you can keep all the money you earn, as long
as you don't ask what's become of the money you "pumped up" to the
Central Committee over the past few decades.[167]

To fully appreciate the consequences of this financial sleight of hand at
the center, it is necessary to examine how local officials used their new-
found independence.

The Rise of Opportunism by Agents: Local Initiatives

Just as the Central Committee apparat had feared, the abandonment of
binding enrollment targets had a sudden and devastating effect on Kom-

somol membership. As Figure 4.3 shows, enrollment dropped like a stone in all regions of the country. Many organizations found youth none too eager to join the discredited league once they actually had a choice. Many local organizations simply stopped trying to attract new members, and the percentage of primary organizations enrolling no new members at all skyrocketed (see Table 4.7). Reflecting the general mood, Mironenko confessed to a Western journalist that even he could not be sure his own son would join the Komsomol.[168]

This erosion of the membership base had dire consequences for the finances of local organizations. As membership fell, so did dues income on which local budgets were now to be directly based. Komsomol activists scrambled to find new income sources to balance their budgets, especially as subsidies from Moscow were cut. Almost overnight, a series of Brezh-

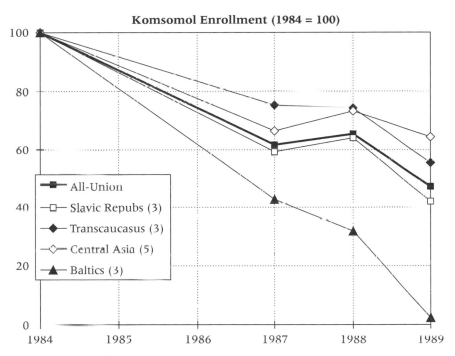

Figure 4.3. Regional Decline in Komsomol Enrollment, 1984–1989 (*Source: Statisticheskii i spravochnyi material* [Statistical and reference materials] [TsK VLKSM, 1990—distributed to delegates of the Twenty-first Komsomol Congress in Moscow], 86–93. Enrollment figures for 1989 were not reported for Estonia and Lithuania, since both republican organizations essentially shut down at the end of that year.)

Table for Figure 4.3. Regional Decline in Komsomol Enrollment, 1984–1989

	1984	1987	1988	1989
RSFSR	1,514,075	858,913	931,870	582,585
Ukraine	621,779	411,693	438,902	319,810
Bielorussia	131,759	73,390	80,170	55,508
Moldavia	55,721	37,292	41,285	29,550
Armenia	40,779	46,142	37,554	23,438
Azerbaijan	149,074	89,388	92,061	89,597
Georgia	66,880	57,646	60,428	29,456
Kazakhstan	287,141	172,159	172,143	138,111
Uzbekistan	318,360	238,411	270,959	246,270
Tadzhikistan	81,735	51,792	59,541	56,750
Turkmenia	63,223	40,152	49,746	45,250
Kirgizia	88,174	53,180	59,683	53,744
Latvia	27,131	11,308	9,906	2,148
Lithuania	50,572	21,707	16,072	0
Estonia	15,227	6,830	3,730	0

Source: See Figure 4.3.

nev-era programs designed to stimulate small-scale entrepreneurship became the seed for a vast network of new Komsomol businesses. Several programs in particular became the core of a new commercial network run by local Komsomol committees: student construction brigades (SSOs), travel bureaus ("Sputnik"), youth housing complexes (MZhKs), and "centers for scientific-technical creativity of youth" (NTTMs).

Student construction brigades had long been one of the Komsomol's chief economic functions. Begun at Moscow University in 1959, SSOs expanded rapidly to provide millions of rubles of summer work at sites around the country. At its peak, in 1979, the Komsomol was distributing nearly half a million students to construction sites around the country. Though this number fell to 270,000 by 1987, the Komsomol was also coordinating the distribution of another 436,000 students to "labor-deficient" industries like textiles or light industries.[169] Student brigades,

Table 4.7. Komsomol Primary Organizations Enrolling No New Members
(As Percentage of All Primary Organizations)

	1984	1987	1989		1984	1987	1989
All-Union	7	11	21	Kazakhstan	2	7	14
RSFSR	10	15	22	Uzbekistan	2	5	6
Ukraine	9	13	17	Tadzhikistan	10	11	10
Bielorussia	2	7	12	Turkmenia	5	22	30
Moldavia	4	13	15	Kirgizia	3	11	14
Armenia	4	5	23	Latvia	9	28	62
Azerbaijan	1	3	7	Lithuania	12	25	n.a.
Georgia	1	2	9	Estonia	14	22	n.a.

Source: Statisticheskii i spravochnyi material [Statistical and reference materials] (TsK VLKSM, 1990—distributed to delegates of the Twenty-first Komsomol Congress in Moscow), 94, 98–99.

like the Komsomol generally, were supposed to be formed on the basis of "voluntarism" and were supposed to offer valuable indoctrination in "labor discipline." In practice, quotas were set for brigade formation, and brigades were often formed and sent to construction sites that had little use for them. Brigade organizers often drew on the same pool of "professional" laborers, assigning them to choice sites offering high pay. These practices, in turn, undermined many of the ideological aims of the program and often left casual participants eager to avoid manual labor in the future.[170]

In the late 1980s, local committees took over the management of these faltering labor brigades and transformed them into youth employment bureaus, operating on a commercial basis. Taking advantage of the decentralization of authority from the center, local and district committees began to negotiate contracts directly with enterprises for the provision of short-term and permanent employment.[171]

In a similar fashion, local committees took over MZhKs—created to build affordable housing for young families—and transformed them into multipurpose enterprises offering a variety of services on a commercial basis. NTTMs—a campaign begun in the early 1980s to support "scientific-technical creativity of youth" (i.e., young inventors' clubs, etc.)—

were also rediscovered by local committees. Most important of all, new government accounting regulations passed in the wake of the Twentieth Komsomol Congress significantly broadened the ability of local Komsomol committees to transfer funds between their budgets and these enterprises.[172] Local committees could use the NTTM or MZhK structure to create, in effect, wholly or partly owned subsidiary business—investing Komsomol resources and using profits (or interest on loans) to close gaps in their operating budgets. By early 1991, over 4,000 successful enterprises were operating under direct Komsomol auspices.[173]

More informally, many committees used the assets of local or primary organizations, over which they suddenly had control, to support commercial operations of varying scope. Cafes, video bars, discos, and travel bureaus were founded or expanded with loans directly from Komsomol budgets; new concerns also used Komsomol printing presses and even operated out of Komsomol offices.[174] While such ventures provided operating income for local and regional Komsomol activities, it quickly became clear that they might also provide Komsomol activists with more stable and lucrative employment than could their troubled parent organization. With budgets now in the hands of local officials, Komsomol bureaucrats in Moscow could do little to control or even monitor the activities of such burgeoning commercial enterprises.

The development of new sources of income empowered local committees to assert their independence from higher organs. In Moscow, for instance, the gorkom considered itself effectively independent of control from both the Central Committee and the Moscow Party Committee by 1990.[175] Sensing that control over Komsomol resources would be an important tool in the establishment of careers in the "private sector," many local committees paid little more than lip service to the democratic ideals proclaimed at the Twentieth Congress. Only one-third of all vacancies on local committees filled after the Congress were contested.[176] In February 1990, for instance, I attended the city-wide conference of the Moscow Komsomol. At this two-day meeting, the gorkom engineered a sweeping organizational restructuring that, miraculously, left the composition of the gorkom virtually intact.[177]

When competitive elections were held, quorums were often difficult to achieve: disaffected rank-and-file members were unexcited by the entrepreneurial activity now dominating the affairs of local committees, and most happily seized the opportunity to walk away from a league they had not wanted to join in the first place.[178] Many members were probably unaware of how their membership dues had been "invested," since Komsomol budgets remained unpublished prior to 1990. Enrollments continued to plummet. Many primary organizations simply dissolved, but at many others, business profits more than offset lost dues.

In the non-Russian republics, Komsomol assets were pressed to serve not the almighty ruble but the rising tide of nationalism. Komsomol newspapers, buildings, automobiles, presses, and personnel were valuable resources in the nascent struggle for national independence. In 1985 and 1986, for example, enrollment in the Estonian Komsomol began to drop off sharply, as the organization became increasingly identified with "imperial" Moscow.[179] Estonian Komsomol officials tried to alert their Moscow superiors that ethnic factors were beginning to erode the stability of the republican organization. They planned to utilize their upcoming Congress, in February of 1987, to recast the Estonian Komsomol along national lines, and thus revive it. However, much of the Congress's debate was preempted when Mikhail Gorbachev made a last-minute decision to stop in Tallinn on his way home from Riga in order to address the meeting.[180] All talk of nationalist drives was quickly shelved, for fear of offending Gorbachev. Estonian Komsomol leaders were forced to settle for proposing a new charter to Moscow that would restructure the Komsomol along "federal" lines. These changes were ignored until 1990, too late to help the Estonian Komsomol.

Facing a similar erosion of its membership base, and sensing that Moscow's dominance might be near an end, Komsomol officials in Lithuania declared their independence from the All-Union organization in 1989. A rival wing of the organization, composed chiefly of Russians, promptly declared its intention to remain loyal to Moscow and claimed the assets of the Lithuanian Komsomol for itself. In late 1989, as Viktor Mironenko watched from the hall in horror, the Estonian Komsomol voted to simply shut its doors altogether. Over a three-month transition period, it parceled its assets out among newly privatized businesses, political parties, and a rump all-Russian Komsomol.

Responses of the Center

As agents began to break away at the street level and in the republics, the Komsomol Central Committee seemed paralyzed. Central Committee plenums in 1989 and 1990 debated a reorganization of the youth league to accommodate more autonomy for local actors, and yet another new charter was drafted for consideration at an Extraordinary Congress. A Central Committee commission was dispatched to Lithuania to try to reconcile the rival Komsomols, but the mission achieved nothing.

In a sharp break with tradition, debates at Central Committee plenums were published in *Komsomol'skaia pravda* (the Party began a similar practice several months later). However, since the Central Committee had never acted as a real policy-making—or even deliberative—body, members often used their speeches to simply make points with readers back home. No sense of direction emerged from the angst-ridden deliberations over the league's "fate," and the published debates did little to revive interest among the mass membership. Instead, the chaotic transcripts merely spread the impression that top officials were incapable of controlling affairs at any level of the Komsomol's operations.

By 1989, not only republican organizations but also Komsomol committees in Russian regions like Volgograd, Sverdlovsk, Novosibirsk, Moscow, and Leningrad took advantage of the apparent vacuum at the center to promote their own agendas; a prominent demand was control over Central Committee assets.[181] Eager to pacify workers at the local level—and to stem the flow of activists going into full-time commercial activity—the Central Committee approved a significant pay raise for Komsomol organizers effective 1 September 1989, to be covered by a special subsidy from its own funds.[182] At least some regional committees took this a step further and gave primary organizations the right to set their own pay scales.[183]

Moves such as these exacerbated the Komsomol's recruitment problems. As the youth league became more of a cross between "Junior Achievement" and a primitive business school, it attracted activists interested chiefly in learning to make money. Enticing them with higher pay only pandered to this perverse incentive, creating a classic example of "adverse selection."[184] These budding entrepreneurs, brimming with free-market enthusiasm, proved hostile to centralized control and uninterested in political indoctrination of the mass membership. Paradoxically, with each new activist, the odds of a Komsomol revival grew dimmer.

Central Committee bureaucrats found themselves with a dwindling set of tools for convincing lower levels of the Komsomol hierarchy to acknowledge their continued authority—or even their de jure "ownership" of Komsomol property and funds. They persisted in their efforts to control the pork-barrel—negotiating with ministries for delivery of various goods and services to local committees[185]—but these measures were less vital to local officials, who could now use their own funds to make purchases directly. Furthermore, as Komsomol's annual army of student laborers became splintered among hundreds of decentralized youth-employment bureaus, ministries had less to gain from cooperation with Central Committee officials. Komsomol apparatchiks could no longer threaten to withhold the most productive seasonal employees from a ministry's top priority project.

As all this was going on, the Central Committee took no firm actions to reclaim Komsomol assets invested in pornographic video salons or expropriated by Baltic nationalists. With each passing month, it appeared not just unwilling, but increasingly unable, to resolve even its most basic dilemma: was the Komsomol to retain its mass membership, or was it to return to its roots as an elite vanguard of highly committed activists? Unclear of their marching orders, even relatively loyal committees allowed enrollments to stagnate. Instead of signaling a policy on this key question, the Central Committee apparatus moved quietly but decisively to hedge its bets.

As noted earlier, the finances of the Central Committee were gradually separated from those of other levels of the organization. Beginning around 1988, apparatchiks began to shift Central Committee assets to dozens of "self-financing" commercial centers, including banks, tourism bureaus, and publishing ventures. By 1990, these operations employed hundreds of former Central Committee staff.[186] In addition, remittances from these supposedly independent ventures covered almost the entire wage bill of workers who remained on the Central Committee after 1989.

More significantly, the Central Committee established a "Commercial Youth Bank" in 1988 with a starting fund of 250 million rubles. Though the bank was supposed to lend exclusively to youth ventures, it soon changed its name to "Finistbank" because, according to Mironenko, potential business partners were put off by the appearance of "youth" in the bank's name.[187] By 1990, the Central Committee had deposited another 500 million rubles into this bank—a significant share of Central Committee assets.[188] Finistbank and other Komsomol banks (like the giant Menatep) soon became major players in the new world of Soviet commercial banking; by April 1990 Finistbank was the second largest commercial bank in the country[189] This use of Komsomol funds was not universally popular, as suggested by this published exchange between Viktor Graivoronskii, a disillusioned Moscow raikom secretary, and two assistant heads of the Central Committee's finance department, Aleksandr Antonov and Aleksandr Starikov:

> *Graivoronskii:* This bank was created to assist Komsomol organizations, but what is happening? It charges them interest for this money.
>
> *Starikov:* At 5–7 percent, this is much less than commercial banks charge.
>
> *Graivoronskii:* But it produces the following paradoxical situation: Komsomolites are being charged interest for the use of their own money!
>
> *Antonov:* Yes, apparently there is something of a paradox here.
>
> *Starikov:* But money has to make money![190]

Looking back, Mironenko gave a similar justification for the Central Committee's move into the world of high finance: "We decided that funds should not lie idle."[191]

There were two important practical consequences of this initiative. First, Central Committee banks could certainly be expected to support the commercial ventures of former Central Committee staffers or their network of associates. Equally important, assets transferred to "commercial" concerns from Central Committee accounts could no longer be claimed by any organization wishing to leave the new Komsomol "federation."[192]

As details of these transactions became known in 1989–90, the Central Committee bureaucracy appeared to be preparing itself for the possibility of the Komsomol's fragmentation. This was also the interpretation attached to the Komsomol's only concerted effort to redefine its policy role in the new, deideologized Soviet state structure. In 1986, Mironenko revived the idea of a "Law on Youth" that would clarify social welfare policy toward the younger generation and, not coincidentally, clarify the Komsomol's role in implementing that policy. However, when the draft law was finally presented to the revamped Supreme Soviet in 1990, its proposed "Ministry for Youth Affairs" was criticized by several deputies as a haven for Komsomol bureaucrats trying to flee a weakened and shrinking organization. Mironenko did little to lessen this impression when he disingenuously offered to help finance the new ministry out of Komsomol funds.[193]

This energetic contingency planning within the Central Committee bureaucracy was not lost on local and regional officials. Recognizing that the center was planning for the eventuality of life after Komsomol, they began to make similar preparations.[194] City, regional, and republican committees began investing assets in the rapidly growing network of commercial banks or venture funds, and many gorkom and obkom officials began careers in finance with assets that once belonged to Komsomol committees. Other activities were almost totally disregarded; many Komsomol committees even failed to attract a quorum to nominate deputies for Russian parliamentary elections in 1990.[195]

Transfers of assets out of Komsomol accounts began to accelerate with the announcement of an Extraordinary Congress to be held in April 1990. If the Congress could not salvage the league's future, its dissolution would cut off the dwindling (but still significant) flow of membership dues and, more important, trigger a definitive accounting and disposition of the assets of Komsomol committees. When this day of reckoning came, it was certainly in the interest of entrepreneurial local officials to have "invested" most or all of these assets in private, commercial ventures. With this realization, the "bank run" was on and the authority of the league's Central Committee was irrevocably undermined.

Endgame

In April 1990, the Komsomol convened an Extraordinary Congress to recast itself as a less political "federal" organization and thus dispel rumors of its imminent demise. But the genie could not be forced back in the bottle. Addressing delegates on the eve of the Congress, Gorbachev was asked by one delegate to comment on the possibility of a Komsomol collapse, but his reply—"Everything . . . is for you to decide"—offered little guidance.[196]

Both Lithuanian youth leagues were represented, but hopes of a reconciliation were dashed when it became obvious their leaders were barely on speaking terms.[197] The Georgian Komsomol attended as observers, the

Estonian Komsomol was represented only by its quisling ethnic-Russian league, and Armenian and Azerbaijani delegates were carefully seated on opposite ends of the hall. The Congress met for eight days—two longer than originally planned—and the proceedings were pure chaos from the first hour. The agenda and rules of debate were not even approved until the third day; organizers of the first session were so distracted by factional bickering that they forgot to sing the Soviet national anthem.[198]

The Congress nearly broke up several times in disagreement over what to name the revitalized Komsomol. Mironenko worked desperately to find a formula that would permit all extant local organizations to sign on to the "new" federation, regardless of their individual goals.[199] The question of control over Komsomol property was cleverly finessed in the waning hours of the Congress, after a proposal to give republican organizations line-item veto power over the Central Committee's budget won a plurality of votes but not a majority. Mironenko was able to push through a much weaker clause declaring that Central Committee property would be "collectively managed" by constituent members of the federation—through their representatives on the Central Committee.

Clearly exhausted by the week-long tightrope act, Mironenko unexpectedly withdrew his name from nomination for reelection. He claimed a younger man was needed to take the Komsomol to its next stage of revitalization. The newly elected leader, Vladimir Ziukin—a scant year younger than Mironenko—promptly declared the Komsomol independent of Party control.[200] Significantly, the only major policy proposal receiving strong endorsement at the 1990 Congress was the preservation of tax breaks for youth-run (i.e., Komsomol) enterprises—a policy promoted successfully by Komsomol deputies in the Soviet Parliament.

Ziukin's eighteen-month tenure proved to be a caretaker stewardship, as Komsomol-founded businesses expanded and diversified. Central Committee bureaucrats had lost both the desire and the capacity to influence lower-level committees. As these ventures consolidated their operations, many officials dropped the Komsomol fig leaf and became full-time employees of the new commercial structures.[201] Communist Party officials in many regions observed the success of Komsomol officials in transforming their political power into economic power and began an analogous transfer of Party assets into the private sector. This is discussed further in Chapter 7.

After the coup, it was no longer possible to speak of the Komsomol's political aims. Central Committee staffers and local committees had, in effect, seized and divided the chief assets of the organization, leaving little more than a shell. Central Committee members debated how best to restructure Komsomol's leading organs "so that only those who can make money can continue in office."[202] In the end, however, there was no constituency for a national youth league. In September 1991 the Komsomol convened one last Congress to divide up its remaining assets. The tone of discussion at the sparsely attended meeting reinforced the sense that, with the collapse of central authority, everyone's attention was on defining the property rights of the organization's twenty-three successor committees. Even Ziukin, the final head of the Komsomol, suggested that he might leave politics for good and give business a try.[203]

Summary

At a discussion of Komsomol strengths and weaknesses at the Institute of Youth (formerly the Higher Komsomol School) in November 1990, I was taken aside by a historian who had, like many scholars at the institute, begun her career as a Komsomol official. "Many of us in the Komsomol worked very hard on issues like housing for young families," she said to me, earnestly. "For many of us, that was the most important work in our lives, because there was nobody else to care about such issues, if not the Komsomol."

Genuinely committed activists are an important element of the Komsomol legacy. But they could not counteract the massive organizational problems associated with leaders unenthusiastic about leading and followers equally unenthusiastic about following. The collapse of the Komsomol was not the consequence of any conflict among its leadership or its Party bosses, nor was it a response to an eruption of discontent emanating from its grass roots. It did not split into reformers and conservatives, nor did its demise benefit any social group other than its former employees.

To understand the Komsomol's collapse, it is necessary to trace the changing incentives confronting individual officials. The Komsomol closed off many channels of information (like sociology or internal feedback) that could have provided direct measures of success or failure in its mission of "indoctrination." Supervisors at each level were therefore obliged to set concrete performance targets, especially for membership growth, in order to exercise control over their subordinates. These subordinates—at each rung of the ladder down to street-level primary organizations—exercised considerable latitude in deciding how to meet these performance targets. Many chose to force enrollments with little attention to the rigors of ideological training, while others found it simpler just to falsify statistics.

When demographic shifts made it no longer possible for local officials to continue concealing the "hidden actions" that facilitated plan compliance, the center took steps that could have been viewed as a reasonable strategy for revival. Binding targets were replaced by a fiscal incentive, and local committees got the power to create new programs tailored to local needs. Unfortunately, when they abandoned budgetary control and membership targets, Komsomol officials also dismantled the primary information channels of their system of hierarchical administration. Komsomol assets were far more important than dues, especially in the Wild West economic environment of 1987. Perceiving signs of weakness at the center, local agents rushed to appropriate those assets over which their committees could assert control. The ensuing "bank run" emptied the Komsomol's coffers and provided much of the seed capital for the first generation of post-Soviet entrepreneurial activity.

As a final note, it is interesting to observe that opportunism by local actors was not particularly facilitated by distance from Moscow. More remote Komsomol organizations did benefit from greater information asymmetries, permitting them to deviate from accepted Komsomol practices with relative impunity (especially in non-Russian republics, where language differences complicated monitoring from the center). On the other hand, organizations like the Moscow City Komsomol became hotbeds of radicalism under the very noses of the Central Committee, perhaps because they were among the first to sense the weakened authority of central organs. In either circumstance, the internal dynamics among multiple agents and distant principals converted the perception of weakening authority into a very real breakdown of hierarchical control.

5 | Job Assignments for University Graduates

"You have a rare specialty. In other words, nobody needs it."

—Job placement committee to graduating Sinologist, c. 1958 (quoted in *Moskovskii universitet*, 25 May 1988)

From the end of the New Economic Policy (NEP) until 1991, all graduates of higher-education institutions in the Soviet Union were obligated to repay the state for their education by submitting to a mandatory job-assignments process. In return for state provision of free higher education for all qualified applicants, "young specialists" were required to work for three years at a job assigned to them on graduation.

Like many aspects of central planning, the job allocation and assignments system for college graduates (known in Russian as *raspredelenie*, or "distribution") was flimsy at best. Even as General Secretaries Brezhnev and Gorbachev stressed the need to better exploit the creative and entrepreneurial energies of the growing technical intelligentsia, administrators paid curiously little attention to the process by which nascent Soviet "yuppies" received their first jobs. Between mid-1989 and mid-1991, however, the raspredelenie system suddenly fell apart. With its demise vanished not only the state's capacity to mobilize highly educated personnel but also the state's ability to guarantee employment for the least experienced cohort of the labor market. As a consequence, college graduates in 1991 faced new freedoms but also grave new uncertainties.

Like the disintegration of the Komsomol, the collapse of raspredelenie provides important clues to the nature of authority in Soviet institutions and why that authority weakened. Unlike the Komsomol, though, the several bureaucracies that together managed job assignments did not completely disintegrate. This chapter, like the previous one, begins with a discussion of the historical and organizational background. It then examines the relative significance of elite controls, social pressures, and institutional rules prior to the 1980s. Finally, I consider the dynamics of the breakdown directly.

Background

History

In the 1936 Stalin Constitution, the USSR guaranteed to all its citizens the "right to guaranteed employment and payment for their work in accordance with its quantity and quality."[1] At the same time, it stressed that work was the "duty and honor of every able-bodied citizen."[2] Thus, in the formulation that typified the attitude of the socialist state toward labor from its earliest days, the guarantee of universal employment came attached to an obligation to work.

The 1977 Brezhnev Constitution, while reiterating the 1936 document's sentiments on the importance of practical labor, presented a slightly softer line on the question of labor obligations. It declared: "Socially useful work and its results determine a person's status in society . . ., the state helps transform labor into the prime vital need of every Soviet citizen."[3] In addition to making explicit what the earlier Constitution took as a given—that the obligation to work was a manifestation of socialist man's desire to engage in useful labor—the Brezhnev draft also guaranteed citizens the "right to choose their trade or profession, type of job and work in accordance with their inclinations, abilities, training and education, with due account of the needs of society."[4]

For graduates of postsecondary educational institutions—including five-year universities and institutes known as VUZy *(vysshee uchebnoe zavedenie)* and two-year specialized secondary schools known as SSUZy *(srednee spetsial'noe uchebnoe zavedenie)*—this formulation merely captured the long-standing realities of their situation.[5] In the Soviet system of higher education, as in the British or other European systems, applicants to institutes and universities applied directly to the departments in which they hoped to specialize. The Soviet system, however, discouraged multiple applications, often channeling students into neglected specializations in which they had minimal interest in order to avoid intense competition (or excessive bribery costs). The structure of the Soviet educational system is schematically portrayed in Figure 5.1.

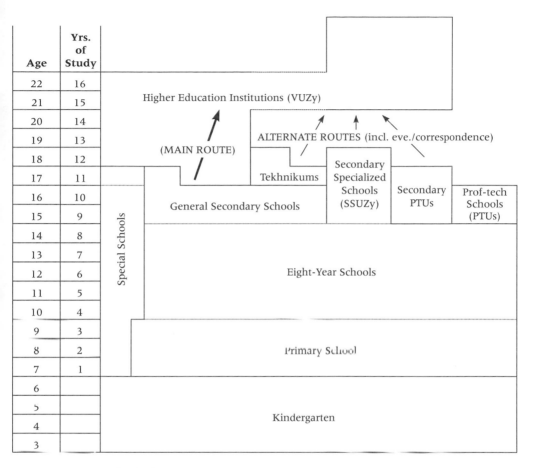

Figure 5.1. The Soviet Educational Structure (*Source:* David Lane and Felicity O'Dell, *The Soviet Industrial Worker* [Oxford, England: Martin Robinson, 1978], 98.)

The choice of educational specialization had important consequences upon graduation. Since the Constitution guaranteed a job only "in accordance with their . . . education" and "with due account of the needs of society," graduates were required to submit to a mandatory assignment process for their first jobs after completing institute or university. These so-called "young specialists" received special legal guarantees of housing and employment in their specialization for the three-year duration of this first assignment.

The assignments process, in practice, was tied integrally with the overall system of economic central planning. Annually (within the guidelines of the Five Year Plan), industrial enterprises and other employers submitted to Gosplan[6] their requirements for "young specialists" for the following employment season (two years away) and projected needs for specialists over the coming five years.[7] The five-year projections were used by Gosplan to formulate target admissions figures for university and institute faculties (i.e., departments) for the coming year. The more immediate requests for young specialists were combined with forecasts of the anticipated number of graduates from the nations' institutes and universities and compiled into a national plan "for distribution *(raspredelenie)* of specialists" for the following year. This painstaking process, requiring coordination of specific inputs from hundreds of thousands of employers and educational institutions around the country, dragged on for many months. Computers were first utilized only in the late 1970s, and it is unlikely the raspredelenie system was ever fully computerized.[8]

Gosplan, however, did not assign specific postings to individual graduates. Instead, it only assigned quotas to each ministry supervising higher education institutions.[9] Each ministry, in turn, produced a plan for assignments down to the level of specific VUZy.[10] Within each VUZ, "committees of personal raspredelenie" were formed near the end of each school year to match specific graduating students to specific postings. These committees consisted of representatives from university administration, the Komsomol, and trade unions. No student representation beyond Komsomol was provided. In theory, preference was given to students with the highest grades in each department, but political loyalty (measured through Komsomol activity) also played a role, as did personal connections and outright bribery.[11]

Under Stalin, few exceptions were granted to mandatory job assignments, which fell under the same harsh disciplinary regime that covered most wartime labor. Graduates ignoring assignments faced up to six months in prison. Gradually, under Khrushchev, more flexibility was introduced into the system. Criminal sanctions were dropped, and allowances were made in the raspredelenie guidelines for students to be exempted from the assignment process in the event of poor health, family hardship, marital circumstances, or a lack of appropriate vacancies. These graduates received a right to "open placement."

Students were entitled to a one-month vacation upon graduation. They were then expected to report to their new jobs to spend the next three years. Arriving at their new place of employment, they presented their assignment papers and in return received housing, reimbursement for their travel, and a specific work assignment. Employers were obliged to report the young specialist's arrival to the relevant assigning ministry and to record his or her progress during the next three years in the employee's "work book." It was illegal for any enterprise to hire a recent graduate who had not been assigned to it or who could not produce a work book which documented that he or she had completed three compulsory years at an assigned posting.

For all its faults, the Soviet higher-education system was able to manage an impressive explosion of educational opportunity throughout the country in the postwar years. Figure 5.2 shows this trend, triggered by Khrushchev's introduction of universal secondary education. The impact on the workforce of this rapid growth of higher education became particularly marked during the 1960s and 1970s (see Table 5.1).

Because of the increase in VUZ enrollments, the number of students subject to the VUZ raspredelenie system also grew dramatically—by 49 percent between 1970 and 1980 alone.[12] By 1980, 95 percent of all graduates of daytime divisions of VUZy received raspredelenie assignments (the remaining 5 percent, presumably, found ways to qualify for open placements). This figure reached 98 percent by 1985.[13]

While the job-assignments system was able to process a steadily increasing flow of manpower through the 1980s, it was plagued by two chronic problems from its earliest days: assignees who didn't show and

Table 5.1. Higher Education and the National Workforce

Graduates of VUZy	1940	1960	1970	1980	1985
Employed in national economy (in millions)	0.9	3.5	6.8	12.1	14.5
Percentage of national workforce	1	4	6	10	11

Source: Narodnoe khoziaistvo SSSR za 70 let [70 Years of the USSR Economy] (Moscow: Finansy i Statistika, 1987), 411, 418.

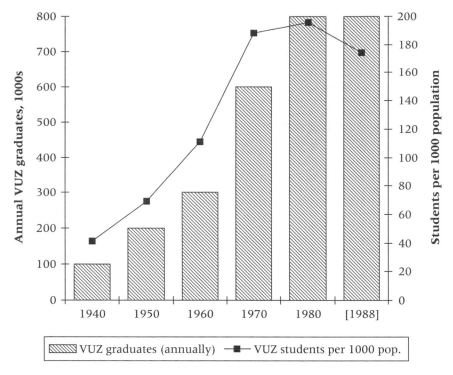

Figure 5.2. Growth of Higher Education in the Postwar USSR (*Source: Narodnoe obrazovaniie i kultura v SSSR* [Education and culture in the USSR] [Moscow: Finansy i Statistika, 1989], 7. Roughly 35–45 percent of graduates were not full-time students but rather received diplomas from evening or correspondence divisions of VUZy. Many of these students were already employed while working toward degrees and were not subject to mandatory raspredelenie. Full-time, daytime divisions produced 55 percent of graduates in 1970, with this share growing to 64 percent by 1985. See *Molodezh' SSSR* [Youth in the USSR] [Moscow: Goskomstat, TsK VLKSM, and VKSh pri TsK VLKSM, 1990], 110.)

employers who didn't want them. Together, these shortcomings set up a vicious cycle of wasted human resources.

No-Shows

The problem of graduates who failed to appear at their designated places of employment plagued the raspredelenie system as early as the 1950s. While documentation of the phenomenon was far from systematic, the problem seems to have been particularly vexing in the Caucasian republics, where often more than half the graduates of particular educational institutions failed to show up at their assigned workplaces.[14] In 1963 the Komsomol First Secretary told the Komsomol Central Committee that shortcomings in raspredelenie were the result of "gaps in ideological work among students." "In the end," he reminded Komsomol officials, "the most important thing is that young specialists, upon finishing institute . . . serve their people *(narod).*" At the same meeting, a secretary of the Moscow State University (MGU) Komsomol organization acknowledged Pavlov's criticism and noted:

> This year at the university, the raspredelenie of young specialists has been considerably more organized than in previous years. A large number of graduates wanted to work in far-off regions, and their requests have been satisfied. Refusals of assignments fell significantly, but there were still some cases. Each refusal is a serious defect in our upbringing work, and Komsomol organizations react very harshly to any such incident of irresponsibility on the part of graduates.[15]

Incidents of noncompliance with raspredelenie assignments continued to plague the system throughout the 1960s and 1970s, encompassing both graduates failing to show at their assigned jobs and specialists fleeing these jobs before completing their three-year commitment. The Caucasus remained a particularly troublesome area. In 1974, for instance, Geidar Aliev, head of the Azerbaijani Communist Party, scolded that republic's Komsomol Congress for failing to improve the compliance rate of assignees:

> We spoke about this at the last Congress, but the situation has not changed. The number of higher pedagogic school graduates who fail to turn up at their assigned places is large , , , But this holds true not only for the higher pedagogical schools. In 1973, out of the 1,335 graduates of the Polytechnic Institute, only 838, or 62 percent, turned up at the places to which they were assigned; corresponding figures were 66 percent for Azerbaijan State Conservatory, 75 percent for the Institute of the Arts, and 77 percent for the Institute of the National Economy. Where are the rest?[16]

Of course, assignees hardly disappeared into thin air. In many cases, no-shows were helped by authorities or at least by loopholes in the system. One newspaper report in 1973 lamenting the shortage of foreign-language teachers in rural schools claimed that roughly half the graduates of teacher-training institutions in Georgia, Uzbekistan, Azerbaijan, and Kazakhstan were exempted from the mandatory assignments process. The author noted that the situation was similar in major cities such as Moscow, Leningrad, and Kiev.[17] Presumably, loopholes in the assignments guidelines intended for graduates in poor health or with special family situations were also made available to children of well-connected parents.

Compliance with job assignments seems to have been particularly sensitive to geographical considerations. Graduates often refused postings far from either their family or university home. Graduates of Moscow VUZy, in high demand at many enterprises and research institutes, were particularly reluctant to leave Moscow, for fear they would never regain a Moscow residence permit.[18]

Graduates' aversion to distant assignments was often exacerbated by seemingly arbitrary personnel flows between distant regions. The chairman of the Khabarovsk krai *ispolkom* (executive committee), for instance, blamed his region's labor shortages on the failure of graduates from outside the region to appear at Far Eastern assignments. Those who did appear were unable to adapt to the harsh conditions and quickly left. At the same time, he complained, planners were sending many natives of the region, graduating from local VUZy, to jobs in the west.[19]

During the 1980s, according to figures collected by the State Statistical Committee (Goskomstat), roughly 10 percent of daytime-VUZ graduates assigned jobs through the raspredelenie system failed to appear at their assignments, and a further 5 percent of those who did appear were no longer on the job six months later.[20] While these figures—which varied little from 1980 to 1987—suggest the overall scale of the no-show phenomenon, they miss two of its most significant aspects.

First, raspredelenie noncompliance, as I have suggested above, tended to be concentrated in certain specialties and regions. Enforcement remained particularly lax and corrupt in the Caucasian and Central Asian higher-education systems, for instance.[21] At the same time, throughout the country teachers or agricultural specialists posted to rural jobs— the majority of assignments in both professions—remained consistently more likely to shirk these assignments. In 1987, Goskomstat conducted a special study of assignment patterns of graduates of teaching institutes and found that two-thirds of the no-shows had been assigned to rural schools. No-show rates for these teacher-designates were particularly high among graduates of VUZy in Azerbaijan (42 percent), Tadzhikistan (40 percent), Georgia (32 percent), Uzbekistan (18 percent), and Armenia (15 percent).[22]

Second, and perhaps more significantly, official statistics underestimated the true scale of the no-show phenomenon since they were collected almost entirely from the enterprises to which young specialists were assigned. As discussed in the following sections, these enterprises often had little incentive to provide planners with accurate information about manpower flows.

No Jobs

Graduates who reported to their designated job placement were not always rewarded for their sense of duty. Though statistics here are even less comprehensive than for the phenomenon of no-shows, officials throughout the raspredelenie system acknowledged that assignees were frequently either denied jobs in their specialty (despite legal guarantees) or denied jobs altogether.

In the Russian Federation, enterprise refusals to accept assigned graduates rose from 4.2 percent in 1965 to 7.2 percent in 1970.[23] In 1978, a Soviet official indicated that "at least 5 percent" of specialists are turned away due to a lack of jobs in their specialty or a lack of housing (which enterprises were obliged to provide for assignees).[24] Reports in the central press cited cases of outright refusals by ministries or enterprises to accept young specialists according to plan, particularly where assignees came from different regions or ethnic groups.[25]

More widespread than outright refusal, however, was the assignment of graduates to jobs unrelated to their education. This was, for many managers, a much simpler solution than sending assignees away. These managers had, after all, requested a specific number of specialists earlier in the two-year planning cycle. By providing menial but well-paid work for them, or by looking the other way as the specialists drifted back home, they might avoid an official complaint which could cast doubt on subsequent planning requests.

Because much of this misallocation of labor was clandestine, it is difficult to provide reliable estimates of the frequency of this practice. The central press throughout the 1970s reported selected cases of engineering graduates sent to work on the assembly line or as janitors. One Party worker from Tashkent complained in a letter to *Pravda* that enterprises in the city were employing trained engineers as trash collectors and cleaners in order to have them available for "fire brigade" reassignments in the event one enterprise fell behind plan targets.[26] Another letter investigated by *Pravda* told of graduates from Moscow's prestigious Bauman Higher Technical School who were sent to a machine tool plant in Krasnodar only to receive janitorial, custodial, and gardening assignments for their entire three-year tenure.[27] These and other cases reported by the Soviet press suggest an oversupply of engineers so substantial that they could be spared more easily for menial assignments than skilled workers.[28]

The misallocation of higher-education graduates was of sufficient concern to policy makers by 1973 that draft guidelines for republic-level legislation on public education under discussion by the Supreme Soviet declared directly: "Persons completing . . . higher education institutions are provided with jobs in their specialties." A discussion about this clause ensued in the press, pitting advocates of an absolute guarantee of appropriate employment (which would simultaneously shackle graduates to their VUZ specialization for the full three years) against proponents of a more flexible formulation. In the end, the compromisers won a small victory, and graduates were only guaranteed "jobs in accordance with the specialties and skill categories they have obtained."[29]

The first reliable estimate of underemployment among young specialists was finally made by Goskomstat in January 1988. A nationwide survey of specialists in industrial enterprises found that only 59 percent of recent graduates (i.e., graduates of universities and institutes, 1985–87) were working in the fields in which they received their degrees. Of those working in other fields—many in production-line jobs—half claimed that no jobs were available in their fields at their assigned enterprises. Another 24 percent indicated a preference for work outside their educational specializations citing higher pay or greater interest. Among older specialists working outside their specialties, unavailability of jobs was far less significant than pay differentials or the nature of the work.[30]

Recent graduates were also asked directly about their experience with raspredelenie. Forty-four percent of all young specialists surveyed indicated that on arrival at their assigned jobs, they were not offered work corresponding to their educational specializations. Sixty-one percent said they were not provided housing.[31]

Distortions in the Young Specialist Labor Market

The failure of many enterprises to honor their commitments to the graduates they had "ordered" was tied to the reluctance of many of these graduates to submit to mandatory job assignments. Aware that some assignees would fail to show for less desirable jobs and that others would appear under duress or only because their poor academic performance offered few alternatives, employers naturally requested more specialists than they really needed. In the worst case, their real personnel needs would not go unfilled by more than a few bodies. In the best case, managers might actually be able to select the best specialists from among those compelled to appear at their factory or institute.

Because two years would elapse between submission of planning requests to Gosplan and the arrival of graduates, managers added a further buffer to their requests for specialists to guard against unforeseen contingencies. They were following the same planning logic that led to chronic hoarding of all productive inputs—in this case human capital—throughout the Soviet economy.[32]

Reports in the Soviet central press often described variations on this abuse of the raspredelenie system. In 1970, *Pravda* reported the case of thirty-two graduates of Penza Polytechnic Institute specializing in textile machinery who were assigned to distant jobs outside their specialty despite a shortage of textile engineers in Penza Oblast. The mother of one of these graduates complained to the paper that her daughter had been assigned to a laundry trust in Cheliabinsk which employed no textile engineers at all but was requesting them for use in future plants (which would be more modern). "Who are we to refuse specialists?" the plant manager calmly told *Pravda*.[33] A decade later, an official at Kishiniev State University complained that "a number of ministries turn in statements of requirements 'just in case,'" only to find some "compelling" reason to break their commitment once the unneeded graduates arrived.[34]

Pravda chastised managers for simply overinflating planning requests rather than intensifying efforts to retain specialists assigned to them. The paper called the resulting situation a "personnel hodgepodge" in which graduates were needlessly directed to distant postings where they had little desire to work. *Pravda* noted that despite the assignment of several Kazakh Polytechnic graduates to jobs outside the republic, twenty-eight graduates from Erevan Polytechnic were assigned to Kazakhstan. Of these "only seven arrived, four of whom shortly thereafter left jobs without authorization. The remaining three have made tenacious efforts to get themselves fired."[35]

While some young specialists were content with work on the production line or as janitors, others saw in their redundancy an opportunity to escape from an assignment they may have wished to avoid in the first place. Once managers had selected and retained those specialists they needed, it was often in the interest of these surplus assignees to permit the violations of their raspredelenie rights (i.e., guaranteed housing and employment in one's educational specialization) to go unreported, since a complaint lodged against their employers would merely entitle them to another, possibly worse, assignment. Similarly, employers had little incentive to complain if these assignees simply disappeared, drifting back home in search of more amenable work—they would be spared the cost of housing these unneeded bodies without placing subsequent manpower planning requests in doubt.

As a consequence of this tacit collusion between unenthusiastic employer and unwilling employee, much of the underemployment of young specialists went unmeasured. Subsequent manpower planning requests therefore went unchallenged. The country went on educating more specialists than it needed, all buoyed by a legal entitlement—if they chose to pursue it—to three years of work in their specialties.

This predicament might be better understood by a simple example. Suppose the manager of a ball-bearing manufacturer in Sverdlovsk in 1970 anticipated a need for six mechanical engineers in 1972. In 1970, he would request fifteen engineers from Gosplan, which might adjust that figure downward to twelve. In 1971, planning documents would be sent to the Ministry of Higher Education instructing it to allocate twelve new graduates to this plant. Six engineers from Urals Poly might be assigned, along with six from Moscow. Of these twelve, perhaps eight would actually appear in the fall of 1972, by which time the manager might actually need only four. He will report the proper arrival of all eight, then choose the best four and put them to work as engineers. The other four might receive jobs as bookkeepers or workers or janitors, and during the course of the next year, they would either drift back to Moscow or look for new work around the factory. Thus, only four engineers would actually be employed as engineers at the plant, but planners in Moscow would continue to think the accurate figure is eight.

If we now duplicate this scenario at all ball-bearing factories in the country, the *perceived* demand for ball-bearing engineers would be twice the *real* demand. Hence, Gosplan was authorizing the training (i.e., admission to VUZy) of twice as many ball-bearing engineers as the country really needed. The hidden underemployment of graduates led directly to the overproduction of specialists. This, in turn, exacerbated underemployment and led to frustration among graduates who found their educations wasted at the workplace.

Overenrollment in the higher education system was a major theme of the only full-length discussion of the raspredelenie system to be found in Soviet libraries as late as 1991. This study criticized the assignments process for lacking long-range planning perspectives and for failing to hold managers accountable for their planning requests. But some of its sharpest criticisms were aimed not at raspredelenie per se, but at the higher-education system for graduating two or three times as many specialists as the economy needed.[36]

With VUZ enrollments at record levels throughout the 1970s, Soviet sociologists, policy makers, and educators took turns bemoaning the phenomenon of the "eternal student." These secondary-school graduates would apply year after year to different VUZy—shunning a factory or farm job and often selecting a specialty on the basis of odds favoring admission—until they finally gained admission. Many feared the lure of higher education was making it an end unto itself, swamping the state's efforts to direct students' vocational choice to economically needed professions. Consequently, many students ended up in majors in which they had little intrinsic interest, only to find themselves bound to them for three more years after graduation. This was especially problematic in teaching and agricultural specializations, where VUZy were abundant and competition less intense.[37]

The shift in educational expectations is evident in the statistics on activities of secondary-school graduates. One survey in the early 1970s found that 80 percent of secondary-school graduates wanted to continue their education, while only 5–7 percent wanted jobs.[38] Table 5.2 shows a clear shift during the late 1970s and 1980s toward continuing education on the part of graduates of general (i.e., nonvocational) secondary-school graduates. At roughly the same time, the USSR Minister of Education was warning that only 10–13 percent of secondary-school grads could expect to begin full-time VUZ studies within a year of their graduations.[39]

For many planners and policy makers, the most disturbing aspect of secondary-school graduates' fixation on acquiring higher education was their reluctance to accept factory or other manual employment, even while waiting to reapply to an institute. An official in the Russian Republic's Labor Resources Committee complained that 57 percent of all secondary-school graduates were "biding time" as secretaries or messengers while waiting to apply to VUZy again; at the same time, he noted, tens of thousands of industrial and construction jobs were unfilled.[40]

Many of these "eternal students" were graduates of the ten-year general secondary schools, thought to provide the best preparation for higher education. They had thus received none of the practical training provided by the vocational secondary schools established under Khrushchev. Consequently, when these young people eventually received nonspecialist work (either after abandoning attempts at VUZ admission or following raspredelenie), they were generally assigned to unskilled manual labor—the least satisfying category of jobs.[41] These assignments were particularly frustrating for graduates of higher education; one panel study of Novosibirsk youth in the 1970s found those who failed to gain admission to VUZy and eventually settled for manual labor were more satisfied with their work than most VUZ graduates assigned to jobs at which their educations were wasted. The author concluded, "Perhaps higher school does not so much quench one's thirst as sharpen it."[42]

For some of these thirsty but vocationally adrift graduates, assignment

Table 5.2. Trajectories of Graduates of Ten-Year Schools (as percentage)

	1968	1974	1977	1981	1984	1985
Went to work	55	53	53	44	40	39
Continued full-time study	45	47	47	56	60	61

Source: Argumenty i fakty, no. 6, 1987, 7.

to blue-collar or even custodial jobs may have been a relief. Though these jobs were boring, they at least offered a rapid exit from a profession many entered only in desperation. The rest found themselves victims of a planning system which based its targets for higher-education enrollments on flawed estimates of the demand for specialists and then bound many of these surplus graduates to jobs which wasted their training and frustrated their aspirations.

Throughout the period of expanding higher-education enrollments, the Soviet Union's real need for trained specialists could be met—despite the flagrant waste of many graduates assigned to menial jobs—by the steady expansion of the pool of specialists available to the economy.[43] As VUZ enrollments began to plateau in the mid- to late-1970s, however, planners began to devote greater attention to using specialists more efficiently. Before looking at this initiative, which set in motion events that would destroy the raspredelenie system, I will consider how the job-assignments process functioned at the street level: How effective were elite-level controls, how influential were societal interests, and how important were information asymmetries and hierarchical structures?

Institutional Dynamics of Raspredelenie

Elite Controls

Guidelines for raspredelenie were set by the USSR Ministry of Higher Education (MinVUZ). Consequently, raspredelenie was treated as an element of overall policy toward education, rather than toward labor or industrial production. Under Khrushchev, the focus in educational reform was to raise the profile of vocational training throughout the educational process and to stem the trend toward shrinking worker and peasant representation in higher-education establishments. Khrushchev was chiefly concerned with reintegrating education with production; he encouraged extensive reliance upon "production practice" as a key part of the educational curriculum.[44]

It is not surprising that Khrushchev had little patience for graduates who shirked their responsibilities and failed to appear at their production jobs. In his view, education should serve the economic system and not vice versa. In 1963, Khrushchev approved a statute delaying the award of VUZ diplomas by a year and making their receipt conditional on graduates remaining in their assigned jobs.[45] In 1964, VUZy were given the additional power to deprive graduates of their diplomas for violation of raspredelenie guidelines.[46]

This strengthening of raspredelenie discipline had been strongly promoted by the Komsomol, apparently over the objections of the Ministry of Higher Education.[47] MinVUZ had presided over a gradual relaxation of the raspredelenie guidelines, through successive revisions in 1954, 1955, 1957, 1960, and 1963. Rights of assignees were more clearly spelled out, the circumstances under which "open placement" could be permitted (health, family, etc.) were gradually widened, and raspredelenie committees at VUZy were given greater authority. The new hard line appeared to represent a step backwards, the start of a possible reversion to the Stalin-era labor regime.

Brezhnev was less obsessed than Khrushchev with the social composition of Soviet institutions, however, and put less faith in the motivating force of ideology. Brezhnev's fixation was science and technology: he wanted a "scientific-technical revolution" in production, and, even more important, he felt that "scientific management" would revitalize the socialist system.

The implications of this shift of emphasis were significant and immediate for educational policy in general and raspredelenie in particular. Brezhnev did not share Khrushchev's dream of blurring the lines between education and production; instead, he dreamt of rescuing Soviet production by harnessing new technologies in industry and "rationalizing" its system of management. He envisioned specialists not as simply highly educated workers sharing workers' values, but as a distinct elite with new, "scientific" skills and approaches. One of his first acts in the field of education, on 3 September 1966, was to unlink the realms of education and production and abort Khrushchev's experiment with deferred diplomas; diplomas would once again be granted immediately upon graduation and not linked with any future work performance.[48]

Although Brezhnev devoted relatively little direct attention after this to higher education, he did endorse a higher-education reform package in 1972.[49] The main stress in this program was on improving the training of scientists and engineers, and particularly teachers of science. It also established a "Council for Higher Schools" within the Ministry of Higher and Secondary Specialized Education to develop "scientifically based recommendations" for improving VUZ operations. Though previous Council of Ministers resolutions on higher education automatically generated a new set of raspredelenie guidelines (if only to fine-tune the rhetorical emphasis), Brezhnev's 1972 initiative was sufficiently vague that it produced only one minor adjustment to the raspredelenie guidelines that had been in force since 1968.[50]

In fact, these guidelines remained undisturbed until 1980, when a pair of government resolutions on the training and utilization of specialists prompted the development of a new set.[51] In 1978, the Council of Ministers expressed alarm at the number of specialists wasting their educations and directed planning organs to reduce the number of surplus VUZ graduates in the economy. Among the specific actions ordered were a critical reexamination of the *nomenklatura* (list) of positions requiring higher education, consolidation of subspecialties in different faculties that offered equivalent training, and better monitoring of specialists' activities after graduation (i.e., compliance with assignments and utilization by their employers).[52] In 1979, a joint Party-state resolution pointed to a different set of concerns—the *shortage* of educated specialists in certain key economic sectors (including mining, metallurgy, agriculture, construction, and transportation) and in certain regions of the country (Siberia, the North, Far East, and Non-Black Earth Zone of RSFSR were singled out). The government directed MinVUZ and Gosplan to make job assignments further in advance of students' graduation—by as much as one to three years—and to develop a detailed five-year plan for raspredelenie. In addition, enterprises were instructed to work more closely with VUZy, offering their facilities to students for internships and "improving the material base" of VUZy.[53]

Together, these instructions clearly reflect Brezhnev's faith in "scientific management" of the specialist labor market. If graduates and enterprises alike were showing signs of resisting planning directives, then the solution must be to envelop them in a larger, more comprehensive plan. Making students aware of their eventual assignment well in advance of their graduation and encouraging students to begin work even before they left school (through internships) could only strengthen the bonds between specialists and their future workplace. Taken to its logical extreme—a five-year plan—students entering a five-year VUZ could receive their future job assignments before even enrolling.

In his expansive examination of Soviet labor policy under Khrushchev and Brezhnev, Peter Hauslohner argues that these changes to raspre-delenie were part of a concerted and almost frantic effort by the Brezhnev regime to regain control over its unproductive and shrinking labor pool.[54] On the one hand, a close look at the origins of these decrees supports Hauslohner's contention that they represented a realization by the political leadership that its massive investment in higher education was being systematically underexploited. However, his implication that reform of the raspredelenie system was considered in the broader context of labor policy is difficult to substantiate. While Hauslohner assigns a major role in the formulation of late-Brezhnev labor policy to the reorganized State Committee for Labor and Social Problems (Goskomtrud), officials of Goskomtrud and Gosobrazovaniia (the State Committee on Public Education, the Gorbachev-era successor to MinVUZ) told me that Goskomtrud played no significant role in the development of raspredelenie policy.[55] Goskomtrud's public silence on issues of specialist training and assignment seems to confirm their account.

The apparent divorce of raspredelenie policy from labor policy suggests more than just a breakdown of interorganizational communication. It points to a more fundamental question about the nature of central policy guidance on raspredelenie within the central planning framework. Given the need for VUZy and employers to coordinate personnel flows through a centrally developed interrepublican and interdepartmental plan—and the sheer logistics of Soviet resource management offered little alternative—how important were central directives anyway? What parameters did they allow policy makers in Moscow to influence?

The lack of any significant variance in the issues addressed by central policy directives suggests one answer: efforts at policy reform produced more rhetoric than results. For over forty years, official evaluations of the raspredelenie system focused on a strikingly similar set of shortcomings. For instance, in 1948, the USSR Council of Ministers cited the following key weaknesses in raspredelenie: (1) neglect of rural postings in favor of assignments in large cities; (2) planning requests from enterprises going unchallenged by planners; (3) no independent measure of demand for specialists; (4) no coordination of student admissions and raspredelenie needs (ministers were particularly concerned that departments of mining and metallurgy were often filled predominantly with women, who rarely pursued careers in these fields); (5) poor ideological work in universities;

(6) poor attention by employers to properly receiving assignees and meeting their housing and professional needs.[56]

Though the Council of Ministers would pass no fewer than seven resolutions on the training and utilization of specialists with higher education during the tenures of Khrushchev and Brezhnev, the targets of official concern remained remarkably similar.[57] Policy makers repeatedly complained of inflated requests by employers, problems estimating the real demand for specialists, poor supervision of graduates' arrival at assigned posts, gaps in ideological indoctrination of graduates, lack of coordination between admissions and raspredelenie plans (particularly when they resulted in overlapping cross-regional assignments), and maltreatment of assignees by their new employers.[58] With the exception of the short-lived Khrushchev experiment with deferred diplomas, none of these government resolutions raised fundamentally new concerns or produced any alteration in the essential structure of raspredelenie. Assignments coordinated by central planning organs were still based upon needs submitted by prospective employers, and they remained binding on graduates for three full years.[59]

New guidelines produced new actions only in the realm of planning, particularly in the area of information gathering and exchange. The reforms of the late 1970s, for example, led to several adjustments to assignments-planning procedure: plans were to be developed as long as five years before students actually graduated, and the State Statistical Administration was to monitor these plans by collecting new data on specialist utilization and compliance with raspredelenie directives. The 1980 MinVUZ regulations specify in agonizing detail the paperwork to be completed at each stage of the development of a central plan for raspredelenie by Gosplan as well as by VUZy and enterprises during the actual assignments. Assignees and employers were instructed to sign a new "labor agreement" in which both parties' obligations—already mandated by existing law—would be reiterated.

Thus, the raspredelenie system seems to have resisted persistent efforts by Soviet leaders to effect even minor changes. The most sweeping attempt at reform in twenty years produced little more than dramatically expanded documentation. In the centrally planned system, however, documentation was more than a mere description of reality—it was reality.

Societal Interests and Policy-Relevant Data

If officials in charge of raspredelenie were unmoved by appeals from above, how sensitive were they to pressures from below? Were they concerned that the job-assignments system seemed deeply dysfunctional?

In 1970, the head of raspredelenie for the Russian Republic's Gosplan admitted that the assignments system was "quite haphazard." He explained, "we don't know the economy's true needs for specialists."[60] Several years later, *Pravda* also branded many assignments "haphazard": "Personnel requests received from the localities do not always give a good idea of the nature and conditions of the work that lies ahead of graduating students."[61]

Both of these critiques zero in on the single weakest link in the multistep raspredelenie process: the requests for specialists submitted by future employers. Requests *(zaiavki)* were submitted two full years before the graduation of requested specialists. Prior to 1980, there was no independent check on the veracity of these requests. More important, neither was there any evaluation post hoc of the reasonableness of specialist staffing levels. The state had little but anecdotal evidence on how well specialists were being utilized by their employers. The chief cause of this gap lies in the data collection system itself: according to officials at Goskomstat, all data related in any way to employment in the USSR came directly from *employers themselves.*[62]

Appearing at their new assignments, VUZ graduates presented their assignment papers, at the bottom of which were small stubs to be filled in by their new employers confirming their arrival. Employers returned these stubs (clipping them off with scissors and embossing them with the official organization seal) to relevant ministerial and VUZ officials attesting to the graduates' timely arrival and to their provision with housing, appropriate positions in their specialties, and so forth. Sampling was not used to collect data; all figures, as one Goskomstat official explained, were "composite" *(svodnye).*[63] In other words, each young specialist portrayed in state statistics as arriving on the job was represented by a clipped stub in regional Goskomstat or ministerial files. For this reason alone, subsequent career developments of these specialists were swallowed up in the enterprise's aggregate personnel figures. If policy makers wanted statistics on the percentage of assignees who remained at their jobs after one or three years, they would need to either add new stubs to graduates' documentation or instruct enterprises to collect these specific data and trust them to report them accurately.[64] Using standard Goskomstat procedures, there was no way to ascertain what these young specialists were actually doing on the job.

In fact, although the 1978 Council of Ministers resolution clearly instructed Goskomstat to "develop a system of indicators to measure the effectiveness of the utilization of specialists in the national economy," Vladimir Korolev, head of Goskomstat's Sector of Labor Statistics, insisted as late as 1991 that measuring the "real demand" for specialists in the national economy was simply "not our [i.e., Goskomstat's] job." According to Korolev, Goskomstat had never even attempted to assess the real demand for VUZ graduates.[65]

This second assertion may not be entirely true. According to Galina Gorbei, deputy chief of Goskomstat's Department of Social Statistics and Korolev's supervisor, Goskomstat did conduct research on different methodologies for estimating real demand for specialists, beyond simply relying on enterprise zaiavki.[66] In the context of these investigations, according to Gorbei, her department conducted an "internal study" to investigate the hypothesis (which had already been incorporated into state and Party declarations) that some key professions were training too few specialists while other specialties were producing surplus graduates. The study, conducted "sometime around 1984," was performed in collaboration with Goskomtrud—an interesting partner, since it played no role in development of either VUZ admissions policies or raspredelenie guidelines. It was, Gorbei told me, a "big study," producing "lots of tables."

According to Gorbei, these tables contradicted conventional wisdom about the specialist labor pool: they suggested there was no overall imbalance between the supply and demand of specialists in particular disciplines. Instead, Goskomstat data seemed to reveal regional imbalances in some vocations; taken together, these imbalances pointed to problems not in the total number of specialists being produced in given fields but rather in their distribution. The problem, it appeared, was that too few graduates were staying in their assigned jobs after their three-year assignment had expired.

This analysis—the first scientific look at supply and demand in the specialist labor market—had little or no impact on the ongoing debate over specialist training and assignment because few people knew of its existence. The Party continued to assert that key sectors were suffering from severe shortages of educated personnel. According to Gorbei, Goskomstat "never thought to publish [the study], perhaps because it failed to confirm the initial hypotheses." The study simply languished in official archives, where it probably remains today.[67]

Rather than measuring specialist "demand" independently, Goskomstat's solution to its post-1978 task of evaluating "the effectiveness of the utilization of specialists in the national economy" was to determine whether specialists were using their education on the job. The simplest approach to this task—using data already supplied by enterprises—was to count the employees with higher education in positions not explicitly requiring that level of education (as categorized by Goskomtrud and Gosplan).[68] In 1987, Goskomstat finally overcame significant opposition from Party officials and published a small footnote to its annual report of the number of specialists in the workforce. According to this note, "In several branches [of the economy], the policy of irrational utilization of diploma-holding specialists continues. About four million of these individuals are working in positions that do not require this level of training."[69]

The figure of four million underutilized specialists represented approximately 12 percent of all specialists in the Soviet economy. According to Gorbei, Goskomstat was permitted to publish this figure only when the demands of glasnost' could be added to the long-standing imperative to better inform the debate over manpower policy.[70] In other words, policy makers who dealt with specialist labor distribution actively opposed disseminating any information that would give added urgency to the need to overhaul that system, at least until disseminating information became a political end unto itself. Even then, Goskomstat still failed to report the percentage of employees without VUZ diplomas holding jobs designated for specialists. Without both sets of data (i.e., employees wasting the education they have and employees coping without the education their position supposedly needs), conclusions about the accuracy of enterprises' reported demand for specialists remained merely guesswork.

Gosplan's quotas for specialist training and assignment relied upon precisely such guesswork. Gosplan used data on the percentage of specialists working either below their educational levels or outside their specialties as a "corrective" for evaluating zaiavki from enterprises.[71] If that figure for an industrial branch or large employer was 15 percent, Gosplan might then adjust enterprise requests downward by 15 percent to compensate for this "wastage" of human resources. Naturally, this procedure further reduced enterprise managers' incentives to provide accurate information on employment patterns to Goskomstat.

Goskomstat's January 1988 survey of specialists was its first significant effort to collect data on the specialist labor market without relying solely on employers. Researchers used a national sample of 10,700 graduates of VUZy and SSUZy; previous surveys of specialists were limited to samples of a few hundred at most. The results were included in Goskomstat's *Trud v SSSR (Labor in the USSR)*, published in 1988 for the first time in twenty years. Other data from this survey were included in several other statistical yearbooks published by Goskomstat between 1988 and 1990 in a glasnost'-inspired wave.

Included in this orgy of statistical openness were several time-series, incorporating data collected for years but never published. No-show rates of graduates at their assigned jobs, for instance, were first published in 1990 but covered the period after 1980.[72] These were presumably the figures used by planners in evaluating the efficacy of the raspredelenie system during the 1970s. The simple publication of these figures, however, does not automatically validate them. As suggested earlier, employers had powerful incentives to report the arrival of assignees and then tacitly permit them to slip away, especially if they had no housing or appropriate jobs to offer.

While there is no simple way to assess the quality of Goskomstat's data, even a cursory examination of parallel statistics kept by the Komsomol (which participated in raspredelenie commissions at VUZy and also organized young specialists at enterprises) hints at basic confusion over the simplest facts. Komsomol data suggest a slightly more serious no-show problem and a far more troublesome attrition problem. Table 5.3 compares Goskomstat figures (available for 1980, 1985, 1987) and Komsomol figures (available for 1982 and 1987).

Thus, despite the persistent stress on better data collection running throughout state and Party initiatives on job assignments, performance of the raspredelenie system through the 1980s was still monitored by unreliable data, most of it supplied by the very enterprises whose assign-

Table 5.3. Goskomstat and Komsomol Data on Raspredelenie

	1980	1982	1985	1987
No-Shows of VUZ graduates (Goskomstat data)	8.9%	—	9.4%	8.0%
No-Shows of VUZ graduates (Komsomol data)	—	**12%**	—	**12%**
Assignees no longer on job after nine months (Goskomstat)	5.1%	—	5.4%	5.2%
Assignees no longer on job after one year (Komsomol)	—	**n.a.**	—	**20%**

Source: Goskomstat: *Molodezh' SSSR* [Youth in the USSR] (Moscow: Finansy i statistika, 1990), 143; Komsomol: TsA VLKSM, f. 6, op. 19, d. 278 (1 March 1982), and TsA VLKSM, f. 6, op. 20, d. 186 (1987).

ment practices were under scrutiny. Even in the late 1980s, as state policy was mandating a greater reliance on long-range planning for admissions and assignments, no independent method was even under development for authenticating enterprises' estimates of their demand for VUZ graduates. Two questions now arise: Why were policy makers satisfied with the poor quality of data presented to them? And why were statisticians and social scientists incapable of providing better data?

The answers to these two questions are linked: analysis only improves if analysts perceive a sincere demand for better research. While policy makers, in theory, were exhorting street-level bureaucrats to produce better information about the utilization of specialists at the workplace, in practice they rarely relied upon such information to drive the policy process. Consequently, much of the data reaching central policy makers remained anecdotal—originating from the planning and monitoring loops of the economic bureaucracy rather than from research institutes or scientific studies.

In August 1978, for instance, the Biuro of the Komsomol Central Committee considered a resolution on raspredelenie, in direct response to the Council of Ministers resolution on the subject earlier that year. The resolution contained the standard toothless urgings for VUZ Komsomol committees to play a "more active" role in the conduct of raspredelenie commission proceedings and to "foster in students love for their chosen profession and ensure strict fulfillment of the plan for raspredelenie of graduates."[73] Unencumbered by any reputation for boldness, the Komsomol leadership was doing little more than recycling the themes of the government decree, which itself rehashed messages at the core of state policy since Khrushchev.

More revealing in its banality was the deliberative process that produced this Komsomol policy document. According to the protocols of the Biuro meeting, the draft resolution was presented to the Komsomol leadership at its regular weekly meeting, accompanied by a four-page analysis of raspredelenie policy prepared by Komsomol's department on students. This memo praised the growing practice of direct VUZ-enterprise ties, citing no aggregate statistics but mentioning specific programs at Kishiniev, Sverdlovsk, and Rostov. The authors warned that too many students were being granted the right to arrange their own placements but then cited raw numbers that showed only 5 percent of graduates in this category (they neglected to add that this percentage was falling steadily). On the problem of no-shows, the memo offered no aggregate data at all, limiting illustration of the problem to specific examples: no-show rates for graduates from Volgograd oblast (12 percent) or no-shows of pedagogical grads from European Russia for assignments in Novosibirsk (14 percent). Finally, the memo merely noted that "many" specialists were employed in jobs not utilizing their education.[74]

On the basis of this idiosyncratic analysis, Komsomol bureaucrats reached the unspectacular conclusion that Komsomol supervision of raspredelenie was inadequate. The Komsomol top leadership endorsed this finding and the accompanying resolution without any substantive debate or discussion.[75] The need for probing discussion was, in fact, as superfluous as the need for more subtle analysis of more comprehensive statistics. What mattered, in the wake of the Council of Ministers' imprecise instructions, was to start the bureaucratic paper trail, placing the issues flagged in the government decree on the "agenda" for monitoring and supervision. The Biuro's resolution, in turn, spawned a 1980 decree from the Komsomol secretariat castigating the Alma-Ata Komsomol for insufficient progress in implementing the 1978 Biuro resolution. By elaborating the specific shortcomings found in its investigation in Alma-Ata, the Komsomol bureaucracy could finally signal to its VUZ-level secretaries exactly what indicators of raspredelenie it would be monitoring in the future.

This was how statistics were employed in shaping the raspredelenie program: not as inputs to a planning system which generated detailed policies but as selective indicators of bureaucratic performance in pursuit of abstract and unvarying goals. Fundamentally, policy was only defined when these indicators were selected, since they would then directly and forcefully focus the goals of street-level bureaucrats. Statistical agencies, consequently, enjoyed little latitude in collecting new data on raspredelenie on their own initiative. New data were not inputs to the policy process; they were, rather, the very implementation of new policy. New statistics were collected when—and only when—state and Party decrees mandated their collection.[76]

As was the case with indoctrination, one of the few sources of "independent" information on job assignments (i.e., collected outside the planning bureaucracy and not used to judge actors' job performance) was sociology. Sociologists working on the Soviet education system devoted considerable attention to the question of specialist training, but their focus tended to be the process of vocational choice and the influence of social background on academic performance and vocational satisfaction. Sociologists also attempted to measure the "prestige" of higher education, seeking to understand fluctuations in the number of applicants for different educational institutions.[77]

One recurring conclusion of these analyses, which often tracked students from secondary school through their first jobs, was that students gave little thought to their choice of profession until they were saddled with a job they hated. The clear implication of this finding was that state programs designed to shape students' vocational preferences and channel them toward economically needed professions were ineffective. Instead, students often disassociated their choice of school from their choice of profession, only to find themselves bound to that profession when the time came for raspredelenie. Programs designed to raise the prestige of skilled labor jobs, as an alternative to higher education, were having little effect. High-school graduates wanted higher education, even if society had no pressing need for so many VUZ graduates; what society needed was more skilled workers with vocational training. In the words of Vladimir Shubkin, a prominent sociologist, "the pyramid of occupational demands is the inverse of the pyramid of occupational preferences."[78]

Once they located the roots of the problem in the poor regulation of secondary students' vocational choice, however, sociologists offered no real alternatives to policy makers. Shubkin's recommendations, based on a ten-year panel study of secondary-school graduates from Novosibirsk, centered on ways of reshaping students' preferences. Noting that students aspired to a socioeconomic stratum just above that of their parents, Shubkin urged policy makers to focus on restructuring the hierarchy of occupational prestige. Even before Shubkin's final results were published, some industries were already working to raise the prestige of understaffed positions.[79]

Shubkin's influence on policy was more the exception than the rule. More common was the experience of Filip Filippov, a sociologist who rose during the 1970s to become director of research on education and youth at the Academy of Sciences' Institute of Sociology. Filippov reported that sociologists encountered regular "interference" from ministries, particularly from the Ministry of Higher Education.[80] The publication of a landmark empirical study on higher education was delayed by a full five years.[81] According to Filippov, he found himself under growing pressure during the 1970s from Party and Ministry officials to "give an apologetic interpretation" to his survey results—that is, to find sociological excuses for ineffective admissions and vocational policies.[82]

However much he remembers himself as a crusader muzzled by bureaucratic disinterest, Filippov was actually noncontroversial for most of his career. When the Komsomol Central Committee solicited policy proposals from a broad spectrum of public figures on the eve of its Eighteenth All-Union Congress, Filippov offered an insightful diagnosis but prescribed weak remedies. In an unpublished letter to the Central Committee, Filippov noted that the education of the labor force had outstripped the educational requirements of the workplace. As a result, he argued, frustrated young workers were shunning "objectively necessary" positions requiring physical labor. His recommendations amounted to little more than expanding ideological indoctrination in the schools and strengthening discipline among students, both of which would facilitate their absorption into the labor force. His most concrete proposal was greater professional training of sociologists to study youth problems.[83]

In both his avowed wish to be free from outside interference in his work and his timidity in joining the policy debate even when invited, Filippov was typical of many social scientists studying issues related to youth, education, and employment. Even in the warm glow of glasnost', a Soviet researcher reviewing twenty years of sociological studies of raspredelenie could find no more profound result than the following bromide: "The defining role in [students'] choice of professions, according to most scholars, is played by [students'] interest in them."[84]

Certainly, no sociologist looking at raspredelenie was ever bold enough to address the imbalance between the "pyramid of occupational preferences" and the "pyramid of occupational demands" as dismissively as the director of the Leningrad Machine Tool Association:

> Of course, a person is lucky if he finds work that coincides with his calling. But the idea that labor must bring satisfaction is an insidious myth. We must tell the younger generation honestly and straightforwardly that, under socialism, labor is first and foremost work. Real labor cannot be a game or amusement.[85]

Not all potential analysts were completely divorced from policy formulation. All-Union and republican education and labor ministries maintained research institutes specifically for the purpose of assisting in the development of social and economic policies.[86] An examination of the work on raspredelenie coming out of these institutes reveals several detailed models of young specialist labor distribution from a planning perspective. With few exceptions, however, these analyses consisted of modeling the system as it presently operated and presented no new data on the behavior of either young specialists or their employers.[87] If academic sociologists were describing an overgrown policy forest by pointing to the same few trees, these think-tank modelers tended not to get past the tangle of roots. Neither community served to inject societal demands and interests into the policy process; instead, distorted data gathered from employers themselves remained largely unchallenged.

Information, Monitoring, and Authority within the Bureaucratic Hierarchy

Although inputs to the policy process were unreliable, officials in charge of raspredelenie retained the final say over guidelines and how they were implemented and monitored. The principal author at Gosobrazovaniia of the 1980 (and 1988) raspredelenie guidelines described the key to the system as "its flexibility." He illustrated this for me with an anecdote:

Some East German colleagues from their [higher education] ministry were visiting and were very interested in our system of raspredelenie. But no matter how we tried to explain to them how it worked, they could not understand it. "This could not possibly work in the GDR," they repeated.

What they were unable to understand was the flexibility *(gibkost')* of our system. In the GDR, I suppose, they would have strictly followed all the rules as published. But for us, it is the flexibility of the system that keeps everybody happy. . . .

For instance, if a factory needs two particularly talented, smart young engineers, the factory manager might call me, and I might call the rector of Baumann [Higher Technical School in Moscow] and ask him to please, as a favor, arrange for a pair of particularly good fellows to be assigned to this factory. It's that simple. Later, the rector might need a favor.[88]

By specifying aggregate figures for the graduation and assignment of specialists but giving discretion over individual assignments to VUZ-level committees, the raspredelenie plan provided plenty of bureaucratic slack for keeping everybody—with the possible exception of the graduates themselves—happy. In addition, provisions were formally included into the plan which increased the discretionary power of enterprises and republican ministries. As an anachronism left from Khrushchev's "worker-specialist" programs, most enterprises and non-Russian district administrations had the right to directly enroll a number of their employees in VUZy, with the provision that they return to their employers upon graduation. Known as "designated training" *(tselevaia podgotovka)*, these programs were essentially affirmative action plans to make higher education available to workers who had pursued the socialist ideal of productive labor. In addition to a limited number of slots in daytime VUZy, almost all slots in correspondence or evening divisions of VUZy were reserved for tselevaia podgotovka.

As with all aspects of the planning system, however, once the program was codified, it developed its own unique pathologies. Officials at MinVUZ chafed at their loss of control over an entire cohort in the admissions and assignment processes. They argued that binding a graduate to his "sponsoring" enterprise would ignore any changes in the student's interests or capacities during his time as a student.[89]

Enterprises, for their part, could barely fill their quota of reserved slots, especially in night and correspondence divisions. Many evening VUZ students were not actually employed at all but were merely failed applicants taking advantage of a backdoor admissions route.[90] Since both VUZy and enterprises had enrollment targets to meet, neither examined students' credentials carefully. Employers bribed workers with vacations and bonuses to induce them to enroll, and many evening and correspondence students turned out to be fictitious. Consequently, those employees who did enroll knew they were "flunk-proof," and academic standards suffered accordingly. According to one report, attendance at evening classes in VUZy of Southern Russia hovered between 5 and 10 percent, and classes were often canceled when instructors failed to appear.[91]

The sad state of tselevaia podgotovka, taken together with the confusion of the East German observers, points to an important characteristic of raspredelenie: flexibility could not be written into the planning system. Bureaucratic actors retained discretionary authority only over processes that were not monitored by concrete performance indicators. Once a measurable target became associated with a specific program—even if that program was developed to make a rigid system more responsive—then actors' goals narrowed exclusively to managing the target data, rather than achieving the broader policy outcome.

As long as VUZ officials were free to make individual job assignments under the umbrella of aggregate plan figures, requests by factories for graduates meeting certain additional criteria (related to their talent or perhaps their likelihood to remain at the enterprise) could be accommodated. And as long as enterprises themselves remained the sole source of data about the workplace performance of young specialists, employers could, in turn, accommodate requests from VUZ administrators for special attention to favored graduates.[92] However, once an informal arrangement became codified and monitored, like tselevaia podgotovka of enterprise employees, then the coin of discretionary authority became quickly transformed into the lead weight of plan fulfillment.

What made plan targets for enrollment or enterprise assignments so burdensome was their unavoidable concreteness; what made them tolerable was their exceedingly avoidable verification. There was no pressing need to challenge the fundamental structure of the monitoring system—and hence the basic principal-agent authority structure of the bureaucratic hierarchies of Gosplan and Gosobrazovaniia—as long as key targets could be met by agents resorting to safety factors like surplus assignees or favors owed to them by other officials. External organizations that played an indirect role in raspredelenie—like the Komsomol, which participated in both placement committees at VUZy and specialists' reception at enterprises—were ineffective as watchdogs.

Komsomol's laissez-faire approach to raspredelenie is curious, since many critics of the placement system pointed fingers at the failure of "upbringing" work at VUZy, which was largely Komsomol's responsibility.[93] Nevertheless, discussion of higher education by Komsomol officials focused almost exclusively on the class composition of the student body, competitiveness levels for admission to different VUZy, and, of course, Komsomol saturation levels. Discussions of job assignments were usually limited to a recitation of no-show and attrition figures (which were collected only after the 1978–79 state decrees, and which, as discussed above, suggested more serious problems than did official Goskomstat figures). Analysis ended with ritualistic calls on enterprises to be held to a higher level of "responsibility" for their treatment of specialists and exhortations for Komsomol committees to strengthen ideological work among students.[94]

If Komsomol officials chose not to meddle in raspredelenie—relieved, perhaps, that they had no concrete task to carry out (and therefore no targets to meet)—other potential watchdogs were neutralized by a lack of resources. Within MinVUZ, for instance, there was a *Gosinspektsiia* bureau whose role was to provide independent data about the performance of officials in implementing policy. After issuing the new raspredelenie guidelines in 1980, the Minister of Higher Education specifically charged this bureau with ensuring compliance with the provisions of the new guidelines, especially provisions about restricting the practice of granting students the right to arrange their own placement.[95] The head of "Gosinspektsiia VUZov," V. A. Severtsev, readily agreed that the primary function of his bureau was to provide policy makers with "unembroidered information" about VUZ operations. At the same time, however, Severtsev complained bitterly that his organization's effectiveness was regularly compromised by the "uninspired" uses to which this information was put. He further charged that policy proposals painstakingly prepared by Gosinspektsiia were "dropped for lack of support," and lamented, "Our powers are less than that of any inspector *(revizor)* at a raion finance department."[96]

On rare occasions, a completely new system for monitoring the performance of the raspredelenie system might be proposed, but the inertia of the planning/monitoring bureaucracy was formidable. For instance, in 1968, economist Aleksandr Birman proposed that graduates be assigned to enterprises on a one-year trial basis. If enterprises accepted the new employee adequately, they would reimburse the VUZ for a part of his education; otherwise, they would be obliged to send the graduate back to his institute "for further schooling." In this way, VUZy would gain an "objective evaluation of the quality of their work."[97]

Naturally, such a system would have greatly limited the "wiggle room" then enjoyed by VUZ officials and enterprise managers, who would both need to adapt to conditions resembling a genuine labor market. The idea was quickly and forcefully attacked by Konstantin Savichev, head of raspredelenie for the Russian Education Ministry, who noted that enterprises already rejected specialists who were sent to them and that under Birman's plan they would have strong economic incentives to reject them more summarily. He ignored Birman's central point: that linking a VUZ's budget to successful placement of its graduates would yield better information about the quality of its graduates. The scheme would leave VUZ officials wholly and directly beholden to enterprise hiring decisions, unable to "negotiate" their way to plan compliance. Savichev, instead, urged a new "statute on the job placement of young specialists" that would make managers "personally responsible" for improper utilization of specialists.[98]

Savichev's call for "responsibility" hinted at a broader shortcoming in implementing raspredelenie guidelines: noncompliance with these guidelines was never punished. In 1966, the brief trial of withholding diplomas until graduates completed part of their job assignments was repealed. After this reversal no further penalties were imposed on errant graduates, except for their obligation to repay the state for travel costs.[99]

The opposition of MinVUZ to any scheme that might delay the awarding of diplomas and grant another organization (i.e., enterprises) some say in whether the diploma was granted at all is understandable. The primary indicator used for measuring overall VUZ performance was the awarding of degrees. Naturally, education officials opposed any loss of control over this activity. Sanctions for raspredelenie violations, they logically argued, should be imposed not on them but on employers.

From the mid-1960s onward, therefore, compliance with placement guidelines was chiefly compelled through the threat of sanctions against employers who either treated assignees poorly or hired specialists who had not completed their three-year assignments. As early as 1967, Savichev himself complained that managers who hired "runaway" specialists (who had abandoned their assigned jobs) were never prosecuted, even though such behavior still represented a criminal offense under prevailing law.[100] By 1980, managerial malfeasance in hiring improperly documented specialists had been reclassified as an administrative rather than a criminal violation, but sanctions for improper hiring or firing of young specialists were never specified, and the sanctions were, it appears, never enforced.[101] Nor were managers who ignored legal guarantees to young specialists of housing or jobs in appropriate specializations ever openly penalized.

Between 1979 and 1987, officials at MinVUZ prepared a draft Supreme Soviet decree that would have delineated financial penalties for violations of raspredelenie guidelines, but this decree was eventually folded into a more comprehensive draft Council of Ministers resolution on higher-education reform. Opposed by enterprises brandishing the newly fashionable rhetoric of enterprise autonomy, these provisions were ultimately dropped when the final document was published in 1987.[102]

Thus managers, like education officials, successfully resisted operational implementation of any raspredelenie guidelines that might get in the way of their chief focus: plan fulfillment. Ministerial supervisors had scant desire to challenge reports of successful plan fulfillment emanating from enterprise (or institute) levels, since their own performance evaluations were also based upon fulfillment of the ministerial plan. Incentives of bureaucratic principals and their agents were closely aligned on this overriding goal, at least at all levels where principals simultaneously acted as agents of higher levels. Consequently, there was no strong incentive for officials within, say, MinVUZ to monitor closely violations of the rules they had written, as long as their short-term plan targets for awarding degrees and distributing job assignments continued to be met. By adhering to the formal procedures outlined by their superiors, street-level bureaucrats avoided any challenge to the authority structure of the organizational hierarchy. In the field, however, agents continued to deviate significantly from prescribed behavior.

Eventually, as one might expect, the search for someone to punish for placement no-shows or attrition led back to the graduates themselves.[103] The Chairman of Gosobrazovaniia, Gennadii Iagodin, proposed in 1988 that graduates receive a "certificate *(attestat)* of qualifications" on completion of their three-year assignments as a sign of having acquired necessary vocational skills at the workplace.[104] Presumably, such certificates could be demanded later as concrete proof of having competed raspredelenie obligations.

Attestaty could, therefore, accomplish much the same goals as Khrushchev's denial of diplomas—depriving "irresponsible" graduates of the documentation necessary to further their careers—without directly involving either VUZy or enterprises. Young specialists themselves would bear the sole burden of ensuring that the certificates were properly conferred (or, where necessary, improperly acquired). However, Iagodin envisioned a reassertion of raspredelenie discipline, denying attestaty even to graduates who were legally exempted from mandatory placement for health or family reasons. Graduates denied jobs in their specializations would receive no leniency, he declared: "Let me reply: don't give them an attestat. Put them through raspredelenie again, and award an attestat only after their three years of work are up."[105]

A mere three years later, Iagodin told me that the attestat was "planned" in 1988 but never really implemented.[106] Under the circumstances, the award of attestaty would have served little purpose by 1991, since the raspredelenie system itself was rapidly falling apart. Iagodin, with no recollection of his earlier advocacy of harsher assignments standards, praised the passing of raspredelenie, calling freedom to choose one's profession "a basic human right."

Between 1988 and 1991, far more changed than simply one minister's interpretation of human rights. But the raspredelenie system was more accurately the victim of continuities than of changes. For even as the economic landscape changed around them, officials responsible for the placement of VUZ graduates remained primarily governed by their need to manipulate short-term performance indicators and their desire to reduce long-term uncertainty about how those indicators would be measured and evaluated.

The Collapse of the Job-Assignments System

The job-assignments system described above was not unlike a rickety old car with worn brakes and perhaps missing a few gears. Such cars don't work quite the way they're supposed to but are adequate for local commuting as long as traffic remains predictable and the owner finds an "accommodation" with the local inspection station. Similarly, the raspredelenie system wasn't quite distributing VUZ graduates around the country with the hoped-for efficiency, but as long as VUZ officials could fine-tune the details of individual graduates' assignments and enterprises held an effective monopoly over information on placements, the system creaked along. In the late 1980s, it ground to a halt.

Prelude: Shifting Priorities

As VUZ enrollments finally began to plateau in the late 1970s, policy discussion focused increasingly on utilizing this large pool of specialists. According to Igor Ivanov at MinVUZ, the goals of Party higher education policy began to shift in 1976 or 1977 from producing more specialists to using them more efficiently. In large part, according to Ivanov, this shift was motivated by the "perception" that by 1976 the education system was finally producing enough specialists overall. The emphasis, therefore, shifted from growth to distribution.[107]

According to Ivanov, Communist Party officials in charge of higher education were the driving force behind a reexamination of raspredelenie policy conducted throughout the first half of the 1980s. New statistics on utilization of young specialists at enterprises were collected in response to the state and Party decrees of 1978 and 1979, but no changes were made in the raspredelenie process beyond the enhanced role assigned to Gosplan in the 1980 placement guidelines. Reports of VUZ graduates being assigned to menial jobs continued to appear in the press throughout this period.[108]

Even some areas singled out in the 1978 and 1979 resolutions proved resistant to change. Directives to consolidate the overall list of specializations in which degrees were offered had little effect. This reform would have necessitated merging and shutting down many smaller departments *(kafedry)* at VUZy throughout the country. VUZ officials responsible for revising the list of available specializations were criticized for lacking the nonacademic experience needed to make a new list useful and realistic.[109] The listing of possible degree categories issued in 1975 featured 466 possible specializations, as detailed as "Sugar and sweetening technologies" or "Fat technologies" within faculties of "Food Technologies," or "Road construction" and "Airport construction" within "Construction and Architecture" faculties. While these may strike Americans either as esoteric postgraduate topics or mundane vocational-school trades ("plumbing, heating, and air conditioning" and "automotive repair" seem particularly well suited to advertisement on matchbook covers), these were actual undergraduate degrees at five-year Soviet VUZy, offered at state expense and guaranteeing three-year jobs in these specialties upon graduation.[110]

Furthermore, on the enterprise side, managers continued to requisition VUZ graduates to fill positions better suited to vocational-school graduates. Despite emphatic mention in the 1978 Party resolution, there was apparently no major review of enterprise nomenklatury to weed out jobs (such as automotive repair) that might be filled by less highly educated personnel.[111] Nor did any new methodology emerge for the direct measurement of economic "demand" for specialists with higher education. VUZ admissions and subsequent placement of graduates continued to be based upon the inflated planning estimates submitted by enterprises. The 1979 directive to move to long-range planning, if it had any effect at all, prompted enterprises to submit even more unrealistic guesses of their need for specialists, in order not to foreclose future options.[112]

The higher-education system, in other words, was continuing to produce specialists who were superfluous by any "rational" calculation and whose employment depended wholly on the continued manipulation of the loose rules of the planning and placement system itself. In this environment of vague regulations and weak monitoring, it is not surprising that key officials responsible for implementing raspredelenie—VUZ rectors and enterprise managers—would increasingly rely on systems of informal contracting to ensure that their actual, specific needs (as opposed to the artificial, tactical "needs" reflected in plan targets) were satisfied.

In 1967, Konstantin Savichev, chief of raspredelenie for the RSFSR Ministry of Higher Education, had proposed a system of "enterprise contracting" to reassign to jobs students who had been admitted to VUZy directly from enterprises through tselevaia podgotovka.[113] Several years later, he broadened this proposal, arguing that planning for raspredelenie should be based on direct VUZ-enterprise contacts rather than through interdepartmental plans compiled through Gosplan. Savichev contended that such direct contacts would shorten the planning process and force managers to present more realistic estimates of their requirements for specialists (this was consistent with his ongoing campaign, mentioned above, to force managers to be more "responsible" for their requests). Eight VUZy (and two SSUZy) around the Russian Republic had already developed a "five-year plan" for placements on the basis of direct enterprise negotiations, encompassing approximately 3,000 graduates per year since 1969.[114]

Even as raspredelenie guidelines elevated the role of Gosplan in long-range planning, Savichev continued to agitate for increased reliance on direct VUZ-enterprise contacts as a corrective to distortions of the planning system.[115] For VUZy, direct ties with employers were often the only solution to having their graduates turned away on reporting for work. Rather than allowing enterprises to guess their need for specialists two years in advance and then forget that commitment, direct contracting with VUZy for the provision of specific numbers of graduates permitted students to actually receive their "practicum" training at the sites of their future employment.[116] In theory, this arrangement should also have reduced attrition by lengthening the adjustment period of assignees.

The terms of these VUZ-enterprise "contracts" apparently varied greatly. At first, enterprises did not subsidize higher education directly, except possibly for paying stipends of workers enrolled under tselevaia podgotovka. Enterprises did, however, fund research at VUZy on a contract basis, provide equipment and furnishings for "practical" components of many curricula, and host students as apprentices. Economists occasionally revived Birman's 1968 plan to place higher education on a more commercial basis by having enterprises reimburse VUZy for specialists they hired, but these proposals now failed even to provoke heated debate.[117] Instead, VUZ-enterprise "contracting" remained quietly outside the planning process, benefiting VUZy by securing preferential treatment for their graduates, and benefiting enterprises by reducing their need to hedge against uncertainty by keeping unneeded specialists "in reserve."

While raspredelenie guidelines through the mid-1980s continued to channel all planning-related activities through Gosplan, the practice of direct VUZ-enterprise contracting for specialists continued to grow. By 1981, forty-seven VUZy in the Russian Federation had agreements in place to train specialists for specific enterprises. According to at least some of these agreements, students were notified of their eventual placement as much two years in advance of graduation and in some cases were allowed to join the enterprise's housing queue at that time.[118] By 1986, Moscow University was relying entirely on "long standing contacts" with employers to place graduates in those departments where raspredelenie could not.[119]

Left undisturbed, informal contracting might have increasingly dominated the practice of job placements at VUZy, while Gosplan preserved for itself the theoretical mission of increasingly detailed long-range planning. Instead, the raspredelenie system confronted an unexpected demand to accelerate and formalize its reliance on placement contracting. Perestroika came to higher education.

Crisis: The Gorbachev Reforms

Mikhail Gorbachev's first comments on the raspredelenie system were similar to those of Khrushchev and Brezhnev before him: he found it wanting. At the Twenty-seventh Party Congress in 1986, Gorbachev declared:

> It is necessary to review the structure of higher and secondary specialized education . . . We must completely overhaul the relations between higher and secondary specialized schools and branches of the national economy, strengthening their mutuality of interests in improving the quality of training and retraining cadres and in a fundamental improvement in their utilization in production.[120]

Gorbachev also announced that proposals were being prepared to accomplish this overhaul. In fact, proposals had been under review for years. In 1984, the Party announced a new reform of the Soviet education system, focused on primary and secondary education. The second stage of that reform, addressing higher education, was already in draft when Gorbachev came to power but was held up to incorporate any new themes proclaimed by the new leader.[121]

The higher-education reforms were finally published in March 1987.[122] The main thematic emphasis of the reforms was unchanged from the days of Khrushchev: closer integration of the education and production systems; better utilization of educated specialists at the workplace; smoother integration of technical innovation into both the educational and industrial systems. The main document addressing raspredelenie was a joint resolution of the Central Committee and Council of Ministers: SovMin 325.[123]

SovMin 325 reiterated calls of the 1978–79 reforms to reduce the number of available specializations, revise enterprise nomenklatury to reflect actual educational requirements of jobs more closely, develop new techniques for estimating demand for specialists, and limit admissions to those engineering specialties experiencing a demonstrable surplus of educated personnel. Its most significant innovation, however, came in its calls for greater cooperation between educational and industrial organizations. SovMin 325 ordered MinVUZ, Gosplan, and all-Union and republican ministries

> in the current five year plan to shift to a new basis for relationships among higher schools, production, and research, anticipating, as a rule, designated training (tselevaia podgotovka) of specialists on the basis of contracts *(dogovory)* between ministries and departments for whom cadres are trained, and MinVUZ, and also directly between enterprises, organizations and VUZy within the limits of the state plan for raspredelenie of specialists.[124]

This formulation elevated VUZ-enterprise contracting to an official, rather than informal, means of placement. It also dealt a major setback to Gosplan, reduced now to planning only at "aggregate levels"—that is, for advisory rather than operational purposes. Gosplan, not surprisingly, opposed this reorganization, since it marked the beginning of a sweeping diminution of its powers that would accelerate with each new economic decree in the package that became known as perestroika.[125]

SovMin 325 included a provision that would anticipate another major theme in perestroika—*khozraschet,* or self-financing. Beginning in 1988, ministries whose enterprises hired young specialists would be obliged to pay 3,000 rubles per specialist to the ministry operating the relevant VUZ.[126] This represented the first introduction of the principle of fees for education, for which Aleksandr Birman had been castigated twenty years earlier. VUZy, however, were restricted in the use of these fees to financing construction and repair of facilities or acquisition of new instruments or supplies. Transfer payments for specialists, in other words, would seed an investment fund for the modernization of the higher education system.

In fact, the practice of payment for specialists was not without precedent. A 1982 report prepared by MinVUZ's research institute, which termed the practice of long-term contracting for specialists "widespread," described one agreement between several VUZy and a mining enterprise in Norilsk. The agreement included a provision for the enterprise to reimburse the participating institutes 5,000 rubles *per year* to offset the training of each graduate covered by the agreement for at least the last three years of his or her education.[127] If such practices were indeed widespread, then the "innovative" guidelines of 3,000 rubles per student to be used for capital investment only must have seemed disturbingly restrictive.

Two critical themes in SovMin 325—decentralization of the planning system by blunting Gosplan's role and legitimizing funding of universities and institutes through means other than the state budget—were consistent with broader decentralizing motifs in Gorbachev's perestroika of the national economy. Taken together, however, they rapidly drove VUZy into the arms of industrial enterprises and out of state control. SovMin 325 was actually just the first of a series of documents issued in rapid succession from 1987–90 that completely transformed the raspredelenie system. Reading through these documents, one can sense officials in Moscow trying unsuccessfully to adapt to and slow down the pace of changes already unleashed among higher-education institutions across the country.

In 1988, new raspredelenie guidelines were issued by Gosobrazovaniia (as MinVUZ had become), consolidating control over many of the VUZy and SSUZy previously administered by different ministries. These guidelines finally implemented the changes decreed by SovMin 325 almost eighteen months earlier.[128] The new guidelines are remarkably similar to the 1980 guidelines, except for the disappearance of any mention of Gosplan in compiling an interdepartmental placement plan. In fact, while the guidelines refer to the implementation of such a plan, there is no indication of where it is to come from.

The clue to this confusion lies in the original language of SovMin 325, which envisioned Gosplan-style planning replaced by negotiations *among ministries* that ran VUZy and enterprises, and only in certain cases between VUZy and enterprises directly. In practice, as I have discussed, direct enterprise-VUZ contacts were already the norm, while there was no real precedent—or arena—for "plans" based on complex interdepartmental negotiations. Gosobrazovaniia's Ivanov, who authored the guidelines, explained that SovMin 325 described interministerial negotiations because "nobody was talking about 'market relations' per se just then." He admitted, however, that most VUZy had interpreted the resolution as license for them to conduct negotiations directly.

The degree of confusion spreading across VUZy is evident in a report on 1988 job placements at Moscow University. L. Lagidze, a raspredelenie official in the philology faculty, complained that ministries that had requested specialists were "acting like one big family": refusing assignees on grounds of "staff cutbacks," then hiring selected graduates individually. Thirty-four of the faculty's graduates specializing in teaching Russian as a foreign language had found jobs on their own, despite the lack of any slots in the annual plan. "So the places are there," he complained, "there's simply a lack of reliable information." The department, announced Lagidze, would be moving to a contract basis for assigning graduates; negotiations were already under way with Intourist, Sputnik, and other employers. "Our hopes rest with the contract system," he declared.[129]

In the spring of 1989, however, another Moscow University official worried aloud that enterprise contracts could prove more of a quagmire than a panacea. Addressing a meeting of the university Party committee, he warned that contracts signed by the university would lack the legal force attached to traditional raspredelenie. "Let's say the university signs an agreement. What next? Next, the student can refuse. We have no legal grounds to send him to that place specified in the agreement *we've* signed."[130]

Later that same year, a new Council of Ministers resolution attempted to clarify the murky question of who was to sign contracts with whom.[131] Enterprises were granted the right to approach VUZ students, or even applicants, directly and offer to finance their education (at a stipend level at least 30 percent above state norms) in return for at least a three-year placement at that enterprise on graduation. In essence, the systems of tselevaia podgotovka and raspredelenie were to be combined, in these cases, into a single scheme of enterprise fellowships for VUZ students. Lucky students would be exempted from the traditional raspredelenie process, and enterprises would gain complete and direct control over which graduates they would hire.

Under this reorganization, which seems clearly to have been dictated by industrial ministries, the VUZy were the unmistakable losers.[132] Enterprises that could handpick new hires would have precious little reason to request, or accept, any students through the traditional raspredelenie process. Yet VUZy remained legally responsible for ensuring the placement of all graduates in appropriate jobs, and "interministerial" negotiated planning seemed as vague and unrealistic as ever. Iagodin, chairman of Gosobrazovaniia, complained that the current assignments system was "ceasing to make sense . . . As soon as we gave the enterprise the right to decide whether it will take on one more engineer or divide that salary among those already working—at that moment the state system of raspredeleniie turned into something quite undefined."[133] Nevertheless, he feebly instructed his subordinates to "prepare . . . suggestions for new functions or the system of raspredelenie of specialists in the current situation."[134]

Before these suggestions could be prepared, however, Gosobrazovaniia attempted to regain some control over the job assignments process by publishing a "standard contract between enterprises and VUZ students."[135] Despite its title—and the thrust of its parent Council of Ministers' decree—this "standard contract" actually had three signatories: the student, the employer, *and the VUZ*. Students were guaranteed a stipend, apprenticeship, a job, and housing; enterprises could negotiate employment obligations longer than three years. VUZy, essentially, acted as guarantors of the agreement. However, the contract also included a provision that would prove crucial later in providing VUZy some negotiating leverage: employers could specify particular courses or skills to be required of students beyond regular academic requirements and were also offered the right to approve students' graduating thesis topics. In other words, VUZy were permitting enterprises to dictate the curriculum of their future employees, potentially shifting the burden of what had been on-the-job training to the VUZ itself.

By the end of 1990, much of the logistics of the old raspredelenie system had been dismantled. Gosplan was no longer even collecting requests for specialists from employers; the unfortunate corollary of this development was that nobody was.[136] Enterprises, facing much more stringent budgetary constraints, could no longer afford to hire unneeded specialists to three-year contracts. Though they had the legal right to recruit individual students for support and ultimate employment, informational constraints discouraged this level of active scouting. They continued to deal primarily with VUZy, particularly partners whose judgment they had come to trust. Universities, meanwhile, were eagerly seeking to augment their own budgets, as phase-outs of state subsidies loomed on the horizon. Contracting directly with enterprises remained the most promising source of such budgetary support.

Thus, in late 1990, the Council of Ministers issued one final decree on raspredelenie, drafted by Gosobrazovaniia at the beginning of the year but reflecting what had in fact become the status quo a few years earlier.[137] Beginning in 1991, all ministries operating VUZy were to define for themselves "the scale and structure of training and procedure for placement of young specialists . . . based on existing ties and contracts *between educational institutions and enterprises.*"[138]

VUZy were free to negotiate fees for the customized training of graduates for specific enterprises, and previous restrictions on the use of these funds were lifted. Recognizing that not all students would benefit from negotiated placements, the decree contained an ominous note: employment bureaus for young specialists were also to be established.

Raspredelenie guidelines retained their legal force, requiring graduating students to submit to mandatory three-year assignments, and the Soviet Constitution continued to guarantee these graduates three years of employment in their specialties. In 1991, Soviet and then Russian parliaments passed Labor Laws guaranteeing free choice of jobs to all citizens, presumably removing the last legal support for raspredelenie. But in December 1990, the VUZ job placement system ceased to function, and everybody knew it. The result was almost immediately a catastrophe for students and VUZy alike: hundreds of thousands of students were stranded without jobs and most VUZy found themselves on the brink of bankruptcy.

While this result was a direct consequence of the surprisingly rapid disintegration of the overall Soviet economy in 1991, it came as no surprise to the officials of the education system. As the final part of this story suggests, they clearly recognized the dangers inherent in basing job placements entirely on VUZ-enterprise contracting. But the VUZ officials seemed unable to resist the temptation to dismantle the old system completely.

Collapse: The Rubble of Raspredelenie

Even as university officials were embracing the idea of direct contracts with enterprises as a solution to their placement and budgetary problems, some saw the outlines of a Faustian bargain. As they rushed to accommodate enterprises' demands, they risked exchanging the constraints and limitations of state control for the tyranny of subordination to industry.

The first prorector of Moscow University recognized in 1989 that in return for a relatively minor financial boost, universities would face mounting pressures to emphasize narrow skills at the expense of more fundamental or theoretical education: "Industry now pays 3,000 rubles per graduate, but the actual cost is more like 30–50,000 rubles. But that's not even the main thing. There is a danger that the employers *(zakazchiki)* will be focused on today's problems, and our graduates, who are trained to take on the problems of tomorrow, will be unwanted."[139]

Another Moscow University official, who headed a Party commission on "improving the academic process," called contracting with enterprises "short-sighted." He warned that only the richest enterprises would be able to enter into such contracts, but not all students aspired to work at these enterprises. He urged the government to continue subsidizing higher education to preserve academic freedoms.[140]

By 1990, even as Gosobrazovaniia worked to recreate a role for VUZy in the emerging system of negotiated placements, its chairman was expressing misgivings about the emerging shape of the new placement scheme. In April, Gennadii Iagodin explained the new procedures in an interview with the Moscow Komsomol newspaper and revealed some defensiveness about the old raspredelenie system and uncertainty about the future:

> *Iagodin:* . . . As soon as we gave the enterprise the right to decide whether it will take on one more engineer or divide that salary among those already working—at that moment the state system of raspredelenie turned into something quite undefined.

Q: Are you saying that it has already ceased to function?

Iagodin: It still functions, at least as long as the state still assumes responsibility for graduates. Gradually we are moving from a planned system of raspredelenie to one in which enterprises begin in the second or third year to approach students, conclude agreements with them, pay them some money as a stipend, and then hire them [upon graduation].

Q: Would a different system of raspredelenie mean there would no longer be three required years of work, considered now by many graduates to be a feudal system that claims its share of victims?

Iagodin: I think there will be changes—these are inevitable. As far as victims associated with unfavorable assignments—the majority of these problems are resolvable, and they are resolved in the field. Let's say a university graduate is assigned to a rural school, but he is an ichthyologist. All his life he's studied fish. Well, let him go and study fish, then.

Q: But Gennadii Alekseevich, you certainly know well that in the field often the most elementary problems go unsolved. . . .[sic]

Iagodin: But they *should* be decided.[141]

One month later, addressing a conference of VUZ rectors, Iagodin's nostalgia for the old placement structure became more understandable. Under pressure of khozraschet, enterprises were choosing to devote increasingly scarce resources to retaining skilled personnel already hired rather than investing in untested new talent. Many enterprises had stopped hiring new graduates altogether, and those that continued to honor commitments under the old mandatory system were neglecting to pay the 3,000 rubles per specialist mandated by the new laws. Iagodin had no illusions about the economic logic at work, declaring, "This [behavior by enterprises] is understandable. Once enterprises were allowed to decide whether to take on a new specialist or offer raises to those already there, many chose the second option."[142]

Nor did he have any illusions about the consequences for students of the new balance of power in higher education. Iagodin estimated that only 50–60 percent of VUZ students would have jobs provided for them through contracts. The remainder, he warned, would need broader education to compete on the nascent and inchoate Soviet labor market. Instead, under pressure to attract enterprise contracts for training specialists, VUZy were narrowing their curricula, even tailoring them for specific enterprises. Graduates trained to work at specific enterprises would actually have *lower* labor mobility should their employers ever cut their labor forces or shut down altogether, as reform economists were urging many to do. Iagodin urged VUZy to offer students additional training outside their specialties: "We must protect our students from the rigidities of the market, since the introduction of khozraschet has effectively destroyed their state system of raspredelenie."[143]

Several months later, Feliks Peregudov, Iagodin's First Deputy Chairman, issued still more warnings that the new world for VUZ graduates would be cruel. Conceding that the state planning system of job assignments was defunct, he urged the parliament to remove the Constitutional guarantee of universal employment. He further called for immediate tax incentives for enterprises to hire VUZ graduates and for unemployment insurance to protect those not hired. Finally, he argued, "the market" would mandate at least a 30 percent reduction in VUZ enrollments in the near future.[144]

Gosobrazovaniia, however, could no longer mandate such a reduction itself. With the planning system dismantled, VUZy contracting directly with enterprises, and enterprise "payments" rapidly replacing state subsidies, Gosobrazovaniia lost all leverage it once had over the universities it still nominally owned and controlled. It could no longer influence curriculum, admissions, or any other aspect of VUZ operations.[145]

Instead of reducing admissions, according to Gosobrazovaniia's Ivanov, as 1991 progressed VUZy continued to admit new students "according to the old plan"—that is, with no reductions at all. "They have not yet sensed the problem," he explained, "and as a result, this year or the next we may have a critical situation."[146] Furthermore, when that critical situation arrived graduates would be on their own, because no progress was being made in establishing employment bureaus for graduates (as mandated by the 1990 Council of Ministers' decree) or in organizing unemployment insurance. Ivanov frankly confessed to me his surprise on learning how much the United States spent on youth employment programs. "We still haven't the faintest idea how much this will cost us," he declared.

In late 1990, Gorbachev announced the formal independence of VUZy from Gosobrazovaniia control.[147] The economics of the system made such a move compelling—state subsidies were being eliminated across the board—but the declaration had little practical effect. VUZy had been acting independently of ministerial control for some time already, relying increasingly on enterprise contracts to pay their bills. But even as khozraschet struck Gosobrazovaniia, it was also striking enterprises with a vengeance. Imminent price increases were forcing skilled workers at enterprises to search for higher salaries, and enterprises were retaining these workers only through offers of immediate raises. Hiring inexperienced graduates was a low priority.

Graduates of VUZy in 1991 faced potentially massive unemployment. In July 1991, *Izvestiia* estimated that only 10 percent of students in institutes and universities were covered by agreements with enterprises.[148] In 1992, the Russian State Committee on Higher Education estimated that just 55 percent of graduates were placed in jobs.[149]

Even prestigious Moscow VUZy found themselves on the verge of bankruptcy, strapped to pay faculty and staff, and unable to attract new teachers willing to accept the paltry salaries attached to the few positions that were open.[150] In July 1991, several VUZy announced plans to charge tuition (of 10,000 rubles and higher) to students directly—thus shifting the onus of seeking out fellowship funding from enterprises back to the students. These fees were ultimately blocked by the Soviet parliament, which declared the move a violation of the Constitutional guarantee of free education. The parliament also banned the collection of fees from enterprises, raising the specter of complete insolvency.[151]

Soviet higher education was thus thrust into the "market era" in a state of deepening crisis. Relatively modest reforms inspired by ongoing informal practices—the marginalization of Gosplan and the formalization of alternate funding sources— had been intended to strengthen the autonomy of educational institutions and increase their receptivity to curricular and technical innovation. Instead, they provided officials at these institutions with incentives to disregard the guidelines of their supervisors altogether.

From the perspective of relationships within the bureaucratic hierarchy, the implications of these minor reforms were fundamental: if budget was increasingly to come from enterprises, in what sense did ministry really "own" VUZy any longer? Just as the MinVUZ most needed to enforce its rules at the VUZ level (to check the erosion of a basic curriculum or prevent the total elimination of mandatory placement without some cushioning transition), it lost its main management tools: control over VUZ budgets and the informational dimension of the planning system itself. The principal-agent relationships at the heart of the organizational hierarchy and the authority relationships they embodied were swiftly and irreparably ruptured.

The collapse of raspredelenie left officials at VUZy uncertain of their role in society, increasingly guided by the short-term dictates of potential employers of their graduates. Graduates who used to chafe at the obligations imposed on them by raspredelenie faced a future in which not only their first three years of work but their very curriculum and selection of specializations were subject to the whims of major employers. And enterprise managers already pathologically suspicious of technological and managerial innovation seemed unlikely to benefit in the long run from the demise of a healthy, independent system of higher education.

Summary

At the end of our final meeting, Igor Ivanov, the Gosobrazovaniia official who had overseen revisions to the raspredelenie guidelines since 1976, explained why he had agreed to help me understand the evolution of the placement system. He felt that any "intelligent person" looking at what had become of the placement system would realize the merits of the old, planned system. Ivanov remembered raspredelenie fondly, describing how, for "85 percent of students":

> It fulfilled their most important need: the need for certainty. They [students] knew they could go through five years without worrying about what they would become or how they were doing and, nevertheless, there would be a job waiting for them. There was no fear of unemployment. They didn't have to worry about tomorrow. And in our system, that sense of certainty, of self-assurance, is most important.[152]

Another interviewee, Vladimir Lepekhin, a Komsomol activist at Moscow University during the 1980s, remembered raspredelenie rather differently. According to Lepekhin, avoiding an unwanted job placement was a major preoccupation of students' final years, "even more than avoiding the draft."[153] This preoccupation yielded results, however: according to Lepekhin, "hardly anyone" ever spent three full years at an unwanted assignment.

That two participants in the placement process would have such different perceptions of how the system worked signals more than just a divergence of interests. Their inability to agree on whether job placements were a benefit or a burden—or, as an interviewer put it to the Chairman of Gosobrazovaniia, "a privilege or servitude"[154]—pointed to the ultimate weakness of raspredelenie: actors in one part of the bureaucratic hierarchy were insulated from actors elsewhere in the system. The profound irony, in retrospect, is that this compartmentalization of the system had also been largely responsible for its resilience during the Khrushchev and Brezhnev decades.

Central policy makers and political leaders recognized the shortcomings of the placement system. They recognized that the country's massive investments in higher education were not yielding benefits for the economic system and regularly called for changes. Yet for decades their calls did little to alter the fundamental nature of the placements system because successive reforms left intact the basic system of performance targets and indicator monitoring. Employers still had strong incentives to request more specialists than they would ever need, and VUZ officials had strong incentives to create informal mechanisms to ensure acceptable placements for the best—or "most favored"—graduates. These mechanisms served enterprises' interests as well, as long as they remained outside the planning process and, therefore, did not create a new set of performance indicators.

The centrality of improving the monitoring system for placements was clearly recognized by policy-making officials. New data were ordered collected, but these were never formalized as performance indicators for evaluating individual actors at either VUZy or enterprises.[155] This incentive structure remained essentially intact when perestroika came to the job-assignments system. The collapse of the system was not a consequence of radical restructuring dictated from the Kremlin—the 1987 reforms did little more than formalize a system of ad hoc contracting which had been in place for some years. Nor was it a response to any sudden revolt of students demanding greater vocational freedom or enterprises denying them places. Instead, reforms intended to make agents in the education hierarchy slightly more responsive to their counterparts in industry acted like organizational solvents, dissolving the monitoring and control mechanisms that kept VUZ officials under ministerial control. Acting largely on their own initiative, these street-level officials tossed aside the old system of raspredelenie, replacing it with a market-based system that solved short-term budget-balancing problems but introduced grave uncertainties for the future.

Not only was the institution of raspredelenie destroyed, but the organization of state control over higher education fragmented decisively. Unlike the Komsomol, Gosobrazovaniia did not completely disintegrate. Instead, VUZy made a sharp transition from hierarchical to market-based control. Though this shift mirrored the "marketization" of Soviet society, it was vigorously resisted by the government officials in charge of higher education. These officials proved unable to enforce their authority decisively once VUZ-industry contracting processes were unleashed. As this is being written, Russian officials continue to fight the wave of privatizations of VUZy that began with the breakdown of raspredelenie.

In the end, the real victims of the collapse of the job-placement system were the VUZ graduates. Forced to compete in a newly competitive labor market, most students found themselves disadvantaged by their narrow education and by the dislocation of former ties between institutes and employers. Their ultimate victimization can be traced not to a failed reform policy but rather to the inability of actors in the old hierarchy of higher education to cooperate in the creation of institutions adapted to the new economic climate. Instead, the old hierarchy crumbled, and officials responded opportunistically, pursuing short-term benefits at the expense of both the long-term stability of their own institutions and the best interests of their own students.

6 | Universal Military Service

> "And if your father has not got a few thousand rubles to spare? Then
> you could cut off your finger with an axe. Or you could stick a small
> piece of foil on your back when you go for an X ray, so that they
> decide you have tuberculosis and turn you down for the army. You
> could go to prison. But if you haven't the courage for any of these,
> brother, you'll find yourself in that dirty railway wagon."
>
> —VIKTOR SUVOROV, *Inside the Soviet Army* (1982)

According to the Soviet Constitution, military service in the Soviet Armed
Forces was a "sacred obligation of Soviet citizens."[1] This obligation was
primarily discharged by young males conscripted into service for two
years, beginning at age eighteen. Conscription was directed and supervised by the Soviet Ministry of Defense but was organized and administered by thousands of local civilian draft boards throughout the country.
For nearly seventy years after the founding of the Red Army, this system
provided the supply of conscripts needed to staff a standing army that
swelled to over five million.

The Soviet system of universal military service also served an important
socialization function. Lessons in patriotism and loyalty first delivered
through Komsomol channels were to be reinforced and cemented during
army service. In addition, the Soviet Army was to be the great ethnic
melting pot, forging a citizenry both international in makeup and inter-
nationalist in outlook.[2]

In practice, the Soviet Army was more often a school of group conflict
and ethnic strife than of brotherhood. As reports of brutality grew and
the Russian share of the draft pool shrunk, agents in the field—particularly the heads of local military commissariats—continued to focus on the
strict conscription targets handed down by the Ministry of Defense. The
targets remained beyond challenge even as demographic shifts forced a
growing reliance on unhealthy or unreliable conscripts.

In the late 1980s the undisputed authority of the Ministry of Defense
over military manpower policy came into question. In effect, alternate

principals emerged—newly elected parliaments at the all-Union and republican levels—asserting for the first time their constitutional right to
set conscription policy independent of the defense ministry. This chapter
describes how this challenge led to a rapid disintegration of Moscow's
control over the Soviet draft and, very nearly, over the Soviet Army itself.
In marked contrast to the Komsomol and raspredelenie, however, the
system of conscription survived its breakup into fifteen separate institutions; even the problems of insufficient and unfit draftees continued to
plague the post-Soviet draft.

This chapter, like the previous two, begins with a review of the organization and implementation of Soviet conscription. It then considers the
institutional structure for managing and conducting the call-up—with
special attention to the unchallenged authority of the military leadership,
the basic irrelevance of street-level feedback, and problems of monitoring
policy implementation by field agents. Finally, it looks at the successive
crises in the late 1980s that undermined the draft: the demobilization of
students, spontaneous reinterpretations of health and other deferrals,
widespread regional draft noncompliance, and the defense ministry's
unsuccessful efforts to regain control over renegade draft boards.

Background

History

The primary institutions of "local military administration" in the Soviet
system were the military commissariats, or *voenkomaty*.[3] There were over
4,500 of these commissariats throughout the Soviet Union, organized by
the Ministry of Defense down to the raion level. In Moscow, for instance,
each of the city's thirty-three raions had its own voenkomat, each led by
its own high-ranking *voenkom* (military commandant, generally holding
at least the rank of colonel), and all reporting to the Moscow city voenkomat. The voenkomaty were responsible for several aspects of local
military mobilization, civil defense training, and veterans' affairs, but
probably their most important responsibility was the management of the
semiannual call-up for the armed forces.

Each voenkomat supervised the work of the local induction commission *(prizyvnaia komissiia)*, which was headed by the local voenkom. These

commissions (which I will refer to simply as "draft boards") each included representatives of local government and of Party and Komsomol organizations, as well as a doctor. Though they operated under the leadership and control of the military, these draft boards were, strictly speaking, civilian institutions.[4] All matters related to the granting of deferments, assignment to specific service branches, and recommendations to military academies came under the purview of these induction commissions.

Young men were required to register at their local voenkomat between January and March of the year they turned seventeen. Registrees underwent preliminary medical certification, and registration lists were then used to prepare the draft rolls. Eighteen-year-olds were inducted into the armed forces twice annually, in the spring (April–May) and fall (November–December). Draft-eligible youth were required to appear at their local voenkomaty, where they would undergo physical examinations and be classified for service or deferral. Those draftees not eligible for deferments were then assigned to a branch of the armed services and sent off for their two years of service (three years were required of conscripts assigned to naval duty).[5]

Deferments were granted to youth on several grounds: family hardship, education, and health. The family-hardship category was most straightforward, covering individuals acting as the sole source of support for invalid parents, two or more young children, or dependent siblings. These deferments were necessary because enlisted men's pay was miserly, providing little more than pocket money.

Educational deferments were provided to full-time students of higher educational institutions (VUZy) and some specialized secondary institutions offering reserve officers' training (I refer to these programs in this chapter as ROTC, though the analogy to the American Reserve Officer Training Corps is imprecise given the Soviet right to free education). Soviet VUZy, as a rule, provided mandatory ROTC training, though these programs varied widely in quality and rigor. Since educational deferments were granted to students at all full-time VUZy, applicants often resorted to bribes or turned to less competitive institutes in which they had little genuine interest in order to take advantage of this avenue of draft avoidance.[6] As I discuss later in this chapter, student deferments were sharply curtailed after the invasion of Afghanistan.

Health deferments were subject to the broadest interpretation. Draft boards were required to form special commissions to conduct medical certification for each draftee. These boards were headed by the draft board's chief doctor but were supervised by the Central Military Health Administration of the Ministry of Defense. Medical classifications were strictly defined in a lengthy set of guidelines issued by the Ministry of Defense, assigning each possible physical or mental condition to a particular classification. Inductees could be classified fit for military service, permanently unfit, or in need of convalescence (i.e., medical treatment followed by recertification). Within the category of "fit for military service," inductees could be classified in several ways, chief among them fit for combat duty (i.e., *godnyi k stroevoi sluzhbe*) and fit for noncombat duty *(godnyi k nestroevoi sluzhbe)*. The latter classification often resulted in inductees being sent to support branches of the service but did not result in a draft exemption.

Individuals seeking to evade military service were most likely to seek a medical deferment. The guidelines governing military classifications, though not strictly secret, were never published; appeal of decisions by medical certification commissions was therefore quite difficult.[7] According to anecdotal evidence, when voenkomat officials accepted bribes to arrange deferrals, the category of deferment was almost always medical.[8]

Draft boards were also charged with nominating youth for admission to the country's network of 140 higher military schools. These schools were responsible for training the army's active officers corps (the reserve corps was theoretically trained through ROTC programs at VUZy and SSUZy). These schools were geared to preparing officers with narrow specialties; for example, two schools, in Cheliabinsk and Voroshilovgrad, were responsible for producing aerial navigators.[9] Although admission was by competitive examination, voenkomaty often had to work hard to meet their quotas for nominees, especially in non-Russian areas.

Finally, voenkomaty were responsible for coordinating local administration of the national program of predraft training. When the length of military service was reduced by a year in 1967, the time available for basic training after induction shrank dramatically. To compensate for this loss, the Law on Universal Military Service called for inductees to receive basic education in military regulations and theory, as well as training in military skills like marksmanship and drilling, before reaching draft age.

This "initial military training" program was administered in the ninth and tenth grades in schools and, less reliably, at workplaces for youth who left school early. In addition, the national quasi-military "volunteer" organization—known by its Russian acronym DOSAAF—offered instruction in specialized skills like driving or radio operation, which could permit draftees to be classified as specialists.[10]

Aside from predraft training, most of the functions of the voenkomaty appear relatively unambiguous. Quotas were delivered for conscripts twice yearly, and twice yearly these quotas were met. Behind this facade of smooth operations, however, the Soviet draft suffered from several nagging problems. Chief among them were open draft evasion, the declining health of inductees, poor predraft preparation of inductees, and patterns of violence and brutality within the conscript force.

Draft Evasion

Cases of open evasion of the Soviet draft during the 1960s and 1970s were rare but not unheard-of. Summary reports of the seasonal draft conducted by the Komsomol (whose representatives sat on draft boards) refer to isolated instances of open refusal to serve. In 1966, for instance, there were 271 such cases nationwide; this figure grew by 250 percent in 1967.[11] In Daghestan, forty inductees refused to serve in 1971; in 1978 scattered refusals were reported in Turkmenistan, Moldavia, Uzbekistan, Armenia, Kirghizia, Daghestan, and Chechen-Ingushetiia.[12] At least some of these outright refusals claimed religious grounds for their objection to military service.[13]

Attempts to evade registration seem to have been more widespread. In 1967, for instance, over 61,000 youth failed to register.[14] In Turkmenistan that year, sixty youth were reported as having fled the republic without appearing at voenkomaty.[15] Evading registration carried far less severe penalties than evading the draft.[16]

Aside from such cases of outright draft evasion, youth seem to have resorted to various ruses to escape active duty. As noted above, the voenkomat system was quite susceptible to corruption, and medical deferments were apparently for sale in most raions. According to Viktor Suvorov, military commissars in Odessa, Kharkov, and Tbilisi were executed for widespread corruption in the granting of medical deferments.[17]

As suggested by the quote introducing this chapter, inductees them-selves often took drastic actions to qualify for medical exemptions. Though self-mutilation represented an extreme approach, many induc-tees tried the less arduous route of simulating psychosis.[18] Attempted suicide was apparently one tried-and-true means of securing such a diagnosis, generally leading directly to a diagnosis of schizophrenia and allowing inductees to trade two years of army service for several months of institutionalization.

Since higher education admissions were also rife with corruption, brib-ery directed toward the rector of a VUZ could often result in an educa-tional deferment. As one ex-Komsomol member wrote to a friend, "You say you want to get into an institute to avoid entering the army. Of course you should. What's the sense of wasting so much time."[19]

Youth on the eve of conscription seem to have engaged in a collective denial of social restraints that may also have been linked to evading service. Several accounts from the 1960s and 1970s suggest that in the months before their induction, large numbers of draftees dropped out of school, quit work, drank heavily, and even engaged in sprees of criminal activity. In Eastern Kazakhstan, for instance, 11,000 youth quit work in the months prior to their induction; 6–7 percent of draft-age youth in one Eastern Kazakh region ended up in jail.[20] Roughly 200 draftees annually in Vinnitska oblast in Ukraine were exempted from the draft in the early 1970s for criminal activity.[21] Similar patterns were noted by Komsomol committees in Primorskii krai in 1971 and in Chechen-Ingushetiia in 1976.[22]

While these rampages may simply have represented a spontaneous letting off of steam prior to submitting to two years of army discipline, there may be a more tactical explanation for this behavior. Youth who were neither working nor in school were considerably more difficult for Komsomol committees to find. And while youth in jail obviously could not be drafted, the 1967 Draft Law also exempted youth under criminal investigation. It is quite possible that a substantial fraction of young men may have actually preferred jail to army service, and the conditions of army life discussed below suggest this may have been a rational calcula-tion. Nevertheless, the ruse was not always successful, as records of the 1968 draft suggest roughly 0.5 percent of the draft pool had criminal records—that is, they were taken into service after their release from jail or correctional camp.[23]

The late 1980s saw an explosion of draft evasion, but much of it was actually sanctioned by governmental action or inaction. Since this phenomenon was actually one symptom of the final disintegration of the Soviet draft, I defer discussion of it until later in this chapter.

Conscript Health

Though it is difficult to sort out genuine medical deferments from those actually disguising draft evasion, there is significant evidence that the Ministry of Defense was concerned over deteriorating health and fitness levels of the conscript pool. In 1968, for instance, just under 98 percent of draftees nationwide were judged medically fit; however, this figure fell below 80 percent in some republics and was reported to be falling in a long list of oblasts.[24] In 1971 the national figure was apparently closer to 94 percent.[25] Oblast-by-oblast reports of the draft in the 1970s collected from Komsomol committees indicate that the proportion of draftees classified as fit for military service (combat and noncombat) ranged from 85 to 95 percent.[26]

In the 1980s the health of the draft pool apparently continued to worsen. In 1980, 92.9 percent of draftees were classified as fit for combat duty; by 1985 this fell to 91.3 percent, and in 1989, despite drastically loosened medical guidelines, it fell to 88.8 percent.[27] At the same time, the health of draftees actually entering the service was also declining. According to Ministry of Defense figures, ill health among fifteen-year-olds rose by 340 percent from 1970 to 1988; by 1988 more than a quarter of fifteen-year-olds failed to meet defense ministry health guidelines.[28] In 1984 a deputy head of the Main Political Administration of the armed forces told the Komsomol Central Committee that conscripts' health was getting steadily worse.[29] According to Ministry of Defense officials, the number of unhealthy servicemen in uniform rose by 29 percent from 1981 to 1989.[30] The poor health of draftees was often linked to poor nutrition, alcoholism, and pollution.

Related to the question of health was the question of fitness. The commander of Soviet Ground Forces, I. Pavlovskii, complained to the Komsomol Central Committee that 35–40 percent of conscripts drafted between 1968 and 1970 failed to reach even "satisfactory levels for physical preparedness of a young soldier."[31] The blame for these poor fitness levels was often laid at the feet of Komsomol.

Predraft Training and Indoctrination

Predraft training programs fell for the most part into the category of "indoctrination," and therefore became largely the responsibility of the Komsomol (see Chapter 4). Alleged shortcomings in Komsomol's work in "military-patriotic upbringing" became a frequent source of friction between the youth league and representatives of the Ministry of Defense (chiefly through its Main Political Administration). Following the Komsomol's own pattern in assessing work in "upbringing," the defense ministry never sought underlying causes of the lack of preparation evident among many draftees; instead, it repeatedly called on the Komsomol to "intensify" its efforts. The Komsomol's reflexive response was to look for quantitative indicators by which to evaluate the efforts of its field organizations.

One target figure monitored closely by the youth league was the level of Komsomol membership among draftees. By the 1970s, Komsomol committees were reporting saturation levels of 70–80 percent among conscripts, well above the national average among Komsomol-age youth.[32] This is unsurprising since conscripts were often ordered to join the Komsomol, either before or after their dispatch from the voenkomat. Enrolling draftees was an easy source of membership growth for local committees, even if these members were then supposed to be transferred to their army unit's Komsomol organization. In practice, as noted in Chapter 4, draftees often remained on the membership rolls of their home committees indefinitely.

One major program in which the Komsomol participated was the awarding of fitness medals *(znachki)*. With names like "Ready for Labor and Defense" (GTO) or "Ready for the Defense of the Motherland" (GZR), these znachki were supposed to be given to youth who passed a series of skill tests. The GTO medal, for instance, required recipients to complete a program that included running, skiing, shooting, swimming, and orienteering. The percentage of draftees holding these znachki was uniformly in the high nineties, but many conscripts proved unable to satisfy their norms in practice. A study of 80,000 draftees carried out by the Ministry of Defense in the late 1960s found over a quarter unable to swim.[33] A Komsomol secretary complained to the Central Committee about "formalism" in the award of fitness medals, noting that while 97 percent of draftees in 1971 held the newly created GZR znachok, over 30 percent proved unable to meet its basic requirements.[34]

More serious complaints about predraft preparation concerned poor skill levels among draftees, particularly language skills. Predraft training classes were often poorly taught or suffered from a shortage of supplies or qualified instructors.[35] Even when training was adequate, students often lacked the Russian language skills to utilize much of the standardized course materials. Roughly 10 percent of the Soviet draft pool spoke Russian poorly in 1970, but this deficiency was particularly serious among Muslim conscripts.[36] In the 1970s, the Muslim share of the draft pool grew steadily, rising from 25 percent in 1970 to 34 percent in 1979.[37] During this same period, the percentage of conscripts from Turkmenistan with poor or no Russian-language skills rose from 4 percent to 13 percent; in Kazakhstan it rose from 1 percent to nearly 19 percent.[38] In 1980, 21 percent of draftees from Uzbekistan spoke Russian poorly or not at all.[39]

Minority conscripts unable to understand the commands of their Russian superiors was a scenario that deeply worried military commanders, particularly once they began confronting Islamic guerrillas in Afghanistan. In the early 1980s the Ministry of Defense began operating Russian language camps for non-Russian conscripts and published several Russian-language textbooks aimed at draftees.[40] Language skills remained a serious problem, however, and fueled the trend toward ethnic segregation already prominent within the ranks of enlisted men. This segregation often led to violent clashes.

Violence among Servicemen: "Dedovshchina" and "Gruppovshchina"

Life as a conscript in the Soviet army was violent and degrading. Though the general level of violence in conscript units received little publicity before glasnost', there was a long history of flagrant disregard for disciplinary norms. In 1965, for instance, the Ministry of Defense was forced to pay the Ministry of Railways 15,000 rubles to cover damage done to trains carrying recruits from assembly points to their service units. According to the Soviet General Staff, drunken conscripts broke over 50,000 windows in railway carriages in a single night.[41] Apparently, this night of rioting on the rails was an enduring tradition, linked with the practice of parents toasting their departing sons until they were—in the words of one general—"too drunk to stand."[42]

The wild sendoff was apparently an appropriate introduction to army life. An inspection team in Uzbekistan in 1981 found that virtually all inductees had left at home all items essential for daily life, such as pens, watches, razors, out of fear they would be stolen.[43] This provided strong confirmation of a sociological study conducted around the same time that found that at least 40 percent of draftees formed their preconceptions about Army life not from predraft training sessions but from letters from acquaintances in the service.[44]

Once settled into their new units, conscripts found themselves in a world in which theft was perhaps the least of their worries. Soldiers were placed into a brutal seniority system in which incoming recruits were subject to severe hazing from officers and senior enlisted men. Known broadly as *dedovshchina* (from the Russian *ded*, or "old man"), the phenomenon was often referred to in official circles as "nonregulation relations" *(neustavnye otnoshenie)*.

Dedovshchina could take a wide variety of forms.[45] Some practices—like forcing newcomers to shine elders' boots or clean their weapons—would not seem out of place at many institutions attempting to enforce norms of unquestioning military obedience. In many units, however, hazing extended to regular beatings or floggings of new recruits.

A cousin of dedovshchina was *gruppovshchina*, or group violence. Initially far less widespread than seniority-based violence, group violence became more common as non-Russians began to make up a larger share of the draft pool. The Deputy Director of the Main Political Administration of the armed forces noted in 1983 that "nationalistic manifestations" were increasingly observed, as the army brought together young men "with insufficient practical experience in associating with people from other nationalities."[46] A military sociologist noted that the non-Slavic conscripts "tend to group together."[47] Ethnic gangs began to arise within units, often pitting Baltic conscripts against Russians or Russians against Central Asians or Transcaucasians. By the late 1980s, some units were completely dominated by non-Slavic groups, even to the extent of ethnic ties taking precedence over seniority.[48]

With the introduction of glasnost' in the mid-1980s, many of the most violent manifestations of hazing and ethnic conflict came into the open.

Iurii Poliakov, who had pilloried the Komsomol in his novella *Incident at the District Level* succeeded in 1987 in publishing a frank exposé of military hazing entitled "One Hundred Days until the Order."[49] The military responded with a wave of scorn (and even banned the journal *Iunost'* from military libraries) but the floodgates were opened.

Though the Afghan War almost certainly raised the level of tension within combat units, there is little reason to suspect that the stories which appeared in print described practices new to the late 1980s. Rather, these discussions of dedovshchina and gruppovshchina finally revealed the details behind what came to be labeled "negative traditions" within the military.[50] One especially brutal, but not atypical, account described a new recruit who was punished by his comrades for requesting a transfer after receiving an "initiation" beating. Trapped late at night on a transport train three days before his transfer, the young recruit was beaten, burned, and raped by seven of his fellow soldiers. He responded by shooting them all, as well as a civilian conductor. After describing his trial and subsequent descent into insanity, the author concluded:

> Bullying in military units has been condoned for a long time, and today it remains the main problem. A batch of new recruits is taken into the army every six months. Nearly every "new boy" has to suffer the "pleasure" of these "non-regulation" associations.[51]

Still other accounts of internal violence were collected by groups of parents investigating deaths or beatings of their children. In 1990, representatives of these groups began publicizing their assertion that 4,000 servicemen were suffering "noncombat deaths" each year—20 percent of these suicides.[52] This figure, which was denied by the Ministry of Defense but endorsed by a Presidential commission investigating the problem, would be equivalent to over ten deaths *every day*. Particularly notorious—for reasons I discuss later in this chapter—were military construction battalions.

While defense ministry officials may have privately seen dedovshchina as an unfortunate consequence of practices that enforced hierarchical discipline, the same could hardly have been said for gruppovshchina. By the late 1980s, ethnic violence in the military was also receiving extensive and disturbing press. Two prominent Uzbek writers described the case of one Uzbek recruit from Ferghana who supposedly died of "illness" in

August 1989. His body was returned home as "unaccompanied baggage," but an investigation of the corpse revealed murder.[53] Another Uzbek writer claimed in 1990 that 430 Uzbek conscripts had been returned home the previous year in "zinc coffins"—sealed so that the cause of death could not be investigated.[54] Similar stories concerning recruits from other republics fueled anti-Moscow sentiments in the provinces.

Institutional Dynamics of Conscription Policy

Trends like group violence in the army ranks were far more ominous than mass inductions to the Komsomol or the poor care given to young specialists. Yet draft quotas could not be challenged, regardless of the increasingly desperate consequences of filling them from a shrinking draft pool. Meeting these quotas often forced street-level officials to violate the spirit, if not the letter, of conscription policy.

Elite Controls

To what extent was conscription policy at the voenkomat level fully controlled by the top leadership in the Party and military?

The approach used in previous chapters to study elite controls—examination of reform initiatives and responses from the field—is less helpful here. Soviet draft policy underwent little significant change from the 1967 Draft Law until the late 1980s. Details of conscription policy therefore reduced to technical calculations of conscript supply and force demands.

Until the late 1980s, there was no open discussion of the Soviet draft by top Party or defense officials beyond simple reaffirmations of the "sacred duty" of all Soviet youth to serve in the armed forces. The universality of military obligations was an unquestioned principle after the 1939 Draft Law dropped class-based distinctions. No Soviet leader ever suggested that military service was anything but supremely beneficial for both the state and the young citizen. In fact, for all intents and purposes, military control over the draft was so absolute that any public discussion of the Soviet draft was essentially taboo until about 1987.

Consequently, adjustments to draft policy were never linked to any broader move toward selective service. Three such adjustments were made under Brezhnev: the restoration of educational deferments for full-time students in 1965, the new Draft Law in 1967, and the discontinuation of educational deferments for most full-time students in 1980. The 1965 reestablishment of educational deferments was a direct consequence of a rapid expansion of the draft pool (as the postwar generation reached draft age)—the number of eighteen-year-olds grew from under one million in 1962 to over a million and a half in 1965.[55] It was no longer necessary for military manpower purposes to maintain draft levels at pre-1965 levels, and student deferments could be reinstated.

By 1967, the pool of eighteen-year-olds was over two million, allowing the length of service to be reduced to two years (three years for seamen). The reduction of draft age from nineteen to eighteen was also a direct consequence of the abandonment of Khrushchev's experiment with 11-year secondary education and a return to ten-year schooling. In neither case did the underlying rationale of the policy shift receive any attention. Instead, the propaganda surrounding the 1967 Draft Law focused on the need for civilian institutions to shoulder a greater burden through pre-draft training programs.[56]

Similarly, by 1980 the pool of eighteen-year-olds began to shrink, just as military activities in Afghanistan required an increase in the intake of conscripts. Educational deferments were therefore restricted only to full-time students attending VUZy on a list prepared annually by the Defense Ministry and Gosplan. The intent of this loophole was to exempt students at institutions whose mission was somehow linked to the military-industrial complex; most entering students suddenly found themselves subject to the draft.[57] However, the decision received very little attention and even less explanation.[58] Even the list of institutions qualifying for exemptions remained secret, permitting the Ministry of Defense to fine-tune the conscript supply from year to year. The translation of manpower needs into conscription policy was automatic; there was no need for top officials to either justify it or attempt to lessen its disruptive consequences for both schools and students.

When military policy finally came under open scrutiny in the late 1980s the response of top officials reflected this history of unquestioned authority. Poliakov's exposé of dedovshchina was banned from military libraries, and its author denounced. Blame was deflected to civilian authorities, as in this typical comment from the commander of air defense forces: "If such things happen, it is not the army that is guilty, it is rather a reflection

of the education that young men are getting in the pre-army environment."[59]

As discussed below, early criticisms of the army's policy of drafting
students were met with undisguised venom coupled with ominous warnings of the dangers of applying glasnost' to military affairs.[60] Finally, a
November 1988 article suggesting a shift to a professionalized army, with
an accompanying cutback in conscription, forced the Ministry of Defense
to defend its policy of universal conscription explicitly.[61]

In a sharp break from historical precedent, the military's position failed
to receive the unquestioning endorsement of the Party First Secretary. At
a forum for Moscow students in 1988, Gorbachev—the first Soviet leader
not to serve in the military—was asked, "Why do we need such a big
army?" He responded, "We must take a good look at the questions of
army service and the draft. I think the question of duration of service will
come up, and it may be changed."[62]

Never before in Soviet history had a Party leader suggested that draft
policy was not sacrosanct, nor had one ever signaled that adjustments in
policy were responses to anything but shifting demographics. Gorbachev's
comment suggested for the first time that the defense ministry might not
be able to unilaterally set draft policy, and it encouraged a flood of
responses from the grass roots. The next section looks at some of these
responses.

Societal Interests and Policy-Relevant Data

It is difficult to search for the influence of social forces or street-level
actors on the policy process prior to 1989 because there was no policy
process to speak of. As already noted, policy shifts emerged from a
technical assessment of the changing shape of the draft pool, with little
apparent concern for the social consequences of particular policy choices.
The military's response to social changes—like deteriorating language
skills or discipline among draftees—was to demand that institutions like
the Komsomol or schools improve their efforts at training the predraft
cohort.

Ministry of Defense officials made regular appearances before the Komsomol Central Committee to complain about poor "military-patriotic upbringing" work. Komsomol officials were taken to task not merely for

failing to indoctrinate students before they were drafted but also for failing to conduct effective indoctrination work within the armed forces. One frustrated Komsomol leader finally called on the Ministry of Defense to assume some of the burden itself: "Comrades, I have a suggestion for the Ministry of Defense. Criticizing Komsomol for poor work in military patriotic upbringing of youth, it hardly rushes to take its own measures to correct the situation."[63]

The defense ministry, for its part, accused the Komsomol of playing too small a role in the draft process overall. After visiting a Moscow voenkomat, a military reporter complained that most Moscow raikom Komsomol secretaries "knew about military service only second-hand."[64] It seems clear that defense ministry officials had little interest in discussing the causes or implications of social problems with the Komsomol officials, who were confronting them on a broader scale.

This does not mean that military planners were blind to signs of discontent. In 1980, two sociologists, including one from the Institute of Military History of the Ministry of Defense, surveyed 2,000 youth in the Baltics and Moscow to investigate their attitudes toward army service.[65] The authors found that 86.5 percent of new recruits "recognized the social importance and necessity" of military service, implying that a remarkable 13.5 percent did not recognize this basic tenet of patriotic upbringing. Even more disturbing, 42 percent of surveyed recruits cited "military discipline and obedience" as their chief fear about army life, perhaps reflecting concern over hazing.

While this study showed remarkable frankness, particularly in its detailed discussion of the shortcomings of military and Komsomol indoctrination programs, it must have ruffled numerous feathers in the Army Political Administration and DOSAAF. The following year, the same authors (one of whom was a lieutenant general) published a virtual retraction, lavishly extolling the virtues of the Army's "upbringing role."[66] For the most part, sociological research that touched on military issues restricted itself to investigations of the prestige of military professions.[67]

Though the military may have been averse to openly confronting social problems affecting the draft, the war in Afghanistan generated a stream of spontaneous feedback. The fate of conscripts posted to Afghanistan was shrouded in uncertainty, especially because coverage of the war in the Soviet press was cryptic at best. It appears that as early as the fall 1981 call-up, the dispatch of new recruits to their military units was being disrupted by parents who feared that their sons might be sent "somewhere far away."[68] In May of the same year, a Komsomol team investigating the draft in Uzbekistan expressed concern over the absence of "supplemental work to broaden the political horizons" of Muslim draftees who were being sent directly into combat situations in Afghanistan.[69]

Several years later, as press coverage of the Afghan war grew more detailed and more combat veterans returned to civilian life, resistance to army service became more intense. At the same time, the guidelines for granting educational and (as discussed in the next section) medical deferments remained unpublished. Isolated instances of draft evasion began to rise, and Party committees received a flood of letters concerning Afghanistan and the draft.[70]

At roughly the same time, grass-roots groups began to coalesce—not of draft-age youth but of their parents—dedicated to reforming the draft system and to keeping their own sons out of uniform. Working together with newly elected institutions like national legislatures, these groups eventually exerted significant pressure on the Ministry of Defense for draft reform, pressure which the Ministry was wholly unaccustomed to dealing with. Later, this chapter describes how they were able to capitalize on violations of the Draft Law committed by local draft boards anxious to meet induction targets set by Moscow.

Information, Monitoring, and Authority within the Bureaucratic Hierarchy

As I have already suggested, draft policy was truly run "by the numbers." Draft boards (not unlike Komsomol committees) received firm targets for inductees, and (unlike the Komsomol) these targets were always met. As noted in previous chapters, any management system relying entirely on quantitative performance indicators invites hidden action problems in areas not directly covered by a numerical target.

The artificial awarding of fitness medals described earlier was among the most egregious examples of this problem. Medals were awarded almost universally, with little regard for whether recipients could actually meet prescribed fitness norms. These problems were not discovered, though, until inductees reached their voenkomaty or their military unit, long after offending Komsomol or DOSAAF committees had met their performance targets.

A similar, more troubling, trend was evident in the recommendation of young men for admission to military schools. Local voenkomaty received quotas, equivalent on the average to three nominees for each opening.[71] In assigning quotas, planners strove to achieve some ethnic integration in the composition of the student body and particularly to encourage applications from indigenous nationalities to schools located in non-Russian republics.

Even though military schools offered an alternative to conscript duty, draft boards seem to have needed extreme measures to meet their quotas. In 1968, for instance, four military academies reported that 9–12 percent of candidates sent to them by local draft boards actually refused to enroll. More than half of the rest failed the entrance examinations. That year, some academies found the candidate pool so thin they were forced to enroll candidates who had failed basic entrance requirements: 29 percent of the incoming class at the Poltava Artillery Academy had unsatisfactory examination grades, while the same was true of 45 percent of new students at the Sumskoe Artillery Academy.[72]

This problem remained chronic throughout the 1970s, despite complaints from the Ministry of Defense about poor screening of candidates. In 1971 Alma-Ata sent 781 candidates to military schools; of these, seventy-seven were returned for poor health, twenty refused to apply, and over 300 failed entrance examinations.[73] Of 358 candidates sent to military schools in 1976 by draft boards in Daghestan, 115 failed basic entrance examinations, twenty-one were returned on grounds of poor health, and ten refused to apply.[74] Refusals to apply were more common from non-Russian nationalities: in 1979, 23 percent of Uzbek candidates sent to the Tashkent Tank Academy flatly refused to take its entrance examination.[75] Clearly, in recommending candidates to these military schools, local committees were chiefly concerned with meeting quotas for youth sent, whether or not these youth eventually enrolled.

Similarly, whenever the pool of youth eligible for basic service grew tight, local committees gave top priority to satisfying quantitative—not qualitative—targets. In 1965, for instance, just as the number of eighteen-year-olds nationwide was recovering from record lows, the General

Staff complained about the quality of conscripts assigned to the strategic rocket corps. Apparently few draftees were volunteering for these highly sensitive units, and the youth assigned by local voenkomaty were "morally unstable individuals with convictions for various crimes and engaged in correspondence with relatives living in capitalist countries."[76]

In the late 1970s, as the eighteen-year-old pool again began to shrink, local committees again filled their quotas with the help of juvenile delinquents and ex-convicts. In Uzbekistan in 1980, for instance, 2,437 youth with criminal records were drafted, an 8 percent rise over 1980. Fourteen percent of these draftees were reported to be "serious criminals," whose crimes included rape or murder.[77] Though youth with prior criminal convictions were not, strictly speaking, exempted from military service (unlike youth actually in jail), they were considered among the least reliable of troops. Often they were assigned to noncombat units like railway troops or military construction brigades. By 1988, 50,000 draftees nationwide had criminal records.[78]

The restriction of educational deferments in 1980 mentioned previously was another essentially automatic response to the difficulty being encountered by local draft boards in meeting their draft quotas. By 1987, even this measure was proving insufficient, as the pool of eighteen-year-olds remained below historic levels. Consequently, the Ministry of Defense turned to the next class of deferments: those granted to conscripts in poor health. As the Minister of Defense himself explained several years later with uncharacteristic frankness, "In the 1980s, due to the sharp deficit of draft resources, the Ministry of Defense, in accord with leading national institutions of public health, was obliged to lower the health requirements for citizens drafted into the army and navy."[79]

In 1987, new medical guidelines were issued, sharply limiting the conditions for which draft boards could grant medical exemptions.[80] Youth with cardiovascular diseases, with histories of pleurisy, asthma, and tuberculosis, with digestive disorders, with histories of mental disorders, and with dozens of other chronic medical conditions were no longer exempted from service. As a consequence of this new policy, the overall health of new conscripts fell dramatically. By 1990, the head of the Railway Troops estimated that a remarkable 70 percent of his soldiers were chronically ill, 40 percent of them too ill to carry out their duties.[81]

Furthermore, since the new regulations were never published, appeal of the decisions of medical certification reviews was virtually impossible. Local draft boards were thus always able to meet their induction targets by simply bending already weak guidelines even further. In the two years following the new regulations, 10,000 to 14,000 conscripts were released from service each year after proving unfit to serve.[82] The improper classifications of these youth during call-up was blamed on the use of unqualified doctors for examinations and on "inadequate examination of draftees . . . and shortcomings in the organization of medical certifications."[83]

Draft policy was thus constantly rewritten to match changing demographics: if the draft pool shrank, deferment guidelines were adjusted to expand the pool. These adjustments exacerbated information asymmetries at the street level.[84] Secret medical guidelines enabled many draft boards to meet their quotas with conscripts who would later prove unfit to serve. While this permitted defense planners to continue setting conscription targets without regard for the appropriate or sustainable size of the draft contingent, it also demonstrated the limits to hierarchical control at the street level of even this most powerful institution. Quantity of inductees was easier to track than quality.

Though local draft boards must have known that sending ill or mentally disturbed young men to confront dedovshchina was tantamount to a death sentence, the power of the Ministry of Defense and its capacity to monitor the raw number of conscripts dispatched to units left them with little alternative. Beginning in 1989, however, alternatives finally presented themselves.

Crisis and Breakdown of the Conscription System

Student Deferments and Demobilization

In the spring of 1982, for the first time in seventeen years, full-time students at daytime VUZy were drafted into active service. Over the next few years, in order to sustain the size of the draft pool in the face of adverse demographics, the number of VUZy whose students were entitled to educational deferments dwindled steadily. As already noted, this list remained essentially secret, so neither students nor educators could say with any certainty throughout this period who would be drafted and who would be able to continue their studies uninterrupted.

In 1985, the first students were drafted from the physics faculty of Moscow University, one of the most prestigious departments in the country.[85] This development suggests that by the mid-1980s the list of exempt institutions must have already been quite short. Students were drafted after their first year, interrupting their education in midstream.[86] Upon returning to their universities, many students found it difficult to pick up their studies; most universities did little to ease the transition. The first contingent to return to the Moscow University physics faculty, for instance, complained about the lack of remedial classes to help them adjust. To make matters worse, this contingent of returnees promptly found themselves obliged to join their classmates in gathering the harvest (a typical Komsomol-organized labor brigade program), despite a MinVUZ decree exempting returnees from the army from this obligation. Two students who attempted to boycott the harvest work were expelled from the Komsomol—a decision supported by the university newspaper.[87]

In the spring of 1987, at about the time the first group of conscripts was returning to elite institutions like Moscow University, a group of educators participated in a roundtable discussion published in the influential weekly *Literaturnaia gazeta*. They forcefully complained that the draft of students was having a serious impact on the health of the nation's educational and research establishments.[88] The article contained an unprecedented critique of the Ministry of Defense's draft policy. One historian remarked, "Those [students] returning from the army follow instructions well, and are wonderfully organized, but there will be no Newtons among them. Apparently their creative capacities atrophy and die."

Another historian in this exchange noted that German science outstripped that of France and England after World War I because, unlike its opponents, Germany had not sent its young intellectuals into the trenches. He concluded, "For this reason I am absolutely agreed that it is stupid and short-sighted to draft students into the army."

The army's response was swift but less than effective. Just a week later, General Dmitri Volkogonov, of the army's Main Political Administration, dismissed the educators as "mistaken," asserting that the army was itself an important school for building character and providing skills and emphasizing the need for military service to be truly universal.[89] Shortly after that, the Deputy Chief of the General Staff, Mukhmet Gareev, reiterated this argument in the pages of *Literaturnaia gazeta,* citing studies showing that 85 percent of student-conscripts completed their studies after their release from the armed forces.[90] The military continued to hammer this point home in a series of articles extending into the fall.[91] In December 1987 Defense Minister Iazov met with a group of writers and angrily mocked the educators calling for the deferment of science students.[92]

Though the issue appeared dormant in early 1988, by that fall another class of returnees was struggling to readjust to student life, and the educational establishment was again campaigning in the press for reinstatement of student deferments.[93] In September 1988, thirty members of the prestigious Academy of Sciences signed an open letter to Gorbachev protesting the draft of full-time students.[94] Throughout the fall, a remarkable series of protests and demonstrations was organized by students at several universities around the country. At one of the most serious of these, a boycott staged at Kiev University in October 1988, students protested the call-up of seventeen recent graduates for a *second* tour of active duty. The rector of the university, addressing a conference of students, asserted that educational deferments would be reintroduced "experimentally" at twenty-five VUZy nationwide, including Kiev University. After some minor concessions were made—like making military training classes voluntary for students in the second year and relaxing dress codes for these classes—students went back to class.[95] Similar grassroots grumblings at Moscow University were also quelled by promised adjustments to the military training curriculum and proposed hikes in stipend levels.[96]

The parents of students called up for military service were less easily placated. In the spring call-up of 1989 several students of the Moscow Energy Institute (MEI) were drafted for active duty. Six of the top nine students in the first-year class were among the draftees, including eighteen-year-old Petr Kirbasov. Kirbasov's mother, Maria Kirbasova, began writing a series of letters to officials at the Ministry of Defense, protesting her son's assignment to a training program in radar technology rather than in his specialty of computer science. Kirbasova's appeals, frequently coupled with similar requests from other mothers of MEI students, were uniformly rejected by defense ministry officials, though they did agree to transfer Petr to a computing center in Kuibyshev after he completed his training.[97] The mothers were not placated and continued agitating through the winter for the release of students from military service, but these appeals were routinely referred to officials at the Ministry of Defense, who took little notice of them. Nevertheless, in the course of that summer the "Committee of Soldiers' Mothers" (KSM) was born, operating out of the offices of the newly assertive MEI Komsomol committee.[98]

The tenor of the draft debate changed swiftly after October 1988. As I have already noted, on 29 October Gorbachev suggested for the first time to a group of students that the terms of the draft could be open for review.[99] Shortly after that, addressing the United Nations on 7 December, he announced a unilateral 500,000-person reduction in the size of the Soviet armed forces.

Gorbachev's U.N. announcement suddenly altered the demand side of military manpower planning; indeed, given the difficulty encountered by local committees in meeting their draft quotas, Gorbachev's unilateral decision may be viewed as a brilliant tactical retreat. Roughly 350,000 of the troop reductions were designated to come out of the enlisted force, presumably reducing quotas nationwide for draftees by at least 150,000 annually.[100]

Ministry of Defense officials—perhaps aware of Gorbachev's own feelings about educational deferments (he had benefited from one himself at Moscow University in the 1950s)—wasted little time signaling that a concession to the educational community might be forthcoming. The following week, the chief of Combat Training for Ground Forces declared that the draft of students had always been regarded as a temporary measure and that the planned restructuring of ground forces would soon permit combat readiness to be maintained "without enlisting students for military service."[101] Several weeks later, Colonel Aleksandr Rutskoi suggested that students would probably make better soldiers if their service came after graduation.[102]

It therefore came as little surprise when, on 12 April 1989, the Supreme Soviet reinstated educational deferments for students at full-time VUZy.[103] The decision was one of the last acts of the old Supreme Soviet—a new Congress of Peoples' Deputies had been elected in late March 1989. In fact, the timing of the reinstatement of educational deferments was probably linked to those elections, since several senior military officials were defeated in their campaigns by younger officers promising military reform. By announcing the military deferments through the outgoing Supreme Soviet, the Ministry of Defense may have thought it was depriving the newly elected Congress of a major political issue.

If this was part of their thinking, army officials badly miscalculated. The April order was to take effect with the 1989 draft, but students drafted in 1988 were expected to serve out their terms. Included in this group were many children of the founders of the Committee of Soldiers' Mothers. Still stinging from the neglect to which they had been subjected at the hands of the military, these grass-roots activists began to work with their newly elected deputies to win the immediate release of all students from the ranks of the military.[104] For their part, these deputies—particularly those elected on the Komsomol's slate—saw in the KSM's demands a chance to demonstrate the power of the new Congress by taking on the powerful defense ministry on an issue with broad popular appeal.

Working closely with several deputies, the KSM fashioned a sophisticated media and lobbying campaign targeted to reach deputies before the Congress of Peoples' Deputies convened on 25 May. As the Committee's activities began to receive coverage in the Soviet press, its ranks began to grow around the country. KSM affiliates sprang up in the Baltics and in several regions across Russia, where it attracted parents whose sons were victims of dedovshchina or were drafted into service despite ill health. Deputies from all over the country found themselves inundated with letters and telegrams from parents of students, complaining that their sons had been assigned to military construction brigades or had suffered attacks or other severe hazing. An appeal to the Congress told of students whose senior officers pledged, "We'll beat the higher education out of you."[105]

Moskovskii komsomolets, the widely read Moscow Komsomol newspaper, began regular coverage of the KSM's affairs, which included a vigil outside the Kremlin: as deputies entered the Congress, the mothers handed them leaflets describing the violence within the military ranks and calling for the immediate demobilization of students. Historians uncovered a little-known decree from 1943 releasing students from service at the wartime front.[106] Representatives of the KSM attempted to press their case with a fellow mother—Raisa Gorbacheva—apparently with some success.[107]

On 25 June the KSM organized a demonstration at a *Moskovskii komsomolets* festival in Gorkii Park that attracted several hundred mothers.

During the proceedings, a poll was taken of student-soldiers attending the festival. Contrary to defense ministry assertions that students were utilizing their education in their service, only 20 percent of respondents reported any specialty assignments at all; 10 percent were serving in construction battalions.[108] Though extremely unscientific, the poll's results were prominently reported on the morning news the following day, just as the newly chosen Supreme Soviet convened to begin confirmation hearings for a new Cabinet of Ministers.

The lobbying campaign reached its climax the following week, as Dmitri Iazov appeared before the Supreme Soviet to be confirmed as Soviet Minister of Defense.[109] Iazov acknowledged that he had received hundreds of inquiries from deputies asking if the 176,000 students drafted during 1987–88 could be released from service. Ignoring the well-publicized KSM poll, he addressed the issue directly:

> I reply, these 176,000 students are the best trained component of the Soviet Armed Forces. They have passed through special training and are now division commanders, commanders of tanks, military machinery, infantry and artillery. Therefore, we would have to release 176,000 of our junior officers corps.
>
> This would, without doubt, affect the combat preparedness of our Armed Forces. Whatever decision you take, I ask you to consider precisely this. It is presently impossible to release the comrades, and they should serve out the term of service dictated by law.[110]

In questions and subsequent debate, deputies were relentless in their attack on draft policy. A whole series criticized Iazov's evasive answers to questions of dedovshchina and gruppovshchina and announced their intention to vote against his nomination. The question of students was raised repeatedly, along with the issues of ill health of conscripts. Several deputies referred explicitly to the "mothers' appeal" and called on Iazov to revisit the "question of the 176,000"; one deputy even suggested as a possible compromise reclassifying these students as medically unfit.[111] Finally, after several hours, Gorbachev may have sensed that Iazov's nomination was in trouble. Donning his hat as chairman of the Defense Council, Gorbachev offered a rambling endorsement of Iazov. However, he signaled that his own position on demobilizing students was not as inflexible as that of the Defense Minister:

About students. I think we should work through this question and take it to a conclusion. That is the mood of the Supreme Soviet and of our people. I have already received quite a packet of letters myself. And here Boris Nikolaevich [Yeltsin] has just presented me with several thousand more. I can't figure out where he got all of them from. And there are others. That's the mood today. We can't just brush it off with answers about difficulties (who doesn't have difficulties these days?) but we must find a solution.[112]

Iazov was confirmed with just forty votes more than the required 216—a remarkably slim margin for an incumbent Defense Minister. Eight days later, the other shoe dropped. On 11 July Prime Minister Nikolai Ryzhkov strode into the afternoon session of the Supreme Soviet and curtly announced that the government proposed to release all students drafted in 1987–88 by the end of the following month.[113] The two-sentence resolution was approved by a show of hands, with just five dissenting votes.

The decision was a stunning defeat for the Ministry of Defense—the first public indication that its position on draft policy might no longer be definitive. The policy reversal took it by surprise; apparently it was not immediately clear whether the figure of 176,000 may have underestimated the total number of affected conscripts.[114] Also caught off guard was the nation's higher education system, which suddenly had to accommodate an extra 176,000 students.[115] The decision affirmed the power of the new Supreme Soviet, through which the demobilization campaign had been waged. The national legislature suddenly became a forum through which grievances could be redressed.

The consequences of this loss of control over draft policy were immediately clear to military officials. In August 1989 G. Krivosheev, Deputy Chief of the General Staff, lashed out at the coalition of media and parents' groups who had succeeded in reversing policy on students. He was particularly critical of the opening rift between institutions claiming to make defense policy, complaining, "Characteristically, after announcing the Supreme Soviet decree, Central TV commentators declared, 'This is our first victory. A victory for the Supreme Soviet of the USSR.' One might ask—victory over whom?"[116]

In response, Krivosheev recast the student draft issue as one of class equality. Noting that the draft pool remained smaller than usual, and that children of the intelligentsia were proportionately overrepresented among VUZ students, he warned, "it will be necessary to call to active service all rural and urban working youth, lacking right to deferral." Ominously, he invoked historical antecedents: "In all, I would very much want to believe, that we will not reach the point where it will be necessary to return to the old, romantic name for the military detachment of our society—the Workers' and Peasants' Red Army. However, that is where it appears we are heading."[117]

Continuing this line of argument, the Ministry of Defense launched a major campaign to reinforce the principle of universality of military service.[118] Its concerns were proven to be well founded, as the decision on students unleashed a wave of new demands for broadening the categories exempted from military service. Several letters published in the press called for the demobilization of rural youth—whose exodus from the countryside was already causing severe social problems—either instead of or in addition to VUZ students.[119]

Of more concern to the military, however, were the new initiatives launched by the KSM, now a potent national force. Privately, leaders of the mothers' group made no secret of their desire to "break" the draft, in order to force the introduction of a volunteer army.[120] The mothers began to work closely with deputies on several Supreme Soviet Committees—including the Committee on Public Health and the Committee on Youth Affairs—who were themselves eager to establish their legitimacy as participants in the formulation of defense policy. Letters from the KSM to the Ministry of Defense were now answered promptly. One proposal introduced by the KSM to the Supreme Soviet, calling for the extension of educational deferments to evening students, brought a prompt reply from First Deputy Defense Minister Moiseev. His letter recalled the defense ministry's recent defeat over daytime students, and his tone mixed annoyance with a trace of alarm:

> Taking this decision [exempting daytime students] has already placed the armed forces in an extremely difficult position. If it is extended to students in other categories, then there will practically be nobody left to serve in the army and navy, and the level of preparedness of these forces will become critical.[121]

The primary focus of the KSM and Supreme Soviet following their victory over students was not evening students, however, but ill or victimized conscripts. Local draft boards, now unable to draft students, were resorting to extreme measures to meet their 1989 quotas—including the induction of an even greater proportion of ex-convicts and invalids. The Ministry of Defense, already off-balance and showing unprecedented weakness, was forced to justify the guidelines used by draft boards to withhold medical exemptions and to assign many unfit draftees to military construction battalions.

Medical Deferrals and Military Construction Battalions

As discussed earlier in this chapter, the Ministry of Defense issued revised medical guidelines in 1987 that removed medical exemptions from many chronically ill youth. According to the 1987 order, many of these unhealthy conscripts were classified as "fit for noncombat duty"; in practice, this meant that many were assigned to military construction brigades.

The 1967 Draft Law provided three medical categories for draftees: fit for service; temporarily unfit and entitled to a recuperative period; and permanently unfit. The category of "fit for noncombat duty" appears to have developed over the years as a sort of reserve, which local draft boards tapped to fill their induction quotas. The 1987 medical guidelines expanded this category dramatically, including in it many conditions previously leading to temporary or permanent medical exemptions. In addition to reclassifying several chronic conditions as "fit for noncombat duty," it also ranked the different service branches according to the physical "grade" required of inductees. This list is reproduced as Table 6.1. The most fit category of inductees fit to serve was Grade 1; the least fit was Grade 6, which included conscripts with a wide range of birth defects and chronic diseases.

As this table shows, even though military construction brigades were often assigned the most arduous tasks in the most inhospitable climates, from 1987 onward they received the least fit conscripts. In addition, the Chief of the Railway Troops complained that local draft boards were not treating his branch as "other combat units," despite military regulations, and therefore he was also receiving the least fit category of draftee for service that involved long stretches in harsh field conditions.[122]

Table 6.1. Ranking of Military Service Branches by Physical Demands

Physical Grade	Service
1	Special Designation Troops *(Spetsnaz)*
2	Naval Infantry Units
2	Border Guards
2	Paratroopers
3	Submarine and Naval Surface Units
3	Tank Forces
4	Rocket Forces
4	Antiaircraft Rocket Forces
4	Chemical Forces
4	Internal Troops
4	Local Rifle Forces
4	Radio/Radar Units
5	Communications Units
5	Naval Ground Support Units
5	**Other Combat Units**
6	**Military Construction Brigades**

Source: Ministry of Defense Order No. 260, 9 September 1987, Appendix 4, 230.
Higher numbers for physical grade correspond to greater degrees of physical limitation or incapacity. Emphasis added.

Under questioning by committees of the Supreme Soviet during 1989 and 1990, military officials finally revealed their clandestine practice of filling draft quotas by relying on unfit conscripts. The Deputy Head of Military Construction stated openly, "[In accord with] Ministry of Defense Order No. 260, individuals with serious deficiencies in their health or physical development have been placed into the military construction battalions."[123]

The Director of Military Medicine, who directed the system of medical certification for draftees, told the Supreme Soviet, "From 1987 to 1989, among young draftees taken into the army and navy, 97–98 percent were healthy and fit for combat duty, but 2–3 percent had medical deficiencies and were classified as fit for noncombat duty and sent principally to military-construction brigades, where they comprised 20–25 percent of the total force level."[124]

In October 1989 the Ministry of Defense attempted to regain the initiative by issuing a new order amending the guidelines for medical deferments. Several of the most egregious instances of misclassification were changed, but the medical guidelines remained more harsh than those in force prior to 1987.[125] The introduction of these amendments, which were also never published, had the perverse effect of demonstrating the depths of the problem: within one year, 80,000 servicemen were released from active duty.[126] Military officials promised to issue revised guidelines by 1991, abolishing altogether the category of "fit for noncombat duty."

The revelations that 80,000 conscripts had been improperly drafted and that nearly a quarter of military construction troops were chronically ill (in addition to the 40–70 percent of railway troops) was only half of the ugly truth. The other half, also revealed to the Supreme Soviet, was that to meet draft quotas, local draft boards had continued and expanded their practice of drafting young men with criminal records. According to standard practice, these draftees were considered only marginally reliable and were therefore also generally assigned to military construction or other noncombat units. In his difficult appearance before the Supreme Soviet, Defense Minister Iazov admitted that discipline had become a major problem on construction brigades: "To our great regret, we are drafting into construction units *over 100 thousand* of those who have completed their assigned [prison] terms, and, naturally, this introduces to these units a certain jailhouse order, certain undesirable aspects."[127]

Finally, the Ministry of Defense was forced to admit that these military construction troops, on whose account it was drafting unhealthy and undisciplined youth, were actually often employed in the civilian rather than military economy. As Iazov told the Supreme Soviet:

> The next group of questions I have received concern construction units and brigades. Well, you know that construction units, road crews, railway troops—all are capable of fulfilling tasks in the civilian economy. If you decide these units should not exist, that would be better and easier for the Ministry of Defense. But I would not want to pursue the course

that is easiest for us. We are building roads in the Non-Black Earth Zone—there are twenty-two brigades there. I ask you, do we need roads, or not? Of course we need them. So who is capable of building roads in such isolated places. Obviously, an organized force.[128]

In fact, construction brigades were assigned to projects in twenty-one ministries, ranging from the Chernobyl cleanup to factory construction. Military builders were paid roughly seven rubles per month, far less than were alternative sources of labor.[129]

By 1990, then, a frightening picture had begun to emerge of life inside a construction battalion, or *stroibat*. Unhealthy conscripts were teamed with hardened, often violent criminals. Work conditions were long and arduous, pay was low, and benefits were few. A shortage of officers left many battalions under the command of a sergeant or petty officer. Since medical and sanitary conditions were worse in non-Russian regions, many Central Asian inductees were assigned to stroibaty. Gruppovshchina and dedovshchina were rampant, and many soldiers fled their units.[130]

Many of these "deserters" fled to local KSM organizations, which offered safe haven and counseled conscripts' parents on how to process complaints. At the same time, the Supreme Soviet and KSM began to lobby for the complete disbanding of military construction units, claiming they violated international treaties banning the use of forced labor. In the summer of 1990, the Ministry of Defense notified several civilian ministries that military construction brigades assigned to them would be withdrawn from the beginning of 1991.[131] Howls of protest poured into Moscow from local governments and managers claiming that important projects would have to be abandoned without the availability of this essentially free labor.[132]

By the fall of 1990, it was becoming clear that construction brigades were still at work in civilian ministries and that violence within military ranks was continuing to escalate. After meeting with KSM leaders, Gorbachev issued a Presidential order disbanding all military construction units in civilian ministries effective 1992 and ending the use of conscript labor in these units beginning with the fall 1991 draft season. Gorbachev also appointed a Presidential commission, to include soldiers' mothers and Supreme Soviet deputies, to investigate the causes of noncombat deaths in military units.[133]

Once again, the Ministry of Defense had publicly lost control over the formulation of draft policy. This time, however, it found itself besieged from several directions. At the policy-making level, a committee of the USSR Supreme Soviet, headed by a young reform-minded major, Vladimir Lopatin, began drafting a new set of guidelines for military reform. These guidelines would lay the foundation for shortened terms, alternative service, and a rapid transition to a professional, volunteer force. The Supreme Soviet also began to draft a law creating alternative, nonmilitary service for conscientious and other classes of objectors.

Challenges to Hierarchical Authority

At the street level, local draft boards began responding to pressures from local groups and, for the first time, failed to fulfill draft quotas. In essence, these field agents realized for the first time that the Ministry of Defense might not be the only source of orders on conscription policy. Even more significant, they began to acknowledge that other institutions, like the Supreme Soviet, might also have the right to exercise authority over their actions.

The Committee of Soldiers' Mothers organized meetings of parents in dozens of cities to advise parents on how to secure deferments for their sons. The KSM obtained and distributed copies of the unpublished guidelines for medical deferments so that draftees could arrive at their voenkomat fully laden with medical documentation and prepared to argue for a classification of "unfit for active duty."[134] Responding to the uncertainty over the authority of the Defense Ministry, draft boards nationwide began to grant deferments far more liberally, particularly on medical grounds. In Moscow, defense officials announced with alarm that only 22 percent of the draft pool was actually drafted in 1990, with medical exemptions more than doubling since 1988.[135]

The shift was most striking in the non-Russian republics. Here, beginning in 1989, local draft boards had to contend with more than just conflicting pressures to meet draft quotas and adhere more closely to deferment guidelines. They also had to respond to instructions from republican legislatures to follow republic-level guidelines in addition to—or instead of—those of the Ministry of Defense. In effect, these republican legislatures declared themselves to be the true "owners" of local draft boards, with authority to dictate local draft policy.

During 1988 antidraft sentiment began to pick up in the non-Russian republics. Independence-minded popular front movements, especially in the Baltics, began calls for authorities to stop drafting young men into an "army of occupation."[136] Attacks on Baltic conscripts during their terms of service fueled demands for Baltic soldiers to serve within the boundaries of their home republics. During the spring 1989 draft season the Lithuanian Party chief and Estonian prime minister separately asked Defense Minister Iazov to allow recruits from their republics to serve locally. Iazov offered no policy concessions but promised to allow more Baltic conscripts to serve within the Baltic military district.

In the summer of 1989, after the defense ministry's defeat on the question of drafting students—and its ignominious withdrawal from Afghanistan—official resistance to the draft became more tangible in several regions of the country. On 22 August 1989, one day before the fiftieth anniversary of the Hitler-Stalin pact, the Lithuanian Supreme Soviet declared Lithuania's annexation by the Soviet Union to be illegal. One month later, it passed a law "On Military Service of Citizens of the Lithuanian SSR," restricting service of Lithuanians in the armed forces to the Baltic military district, establishing a national militia, and suspending the draft to military construction battalions. In a separate order, the Supreme Soviet established "commissions on military service" at the district level to serve as watchdogs over voenkomaty, to ensure compliance with the new law as well as adherence to guidelines for medical and other deferments.[137]

In Georgia, a series of hunger strikes and sit-ins staged by draftees led to widespread acts of defiance and a Defense Ministry promise that more Georgians would be allowed to serve their time within the Georgian republic.[138] Similar activity—including "systematic picketing of voenkomaty, disruption of the dispatch of draftees to their military units, and even direct attacks on voenkomaty"—was reported by military authorities in Latvia, Estonia, Moldavia, and the Western Ukraine.[139]

According to Grigorii Krivosheev, the top General Staff officer in charge of mobilization, this campaign of draft resistance "had the tacit approval of local and republican organs of Soviet power."[140] Military officials complained publicly that local Party and state officials in several republics were refusing to take action against those evading or disrupting the draft. Calls from draft officials for assistance enforcing conscription were apparently ignored by local authorities in Armenia, Azerbaijan, Georgia, and Ukraine.[141] A Party raikom secretary in Georgia replied to the voenkomat's request for assistance with the statement, "I'm with the people, and the people don't want to serve." In Armenia, a military commissar (voenkom) was beaten by an angry crowd. As a result of these disruptions, the Soviet draft in 1989 reportedly fell short of its target by 23,500 men.[142]

The situation in the Baltics and Transcaucasus deteriorated in the spring of 1990, as several other republics followed the Lithuanian example and passed laws requiring draftees to serve within their home republics or local military districts. In addition, several republics passed laws creating "alternative service" for conscripts not willing to serve in the army—essentially legitimizing draft evasion by local conscripts.[143] According to Krivosheev, several republics began denying voenkomaty access to financing, transportation, and other technical support; further attacks were reported on voenkomat officials. By the fall of 1990, after local elections were held in most republics, draft boards in several regions—particularly in the Baltics and Western Ukraine—found themselves effectively under siege, operating without electricity or running water.[144] Even in Moscow, draftees arriving at their dispatch points were met by picketers, who succeeded in disrupting the sendoff.

These local developments produced two trends that seriously undermined the draft in many regions. First, draft evaders went unpunished. In the Baltics, draft evasion often took the form of "alternative work service" and was therefore legal under republican laws. Even in Moscow, voenkomat officials conceded that pursuing evaders "requires the cooperation of government and law-enforcement officials at the local level. But they are actively obstructing the implementation of all-Union laws."[145]

At the same time, local draft boards, when they could meet, were granting far more deferrals on recognized grounds—even if this put induction targets out of reach. According to the Ministry of Defense, the conscription rate nationwide fell from 54 percent in 1989 (after the reintroduction of student deferments) to 51 percent the following year, and to 43 percent by mid-1991. In many parts of the country, local chapters of the Committee of Soldiers' Mothers held weekly meetings to advise parents on how to qualify their sons for legal deferrals on medical and family hardship grounds. Some KSM members even began working directly with several draft boards as unofficial "consultants."

The results of this wave of regional noncompliance were devastating for the national draft. Officials were forced to acknowledge a shortfall of 135,000 in the 1990 draft and, more disturbing, nonfulfillment of the conscription plan in a whole series of individual republics. Noncompliance spread as individual republics observed their neighbors' shortfalls going essentially unpunished. Dynamics of successive draft seasons by republic are depicted in Table 6.2.

In making these draft figures public, the Ministry of Defense may have been hoping to arouse alarm among law-abiding citizens, or at least to scare some of the legislators in the USSR Supreme Soviet. No previous draft reports had ever admitted to underfulfillment of national or republican plans. It seems more likely, however, that this publicity served instead to advertise the weakness of the defense ministry and its deep dependence on local agents (both draft boards and local law-enforcement officials) for successful implementation of draft policy. Given the growing independence movements in the republics, realization of the Ministry's weakness probably helped noncompliance spread.

A bank run was on, as local draft boards placed voenkomat resources at the disposal of republican leaders, rather than the Ministry of Defense. By the spring of 1991, however, the defense ministry was attempting to reassert its authority over local conscription policy.

Responses of the Ministry of Defense

Unlike the street-level administrators discussed in previous chapters—local Komsomol committees or VUZ officials—local draft boards were unable to build up "safety margins" to enhance their autonomy from superiors. While it was dependent on local authorities for draft implementation, the defense ministry still controlled data about the draft not easily obtained by the local legislatures seeking to replace it as the authoritative source of draft policy. In some republics, like Estonia and Lithuania, local and district committees were established alongside draft boards to remedy this problem and keep republican officials fully informed about induction activities.

The defense ministry's advantages extended beyond the control of

Table 6.2. Conscription as Percentage of Plan, by Republic

Republic	Spring 1989	Spring 1990	Fall 1990	Spring 1991
RSFSR	100.0	98.6	95.4	100[a]
Ukraine	97.6	99.4	95.1	100[a]
Bielorussia	100.0	98.9	90.4	100[a]
Lithuania	91.6	33.6	25.1	12.3
Latvia	90.7	54.2	39.5	30.8
Estonia	79.5	40.2	35.9	30.3
Moldavia	100.0	100.0	96.0	81.4
Georgia	94.0	27.5	18.5	8.1
Armenia	100.0	7.5	20.5	16.5
Azerbaijan	97.8	100.0	84.0	100[a]
Kazakhstan	100.0	99.2	100[b]	90
Uzbekistan	100.0	87.4	85.6	81.4[a]
Kirghizia	100.0	89.5	100.0	90
Tadzhikistan	100.0	92.7	93.4	90
Turkmenistan	100.0	90.2	96.1	90
All-Union	n.a.	n.a.	96.4	91.4

Source: Spring 1989, 1990 from *Krasnaia zvezda*, 12 July 1990, 1; Fall 1990 from Krivosheev testimony, Komitet po molodezhnoi politike, Verkhovnogo soveta SSSR, unpublished stenogram of Hearing, 4 April 1990; Spring 1991 (and Fall 1990 All-Union) from *Izvestiia*, 22 July 1991, 2.

a. In Russia, Western Ukraine, and Azerbaijan reports of full compliance with plan targets in 1991 are contradicted by first-hand accounts of widespread disregard of the draft and may have been achieved either by false reporting or by simply lowering targets. The unreliability of these 1991 figures is reinforced by a 27 July 1991 interview with an Uzbek official, who called the 81.4 percent compliance figure reported earlier by *Izvestiia* "clearly a mistake." This official claimed the draft plan "has been fulfilled by 101.8 percent," but went on to note that this included conscripts drafted into "nonmilitary formations" comprising "youth who for various reasons are not being drafted to do actual military service and will work in the national economy."

b. Even total fulfillment of the conscription target did not automatically imply the absence of resistance to the draft. In Kazakhstan in fall 1990, for instance, 1,500 young men evaded the draft, but the draft boards were able to meet their targets anyway.

information. As 1991 began it still controlled a formidable troop force, and republican governments did not. Fearing a further erosion of control over conscription activities at the street level, it moved to reassert its primacy on several fronts.[146] Most spectacularly, on 7 January 1991, the Ministry of Defense announced it would use airborne troops to enforce the draft in the Baltics. In Estonia, the Prime Minister of the republic instructed all Estonian youth serving "alternative service" (roughly 8,000 had avoided the draft in this way) to take an immediate "winter vacation"; he further suggested they not stay at home.[147] In the end, these troops were used not to enforce the draft but to assault government buildings in Lithuania and Latvia. After the deaths of fourteen civilians in Lithuania and four militiamen in Riga, the defense ministry withdrew airborne troops on 30 January.

The unsuccessful Baltic deployment severely worsened the position of the Ministry of Defense. It had shown itself unable to reassert control over breakaway republics. Accordingly, it became more urgent for it to neutralize the institutions which had challenged it. Reporters covering stories of dedovshchina, gruppovshchina and other "negative manifestations" including draft evasion and desertion found themselves called up for service.[148] The same fate awaited some of the more outspoken young deputies in local soviets.[149] Mothers active in the KSM found themselves viciously attacked in the press and blamed for raising sons in ill health and lacking the discipline to resist dedovshchina.[150] The settling of scores extended all the way to the Council of Ministers: on 19 July 1991 Gennadii Iagodin was fired from his post as chairman of the State Committee on Education, reportedly at the urging of Minister of Defense Iazov. Iagodin's dismissal, which was overturned by Gorbachev when he returned from abroad several days later, was reportedly a payback for his support of educational deferments.[151]

Education deferments also came under renewed attack. In December 1990 two contending proposals for military reform were published—one authored by Vladimir Lopatin, the young reformist major, and the other prepared by the Ministry of Defense. The Lopatin plan, prepared by a group of deputies in the USSR Supreme Soviet, envisioned a fairly rapid transition to a professional, volunteer army, supported by territorial militias and allowing alternative service during the transition. The defense ministry draft, though far less radical, also offered significant reforms, including a reduced term of service (eighteen months army, two years navy), alternative nonmilitary service, and broader participation on local draft boards. The defense ministry draft was adopted as the basis for discussion.[152]

By April, however, it was becoming clear that the Ministry of Defense had little intention of permitting deputies to amend its plan, even though it required parliamentary passage. A Supreme Soviet Committee meeting to consider draft policy was told flatly that the number of draftees was a "state secret."[153] Furthermore, it was told that the Presidential order to disband military construction battalions in the civilian economy had been implemented in seventeen ministries but that stroibaty would remain in four civilian ministries until at least 1994. These remaining battalions, according to mobilization chief Krivosheev, comprised over half the military construction troops serving on nonmilitary projects.

Under questioning by deputies, Krivosheev revealed a link in military plans for stroibaty and alternative service. By offering a thirty-month tour of nonmilitary service on construction projects to conscientious objectors (fifteen months for graduates of higher education), the defense ministry could "eliminate the need for military construction brigades in the civilian economy." A deputy from Latvia expressed "astonishment that the respected speaker sees alternative service as a direct replacement for stroibaty."[154] He explained that those deputies drafting legislation on alternative service envisioned medical or community service, not construction projects.

In a particularly jarring declaration, Krivosheev announced that the navy had unilaterally reduced terms of service from three years to two, effective immediately. Several deputies supported this outcome but objected to the manner of the decision. Shortening the naval tour would, for instance, revive pressure to suspend deferments, limiting the policy options open to the Supreme Soviet; more disturbing, if the defense ministry could shorten terms without parliamentary approval, it could also lengthen them. The admission led to the following tense exchange:

Krivosheev: The Supreme Soviet is reviewing the documents. But in spite of the fact that no decision has been reached, we continue to fulfill the plan and this year we are beginning to demobilize those who were supposed to serve a third year. And next year we will shift to a two-year term of service.

V. Minin (deputy): On what basis will you make this shift?

Krivosheev: On the basis of the Ministry of Defense. We have received *oral agreement* from the President and government. But not yet from the Supreme Soviet.[155]

Finally, Krivosheev revisited the question of drafting students, repeating defense ministry objections to educational deferments. He suggested that if deferments of VUZ students were "temporarily suspended," the term of service could be reduced to eighteen months. He added, disingenuously, "That is for you to decide, comrades people's deputies."

Later that afternoon, V. Bespalov, the military commissar of the city of Moscow, put the defense ministry's case more bluntly: either the Law on Universal Military Service should make service truly universal, or the Supreme Soviet should write a new law. He further suggested that, to set the proper example for the younger generation, only citizens who had served in the armed forces would be eligible to hold a government position. "This is how it is done in civilized countries," he declared, grandly. He was certainly aware that his screening criterion would exclude from public office none other than Mikhail Gorbachev.

During the spring, military officials sought to portray the state of the draft as exceedingly grim—so grim, in fact, that drastic measures were warranted. In a departure from historical precedent, they suggested that the induction order be signed by the Cabinet of Ministers rather than by the Ministry of Defense. In this way, one official argued, it would be legally binding on civilian organs like local draft boards.[156] Such a proposal would also give the army the legal justification to send troops to enforce decisions of local draft boards directly, without relying on less cooperative local authorities. Throughout the spring of 1991 Moscow was rife with rumors that troops were scouring the Metro for draft-dodging youth.

On 17 June Minister of Defense Iazov told a closed session of the Supreme Soviet that the armed forces were 353,000 men short owing to recruitment and conscription problems and that only 6 percent of the draft target was being met in Georgia, Armenia, and the Baltics.[157] Iazov complained that every republic was refusing to surrender conscripts to serve outside its own borders, and he warned that, without drastic action, the armed forces might face a 21 percent manpower shortfall by the end of the year.

The following month, Supreme Soviet deputies revealed that the military service law being shepherded toward approval by defense ministry officials no longer contained a provision for higher educational deferments.[158] General Staff officials admitted that the educational deferment had again been dropped. They defended the move on grounds of social equity (i.e., resuming the student draft would permit the army to preserve health and family deferments utilized by workers or rural youth), manpower shortage (1990 draft totals were said to be just 68 percent of 1980 totals), and the continued decline in the size of the draft pool.[159] Most significantly, the draft Military Service Law was said to be on its way to the Council of Ministers for consideration by 20 July 1991, and "the basic refinements to the draft are being carried out by the Ministry of Defense" working through a "special subcommittee" created to draft the law.[160] The Ministry of Defense had usurped control over the legislative agenda from the Supreme Soviet and was using this control to reverse its painful defeat just two years earlier.

At the beginning of August, Iagodin, back in his post at the head of Gosobrazovaniia, warned that Defense Minister Iazov had formally asked Gorbachev to sign a decree suspending student deferments effective with the 1991 fall draft. The Supreme Soviet would be bypassed altogether.[161] Gorbachev's response to this request is unknown, because on 19 August he found himself prisoner of a conspiracy led in part by the Defense Minister himself.

Final Fragmentation: After the Coup

After the collapse of the August coup attempt, the new chief of the Soviet General Staff, Vladimir Lobov, wasted little time in announcing that the armed forces would not, after all, resume drafting students.[162] The creation of the Commonwealth of Independent States in December and the announcement several months later that Russia would form its own Ministry of Defense effectively left draft policy in the hands of individual republics. In most post-Soviet states conscription has continued but at varying levels of comprehensiveness and effectiveness.

In Russia conscription levels continued to slump. In many parts of the country, including virtually all Moscow raions, representatives of the Committee of Soldiers' Mothers continued to serve as volunteer members of draft boards. In the spring 1992 draft, almost 50 percent of draftees called up in Moscow received medical deferments.[163] Overall, the conscription rate in Moscow slumped to a meager 9 percent (this is presumably comparable to the 22 percent figure from 1991).[164] Enforcement of the draft also remained problematic: while defense officials claimed that 7 percent of conscripts in Russia were no-shows, only thirty-eight were prosecuted for draft evasion.

In February 1993, the Russian parliament passed a new law on military service.[165] While universal military service remained a fundamental principle, the law also contained provisions for "alternative service" (to be defined in separate legislation) and "contract service" (i.e., volunteer service as a first step toward a professional force). Educational deferments were retained, but not without renewed opposition from military officials. Also retained were categories of medical certification like "limited fitness for military service." Both deferments and medical classifications were subject to administrative, not just legislative, adjustment. In a tacit acknowledgment of the severity and self-perpetuating nature of intraservice violence, a special draft exemption was created for brothers of conscripts killed while in service. Finally, draft boards were made more definitively civilian institutions, no longer chaired by the local military commissar but rather by the city or district "head of administration."

The new law in Russia solved none of the agency problems faced by military planners. Defense officials remained dependent on local, civilian organs to supply them with conscripts, and the impoverished force's offer of "contract service" has not stopped the decline in manpower levels.[166] The shortages are almost certainly exacerbated by the norms of allowable noncompliance established in recent years—draft boards have been far more liberal in granting deferments, even if that means failing to meet conscription targets.[167]

During 1995 the Russian defense ministry was again targeting student deferments and restored the length of conscript service to two years.[168] The Committee of Soldiers' Mothers continued its fight against this retrenchment, but the mothers' vigorous opposition to the war in Chechnya won them few allies in Yeltsin's inner circle. The military has apparently reconsolidated its control over the conscription system, though the potential for further fragmentation exists.[169] A decisive 1995 Duma debate on conscription policy was held in secret.

In the non-Russian republics, the potential for these conflicts may be less severe.[170] In Caucasian republics engaged in regional conflicts, or in Central Asian republics still essentially under single-party rule, civil-military disputes over draft policy may be stifled for some time to come. In that case, military planners may confront the same hidden action problems encountered by Soviet counterparts throughout the 1960s and 1970s, but probably not the open challenge to their authority which undermined centralized control over conscription after 1989.

Summary

Unlike the Komsomol or the system of postgraduation job assignments, the military draft did not end with the collapse of the Soviet Union. However, it did share many of the problems of its sibling institutions prior to the Soviet collapse. For decades, the capacity of the Soviet system to mobilize its citizens for the draft was eroding, and the army was developing an increasing class bias. Deviation from the norms of universal conscription was long the rule rather than the exception.

As the Soviet draft pool shrank, inflexible quotas forced local draft boards to induct young men who were increasingly unfit or unsuited for army service. This behavior, in turn, provoked a wave of grass-roots protest that worked symbiotically with newly autonomous or newly elected representative bodies eager to establish their own power. Early setbacks for military planners on issues like the draft and demobilization of students punctured their shield of invincibility and opened the door for more serious challenges.

The sudden loss of control over draft policy by the Ministry of Defense after 1989 did not result from any direct policy shift by the Party leadership. Soviet leaders up to and including Gorbachev never wavered in their support for the universality of military service. By itself, the reinstatement of student deferments did not represent an erosion of this principle. The decision merely restored previously existing exemptions for VUZ students. Rather, Gorbachev's great departure from precedent was to suggest that draft policy was itself a topic suitable for national debate. This opened the door for Supreme Soviet deputies to assert themselves and led to the defense ministry's first significant setback.[171]

The decision on students was, at first, not all that far-reaching. The reinstatement of educational deferments was made possible in part by

Gorbachev's announced ground force reductions and was not loudly opposed by defense officials. The demobilization of students already serving could also have been a minor decision—fewer than 200,000 individuals were affected out of a force of nearly five million—had top military officials not resisted it so forcefully. Groups all over the country were able to watch the military's campaign to keep those students in uniform rebuffed by the Supreme Soviet and then see this setback ratified by Gorbachev's government. Many observers in Moscow with whom I spoke agreed that the July 1989 decision to demobilize the 176,000 student-soldiers opened the floodgates.

Contrary to an image that has become popular, the wave of street-level noncompliance that followed the July decision was not exactly a grassroots explosion of draft dodging. It was, instead, a wave of street-level noncompliance by the field agents who managed conscription—by draft boards and local governments. Young men across the country could not have successfully kept out of uniform if local officials had not *allowed* them to do so by granting deferments more liberally, abandoning prosecution of draft dodgers, and acknowledging the instructions of republican parliaments to exempt youth in "alternative" service and to not send draftees beyond republican borders.

The role of glasnost' in the undermining of the draft is also important to note. Prior to 1986, the military's monopoly over the flow of information on the draft was all but total, extending to comprehensive censorship of reporting on army life in general and to military maneuvers in Afghanistan in particular. After the mid-1980s, however, the press began to paint army life as a Hobson's choice between death in Afghanistan or torture at the hands of senior officers or ethnic gangs. The military's angry response to these reports was its first sign of weakness, suggesting it had tried but failed to prevent their publication. Further signs came from ongoing coverage of draft dodging and civil disobedience. The Baltic republics' success in keeping their sons out of the army was watched by groups throughout the country and soon emulated. The Ministry of Defense was unable to perpetuate the myth that military service was honored as a "sacred duty" by citizens in all parts of the country.

Draft board agents ultimately undermined the authority of their Ministry of Defense principals by acknowledging the rights of other principals to set draft policy. Even in districts where Ministry of Defense control was not directly challenged, many draft boards granted deferments that made it impossible for conscription targets to be met; since they were civilian institutions, the military could not directly enforce these targets by simply replacing draft board personnel. Thus, the decisions of local draft boards temporarily undermined the property rights of the Ministry of Defense over the resources necessary to conduct a nationwide call-up; in non-Russian republics, these resources were transferred to the control of the republican legislatures.

In contrast to the previous cases, however, we do not observe a full-scale bank run at the street level of the draft hierarchy. The hierarchy of military commissariats remained mostly intact, shifting their allegiances to republic-level authorities. One explanation for this is suggested by specificity of voenkomat assets. Unlike the assets controlled by Komsomol committees or VUZy, draft board resources were specific to the activity of conscription. Put differently, while Komsomol committees could spend dues money to open video salons or banks, draft boards could not really "draft" youth into nonmilitary organizations. If the draft were to collapse, draft boards would no longer exist and their resources (and their rents) would be dissipated. Though this may have been the ultimate aim of groups like the Committee of Soldiers' Mothers, it was not in the interests of most of the agents at the street level of the draft hierarchy.

The Breakdown of Hierarchy:
Comparative Perspectives

> "Our dominant impression of things Russian is an impression of a
> vast, irreparable breakdown."
>
> —H.G. WELLS (1920)

Reviewing the Case Study Evidence

The case studies presented in the last three chapters offer three views of
hierarchical breakdown after the onset of the Gorbachev reforms. In each
case study, actors at the street level of the hierarchy ultimately defied
those actors who previously had the unchallenged authority to issue
orders to them. The catalysts for the organizational crisis are not identical
in each case however, nor are the resulting institutional structures. These
differences are summarized in Table 7.1.

Each case study considered the nature of hierarchical authority and
control prior to the crises of the late 1980s and the erosion of those
controls under Gorbachev. Guiding each case-study presentation were the
hypotheses developed in Chapters 1 and 2 as tests of contending models
of institutional breakdown. I now return to these hypotheses explicitly
and consider which models are supported or disconfirmed by the evidence
I have been discussing.

Ideological Decay

> *H1.1: Mid- and lower-level bureaucrats exhibited significant levels of ideological
> conformity prior to the breakdown of hierarchical control.*

The data presented in Chapter 3 suggested that cynicism was the norm
not merely among youth but also among the officials of the Soviet youth
program. The perspectives offered by the individual case studies do little
to reverse this judgment. Komsomol secretaries who were supposedly in
charge of indoctrination were actively squelching any members' expressions of zeal that might require special attention on their part. VUZ and

Table 7.1. Characteristics of Hierarchical Breakdown

Case	Catalyst	Outcome
Komsomol	Discontinuation of mandatory growth targets and fiscal devolution to local organizations (greater autonomy for agents)	Disintegration of Komsomol
Job Assignments	"Self-financing" for VUZy and enterprises (greater autonomy for agents)	Transition from hierarchy to market in higher education
Conscription	Liberal draft deferment guidelines approved by republican legislatures (emergence of alternative principals)	Hierarchy intact, but republican control over commissariats

labor ministry officials were criticizing university graduates for shunning job assignments in their chosen field even as these same officials inflated labor demand figures and wasted those specialists who did show up. Military officers in charge of conscription similarly castigated youth who sought to evade service even as they dispatched ill or lame young men to work alongside hardened criminals in brutal conditions.

It seems clear, then, that "true believers" among the administrative elite were in the minority. While the 1980s certainly witnessed a public disavowal of many tenets of orthodox Soviet ideology, the evidence suggests this played little role in the crumbling of the Soviet bureaucratic edifice. Well before the 1980s, ideology had ceased to be the mortar holding that edifice together.

Elite Politics

H1.2: Actions of mid- and lower-level bureaucrats prior to the breakdown were determined by, or at least consistent with, instructions from higher levels of the bureaucracy. Commands from above were implemented, at least in large part.
H1.2a: Once breakdown began, divisions within the administrative bureaucracy mirrored divisions among the elite.

These hypotheses explored the core of elite-driven theories of Soviet and post-Soviet politics, and they find mixed support in the case-study data.

Throughout the post-War period, Komsomol agents at the street level paid little heed to the detailed guidelines that were supposed to govern league work. Top Komsomol officials were given wide latitude by the Party to determine how success in "indoctrination" was to be measured; they defined it in terms that minimally constrained abuses at the street level.[1] Likewise, the year-to-year functioning of raspredelenie bore only a faint resemblance to the way the system was supposed to work. Only in the case of the draft was street-level behavior actually directed—rather than just constrained at the margins—by the authoritative commands of higher-level policy makers.

The details of organizational breakdown, consequently, do not consistently reflect coalitional politics at higher levels. The Komsomol's disintegration was so complete that factional politics seem to have been completely overshadowed by the street-level bank run on league assets. While the conflict among Komsomol leaders over future league policies did serve to preclude any forceful response to street-level opportunism, it was not ultimately reflected in a split of the organization into contending wings.

In the raspredelenie case, similarly, evidence suggests that policy makers were trying to keep up with practices at the street level—particularly with regard to side-contracting between VUZy and enterprises—rather than directing them in any meaningful sense. In the end, raspredelenie was left in the formal guidelines issued by Gosobrazovaniia, even though its implementation was no longer possible at the street level. As late as 1995, Gosobrazovaniia was still attempting to dictate the terms of contracts between VUZy and employers that would bind students to their jobs for at least three years after graduation.[2]

Only in the case of the draft was the fragmentation of the system consistent with the elite cleavages that shaped the struggle over control of the hierarchy. In this case, the challenge to hierarchical authority came initially from outside the institutional hierarchy, rather than below. But, significantly, it was the decision of local draft boards to be guided by republican legislation rather than Soviet law that turned a temporary setback by the defense ministry (over student deferrals) into a challenge to its authority. Organizational fragmentation was not merely a consequence of the breakup of the Union being played out at higher levels but rather an important and integral factor in deciding this conflict.

Societal Interests

H1.3: Street-level bureaucrats prior to the breakdown monitored the demands of and policy impacts on distinct societal groups.
H1.3a: Once breakdown began, divisions within the administrative bureaucracy mirrored divisions in society.

Chapter 3 disputed the notion that the Gorbachev era was accompanied by a generational upheaval of disaffected youth; signs of anomie covered prominently in the press were nothing new to Soviet society. The case studies examined indirect representation of societal interests and found that, while street-level actors or even policy makers may have been aware of some grass-roots demands, they had little impact on the formulation or even conduct of policy. Komsomol and raspredelenie officials collected sociological and statistical data relevant to, respectively, indoctrination and youth employment; even the army conducted sociological studies of draftees. But there is little evidence in any of these studies of a degree of policy responsiveness suggesting that any officials in these hierarchies acted as "representatives" of societal interests.

The Komsomol, which played a role in three of these policy areas and was the designated institutional voice for Soviet youth, did assemble a wealth of data from its own networks and from outside experts. For the most part, these data were either used to illustrate prefabricated official resolutions or were swallowed by meaningless rituals of deliberative policy making like league-wide Congresses. Direct articulation of interests was rare; when opinions were actually sought "from below," they were quickly repackaged and disposed of, leaving little impact on the agendas of either top policy makers or local officials.

Direct articulation of societal interests was most evident in the draft case, where the military establishment had been least concerned about the consequences of conscription policy on other spheres of life. Ironically, the most vocal groups that organized to challenge the defense ministry were not composed of draftees but of their mothers (and, later, their fathers as well). Thus, the attack on the draft and crisis of military manpower policy seems the strongest candidate for a case of "societal capture" of the three cases studied.

This conclusion is not supported by the details of the breakup of the draft hierarchy; more specifically, Hypothesis H1.3a is not supported. The machinery of the draft was fragmented not along social, but along political (i.e., nationalist), lines. Though the authority of the Soviet Defense Ministry was first challenged successfully by an alliance of social groups (mothers) and legislatures (in the newly elected Supreme Soviets), the interests of those groups were not especially furthered by subsequent events. The post-Soviet Russian army has made only halting progress toward professionalization, as the parents' groups had strongly urged, and there has been significant backsliding even on core issues like the student draft. Control over conscription policy seems to be moving out of the hands of the legislatures (at least in Russia) back to the Russian Ministry of Defense, though the ratio of draftees eligible for deferrals remains far above pre-Gorbachev levels. Thus, the breakup of the conscription hierarchy delivered uncertain benefits at best to draftees.

From the perspective of "who benefits" (admittedly a functional measure of interest representation), the conscription breakup more closely resembles the breakup of the Komsomol and the collapse of the job-assignments system. The former benefited few youth other than former Komsomol officials, while the latter presented college graduates with massive employment challenges. These two cases also fail to support H1.3a: the only cleavages that emerged from either the disintegration of the Komsomol or the collapse of raspredelenie were economic alliances. Apparently, bureaucratic actors were chiefly protecting their own narrow interests.[3]

Though the evidence does not support assigning societal interests a direct role in the fragmentation of administrative structures, the case studies did reveal an important contextual role for societal actors. The mass exodus of rank-and-file members from the Komsomol helped trigger the fiscal crisis that precipitated the bank run. In the case of the draft, not only did mothers' groups exert pressure on legislators, but mass demonstrations in the non-Russian republics emboldened legislators to adopt more liberal conscription regulations at odds with Kremlin policy.

In both cases, however, mass publics were responding to the same catalysts that caused bureaucrats to rethink their roles in the hierarchy: limited reform initiatives that appeared as an external shock. As noted in the Introduction, the objective of this analysis is not to explain the Gorbachev shock, but rather why it resulted in the disintegration of once-stable institutions. While societal processes may have reinforced centrifugal tendencies within the administrative apparatus, the case studies provide little evidence that social forces were the source of these tendencies.

"Behavioral" Theories of Institutions

H2.6: As reforms begin and levels of uncertainty begin to escalate, lower-level bureaucrats should react incrementally. They should not depart radically from established rules.

The details of all three cases studies clearly show that bureaucratic actors were capable of dramatic acts of defiance in response to relatively small changes in their decision environment. Rather than reacting conservatively to the uncertainties of reform, street-level actors appear to have been carefully evaluating the consequences of actions taking place around them. Their response to uncertainty, rather than being conservative, suggests a "threshold" effect; a certain level of uncertainty about the clarity of principals' property rights would trigger a decisive defiance of formal lines of authority.

The disintegration of the Komsomol provides the most dramatic evidence of the weakness of behavioral predictions. Once they gained control over their budgets, many local officials showed an enthusiasm for entrepreneurship that would put Donald Trump or Bill Gates to shame. As a consequence, many of these former Komsomol officials are now leading Russia's new business elite. We cannot, therefore, accept the tempting image of bureaucratic sclerosis and blame the demise of the Soviet system on its "rigidity" and "its inability to innovate."[4] Rather, the case studies suggest that Soviet institutions collapsed because they were unable to control the innovations launched by their agents at the street level; they collapsed because they became, in a sense, too flexible.

Neoinstitutional Bank Run

Evidence from all three case studies supports the main elements of the neoinstitutional model, both in its description of the nature and limits of hierarchical control prior to Gorbachev and in its account of a cascading breakdown of authority.

H2.1: Agents in Soviet hierarchies exploited information asymmetries to evade monitoring by principals.

In all three case studies, street-level agents used compliance with formal performance targets to mask their disregard of more fundamental guidelines of behavior. Komsomol officials, for instance, hid problems of their apathetic membership and abandonment of real ideological training behind reports of steadily growing membership saturation rates.

In the case of raspredelenie, problems of monitoring were compounded by the division of responsibilities across two bureaucratic structures, Gosobrazovaniia and Gosplan. The most significant statistics on the shortcomings of the job-assignment process—particularly no-show or dropout rates by graduates or poor utilization of specialists by enterprises—were collected by labor officials, who wielded no direct authority over street-level actors implementing the system. By keeping control over labor statistics and graduation rates, these officials were able to respond to the misallocation of graduates by striking ad hoc side deals.

Information asymmetries were probably least severe within the conscription system, since the number or fitness of conscripts or officer candidates could not be concealed from superiors. Though induction of students and even infirm youth was explicitly directed by top policy makers, street-level actors still capitalized on the slack offered to them by the discretion inherent in secret medical guidelines. Despite growing criticisms of the quality of the draft pool, local draft boards continued to send ill or unfit conscripts to the field.

In none of the organizations studied did planners manage to construct any plan-independent monitoring system—that is, an information system through which planners could reliably monitor the accuracy of agents' reports of their own performance. Indeed, the evidence presented strongly suggests that falsified, or at least highly selective, performance reports were readily accepted from subordinates because they allowed managers to more easily meet their own performance targets.

In each case study, press reports and internal discussions clearly indicate that policy makers had concerns about the qualitative aspects of policy implementation (i.e., the ideological commitment of new Komsomol members or the health of draftees), yet the primary monitored indicators remained the aggregate figures of enrollment or assignment or induction. In the case of job assignments, relevant information was not even compiled: statistical agencies were blocked until the late 1980s from collecting and publishing data related to the real demand for VUZ-educated specialists.

Since actors at even the highest levels of each bureaucracy were simultaneously agents of principals in the Party hierarchy, no policy maker was ever forced to assume the risk associated with his or her performance; all actors hid behind artificial reporting that protected each of them from the unpleasant truths of organizational failure. While Gorbachev's reforms affected the collection and processing of information, they did little to enforce accountability at any link in this long chain.

H2.2: If reforms exacerbate information asymmetries between principals and agents (for instance, by weakening monitoring mechanisms), opportunism by agents should increase.

In the case of the Komsomol, the critical shift in the organizational balance of power came when local committees gained control over their own budgets and were relieved of their obligation to meet enrollment targets. Taken together, these steps gave local organizations the means to ignore central directives and deprived central administrators of the mechanism to issue those directives through the planning system. Komsomol officials responded not by redoubling efforts to enroll new members but by seeking commercial sources of revenue to replace plunging dues and subscription income.

In the case of raspredelenie, the shift from Gosplan-coordinated assignments to "negotiated placement" similarly offered VUZy an independent resource stream (from enterprises) and deprived Gosobrazovaniia planners of their chief means for measuring and controlling the placement of graduates. VUZy responded by offering enterprises unprecedented input into the details of student training, formerly the exclusive purview of Gosobrazovaniia.

In the case of the conscription hierarchy, the internal balance of power shifted not through the empowerment of local agents but by the direct weakening of the previously unchallenged principal. The Ministry of Defense was challenged publicly and successfully on the draft and demobilization of students, guidelines for medical deferments, and policies on construction battalions. In effect, the USSR Supreme Soviet—and republican parliaments, especially in the Baltics and Transcaucasus—emerged as alternate principals. By drafting new laws on military and alternate service (and, in the non-Russian republics, actually passing them), legislators were essentially claiming control rights over the lower levels of the (civilian) draft hierarchy and asserting the right to dictate how draft boards should operate.

H2.3: If opportunism by agents escalates to expropriation of organizational assets, principals' authority to enforce other property rights claims (without resorting to force) will be weakened and opportunism will spread until the hierarchy collapses altogether.

When hidden actions are no longer hidden, the authority relationship at the heart of the principal-agent relationship comes under direct threat. In this framework, hidden action should not threaten the hierarchy because it is anticipated in the "contract" between principal and agent. Agents' activities beyond the bounds of prescribed behavior are constrained by their understanding that the principal can revoke their right to control her resources. When some agents observe others disregarding behavioral guidelines with impunity, therefore, the principal's control over her resources comes into doubt, and an organizational bank run is unleashed. Thanks in large part to glasnost', noncompliance by selected agents could not be easily concealed.

Local Komsomol committees used local assets for purely commercial ventures and to prepare "golden parachutes" in the event of the organization's demise. VUZ officials used income derived from direct contracting to replace ministerial subsidies and permit independence from ministerial control. Local draft boards observed the Ministry of Defense's loss of control over draft policy and its inability to punish draft evaders and they concluded they could allow conscription targets to go unmet for the first time. In each case, defiance of central control spread rapidly, as field agents realized that they could act with impunity.

It is important when considering this to remember that no Soviet organizations were ever designed for the eventuality of a transfer of power—no scenario ever envisioned an end to Communist Party rule. Therefore, whereas American agencies are created by governing parties with constraints to limit the harm they might eventually do in the hands of their opponents,[5] Soviet organizations had no such provisions. The consequences of political change at the center, therefore, were incalculable. Komsomol in the hands of an opposition faction, for instance, would almost certainly purge officials at all levels. With this in mind, the bank run impulse by youth league officials seems even more understandable.

H2.4: Organizations whose assets are less specific are more likely to be susceptible to bank run collapses.

The three institutions at the heart of the case studies controlled organizational assets of varying degrees of specificity. This variance helps explain the different outcomes observed among the cases. The variation among observed outcomes also undermines the reductionist assertion that all three case studies are manifestations of the same systemic processes of breakdown or responses to external pressures. Certainly there were social, economic, and international pressures at work on the Soviet system, but they did not affect all institutions in the same way. Variation among the cases suggests that street-level actors were rationally calculating the costs and benefits of attempting to deploy their local assets outside the bureaucratic hierarchy.

For instance, Komsomol buildings, bank accounts, printing presses, and the like were easily transferred to other uses, and little now remains of the youth league besides the personal networks forged among its officials. Assets at VUZy were more difficult to redistribute, since the organizational collapse did not extend to the breakup of the educational institutions themselves (though in some cases, more profitable faculties were spun off as profit-making schools for managers or lawyers, often in partnership with a Western university). The job-assignments case, therefore, can more accurately be summarized as a transition from hierarchy to market. The conscription system, finally, utilized resources that were specific to the military mobilization of young men. Equally important, the officials in charge of conscription derived high rents from their discretion over the granting of deferments; these rents were highly specific to the conscription process. The draft hierarchy, therefore, did not dissolve but rather redistributed itself among the fifteen new republican principals.

H2.5: The likelihood and pace of hierarchical breakdown will be affected by principals' responses to early episodes of open defiance: punishment of offenders will retard disintegration, while acquiescence will accelerate the level of challenges.

H2.5a: Unsuccessful attempts to punish defiant agents will accelerate the processes of hierarchical collapse.

The Komsomol Central Committee's moves to protect its own assets were clear signals that the employees of the central administration were anticipating a fragmentation of the organization and led to a rapid nullification of its ability to constrain the redeployment of assets by local committees. Similarly, Gosobrazovaniia could do little to halt the incipient "privatization" of the higher-education system, despite its recognition that no safety net was in place for those students who would be left unemployed.

The Ministry of Defense did attempt to reassert control over draft boards in the Baltics, with disastrous consequences. Thousands of other draft boards were then left to reconsider with whom their allegiance should lie as the fragmentation of the country suddenly loomed as a possibility. Extremely high exemption and deferral rates during the first few rounds of post-Soviet conscription suggest that the Russian defense ministry remains even less able than its Soviet predecessor to enforce strict compliance with quotas on the part of local draft boards.

In the remainder of this chapter, I use the neoinstitutional model of hierarchical control and collapse to examine other Soviet and Soviet-type institutions. I begin by looking at other bank run dynamics under Gorbachev, including one notable case where hierarchical controls apparently remained intact. I then look at Chinese institutions, which implemented decentralizing policies similar to those tried under Gorbachev without unleashing a comparable wave of agent defections. Unlike the "structured focused comparison" approach utilized in the case studies, this discussion is not intended to be rigorous; the goal is to demonstrate that the model illuminates the breakdown of the most central institutional pillars of the Soviet system and the relative robustness and adaptability of comparable structures in China.

Additional Manifestations of Soviet Institutional Breakdown

The most significant organizational reforms in the early Gorbachev period affected the economy and were intended to transfer decision-making power from central planners to firm-level managers, in part to alleviate hidden information problems.[6] The 1987 Law on State Enterprises began the shift from mandatory central planning to a less comprehensive system of state orders and introduced "self-financing" for firms and other organizational units. Subsequent legislation provided for the establishment of cooperatives or "small firms" that operated under the umbrella of larger state enterprises but were organizationally and legally distinct.

In theory, these moves implied that the budget constraint faced by managers would become harder, but that they would also have more options available (for example, sale of some proportion of their output at liberalized prices) to respond to these new incentives. In practice, however, the cooperatives and small enterprises established by firm managers enabled them to remobilize many assets of state enterprises into organizational units less clearly owned by state ministries.

These micro-level realignments came to be known as "spontaneous privatization," since a frequent pattern was the de facto expropriation by managers and ministerial bureaucrats of many assets belonging to state enterprises.[7] In many cases, these spontaneously privatized concerns collaborated with state bureaucrats eager to "privatize" the functions of the ministries themselves. In the brief period from 1989 to 1991 many managerial responsibilities previously discharged by the industrial planning hierarchy were internalized by enterprises themselves or shared with horizontally or vertically integrated *kontserny*.[8] Even in those cases where kontserny duplicated many of the functions of ministries, their creation served the same function as more radical forms of enterprise-level privatization: the property rights of state actors at higher levels of the bureaucracy over firm-level assets were either blurred or abrogated altogether.

Once it became clear that the ministerial supervisors were unable (or unwilling, given the rent-seeking potential) to stop enterprise managers from claiming de facto ownership rights over assets, the pace of spontaneous privatization accelerated. New "commercial banks" (themselves the result of spontaneous privatization within state banks) became active financiers of managerial buyouts.[9] Industrial ministries consequently disintegrated *well before* the 1992 initiation of a formal privatization program in Russia. Once privatization was decreed, managers extracted important policy concessions to protect their newly won control over enterprise assets; in other words, the property rights they grabbed in 1989–91 during the enterprise-level bank run proved remarkably durable.[10]

A parallel process was unfolding within the hierarchies of control at the municipal level, particularly over retail establishments. The *New York Times* reported on one typical case in the early post-Soviet days. Under the centrally planned system, employees of a Moscow retail clothing store submitted all of their receipts to a regional administrator. This administrator paid their salaries and authorized all purchases of supplies. When the state announced the store would be sold for 2.2 million rubles, several employees (led by the store manager) hoped to buy the store themselves, guaranteeing their continued employment, but lacked the necessary capital. In anticipation of the sale, the store manager began withholding revenues from the administrator (presumably by inflating prices above official levels) to build up a purchase fund.[11] In addition to facilitating the managerial takeover, the ruse presumably deflated the apparent profitability of the property, discouraging alternate purchasers. On the day of the sale, the manager paid cash.[12]

While the hierarchical links within the branch ministries were disintegrating, a similar process was unfolding within the federal and regional administrative systems of the Soviet state. In 1989, the Soviet government began a restricted initiative to devolve certain functions from Moscow to regional levels, reducing direct transfers from the center while giving regional governments new taxing authority over local enterprises.[13] In short order, subnational budgets came under severe pressure from declining tax revenues (the new Law on State Enterprises essentially wiped out the profits that were to be taxed by regional governments) and reduced subsidies from the center.[14] Consequently, regional officials began seeking new sources of revenue, ranging from ad hoc taxes and fees to joint ventures. Since it was virtually impossible for Moscow to measure the scope of these extrabudgetary revenue flows accurately, the activity of regional officials became more difficult to monitor and control through the standard planning mechanisms of the budget.

As regional and republican governments concentrated on closing their own fiscal gaps and on providing new services to voters in upcoming regional elections, they also began selectively withholding revenue transfers from Moscow. Moscow's response to these trends shows a lack of clear resolve. For instance, in late 1989 the Baltic republics lobbied for and received a special economic status that allowed them to define their own tax and fiscal systems. During 1990, however, the Soviet government moved to restrict their autonomy sharply: Lithuania was blockaded, and Estonia was ultimately forced to forward tax payments it had been withholding.

After Yeltsin's election in the summer of 1990 and subsequent declaration of "economic sovereignty" for the Russian Federation, it became impossible for Soviet leaders to maintain the charade of control over republic-level finances. Yeltsin had the capacity to implement unilaterally a single-channel tax payment system for Russia; other union republics sensed the vulnerability of the Soviet government and quickly followed suit. Coupled with unorthodox revenue-generating schemes at the regional level that were difficult to monitor, Soviet leaders found it impossible to even draw up a consolidated budget for 1991.[15] The center found its traditional revenue sources suddenly choked off. Gorbachev could do little to recapture fiscal resources seized by subnational officials except plead for a substantial role for Moscow in the planned Federation Treaty. Thus, the "bank run" by regional officials was essentially irreversible by early 1991, almost a full year before the formal disintegration of the Soviet Union.

Disintegration of both industrial and federal hierarchies within the Soviet system should have been contained by unitary political structures like the Communist Party, trade unions, and Komsomol. The chaotic collapse of the Communist Party in August 1991 has made it unlikely that we will ever be able to fully document internal Party financing or the behavior of local officials on the eve of the CPSU's collapse. What details we have learned suggest that the collapse of the CPSU followed the Komsomol's pattern closely but that it began later and was interrupted by the August coup. Beginning in 1987 and accelerating after the Nineteenth Party Conference in 1988, local and regional Party committees began filling posts by competitive elections. Carried to its logical extreme this practice implied that principals within the Party hierarchy could no longer summarily replace insubordinate agents if those agents owed their positions to direct elections. It also changed agents' incentives, introducing a new degree of uncertainty over their tenure, since not all risk could be transferred to their principals.[16]

Regional and local Party officials were also granted greater authority over their own budgets, a process stressed at the 1990 Party Congress.[17] However, this devolution of power from the Kremlin was a mixed blessing at best. Declining profitability of the Party's economic activities (particularly publishing), coupled with the unprecedented drop in Party membership (down approximately 20 percent in the eighteen months after 1 January 1990), created severe budget gaps at all levels of the Party hierarchy.[18] As Komsomol officials had already learned, transferring responsibility for budgets in this environment was equivalent to transferring responsibility for deficits. Local Party officials quickly discovered it was simpler—and less uncertain—to seek new revenue sources through commercial activity than through recruiting new members. And with tools for monitoring and sanctioning weakened, officials in Moscow could do little to guarantee that the profits of these activities remained in Party coffers.

Beginning around the Twenty-eighth Party Congress in 1990, regional Party officials began preparing their "golden parachutes"—using Party funds to set up regional banks and enterprises where many would find employment after the August 1991 coup. In June 1991 the Politburo approved the transfer of 600 million rubles of central Party funds to commercial organizations (including those created earlier by the Komsomol and through spontaneous privatization of enterprises), thus insulating these funds from the consequences of the Party's impending disintegration. This action certainly signaled uncertainty in the minds of Party leaders over the fate of the Party and helped accelerate the bank run. At the time of the August coup, Party property at all levels was being transferred to "private" owners in a systematic effort to keep these assets under nomenklatura control.[19]

Not all Soviet institutions fragmented under the stress of low-level opportunism. Most notably, the Russian KGB seems to have survived the breakup of the Soviet Union essentially intact, and many observers have concluded that its power remains largely undiminished.[20] The KGB, of course, was a military organization, drawing recruits from the semiannual draft and employing military discipline. But this alone cannot explain the organizational survival of the KGB, especially given the turmoil that struck institutions of conscription and military mobilization.

Data on the internal dynamics of the KGB are relatively scarce, and I cannot here offer a full account of its response to reforms. Nevertheless, it is possible to suggest some characteristics that may explain its organizational robustness in the context of the neoinstitutional model. Three elements stand out: pervasive secrecy, high relative compensation, and asset specificity.

As the monitoring agency of last resort for all institutions in the Soviet system (including the top leadership), the KGB was able to exercise a high degree of control over publicity surrounding its own operations. While glasnost' produced a KGB campaign to change its public image—complete with a "Miss KGB" and occasional revelations about Stalin-era crimes—it did not unleash the torrent of self-flagellating critiques of current operations endured by the Komsomol, the Party, and even the Army. Contemporary KGB operations remained largely hidden from public scrutiny. An important corollary of this lack of openness was that lapses of discipline in one part of the organization had limited effect on the reputation of the KGB leadership as perceived by field commanders elsewhere in the agency. Top commanders' control over the KGB's assets, therefore, remained unambiguous, and so, in turn, did their authority.

In addition, KGB troops and field commanders were shielded from many of the material deprivations suffered by officers and troops in the regular army. While the press routinely reported on appalling housing conditions for officers or pervasive acts of brutality among conscripts, KGB personnel remained relatively well fed and well housed. By diverting assets to insure their well-being, the top leadership attempted to buy the loyalty of this critical palace guard. In terms of the neoinstitutional model, such a strategy would have raised the perceived riskiness of insubordination. Any attempt to break from the organizational hierarchy would have immediately severed the flow of material benefits to the agent.

Finally, many KGB assets were quite specific, not unlike those of the voenkomaty. The KGB was, according to many accounts, the source of extensive funds for legal and illegal business activity in the post-Soviet environment, so some looting of organizational assets clearly took place.[21] In the case of the KGB, however, most of this activity was apparently confined to the highest levels and was highly clandestine; assets controlled by actors lower in the organizational hierarchy (including reputational assets) were far less fungible. In the regular army, by contrast, many soldiers in the periphery faced a hostile environment within their own units and had little to lose by breaking away; they could improve their lot by trading on their mercenary skills or simply smuggling military hardware.

Chinese Reforms: Successful Decentralization

In China, beginning in 1979, reforms also devolved property rights over many industrial assets and regional fiscal resources from central leaders to lower-level officials.[22] As in the Soviet Union, these reforms gave agents at lower levels of political and economic hierarchies the opportunity and capability to defy principals' authority and break hierarchical controls. In China, however, these controls have strained but not snapped. China-watchers have begun to ask, "Can the center hold?"[23] but to a Soviet-watcher the remarkable feature of Chinese reforms is that the center has held as long as it has.

The Nature of Chinese Reforms

In the early 1980s, economic reforms in China transferred significant autonomy to local and regional governments in two ways. First, in a process akin to spontaneous privatization, local authorities were granted extensive property rights over economic enterprises under their jurisdiction, triggering an explosion of so-called town and village enterprises (TVEs). Second, in a shift analogous to Soviet fiscal decentralization, regions were entitled to keep a significant share of the taxes on regionally "owned" enterprises, passing only a negotiated percentage up to the central government. In many regions, local officials were rapidly transformed into rich industrialists, operating with great independence from hierarchical control.

By the late 1980s, however, the economy in several regions was in danger of severely overheating. Officials at the center attempted to slow economic growth, which in practice meant slowing growth in precisely those regions whose economic success had made them most independent of Beijing. The retrenchment of 1988–91, though imperfectly administered, did succeed in moderating the overall growth rate and driving out the most dangerous inflationary threats.

Since then, however, control over regional officials has been incomplete. Certain regions successfully resisted the imposition of a unified tax code and have evaded attempts to limit investment levels in overheated regions.[24] Furthermore, at its landmark November 1993 Plenum, the Chinese Communist Party leadership agreed to moderate its five-month austerity drive in order to win regional acquiescence in their plans to restructure the banking and fiscal systems.[25]

When contrasted with the Soviet experience, the striking question is how officials in Beijing were able to maintain any measure of control over thriving local economies even in the face of reforms that gave local officials access to resources not directly administered by the center. In Russia, external resource flows acquired by agents made it possible for them to defy hierarchical authority and trigger structural disintegration. In China, although local officials had some success in resisting the intervention of the center, their resistance never triggered the sort of bank run that would render impossible any assertion of authority by leaders in Beijing. How did the Chinese leadership preserve its influence over its local agents as it presided over a reform whose hallmark was devolution of power to regional administrators?

Several mutually reinforcing explanations are possible. First, while the Chinese Communist Party gained new revenue sources from the regional growth explosion, the Party itself avoided internal restructuring along the lines of the CPSU. Second, Chinese reforms clarified rather than obscured property rights and created incentives that addressed rather than exacerbated problems of hidden action and hidden information. Finally, Chinese leaders were more prepared to take decisive actions to preserve their reputation for discipline. I shall elaborate on these in turn.

Whereas Gorbachev's reformers identified "stagnation" as a key shortcoming of the CPSU and Komsomol, Chinese Communist Party (CCP) leaders were forced to rebuild unstable political institutions severely weakened by a decade of Cultural Revolution.[26] (The Chinese youth league needed to be reconstituted entirely and played a far more marginal role than its wealthy Soviet counterpart.) Control over CCP local committees was already highly decentralized, and initiatives to deepen "intra-Party democracy" or devolve power to lower levels of the apparatus never advanced beyond the stage of rhetoric. Instead, "normalization" of Party life was stressed, which in practice meant avoiding further organizational upheaval within the Party.

As economic reform progressed, therefore, and CCP officials at local levels gained access to new sources of revenue retained by local and regional jurisdictions, they did not face the same uncertainties over Party tenure or funding confronted by their CPSU counterparts. Whereas new

forms of economic organization in the Soviet Union became the sponges
for assets withdrawn from the Party or Komsomol, analogous economic
developments in China swelled local Party coffers without triggering an
intra-Party bank run. Intra-Party discipline was only one centripetal factor, however; at least as important were the incentives established by the
economic and fiscal reforms themselves.

Chinese economic reforms depended critically on empowering regional
and rural officials as engines of economic growth. The hallmark of the
reforms was the creation of hybrid organizational forms to control rural
enterprises.[27] These hybrids represented a "virtual partnership" between
enterprise management and local government.[28] Jean Oi has described
this organizational innovation as "local state corporatism," arguing that
it represented a "merger of state and economy" in which "fiscal reform
has assigned local government property rights over increased income."[29]

The delegation of property rights to midlevel administration was not
entirely an innovation of the Deng reforms; the Chinese system had long
been less centralized than the Soviet system. David Granick has argued
that such property rights dated in some cases from as early as 1957 and
were fairly stable since the early 1970s; the Deng reforms, in this view,
changed the scope of these rights.[30] This interpretation has been challenged by Susan Shirk, who argues that even under Deng devolution of
power to local governments ran little risk of "loss of central control"
because the center never lost the power to appoint local officials.[31] The
analysis in this book suggests, first, that it is important to ask *why* the
center has retained this power even as agents increasingly gained the
resources to "defect,"[32] and second, that the critical distinction may be
less the center-periphery allocation of property rights than the way in
which those rights delineated public and private spheres.

Local officials profit from reform both by collection of higher levels of
taxes and by direct profit-sharing in quasi-public rural enterprises. The
reforms have thus created "cadre-entrepreneurs" whose economic interests are tied to property rights that codify local government's role as
shareholder and/or tax authority.[33] These cadre-entrepreneurs—frequently including local Party secretaries—face incentives similar to those
of private businessmen, but they rely on their position in the state bureaucracy to preserve their "quasi-ownership rights."[34] Thus, the Chinese
reforms served to reinforce the state's property rights rather than under-

mine them. Chinese local officials seeking to profit through the commercial deployment of state assets were not driven to move these assets out of the state sector, as in the Soviet case; rather, they faced powerful incentives to keep their state/Party position and accept whatever discipline was necessary to retain it.[35]

The new incentive structure facing officials at the local levels in China is aptly expressed by the use of the term "contracting" to describe the schemes put in place during the 1980s.[36] Beginning in 1981, enterprise managers were guided by "contracts" stipulating either tax or profit targets on a multiyear basis.[37] Since 1987 regional governments were similarly guided by fiscal contracts negotiated with the center, stipulating regional contributions to (or subsidies from) the central budget. These reforms have not weakened the center at the expense of the provinces as some analyses have implied; rather, careful studies of the Chinese fiscal system suggest that "the overall decline in budgetary revenues, rather than a change in the distribution of those revenues between center and local . . . is the more important trend of the reform era."[38]

Walder has characterized the effect of these reforms as producing a shift from "hierarchical authority" to "bilateral contracting," but the more remarkable feature of this transformation is that—unlike in the Soviet case—these new "contracts" have proved enforceable.[39] "State and Party officials" continue to exercise "all rights to control, income flows, and sale or liquidation" from both TVEs and state firms.[40] Regional governments continue to forward tax payments to Beijing.[41] The central government has even been able to partially "recentralize" some fiscal and financial functions, first during the 1988–89 retrenchment and more recently (though less effectively) during 1993–94 "rationalizations" surrounding the Third Plenum of the Fourteenth Party Congress.[42] In China, in other words, policies aimed at decentralization actually produced decentralization, and not a Soviet-style bank run.

In addition to creating incentives for preserving some hierarchical links, the Chinese reforms also left in place—and even strengthened—the management information system previously based on central planning.[43] The planning system itself was dismantled far more gradually than in the Soviet case, avoiding the information vacuum that crippled Soviet leaders.[44] As Kenneth Lieberthal notes, "Reforms have, on balance, shifted control over resources—especially over budgetary resources—to lower bureaucratic levels in the system. But this same reform effort has effectively created greater central-level control over information and skills."[45]

In part, this central-level control is the result of new central bureaus devoted to statistical data-gathering and economic policy research.[46] In addition, however, the tax and profit contracting systems erected in place of central planning gave officials greater incentives to monitor the economic activities of their subordinates. While the soft budget constraint continued to shield branch managers in the Soviet system, Chinese local officials quickly saw the fiscal incentives to maximize their revenue. Their incomes—both their bonuses and their budgets—were directly tied to the economic performance of enterprises under their jurisdiction.[47] In other words, the new Chinese system rewarded local officials for addressing precisely those problems of hidden action and hidden information that the Soviet reforms had only exacerbated.

This Chinese fiscal policy of "eating in separate kitchens" introduced a new challenge to central control, however.[48] Although local authorities directly retained a share of profits on rural enterprises, tax rates were still set at the center (unilaterally, or through negotiations with the regions). Local authorities in economically active areas thus began manipulating the balance between rural enterprise budgets and profit remittances to minimize the revenues that must be shared with the center. They also began to levy ad hoc fees and to raid extrabudgetary funds (i.e., reserves) maintained by enterprises for the purpose of strategic investment. As a result of this fiscal crunch, rural enterprises have been forced to endure increasing levels of micro-level intervention by state actors. The result has been increasing manipulation of profit and budget figures by rural cadre-entrepreneurs, which will make it increasingly difficult for officials in Beijing to monitor field-level activities and maintain their control.

Finally, the CCP's actions in Tiananmen Square during the summer of 1989 can be viewed as an explicit strategy to establish a reputation for punishing transgressions of discipline and deterring waves of opportunism. Reforms were well advanced by this time, however—so the leadership's reputation must already have been well established. As I discuss above, reputational strategies involve trading short-term costs for long-term deterrence. In this regard, the early agricultural successes of the Chinese reforms may have offered it deeper pockets to absorb such short-term costs through the 1980s. More significantly, at the time of the

June 1989 massacre, leaders in Beijing were already implementing an economic austerity program with only limited resistance from state and Party officials.

The "Lessons" of China: The Importance of Institutional Design

A growing number of authors have scoured the Soviet/Russian and Chinese reform experiences in search of "lessons" about the relative merits of rapid or evolutionary reform.[49] Though these authors often arrive at radically different conclusions, most agree that "a gradual strategy requires effective state management of the economy" and that the relative effectiveness of the Chinese state in managing reforms in that country can be attributed to its postponement of political reforms.[50]

The argument at the heart of this book rejects the assumption that organizational integrity and effectiveness are exogenous to the process of reform and examines specific processes that undermined or preserved institutional stability in these two reform environments. The analysis suggests that organizational reforms in the Soviet Union radically weakened authority links within Soviet hierarchies and accelerated organizational disintegration—thus making a gradualist approach impossible—while superficially similar reforms in China left fundamental authority linkages intact.

Previous organizational analyses of centrally planned systems failed to suggest how poor performance could, under certain circumstances, affect or even undermine structure.[51] As Yasheng Huang noted in a comparison of the choice of reform strategies in China and the Soviet Union, "administrative capacities matter."[52] While this is undoubtedly true, the analysis in this book suggests that, during periods of reform, administrative capacities are not fixed. Institutions thought to be "guiding" reforms can be profoundly weakened by the very reforms they unleash. In an environment of rapid change, opportunistic agents at lower levels of the bureaucratic hierarchy may perceive a chance to profit from chaos and seize the assets they have been managing as their superiors lose the authority to exercise discipline. Thus, institutional stability must be viewed as endogenous to models of reform.

The model suggests that the "lessons" drawn from China's relative success must be carefully considered. The "hidden hand" behind the

Chinese market wielded a bloody bayonet, but it also presided over a broad reallocation of property rights. As a consequence, bureaucrats hoping to profit from economic reforms have faced strong incentives to remain in their state and Party positions rather than attempt to "privatize" assets under their control. Some China scholars have called the reforms "botched" because they replaced state intervention at the center by state intervention at the localities,[53] but this same decentralization of quasi-ownership rights may have provided crucial organizational glue for holding the state and Party together.

The model, in other words, suggests that erosion of hierarchical authority is not inevitable. Certain institutional characteristics may help insulate an organization from the centrifugal forces described here, and elements of the institutional reforms themselves or the actions of political leaders can and do affect the calculations of lower-level bureaucrats.

8 | Conclusions and Extensions: Control and Collapse in Hierarchies

"We can lick gravity, but sometimes the paperwork is overwhelming."

—WERNHER VON BRAUN

The collapse of a single central column can topple a great building, yet other buildings survive powerful earthquakes. The challenge to structural engineers is not to understand why tremors occur but rather why certain tremors are sufficient to bring down certain buildings. A devastating earthquake in one part of the globe may reveal new details about the properties of buildings under stress and permit structural flaws to be recognized in buildings thousands of miles away.

Similarly, political scientists must study not merely the nature of political shocks but also the manner in which certain shocks topple certain political systems. Gorbachev may have been the shock that started the Soviet edifice swaying, but this study has attempted to explain why certain institutional pillars collapsed (bringing down the regime) while others remain standing to this day. Institutions that survived the breakdown now serve as the foundations for post-Soviet regimes across the region.

Administrative hierarchies such as those analyzed in this book are crucial to the stability of any state. In any type of regime—from democratic to totalitarian—rulers need an apparatus to be able to rule. Before any set of leaders can think of governing a population, it must first resolve the problem of governing this state apparatus. This challenge, for instance, is at the very heart of Max Weber's analysis of legitimacy and his theory of bureaucracy: Weber characterized it as an inquiry "into the grounds upon which there are based the claims of obedience *made by the master against the 'officials'* and of both against the ruled."[1]

Contemporary "state-centered" analyses often reduce this first component of Weberian legitimacy to a narrow focus on policy implementation. Similarly, theories of public administration assume that power relationships between rulers and officials are clear, stable, and uniform across most institutions of the state. In fact, as the previous chapters demonstrate, the links of authority and obedience in different hierarchies are highly sensitive to factors of institutional design. A lapse in administrative control in one part of the state apparatus—or even the *perception* of such a manifestation of weakness—can spread rapidly until it undermines the essential capacity of a state to govern.

The analysis presented in this book, therefore, is relevant not just to Communist and post-Communist states but to any large decentralized bureaucracy established to extend control across a large political or even corporate system. Crisis and collapse in such systems are not rare and esoteric problems. On the contrary, as Chester Barnard noted, organizational effectiveness and survival "is the abnormal, not the normal condition . . . Failure of organization, disorganization, disintegration, destruction of organization—and reorganization—are characteristic facts of human history."[2]

To be more specific, the theory of institutional breakdown presented in Chapter 2 yields a set of implications for hierarchies in times of reform or crisis:

1. If devolution of control rights over organizational assets exacerbates information asymmetries between principals and agents (for instance, by weakening monitoring mechanisms), opportunism by agents becomes far more likely.
2. If agents had previously been operating opportunistically, devolution of additional control rights could permit them to expropriate organizational assets altogether.
3. If property rights within organizational hierarchies are ambiguous, the loss of control over certain assets may undermine principals' authority to control other resources. Other agents may respond by reassessing the risks of their own opportunism versus the risks of remaining loyal to a weakened organization.
4. If principals do not assume a share of the risk from misappropriation of institutional assets, they will lack the proper incentives to police their agents. This is true at each level of a hierarchical organization.

5. If principals hope to check the erosion of their authority, they must move quickly and unambiguously to restore their reputations by disciplining opportunistic agents and clarifying property rights.
6. Institutions whose assets are highly specific to the official function of an institution are less likely to succumb to an organizational bank run. These hierarchies are likely to prove more robust, since the benefits of defection are significantly reduced.

In the remainder of this chapter, I present some illustrations of these phenomena in non-Communist cases. My intent here is not to offer any further test of the neoinstitutional model but rather to suggest some future directions for research and analysis. I will look briefly at imperial collapse, state strength and corruption, democratic institutions, and corporate governance. I conclude by returning to the post-Soviet environment and considering the significance of the analysis for post-Soviet political economy.

Hierarchical Control and Collapse in Non-Communist Environments

Collapse of Empires and Civilizations

The neoinstitutional model developed here focuses on the micro level—individual actors within specific institutions—and this book has concentrated on individual institutions during fairly limited periods of time. The centrifugal dynamic described by this model may also be relevant to understanding disintegrative processes on a larger scale.

In his account of the expansion and maintenance of the Roman Empire, Edward Luttwak makes repeated reference to the Romans' skill at defending a vast frontier with a "very narrow and very economical base of military power."[3] The secret, for Rome, was to establish and preserve a reputation for ruthlessly putting down even the most remote challenge to its authority in the provinces. This reputation was a critical asset, since Roman troops stationed along the frontier in the early stages of imperial expansion were too thinly distributed to suppress an insurrection and still defend the imperial border. Thus, the "seemingly irrational commitment of resources" devoted to extinguishing the Jewish outpost on Masada was intended to warn other imperial vassals considering defiance that "the

Romans would pursue rebellion even to the mountain tops in remote deserts to destroy its last vestiges, regardless of cost."[4]

As the Soviet case suggests, maintaining a reputation for discipline requires an administrative apparatus that is willing and able to recognize potential threats early and alert political leaders to their existence. The Roman administrative structure began to decay once its government became, in Gibbon's phrase, "weak and distracted."[5] The more general process is described by Herbert Kaufman, who highlights the prominent role of "runaway field administrators" in the collapse of entire states and civilizations. He notes that:

> Whatever the motivation, the upshot was that things went on in the field that central officials did not know about, would not have approved, never intended, and would have overruled had they been sufficiently aware and powerful. (Sometimes field administrators, including military commanders, attained so much power that they could actually defy their nominal superiors.) Whatever the forms of government authority, some systems were in fact almost totally decomposed as a result of administrative fragmentation.[6]

Kaufman's perspective on imperial breakdown shares several important elements with the neoinstitutional model presented in this book, including the decisive role of information asymmetries and the enormous latent power in the hands of local administrators to defy their superiors. This model goes beyond the standard view in which organizational dysfunction leaves empires *vulnerable* to centrifugal tendencies.[7] In the model presented here, those centrifugal tendencies are created by the very mechanisms of rule themselves.

A similar perspective is useful for discussing the most contemporary example of imperial collapse: the demise of the Communist regimes of Eastern Europe. While a detailed discussion of these cases would go well beyond the scope of this book, participants and observers agree that the Soviet refusal to endorse the violent repression of mass protests in East Germany and Poland undermined these regimes' reputations for punishing dissent. Once Gorbachev ruled out the use of Warsaw Pact forces to suppress internal upheavals, apparatchiks from Warsaw to Sofia had to reconsider their expectations about the likelihood of continued Communist rule.

While mass demonstrations or emigration played an undeniably important role in toppling each of the East European regimes, the decision of Communist leaders to negotiate transitions rather than fight for power was equally important. The logic of the bank-run model suggests that these leaders probably had few other options, since the agents who would have carried out any orders were already anticipating the regime's transition.[8] From this perspective, the political and economic success of former Communist cadres across the region since 1989 is unsurprising: the old regimes fell, in part, because these actors had already begun preparing for life after Communism.

This portrayal of imperial collapse is at odds with a contending view that collapse is triggered not by corrosive opportunism from within but by declining marginal-returns to complexity.[9] In this marginal returns model, societies reach a natural limit of complexity, at which point collapse returns them to a simpler state of existence. While intuitively appealing, this perspective offers little guidance to suggest which components of collapsing states are more or less susceptible to disintegration. Since the breakdown of discrete organizational structures throughout the Communist world was far from uniform, theory should help us understand not just the functional consequences of collapse but also the dynamic mechanism that produces it.

State Strength and the Problem of Corruption

Since political scientists brought the state "back in" to political theory almost two decades ago, much effort has been expended on measuring the relative strengths of different states. Unlike international relations, where state strength suggests the capacity to triumph in interstate contests, comparative politics has focused on the strength of a given state's apparatus both in absolute terms and versus society.[10] The focus in these analyses is on the state's ability to implement policies of its choosing, and it has become common to distinguish between state "autonomy" and state "capacity."[11]

State autonomy measures the degree to which state actors formulate policy preferences independently from societal interests.[12] State capacity, on the other hand, measures a state's ability to successfully achieve those goals it chooses to pursue. The model of hierarchical breakdown developed in this book says little about the autonomy of state actors, though a key finding in the Soviet case was that societal interests were minimally represented in state institutions. Despite the relative autonomy this suggests for the state, the "bank run" triggered by regional agents all but crippled Soviet state institutions. In other words, the "bank run" triggered by state agents directly eroded state capacity and by extension state strength.

This analysis adds an important element to theories that rely on state strength. It suggests that state capacity does not increase or decrease uniformly across a state's apparatus but can vary by institution. Some institutions with better monitoring systems and stronger authority linkages can more effectively implement goals established by principals within the state hierarchy.

This observation contributes to two ongoing discussions. First, studies of the effectiveness of economic policy reform cannot look solely at state "embeddedness" in society but must include as a separate concern the basic question of institutional capacity.[13] While the "endogenization" of state capacity has reentered the discussion of economic reform in "transitional" states, these analyses still devote little attention to the differences in institutional design and properties across state systems.[14] These differences were also an important finding of the discussion of Chinese reforms in Chapter 7.

Second, the puzzle of weak "empirical" statehood—sprawling structures with anemic powers—in non-European states may benefit from renewed attention to the institutional structures supporting these states.[15] An analysis of bureaucratic anemia in the Middle East noted the importance of a functioning state administration to effect "the transfer of resources within society"; this incapacity, over time, can prevent the regime from developing domestic bases of legitimacy.[16] The model developed in this book suggests that weak administrative capacities may also threaten the stability of the state far more directly, by signaling the inability of principals to discipline agents within state hierarchies.

In a similar vein, rampant corruption is frequently identified as a threat to state capacity and state legitimacy. Some studies of corruption have portrayed it as an agency problem, using much the same framework employed in this book.[17] These studies have focused on the causes of corruption and prescriptions for combating it; the bank-run model discussed here suggests an important consequence of corruption. A corrupt state apparatus can occlude the data-gathering capacities of bureaucratic supervisors, complicating the task of monitoring the performance of field agents. Further, regimes that tolerate corruption on a large scale are signaling to field agents the laxity of hierarchical authority. Finally, corrupt officials have greater opportunities for accumulating safety margins, insulating them from the potential effects of any attempt to reassert controls within the hierarchy.

For all these reasons, official corruption threatens political stability not merely through the indirect consequences of reducing state capacity but directly by creating a climate conducive to the development of an institutional bank run. The danger of such a situation can be seen in the ill-fated secession of the Russian province of Chechnya: the corruption of Chechnya's military and civil leaders allowed them to accumulate a reserve of money and arms that sustained their defiance of Moscow's authority from 1991 to 1995.[18]

In most cases, however, as the discussion of China shows, corrupt agents require the state to survive for their rent-seeking to continue. They either lack the safety margins required to defect from state service entirely, or the assets they control (like patronage powers) are too specific to state institutions to be sufficiently fungible. In these cases, corruption may threaten state *capacity*, but it may also enhance regime stability—at least against the threat of internal disintegration.

Agency Theories and Democratic Systems

Principal-agent models have been widely used to investigate whether elected officials in democratic polities continue to exert "political control" over the unelected bureaucrats to whom they designate the task of policy implementation.[19] For the most part, these analyses depict executive agencies as agents answerable to a Congressional principal or to multiple principals if Congressional factions or the President are included in the model. In essence, these models apply micro-level theory to macro-level structures, since the depiction of legislative-executive interactions as an agency relationship is an imprecise analogy at best.

At several junctures, however, the literature on agency relations in democratic institutions has remained at the micro level of intraorganizational dynamics, similar to that employed in this book. Kiewiet and McCubbins, for instance, discuss the problem confronted by principals choosing agents who can then use their delegated authority against the principals.[20] "Madison's dilemma," as Kiewiet and McCubbins define it, "arises from agents exploiting the favorable strategic situation in which they are placed."

The true mystery behind Madison's dilemma, however, lies not in the range of solutions devised to constrain abuses of power on the part of agents but rather in the degree to which these abuses of power remain within fairly narrow bounds. To be sure, bureaucratic shirking or outright corruption are common symptoms to be found in democratic institutions, but widespread defections on the part of agents are almost unheard of. The National Reconnaissance Office (NRO), for instance, may have succeeded in accumulating $4 billion in clandestine funds without the knowledge of supervisory officials in the executive or legislative branches, but its administrators would never claim that they had a right to *keep* the improperly sequestered money.[21] Further research into the comparative dynamics of authority relations in different organizational settings could yield important new insights into the nature of democratic control and by extension democratic legitimacy.

The case of education may help bring this puzzle into sharper focus. In the area of public education, monitoring performance is a great challenge to administrators in the bureaucratic hierarchy.[22] Just as "indoctrination" was difficult for Komsomol officials to measure, so too measuring excellence in education requires the use of an artificial set of performance indicators. Furthermore, since personal relationships between teachers and students form the bedrock of the educational interaction, a measure of decentralized autonomy is recognized as a technical necessity in any large and diverse school system. Finally, educators face the problem of multiple principals as they attempt to comply with federal, state, and local guidelines and directives that are often at cross purposes.

Despite all these conditions conducive to the disintegration of a bureaucratic structure, defiance at the street level tends to be limited to inefficiency or petty graft by school administrators. In many instances, teachers resort to defying authority in order to *accomplish* their occupational mission because they find themselves in an untenable bureaucratic straitjacket prepared for them by federal and state regulators.[23]

From the perspective of the bank-run model there are at least two factors contributing to the robustness of the hierarchical order in these school systems.[24] Since educational technology consists primarily of teachers' skills, there are few significant organizational assets available for appropriation. Thus, while "defecting" teachers may abandon the public schools for private education, their departure is not associated with any capture of organizational assets that would signal the weakening of organizational control. In addition, the relatively low compensation and status levels associated with teaching spare administrators from the problems of adverse selection that plague the recruitment in such professions as police officers or prison guards.[25]

We are accustomed to citing "democratic culture or norms" as the explanation for the virtual absence of bureaucratic insurrections in democratic institutions. A closer look at episodes of the breakdown of hierarchical controls, however, is likely to reveal significant variance in institutional design and dynamics that keeps low-level shirking or insubordination from escalating into a more contagious challenge to authority.

Authority Breakdown and Crises of Corporate Governance

Though Western systems are equipped with frameworks for third-party adjudication of ambiguous property rights claims, agency problems in Western corporate hierarchies can also escalate to the brink of disintegration. Such cases often exhibit some of the same characteristics that, according to the neoinstitutional model, made the Soviet system so vulnerable: difficulty in measuring organizational outputs at the street level, monitoring networks susceptible to manipulation by agents, constraints on the capacity of higher-level principals to punish acts of insubordination, limited assumption of risk by principals and agents (a particularly acute problem in both modern corporations and government agencies), and nonspecific assets.

A classic example from the annals of corporate America is the crisis at Sears Roebuck during the 1970s. Sears had prospered as a highly decentralized firm, in which the buyers in Chicago and the sellers in stores around America developed radically different, and often antagonistic, cultures.[26] They also had contradictory performance measures: buyers were rewarded for purchasing large quantities of goods and selling them at low markup, while "field men" (store managers) sought to maximize their revenues by marking up prices as much as possible. Thus, buyers continually pressured field agents to hold heavily promoted sales, which the field men vigorously resisted.

Ultimately, Sears' buyers arranged a scheme whereby third-party suppliers would overbill Sears' store managers for goods and kick back part of this inflated price directly to the buyers in Sears' Chicago offices. This money went into a special fund—known as a 599 account—which buyers would then use to entice store managers to hold sales and move a higher volume of goods (for instance, by reimbursing the store manager for advertising costs). As a consequence of this system, top management in Sears found themselves unable to respond effectively to the rise of discount mall stores in the 1970s because "every numerical indicator was tainted by politics and history."[27] They had no reliable indicators of market share or promotional costs or even profit margins. To their horror, Sears executives had to write off most of a planned dividend disbursement when the true scale of 599 expenditures was finally revealed. Because of resistance from buyers in Chicago and sabotage from the highly autonomous "field men," the process of recentralizing Sears, Roebuck (and eliminating the 599 accounts) took nearly a decade.

Another interesting example of a "runaway agent" was film director Michael Cimino during the making of *Heaven's Gate*.[28] Cimino was filming his epic in remote Wyoming, where United Artists was unable to exercise close control over how his rapidly ballooning budget was being spent. When studio executives finally did visit the set, they discovered, among other irregularities, that Cimino had installed an irrigation system in front of his own house in order to use it in a single shot. As United Artists bickered over a series of personnel changes (effectively splitting the top leadership of the studio), Cimino spent his entire initial budget without producing even an hour of usable film.

What allowed the production to continue was the difficulty of generating a definitive verdict on whether the footage that had been shot might have justified the cost. In the notoriously subjective world of Hollywood filmmaking, quality of output is almost impossible to judge before a film is in front of an audience and reviews and box office figures begin to pour in. Consequently, principals such as studio executives face profound obstacles devising a scheme for evaluating the activities of agents such as directors. Cimino ultimately completed *Heaven's Gate* at a cost of $44 million; when it finally opened, it was the biggest Hollywood debacle in over two decades and destroyed the once-mighty United Artists.

Thus, problems of effectively measuring output, agents controlling the flow of information to principals, and contagion effects of insubordination are not confined to Communist systems or even to public institutions. In a wide variety of environments, such conditions can conspire to elevate standard problems of slack or shirking to the realm of crises of authority within institutions. Nowhere are these problems likely to be more acute, however, than in the successor states to the Soviet Union, where many Communist bureaucratic blueprints are still very much in use.

After the Collapse: Institutions in the Post-Communist States

As these conclusions are written, political and economic reform in Russia lurches along toward an uncertain future, and reform processes in the other Soviet successor states (aside from the relatively progressive Baltics) straggle behind at varying intervals. Throughout the former Soviet empire, the question of "governability" remains atop the political agenda.

Many of the leading political and economic actors in post-Soviet states are precisely those agents who successfully defected from weakening Soviet structures. Perhaps the most prominent example of this comes from the world of banking: many of Russia's most powerful financiers in the early 1990s are the young men who established commercial banks with the help of Komsomol assets in the late 1980s. Many of that country's leading "industrialists" are those managers who took the lead in nomenklatura-privatization—the factory-level bank run discussed in Chapter 7.

The current prominence of these actors derives largely from their success at securing control over the assets they managed at the expense of central administrators. We might therefore reasonably expect that their top priority in the near term will be protecting the new property rights that they "stole fair and square." They are unlikely to acquiesce in any legal or organizational regime that forces them to surrender any of these hard-won property rights.

In addition, we would expect them to have a strong distrust for new institutions of central administration or even central coordination, since they know better than most how easily hierarchical authority can be debased. The features of the organizational environment that facilitated this erosion of authority—particularly closed information flows and the absence of independent rights adjudication mechanisms—have not yet been substantially remedied in the post-Soviet states. For any national or transnational institution to be effective, it would have to rely either on the threat of coercion or on self-enforcing commitments to the institution by independent agents. For the reasons I have just suggested, these commitments will probably remain quite elusive, even where central coordination or vertical integration would potentially confer efficiency gains.

To the surprise of many observers, however, post-Soviet states like Russia, Ukraine, and Kazakhstan have not fragmented into even smaller units. This is a particularly striking development in Russia, where many of the constituent ethnic republics of the Russian Federation (including powerful regions like Tatarstan) declared their own autonomy by 1992. In part, Yeltsin has managed to keep centrifugal forces in check by adopting Chinese-style tactics of particularistic bargaining with individual regional leaders. By signing formal agreements *(dogovory)* with regional governors—including those serving at the President's pleasure—Yeltsin has moved to reconstitute the state structure explicitly as a "nexus of contracts."[29]

Despite these macro-level developments, hidden action and hidden information problems that plagued Soviet organizations continue to afflict their post-Soviet successors. Information flows in the post-Soviet system remain highly distorted, and budget constraints remain malleable.[30] In the Russian economic sphere, architects of privatization explicitly accorded priority to "depoliticizing" firms, to the neglect of fashioning effective governance structures.[31] Privatization gave many managers ownership rights over their firms, and external shareholders had few weapons to use to exert oversight or control.[32]

Under these conditions, the Chinese experience with "hybrid" organizational forms combining state and private ownership may prove important. By allowing regional and municipal actors to hold a stake in emerging regional "holding companies," Russian officials may at least reduce these actors' incentives to undermine the authority and property rights of central authorities.[33] An analogous move might be to make the state's institutional assets more "specific" by shifting from fiscal to regulatory activity as the preferred policy instrument. Either policy direction would lessen the incentive for actors to defect from state administration and would increase their incentives to collect reliable information about the activity of agents.

Since regulatory regimes are notoriously susceptible to corruption, such an approach may institutionalize rent-seeking as the price paid for institutional stability. Unfortunately for reformers in Russia and in other transitional systems where property rights are ambiguous or uncertain, organizational structures are likely to remain unstable unless and until agents perceive clear incentives to accept hierarchical authority once again. As this book has argued, this authority is the very glue of the state and its chief defense against being stolen by its own officials.

Appendix: Data Sources

The micro-economic framework in this study is particularly data-hungry. Since I try to understand what determined the choices made by individual actors at different policy levels, I employ a wide range of data covering, in as much detail as possible, individual decision processes. Fortunately, much of this data covering the entire Soviet period is now accessible to researchers.

I have used interviews and archival material to try to reconstruct the "decision environment" of individual actors at the street or policy formulation level. I drew particularly heavily on material uncovered at the Central Archives of the Komsomol in Moscow. At that archive, I was able to review material from 1963–1987 on a wide range of youth policy issues, including much material that originated outside Komsomol itself. I was able to confirm impressions received from archival materials through interviews with former officials and policy makers. Since these sources raise special considerations about veracity and inferential value, I discuss my use of them below.

Archives

Much of the data presented in this study—especially but not exclusively in Chapter 4—comes from the Central Archives of the Komsomol (TsA VLKSM). The Komsomol archive, like most Party and governmental archives in the Soviet Union, was organized along the structural lines of the Komsomol itself. Material relevant to case studies was often scattered among various *fondy* (funds) and *opisi* (registers). I relied heavily on Fond 1 (Central Committee of the VLKSM) and Fond 6 (Congresses of the VLKSM), but within these collections, documents were often hidden in unlikely places. The Central Committee Collection, for instance, had separate opisi for the individual departments of the apparatus (like "Student Youth" or "Sports and Mass-Defense Work"), but also for the Biuro, Secretariat, Business Office *(upravlenie delami)*, and, cryptically, "Documentation." In addition, each department's opisi contained several folders labeled simply "Reports" *(spravki)* or "Notes to the Secretariat." These catch-all folders contained a varying assortment of documents ranging from ten to 500 pages in length.

I include this brief description to stress that the Komsomol's record keeping was erratic at best. Where voluminous records existed (like stenograms of Central Committee plenums), I sampled as systematically as possible. For more manageable threads, I tried to read through an entire series of documents if they were prepared regularly over a period of time. Unfortunately, this was not always possible. Gaps often appeared, or reports grew thinner and then vanished. Certain classes of documents were labeled "Not for delivery" (particularly those related to the draft or foreign currency transactions) and unavailable for examination, though some of these were delivered at erratic intervals.

It is important to my analysis to try to understand what outcomes were monitored and when, but the preceding summary suggests that it was not always possible to infer this simply from the discontinuities in the archival record. As Carl Sagan noted after the Viking lander found no signs of life on Mars: "Absence of evidence is not evidence of absence." I have tried in this study to respect the difference between these two categories.

Materials from the Komsomol archive are identified in the notes by their originating office and a description of the document. Page numbers for archival documents are given as *listy* (ll.) to distinguish them from pages (pp.) in published material. Photocopying was not permitted at the Komsomol archives, and I have relied on notes taken during my work there. These notes were left with the archivist but were never inspected.

I also had access to a substantial file of correspondence in the possession of Maria Kirbasova, chairman of the Russian Committee of Soldiers' Mothers. I was able to photocopy all of these materials and have tried to identify them as thoroughly as possible in the notes.

Interviews

This study relies on interview data wherever possible to illuminate otherwise hidden processes behind the formulation of new regulations or the collection and evaluation of policy-relevant data. Most of these interviews were conducted during 1990 and 1991 in Moscow and Tallinn. It is worth noting that the politicization of Russian discourse—then and now—is pervasive. Russian officials were particularly reluctant to separate a chronicle of events from their judgment of those events. When these interviews were being conducted, the political atmosphere in the Soviet Union was highly charged. Virtually all interviewees were eager to portray themselves as long-time proponents of reform and readily dismissed any actions in their pasts that might cast such an evaluation in doubt. I have tried, throughout, to draw from these interviews concrete information relevant to understanding what happened at the time policy-relevant decisions were being made. Such use of data, however, is inevitably somewhat selective.

Statistics

A key theme of this study is that actors manipulated data to give the illusion of plan compliance or to conceal activities at variance with official guidelines. Nevertheless, each case study presents certain data that illuminate aspects of bureaucratic performance. In all cases, however, I have tried to avoid using statistics that are contradicted by more reliable or more consistent sources. For instance, if Komsomol enrollment figures for a given year are reported at one level in an internal report a year later and then consistently at a second level in all statistical sources published after that, I have used the latter figure. This rule is not without its pitfalls, however, since the first figure may be a more accurate reflection of street-level activities before they have been "adjusted" to reflect desired levels of growth or saturation. On the other hand, the second figure is the one accepted by policy makers as the baseline from which future trends (and future targets) are to be judged, and therefore—within the world of the decision hierarchy—is more relevant. One exception to this rule occurs in Chapter 6, where I address (in several notes) the difficulties reconciling different versions of the Defense Ministry's reports of conscription levels for 1990–91. There, however, the confusion over these figures is the precise point I was trying to illustrate.

A more vexing problem concerns the comparability of data over periods of time. Frequently, statisticians changed the categories utilized in the middle of a time series, making systematic comparison difficult. For instance, when regional Komsomol officials chose to report fitness levels of conscripts, they shifted among categories of "fit for military service," "fit for combat service," and simply "unfit" with seeming abandon. This lack of consistency made comparison among regions or across time virtually impossible. The possibility cannot be discounted, however, that such obfuscatory reporting was a deliberate strategy on the part of local officials hoping to disguise adverse trends in the conscript pool.

Notes

TsA VLKSM: Central Archives of the All-Union Leninist Communist Union of Youth (Komsomol). These are cited by *fond* (f.), *opis* (op.), *delo* (d.), and where possible by *list* (l.) or *listy* (ll.).

MIK: Personal Archives of Maria I. Kirbasova, Chairman of the Committee of Soldiers' Mothers (KSM)—these sources consisted of photocopied documents related to KSM activities, including correspondence with officials of the Ministry of Defense.

Introduction

1. *An American Engineer in Stalin's Russia: The Memoirs of Zara Witkin, 1932–1934,* ed. Michael Gelb (Berkeley, Calif.: University of California Press, 1991), 211–212.
2. Adam Przeworski, *Democracy and the Market* (New York: Cambridge University Press, 1991), 1.
3. One analysis that did place the spotlight clearly on "the typical soldier or policeman or bureaucrat" was a discussion paper presented by Mancur Olson well before the actual Soviet collapse. It is published as "The Logic of Collective Action in Soviet Type Societies," *Journal of Soviet Nationalities* 1, no. 2 (1990): 8–27.
4. Samuel Huntington, *Political Order in Changing Societies* (New Haven, Conn.: Yale University Press, 1968), 8
5. Valery Boldin, *Ten Years That Shook the World* (New York: Basic, 1994), 68.

1. Control and Collapse: Reformulating Traditional Approaches

1. The discussion that follows draws both from economics and from the work of Kiser and Ostrom on developing a model for the study of the policy-making process. Kiser and Ostrom label their framework "microinstitutional":

Larry Kiser and Elinor Ostrom, "The Three Worlds of Action," in *Strategies of Political Inquiry,* ed. Elinor Ostrom (Beverly Hills, Calif.: Sage, 1982), 179–222. This approach is nicely summarized, slightly refined, and designated "institutional rational choice" in Paul A. Sabatier, "Toward Better Theories of the Policy Process," *PS: Political Science and Politics* (June 1991): 147–156.

2. This formulation, in the spirit of Herbert Simon and Kenneth Arrow, is offered as conventional wisdom by James A. Mirrlees, "The Optimal Structure of Incentives and Authority within an Organization," *Bell Journal of Economics* 7, no. 1 (1976): 105.

3. In this study, "institution" is often used in place of "organization," though the former is a slightly broader concept. This is compatible with but less encompassing than the usage popularized by Peter Hall in *Governing the State* (New York: Oxford University Press, 1986), 18: "formal rules, compliance procedures, and standard operating practices that structure the relationship between individuals."

4. See May Brodbeck, "Methodological Individualism: Definition and Reduction," in *Readings in the Philosophy of the Social Sciences,* ed. May Brodbeck (New York: Macmillan, 1968), 280–303, and Elinor Ostrom, "Rational Choice Theory and Institutional Analysis: Toward Complementarity," *American Political Science Review* 85, no. 1 (1991): 243. I am essentially adopting the distinction between a rational choice *framework* or *approach* and rational choice *theory* employed by Ostrom on 243, n.1. A "framework" merely assumes that decisions are based on some minimally rational calculation of costs and benefits but, unlike a "theory," includes no additional assumptions about the nature of that calculation or the data which go into it.

5. James G. March and Johan P. Olsen, "The New Institutionalism: Organizational Factors in Political Life," *American Political Science Review* 78 (1984): 734–749.

6. Mary Douglas, "Converging on Autonomy: Anthropological and Institutional Economics," in *Organization Theory: From Chester Barnard to the Present and Beyond,* ed. Oliver E. Williamson (New York: Oxford University Press, 1990), 98–115 (esp. 99ff.) Douglas's useful discussion builds upon Barnard's seminal theory of the functioning of executive power.

7. On revealed preferences, see Timur Kuran, "Now Out of Never: The Element of Surprise in the East European Revolution of 1989," *World Politics* 44, no. 1 (1991): 7–48.

8. The term is taken from Michael Lipsky, *Street-Level Bureaucracy* (New York: Russell Sage Foundation, 1980). Kiser and Ostrom call this the "operational choice" level, as distinct from the "collective choice" levels above it ("The

Three Worlds of Action," 206–211). See also Elinor Ostrom, *Governing the Commons* (New York: Cambridge University Press, 1990), 52–53.

9. See, for instance, Herbert Simon, *Administrative Behavior* (New York: Free Press, 1976), Chapter 7; also Jeffrey Pfeffer, *Power in Organizations* (Marshfield, Mass.: Pitman, 1981), Chapter 1.

10. The term "dependency" was used by David Mechanic in "Sources of Power of Lower Participants in Complex Organizations," *Administrative Science Quarterly* 7, no. 3 (1962): 349–364. I return to this point, in modified form, in the discussion of agency problems in the next chapter.

11. Oliver E. Williamson, "Comparative Economic Organization: The Analysis of Discrete Structural Alternatives," *Administrative Science Quarterly* 36, no. 2 (1991): 274.

12. Kenneth J. Arrow, *The Limits of Organization* (New York: Norton, 1974), 64.

13. In part, this was a consequence of the paucity of data on processes internal to Soviet institutions (a condition now largely, but not wholly, remedied by the opening of Soviet archives and greater availability of officials for interviews). Studies of the industrial planning process, which are considered in the next chapter, are a major exception to this black-box treatment.

14. Mancur Olson, "The Logic of Collective Action in Soviet Type Societies," *Journal of Soviet Nationalities* 1, no. 2 (1990): 17. Olson's observation, though merely suggestive, foreshadows the more detailed discussion of property rights and authority within hierarchies in the next chapter.

15. "Comments on 'The Logic of Collective Action in Soviet Type Societies,'" *Journal of Soviet Nationalities* 1, no. 2 (1990): 28.

16. See ibid., 29, where another commentator, Martha Olcott, portrayed the "middle elite" as a "weather vane between the top and the bottom."

17. George Breslauer, "In Defense of Sovietology," *Post-Soviet Affairs* 8, no. 3 (1992): 200.

18. See the matrix, ibid., 202. His third key discriminating factor was different images of "collective elite receptivity to modernizing change."

19. Ibid., 226–27.

20. Alexander Dallin, "Causes of the Collapse of the USSR," *Post-Soviet Affairs* 8, no. 4 (1992): 297.

21. Rasma Karklins, "Explaining Regime Change in the Soviet Union," *Europe-Asia Studies* 46, no. 1 (1994): 30.

22. For other accounts of the collapse that depict it in large part as an ideological crisis, see David Remnick, *Lenin's Tomb* (New York: Random House, 1993) and Zbigniew Brzezinski, *The Grand Failure: The Birth and Death of Communism in the Twentieth Century* (New York: Scribner's, 1989). Brzezinski's book lists the end of "the Party's ideological control over the society's value system"

(77) as just one of the "ten dynamics of disunion"; however, his discussion on the Chinese reforms (Chapter 15) clearly suggests that "ideological flexibility" was the key to the Chinese regime's avoiding Gorbachev's fate. An even more nuanced analysis that gives an important role to ideology is Ken Jowitt, *New World Disorder: The Leninist Extinction* (Berkeley, Calif.: University of California Press, 1992), especially Chapter 6 ("Gorbachev: Bolshevik or Menshevik").

23. See, for instance, Mary Douglas, "Converging on Autonomy: Anthropological and Institutional Economics," in *Organization Theory: From Chester Barnard to the Present and Beyond,* ed. Oliver E. Williamson (New York: Oxford University Press, 1990), 98–115. For a review of the broader debate over "social norms" versus "instrumental rationality," see Jon Elster, "Introduction," in *Rational Choice,* ed. Jon Elster (Oxford, England: Basil Blackwell, 1986). For a more extensive discussion of "non-rationality," see Jane J. Mansbridge, ed., *Beyond Self-Interest* (Chicago: University of Chicago Press, 1990).

24. See, for instance, Raymond Bauer, Alex Inkeles, and Clyde Kluckholm, *How the Soviet System Works* (New York: Vintage, 1961); also Merle Fainsod, *How Russia Is Ruled* (Cambridge, Mass.: Harvard University Press, 1963).

25. Bauer, Inkeles, and Kluckholm, *How the Soviet System Works,* 194–196. Even the case of true believers in a totalitarian system, however, is not an unequivocal demonstration of the power of ideology, since the regime's instruments of coercion made ideological conformity an act of indubitable self-interest. Nevertheless, it is probably undeniable that at various levels policy makers resisted certain innovations solely because they viewed them as ideologically impermissible. In Chapters 3–6, however, I note several instances where actors ignored ideological constraints to facilitate actions in their narrow self-interest.

26. For instance, see Jerry F. Hough, *The Struggle for the Third World* (Washington, D.C.: Brookings, 1986), 259–262; or, more broadly, Vladimir Shlapentokh, *Public and Private Life of the Soviet People* (New York: Oxford University Press, 1989), 227–231. For an analysis that places greater emphasis on the role of ideology, though stressing its tactical utilization in a game-theoretic framework rather than its cognitive consequences, see Scott A. Bruckner, "The Strategic Role of Ideology: Exploring the Links between Incomplete Information, Signaling, and 'Getting Stuck' in Soviet Politics," Paper presented at the annual meeting of the American Political Science Association, Chicago, September 3–6, 1992.

27. Zbigniew Brzezinski and Samuel Huntington, *Political Power: USA/USSR* (New York: Viking, 1965), 191.

28. Brzezinski and Huntington, *Political Power,* 203 ff.

29. Carl A. Linden, *Khrushchev and the Soviet Leadership 1957–1964* (Baltimore, Md.: Johns Hopkins University Press, 1966), 10.

30. For an overview of the debate over the interest-group approach, see Susan Gross Solomon, ed., *Pluralism in the Soviet Union* (New York: St. Martin's, 1983), especially the chapters by Solomon, Hough, and Brown. See also *Interest Groups in Soviet Politics,* eds. H. Gordon Skilling and Franklyn Griffiths (Princeton, N.J.: Princeton University Press, 1971), 253–289; Peter Solomon, *Soviet Criminologists and Criminal Policy* (New York: Columbia University Press, 1978); John Löwenhardt, *Decisionmaking in Soviet Politics* (New York: St. Martin's, 1981).

31. This was even true of studies that argued that Soviet leaders needed to engage in a period of "authority building" to consolidate control among the political elite. See, for instance, George Breslauer, *Khrushchev and Brezhnev as Leaders* (London: Allen and Unwin, 1982) or Valerie Bunce, *Do New Leaders Make a Difference?* (Princeton, N.J.: Princeton University Press, 1981).

32. Joel Schwartz and William Keech, "Group Influence and Policy Process in the Soviet Union," *American Political Science Review* 62 (1968): 840–851. Emphasis in original.

33. Thane Gustafson, *Reform in Soviet Politics: Lessons of Recent Policies on Land and Water* (Cambridge, England: Cambridge University Press, 1981),158. Gustafson delved deeper than most analysts by examining policy implementation. His findings—which assigned an important role to the institutional dynamics of policy formulation and implementation, including the constraints that were placed on the free flow of information about the results of policy—foreshadow some of the main themes of the next chapter.

34. Thomas Remington, "Sovietology and System Stability," *Post-Soviet Affairs* 8, no. 3 (1992): 258.

35. Classic works in the "transitions" school include Guillermo O'Donnell and Philippe Schmitter, *Transitions from Authoritarian Rule: Tentative Conclusions about Uncertain Democracies* (Baltimore, Md.: Johns Hopkins University Press, 1986) and Adam Przeworski, *Democracy and the Market* (New York, Cambridge University Press, 1991). For extensions to the Soviet transition, see Philippe Schmitter and Terry Lynn Karl, "The Conceptual Travels of Transitologists and Consolidoliogists," *Slavic Review* 53, no. 1 (Spring 1994) and Russell Bova, "Political Dynamics of the Post-Communist Transition: A Comparative Perspective," *World Politics* 44, no. 1 (October 1991).

36. Phil Roeder, *Red Sunset* (Princeton, N.J.: Princeton University Press, 1993).

37. Ibid., 245.

38. On p. 248, for instance, he writes that "structural features constrained the coalitional politics by which political actors sought office and made policy."

39. For a representative account employing the "civil society" approach, see M.

Steven Fish, *Democracy from Scratch* (Princeton, N.J.: Princeton University Press, 1994). For the "societal capture" approach, see Minxin Pei, *From Reform to Revolution* (Cambridge, Mass.: Harvard University Press, 1994).

40. Martin Malia, "Leninist Endgame," *Daedalus* 121, no. 2 (Spring 1992): 57–75.

41. See, for instance, Barrington Moore, Jr., *Terror and Progress USSR* (Cambridge, Mass.: Harvard University Press, 1954), esp. Chapter 7; or Richard Lowenthal, "Development vs. Utopia in Communist Policy," in *Change in Communist Systems*, ed. Chalmers Johnson (Stanford, Calif.: Stanford University Press, 1970), 33–116. The primacy of social change as a determinant of political outcomes was also, of course, one of the basic tenets of Marxist analysis.

42. For examples of this approach see Jerry F. Hough, *Russia and the West: Gorbachev and the Politics of Reform* (New York: Simon and Schuster, 1988); Gail W. Lapidus, "State and Society: Toward the Emergence of Civil Society in the Soviet Union," in *Politics, Society, and Nationality inside Gorbachev's Russia*, ed. Seweryn Bialer (Boulder, Colo.: Westview, 1989); and Moshe Lewin, *The Gorbachev Phenomenon: A Historical Interpretation* (Berkeley, Calif.: University of California Press, 1988).

43. Lewin, *The Gorbachev Phenomenon*, esp. 85–100; one frequently cited example of an internal analysis of the Soviet social structure and the demands it was making on the political system is the so-called "Novosibirsk Report" of 1983, reprinted in *Survey* 28, no. 1 (1984).

44. See, respectively, Schwartz and Keech, "Group Influence and the Policy Process"; Jane Dawson, "Social Mobilization in Post-Leninist Societies: The Rise and Fall of the Anti-Nuclear Power Movement in the USSR" (Ph.D. diss., University of California at Berkeley, 1993); and Stephen Crowley, "From Coal to Steel: The Formation of an Independent Workers' Movement in the Soviet Union, 1989–91" (Ph.D. diss., University of Michigan, 1993).

45. Peter Hauslohner, "Gorbachev's Social Contract," *Soviet Economy* 3, no. 1 (1987): 54–89. For a related argument in more detail see Linda Cook, *The Soviet Social Contract and Why It Failed: Welfare Policy, Workers and Politics from Brezhnev to Yeltsin* (Cambridge, Mass.: Harvard University Press, 1993).

46. Jerry F. Hough, *Soviet Leadership in Transition* (Washington, D.C.: Brookings, 1980); Seweryn Bialer, *Stalin's Successors: Leadership, Stability and Change in the Soviet Union* (Cambridge, England: Cambridge University Press, 1980); George Breslauer, "Is There a Generation Gap in the Soviet Political Establishment?" *Soviet Studies* 36, no. 1 (1984), 1–25; Mark Beissinger, "In Search of Generations in Soviet Politics," *World Politics* 38 (1986): 288–314.

47. Jerry Hough once tackled this issue directly in exploring the link between

the participation of women in local soviets and policy outcomes for "women's issues" like day care. See Hough, "The Impact of Participation: Women and the Women's Issue in Soviet Policy Debates," in his *The Soviet Union and Social Science Theory* (Cambridge, Mass.: Harvard University Press, 1977), 140–158.

48. This limitation on leaders' capacities to change policy outcomes directly is less valid in the realm of foreign policy, which is not considered in this study.

2. Control and Collapse: Neoinstitutional Approaches

1. In equating neoinstitutional theories with a "contractual" approach, I am adopting the categories of Moe, who contrasts this with the "behavioral" paradigm of satisficing, limited search algorithms, and "garbage-can" policy making (Terry M. Moe, "The New Economics of Organization," *American Journal of Political Science* 28 (1984): 739–777). I consider the behavioral paradigm briefly at the end of this chapter.

2. Thráinn Eggertsson, *Economic Behavior and Institutions* (Cambridge, England: Cambridge University Press, 1990), 53.

3. Ibid., 40–41.

4. These two elements—combined with methodological individualism and utility maximization—are highlighted by Eirik G. Furubotn and Rudolf Richter, "The New Institutional Economics: An Assessment," in *The New Institutional Economics*, ed. Eirik G. Furubotn and Rudolf Richter (College Station, Tex.: Texas A & M University Press, 1991), 4–5. Methodological individualism and utility maximization were considered in the previous chapter.

5. Oliver E. Williamson, *The Economic Institutions of Capitalism* (New York: Free Press, 1985), 30.

6. For the purposes of neoinstitutional theory, it is not necessary that we assume all actors to be opportunistic, merely that some are and the contracting parties cannot *a priori* tell who they are.

7. I am employing Kreps's definition of bounded rationality: a boundedly rational individual "attempts to maximize but finds it costly to do so and, unable to anticipate all contingencies and aware of this inability, provides ex ante for the (almost inevitable) time ex post when an unforeseen contingency will arise" (David Kreps, *A Course in Microeconomic Theory* [Princeton, N.J.: Princeton University Press, 1990], 745).

8. Merle Fainsod, *Smolensk under Soviet Rule* (Cambridge, Mass.: Harvard University Press, 1958; reprint, Boston: Unwin Hyman, 1989). Jerry Hough also notes this characteristic of Fainsod's study, though he offers a more sanguine

interpretation: "The Smolensk party officials of the 1930s, as I read Merle Fainsod's book, do not seem to have been rigid bureaucrats, but men who creatively struggled to juggle and reconcile a multiplicity of conflicting pressures both from above and below" ("The Bureaucratic Model and the Nature of the Soviet System," in *The Soviet Union and Social Science Theory,* ed. Jerry F. Hough [Cambridge, Mass.: Harvard University Press, 1977], 66).

9. J. Arch Getty, *Origins of the Great Purges* (Cambridge, England: Cambridge University Press, 1985).

10. Eggertsson, *Economic Behavior,* 41. See also Jean Tirole, "Hierarchies and Bureaucracies: On the Role of Collusion in Organizations," *Journal of Law, Economics and Organization* 2, no. 2 (1986): 181–214.

11. This statement of "the principal's problem" is taken from Gary Miller, *Managerial Dilemmas: The Political Economy of Hierarchy* (Cambridge, England: Cambridge University Press, 1992), 75, and also draws on Stephen Ross, "The Economic Theory of Agency: The Principal's Problem," *American Economic Review* 63 (1973): 134–139. For reviews of the basic literature on agency, see Joseph E. Stiglitz, "Principal and Agent," in *The New Palgrave: Allocation, Information and Markets,* ed. John Eatwell, Murray Milgate, and Peter Newman (New York: Norton, 1989), 241–253; Kenneth Arrow, "The Economics of Agency," in *Principals and Agents: The Structure of Business,* ed. John Pratt and Richard Zeckhauser (Boston: Harvard Business School Press, 1985); David E. M. Sappington, "Incentives in Principal-Agent Relationships," *Journal of Economic Perspectives* 5 no. 2 (1991): 45–66; and Eggertsson, *Economic Behavior,* 40–45.

12. Arrow, "Economics of Agency," 38–40. Hidden action is sometimes called "moral hazard," and some cases of hidden information are also known as "adverse selection." Both of these problems flow from the neoinstitutional assumption that agents will behave opportunistically (or, minimally, that opportunism cannot be ruled out *ex ante*).

13. The use of such "forcing targets" is considered in Bengt Holmstrom, "Moral Hazard and Teams," *Bell Journal of Economics* 13 (1982): 324–340; see also James A. Mirrlees, "The Optimal Structure of Incentives and Authority within an Organization," *Bell Journal of Economics* 7, no. 1 (1976): 124–130.

14. For principal-agent analyses of the Soviet system, see Jan Winiecki, *Resistance to Change in the Soviet Economic System* (London: Routledge, 1991), esp. 29–37; Paul Gregory, *Restructuring the Soviet Economic Bureaucracy* (Cambridge, England: Cambridge University Press, 1990), esp. 15–19; John H. Moore, "Agency Costs, Technological Change, and Soviet Central Planning," *Journal of Law and Economics* 24 (1981): 189–214; Gertrude E. Schroeder, "Property Rights Issues in Economic Reforms in Socialist Countries," *Studies in Comparative Communism* 21, no. 2 (1988): 175–188.

15. Winiecki makes essentially this point in *Resistance to Change in the Soviet Economic System*, 29: "[The] manipulation of plan targets and plan fulfillment reports provides an excellent example of how moral hazard is strongly amplified by the lack of markets and muddled property rights structure in the Soviet system."

16. Goal displacement, in contemporary discourse, has a pejorative connotation, suggesting the abandonment of the guidance provided by organizational goals in favor of simple-minded pursuit of short-term performance targets. Initially, however, the term suggested an important means of internalizing organizational rules. See James G. March and Herbert A. Simon, *Organizations* (New York: Wiley, 1958), 38.

17. Janos Kornai, for instance, describes four typical indicator-adjustment strategies employed by reformers seeking to "perfect" the planning system (*The Socialist System: The Political Economy of Communism* [Princeton, N.J.: Princeton University Press, 1992], 405).

18. See, for instance, Anthony Downs, *Inside Bureaucracy* (Boston: Little, Brown, 1967), 148ff. The Party's control over the Soviet Press consolidated its effective monopoly over most monitoring activities.

19. Jerry Hough, for instance, found this for the case of industrial organization in *The Soviet Prefects: The Local Party Organs in Industrial Decision-making* (Cambridge, Mass.: Harvard University Press, 1969). A similar picture for Party-Army relations at lower levels of the military hierarchy emerges from Timothy J. Colton, *Commissars, Commanders, and Civilian Authority* (Cambridge, Mass.: Harvard University Press, 1979).

20. Prior notice of reviews or audits dates at least as far back as Gogol's *Inspector General*. Tirole—who models a three-level hierarchy as principal-supervisor-agent—cites the practice of monitors providing advance notice of their arrival as a typical example of supervisor-agent "collusion," wherein the supervisor does not want to find data unfavorable to the agent ("Hierarchies and Bureaucracies," 185).

21. Furthermore, no incentive mechanism—even in theory can simultaneously maximize output and reveal accurate information, especially if agents' inputs and compensation both depend upon the information they send to principals. See Jeffrey Miller and Peter Murrell, "Limitations on the Use of Information-Revealing Incentive Schemes in Economic Organizations," *Journal of Comparative Economics* 5 (1981): 257–263. Gary Miller also considers this problem in *Managerial Dilemmas*, 138–158.

22. Anthony Downs, for instance, considered the fact that "The major portion of its output is not directly or indirectly evaluated in any markets external to the organization by means of voluntary quid pro quo transactions" to be a defining feature of any bureau (*Inside Bureaucracy*, 24–26).

23. John M. Litwack, "Ratcheting and Economic Reform in the USSR," *Journal of Comparative Economics* 14 (1990): 254–268; John M. Litwack, "Discretionary Behavior and Soviet Economic Reform," *Soviet Studies* 43, no. 2 (1991): 255–279. Though prominent in discussions of centrally planned economies, the "ratchet problem," Litwack argues, occurs in any principal-agent model featuring asymmetric information, in which principals "cannot or do not commit themselves to long-run incentive schemes or tax schedules." Where present, the ratchet problem invalidates the assumption of Niskanen and others that bureau chiefs can be modeled as budget-maximizers (William A. Niskanen, *Bureaucracy and Representative Government* [Chicago: Aldine, 1971]).

24. See, for instance, Joseph Berliner, *The Innovation Decision in Soviet Industry* (Cambridge, Mass.: MIT Press, 1976), 404, 440, or Peter Rutland, "Economic Management and Reform," in *Developments in Soviet Politics,* ed. Alex Pravda, Stephen White, and Zvi Gitelman (Durham, N.C.: Duke University Press, 1990), 168.

25. This assertion is demonstrated for the case of utility-maximizing agents facing the financial and planning environments common to Soviet enterprise managers in Eirik G. Furubotn and Svetozar Pejovich, "The Soviet Manager and Innovation: A Behavioral Model of the Soviet Firm," in *The Economics of Property Rights,* ed. Eirik G. Furubotn and Svetozar Pejovich (Cambridge, Mass.: Ballinger, 1974), 203–216. James Dearden, Barry Ickes, and Larry Samuelson reach related conclusions by distinguishing between incentives for agents to innovate (which can be significant) and the incentives for them to adopt innovations once they become publicly available (which are less powerful). See "To Innovate or Not To Innovate: Incentives and Innovation in Hierarchies," *The American Economic Review* 80 (December 1990).

26. Eugène Zaleski, *Stalinist Planning for Economic Growth* (Chapel Hill, N.C.: University of North Carolina Press, 1980), 484.

27. In other words, agents' performance targets for year x became simply a marginal increase over their accomplishments in year x-1 (e.g., $1.05T_{x-1}$).

28. Michael C. Jensen and William Meckling, "Theory of the Firm: Managerial Behavior, Agency Costs, and Ownership Structure," *Journal of Financial Economics* 3 (1976): 351.

29. See, for instance, Roy Radner, "Repeated Principal-Agent Games with Discounting," *Econometrica* 53, no. 5 (1985): 1173–1198; Jean Tirole, "The Multicontract Organization," *Canadian Journal of Economics* 21, no. 3 (1988): 459–466; Drew Fudenberg, Bengt Holmstrom, and Paul Milgrom, "Short Term Contracts and Long Term Agency Relationships," *Journal of Economic Theory* 51 (1990): 1–31.

30. These findings are nicely summarized in Sappington, "Incentives," 59.
31. Kenneth J. Arrow, *The Limits of Organization* (New York: Norton, 1974), 64. He is paraphrasing Herbert Simon.
32. The notion of "zone of acceptance" can be traced back to Chester Barnard in *The Functions of the Executive* (Cambridge, Mass.: Harvard University Press, 1938). Barnard initially referred to a "zone of indifference," but the concept was reformulated and relabeled by Herbert Simon. It can be thought of as that range of actions covered by the employment contract between principal and agent. On the "zones of acceptance" and neoinstitutional analysis, see Oliver Williamson, "Chester Barnard and the Incipient Science of Organization," in *Organization Theory: From Chester Barnard to the Present and Beyond,* ed. Oliver E. Williamson (New York: Oxford University Press, 1990), esp. 175–176.
33. Holmstrom and Tirole, "The Theory of the Firm," 123.
34. The literature on economics of property rights is extensive; see Eggertsson, *Economic Behavior,* 33–37, for a review of basic principles. In this discussion, I reject Yoram Barzel's assertion in his *Economic Analysis of Property Rights* (Cambridge, England: Cambridge University Press, 1989) that a "property rights approach" is somehow distinct from "agency theory" (11).
35. A parallel argument in which property rights are derived from de facto control over assets, rather than vice versa, is developed in John Umbeck, "Might Makes Rights: A Theory of the Formation and Initial Distribution of Property Rights," *Economic Inquiry* 19.1 (1981): 38–59. Umbeck considers property rights in weakly organized environments, not within organizations.
36. Indeed, Getty's account of the Purges *(Origins of the Great Purges)* could be interpreted as such a reassertion of control over political resources by the center.
37. Schroeder, "Property Rights Issues." Schroeder noted that economic reforms in the absence of property rights reform would likely make agents *less* efficient. Her analysis continued the pioneering line initially pursued by John Moore, who assumed reform would follow a course of reducing agency costs but treated property rights as essentially stable ("Agency Costs, Technological Change, and Soviet Central Planning").
38. Analyses by Boettke and Anderson and by Winiecki have examined the rent-seeking consequences of "quasi-contract" or "nonexclusive" property rights in the Soviet system. Both studies focused on the consequences of economic reforms for generating support or opposition to a reformist coalition, but neither considers how a reconceptualization of property rights might lead to a collapse of organizational structure (Peter J. Boettke and Gary M. Anderson, "*Perestroika* and Public Choice: The Economics of Auto-

cratic Succession in a Rent-Seeking Society," *Public Choice* 75, n. 2 [1993]; Winiecki, *Resistance to Change*).

39. A notable exception is Victor Nee and Peng Lian, "Sleeping with the Enemy: A Dynamic Model of Declining Political Commitment in State Socialism," *Theory and Society* 23 (1994): 253–296. Nee and Lian present a model of hierarchical breakdown similar in some ways to that developed in this chapter.

40. Bengt Holmstrom, "Moral Hazard and Observability," *Bell Journal of Economics* 10 (1979): 74–91; also see Bengt R. Holmstrom and Jean Tirole, "The Theory of the Firm," in *Handbook of Industrial Organization,* ed. Richard Schmalensee and Robert Willig (Amsterdam: North-Holland, 1989), 88–92.

41. Moe, "The New Economics of Organizations," 763.

42. The term was introduced by Kornai in 1980, and is summarized in Kornai, *The Socialist System,* 140–145.

43. At middle levels of the bureaucracy, this is equivalent to saying that, since principals were simultaneously agents to higher levels, they suffered from "moral hazard" as well. At the top of the hierarchy, however, the incentives should have been different.

44. Winiecki makes a similar point in *Resistance to Change* by arguing that the Soviet system protected the "rents" of key officials and industrial managers from any consequences of their job performance.

45. Melor Sturua, *New York Times Book Review,* 2 February 1992, 15.

46. Williamson, *Economic Institutions,* esp. Chapter 4.

47. See Benjamin Klein, Robert Crawford, and Armen Alchian, "Vertical Integration, Appropriable Rents, and the Competitive Contracting Process," *Journal of Law and Economics* 21 (1978): 297–326; Jeffry Frieden also discusses asset specificity in *Debt, Development and Democracy* (Princeton, N.J.: Princeton University Press, 1991), 20–21. The discussion here also draws on a roundtable on "Factor Specificity, Interest Groups, and International Trade" held at the Annual Meeting of the American Political Science Association, Washington, D.C., in 1993. Participants in that panel were Michael Gilligan, James Alt, Ron Rogowski, and Jeffry Frieden.

48. On rents and rent-seeking generally, see *Toward a Theory of the Rent Seeking Society,* ed. James Buchanan, Robert Tollison, and Gordon Tullock (College Station, Tex.: Texas A & M Press, 1980). On the connection between rents and asset-specificity, see Williamson, *Economic Institutions,* 52–56.

49. On the persistence of such networks through bureaucratic reorganizations and reforms, see Dorothy J. Solinger, "Urban Reform and Relational Contracting in Post-Mao China: An Interpretation of the Transition from Plan to Market," *Studies in Comparative Communism* 22, no. 2/3 (1989): 171–185.

50. As I suggest in Chapter 8, these characteristics are not exclusive to Soviet-

type systems. Highly decentralized or dispersed nonmarket hierarchies like empires, public schools, or even large corporations may display some similar characteristics.

51. To be more precise, Andrei's income rights may still be secure, but his transfer rights are threatened and his use rights are in some doubt.

52. Presumably some intangible assets, like reputation, will not be transferable; these assets are highly specific to their current use.

53. Nee and Lian ("Sleeping with the Enemy") develop a similar scenario, based upon Granovetter's "threshold" model of collective behavior. According to their analysis, the likelihood of a Communist Party activist becoming an "opportunist" and defecting from the organization is strongly related to the extent of opportunism among other Party activists. They attribute this to the "demonstration effect" that spreads opportunism from higher-ranking officials through the organization. In the model developed here, the observable opportunism of other agents may also provide still-loyal actors with new information about the *viability* of the parent organization and thus the likelihood of receiving the "sucker's payoff" in the event of organizational collapse. This signaling effect of protest or defection—as distinct from more straightforward demonstration effects—is described for the phenomenon of mass protest in Susanne Lohmann, "Dynamic of Informational Cascades: The Monday Demonstrations in Leipzig, East Germany, 1989–91," *World Politics* 47, no. 1 (1994): 42–101. All of these models are related to the broader class of phenomena known as self-fulfilling prophecies. For a useful discussion of this family of models, see Thomas C. Schelling, *Micromotives and Macrobehavior* (New York: Norton, 1978), 115–119.

54. For a general analysis of this phenomenon, see David Epstein and Sharyn O'Halloran, "The Multiple Principals Problem in Politics," Political Economy working paper, Columbia University, 1994.

55. Charles Tilly, "Revolutions and Collective Action," in *Handbook of Political Science, Volume 3: Macropolitical Theory*, ed Fred Greenstein and Nelson Polsby (Reading, Mass.: Addison-Wesley, 1975), 520ff.

56. This discussion draws on David M. Kreps, "Corporate Culture and Economic Theory," in *Perspectives on Positive Political Economy*, ed. James E. Alt and Kenneth A. Shepsle (Cambridge, England: Cambridge University Press, 1990), esp. 100–116.

57. See Reinhard Selten, "The Chain Store Paradox," *Theory and Decision* 9 (1978): 127–159, as well as the subsequent discussions in David Kreps and Robert Wilson, "Reputations and Imperfect Information," *Journal of Economic Theory* 27: 253–279; and Paul Milgrom and John Roberts, "Predation and Entry Deterrence," *Journal of Economic Theory* 27: 280–312.

58. The discussion of reputation effects in this section draws on the discussion

in Chapter 9 of Drew Fudenberg and Jean Tirole, *Game Theory* (Cambridge, Mass.: MIT Press, 1991) and David M. Kreps, *Game Theory and Economic Modelling* (Oxford, England: Oxford University Press, 1990), 65–72. See also Drew Fudenberg and David K. Levine, "Maintaining a Reputation when Strategies Are Imperfectly Observed," *Review of Economic Studies* 59 (1992), 561–579, and James E. Alt, Randall L. Calvert, and Brian D. Humes, "Reputation and Hegemonic Stability: A Game-Theoretic Analysis," *American Political Science Review* 82, no. 2 (1988), 445–466.

59. Peter Hauslohner, for instance, considered the virtual elimination of the use of violence against members of the ruling elite to be one of the defining "rules" of post-Stalin politics ("Politics before Gorbachev: De-Stalinization and the Roots of Reform," in *Politics, Society and Nationality inside Gorbachev's Russia,* ed. Seweryn Bialer [Boulder, Colo.: Westview, 1989], esp. 44–48).

60. The "behavioral" categorization is taken from Moe, "The New Economics of Organization."

61. March and Simon, *Organizations,* 171.

62. James G. March and Johan P. Olsen, *Rediscovering Institutions: The Organizational Basis of Politics* (New York: Free Press, 1989), Chapter 2; James G. March, "Bounded Rationality, Ambiguity, and the Engineering of Choice," in *Rational Choice,* ed. Jon Elster (Oxford, England: Basil Blackwell, 1986), 142–170; James G. March and Johan P. Olsen, *Ambiguity and Choice in Organizations* (Bergen, Norway: Universitetforlaget, 1975).

63. This stress on the dominance of rules was introduced by the sociological study of bureaucracies. Weber and others stressed the efficiency gains that result from replacing individual discretion with strict specialization and rule-guided patterned responses. For reviews of the current distinctions between sociological and economic approaches to organizational analysis, see Terry Moe, "Politics and the Theory of Organization," *Journal of Law, Economics and Organization* 7 (1991): S106–129, and Christopher Winship and Sherwin Rosen, "Introduction: Sociological and Economic Approaches to the Study of Social Structure," *American Journal of Sociology* 94, Supplement (1988): S1–16.

64. See Graham T. Allison, *Essence of Decision: Explaining the Cuban Missile Crisis* (Boston: Little, Brown, 1971), Chapter 3, and March and Olsen, *Rediscovering Institutions.*

65. Michael Lipsky, *Street-Level Bureaucracy: Dilemmas of the Individual in Public Services* (New York: Russell Sage Foundation, 1980), 17.

66. Raymond Bauer, Alex Inkeles, and Clyde Kluckholm, *How the Soviet System Works* (New York: Vintage, 1961), 85–94. A similar point emerges from a networks analysis of early Soviet state building; see Gerald M. Easter,

"Personal Networks and Postrevolutionary State Building: Soviet Russia Reexamined," *World Politics* 48, no. 4 (July 1996), 551–578.

67. Hough, "The Bureaucratic Model," 49–70. In his earlier study of local Party officials *(The Soviet Prefects)*, Hough had stressed their role in improvising essential horizontal linkages among branches of the vertically structured economic bureaucracy.

68. One of its first and best elaborations of this vicious cycle was Joseph S. Berliner, *Factory and Manager in the USSR* (Cambridge, Mass.: Harvard University Press, 1957). In another example, a comprehensive study of the Soviet oil and gas sectors in the 1980s blamed poor data quality and irrational or conflicting incentives for distorted organizational goals beyond the point of incoherence (Thane Gustafson, *Crisis Amid Plenty: The Politics of Soviet Energy under Brezhnev and Gorbachev* [Princeton, N.J.: Princeton University Press, 1989], esp. 10).

69. For other studies that focused on specific Soviet institutions, highlighting similar features, see Abdurakhman Avtorkhanov, *The Communist Party Apparatus* (Chicago: Henry Regnery, 1966); William Odom, *The Soviet Volunteers* (Princeton, N.J.: Princeton University Press, 1973); and Blair Ruble, *Soviet Trade Unions* (New York: Cambridge University Press, 1981).

3. Testing Theories of Institutional Change: The Soviet Youth Program

1. For an overview, see Allen Kassof, *The Soviet Youth Program* (Cambridge, Mass.: Harvard University Press, 1965).

2. On the logic of "process tracing," see Alexander George and Timothy McKeown, "Case Studies and Theories of Organizational Decision Making," in *Advances in Information Processing in Organizations,* vol. 2 (Greenwich, Conn.: JAI Press, 1985), 21–58.

3. The idea that youth would transform a political system if they grew disillusioned with it actually dates to Plato (see *The Republic,* Book 8). For a broad survey of generational perspectives on political change, see *Political Generations and Political Development,* ed. Richard J. Samuels (Lexington, Mass.: D. C. Heath, 1977).

4. Vladimir Lenin, "Letter to Bogdanov and Gusev," 11 February 1905, in *Lenin on Youth* (Moscow: Progress, 1970), 122.

5. Lenin, "Letter to S. I. Gusev," 15 February 1905, in *Lenin on Youth,* 125. Oblomov was a fictional character famous for his laziness.

6. Lenin, "The Youth International," 1916, in *Lenin on Youth,* 172.

7. Quoted in Louis Feuer, *The Conflict of Generations* (New York: Basic Books, 1969), 303.

8. Ibid., 304.

9. Lenin, "The Tasks of the Youth Leagues," Address to the Third All-Russian Congress of the Russian Young Communist League, 2 October 1920, in *Lenin on Youth*, 236.

10. Lenin, "The Tasks of the Youth Leagues," 251.

11. See, generally, Kassof, *Soviet Youth Program*, 10–21; and Merle Fainsod, *How Russia Is Ruled* (Cambridge, Mass.: Harvard University Press, 1963), 284–95.

12. See Gail Lapidus, "Educational Strategies and Cultural Revolution: The Politics of Soviet Development," in *Cultural Revolution in Russia, 1928–1931*, ed. Sheila Fitzpatrick (Bloomington, Ind.: Indiana University Press, 1978), 78–104.

13. Kassof, *Soviet Youth Program*, 18.

14. See, for instance, Kassof, *Soviet Youth Program*, 141–170.

15. David Robert, "Moscow State University," *Survey* 51 (April 1964): 24–31.

16. Vladimir Semichastnyi, "Address to 8th Komsomol Plenum (28 December 1965)," TsA VLKSM, f. 1, op. 2, d. 472, ll. 20–43. In the text of the speech, the names of individuals were highlighted by capitalization.

17. See, for instance, Bill Keller, "Russia's Restless Youth," *The New York Times Magazine*, 26 July 1987, 14; or Walter Laqueur, *The Long Road to Freedom: Russia and Glasnost'* (New York: Scribner, 1989), 151–163, and the more comprehensive treatments in Nancy Travers, *Kife* (New York: St. Martin's, 1989), and Andrew Wilson and Nina Bachkatov, *Living with Glasnost': Youth and Society in a Changing Russia* (London: Penguin, 1988).

18. *Pravda*, 16 August 1983, 1.

19. See *Radio Liberty Research Bulletin* 212/81, 22 May 1981.

20. *Sovetskaia rossiia*, 13 March 1988, 3.

21. Mikhail Gorbachev, *Perestroika: New Thinking for Our Country and the World* (New York: Harper and Row, 1987), 115.

22. The data examined in this section were made available by the Inter-University Consortium for Political and Social Research. The data for the *Soviet Interview Project: 1979–1983* were originally collected by James R. Millar, et al. The analysis presented here was performed by the author using the SPSS-PC+ statistical package; neither the collectors of the data nor the Consortium bear any responsibility for its findings or interpretations.

23. Naturally, there is some emigré bias in this sample: all respondents did *leave* the Soviet Union, but many either left with their families and played no role in the decision or explained their decision in terms of concerns for others (spouses, children, etc.) rather than for themselves. The role played in and motivation for the emigration decision were entered into any regressions described in this section, and any significant dependence is noted.

24. This set of indicators is borrowed from two studies of support for the American political system: J. Fraser, "Validating a Measure of National Political Legitimacy," *American Journal of Political Science* 18 (1974): 117–134; and Bert and Michael Useem, "Government Legitimacy and Political Stability," *Social Forces* 57 (1979): 840–852.

25. Personal (or political) efficacy here is taken as equivalent to what Almond and Verba termed "subjective political competence"—an individual's belief that he or she can influence government decisions through political participation. See Gabriel Almond and Sidney Verba, *The Civic Culture* (Boston: Little, Brown, 1965), 137.

26. Results not presented here suggest that Komsomol activism is strongly correlated with activism in other regime institutions like peoples' militia or trade unions. Komsomol membership is also correlated with membership in these other mass organizations but not with any degree of activism in them. Joiners, in other words, remained just joiners, and activists were likely to be activists from a young age.

27. Admittedly, the KGB may represent a special case for emigré respondents, though the relationship remained significant in a multiple regression which included the role played in the emigration decision.

28. Not shown in Table 3.2 are the attitudes on wage norms for professionals and academics, which are also not significantly correlated with any form of Komsomol activity.

29. One of the earliest sociological journals, *Chelovek i obshchestvo* [Man and society], regularly published special sections devoted to youth sociology. See, for instance, issues 5 and 6 in 1969. For some background on the history of Soviet sociology, see Elizabeth Ann Weinberg, *The Development of Sociology in the Soviet Union* (London: Routledge and Kegan Paul, 1974) and Vladimir Shlapentokh, *Sociology and Politics: The Soviet Case* (Falls Church, Va.: Delphic Associates, 1985). In addition, I discuss some of the early Komsomol-sponsored public opinion surveys in Chapter 4.

30. *Komsomol'skaia Pravda*, 21–22 July 1961; the results are from a readers' poll which was widely discussed at the time. This series of polls is discussed further in the next chapter.

31. See, for example, B. A. Efimov, "Education and the Socio-Political Advancement of Young Workers," *Sotsiologicheskie issledovaniia*, no. 3 (1977): 47–51; or V. G. Alekseeva, "Informal Groups of Urban Adolescents," *Sotsiologicheskie issledovaniia*, no. 3 (1977): 60–70.

32. M. K. Gorshkov and F. E. Sheregi, "Dynamics of Public Opinion among Youth," *Sotsiologicheskie issledovaniia*, no. 4 (1979): 33–40.

33. Labor discipline is discussed in V. A. Smirnov and V. E Boikov, "Contract

Brigades and the Communist Upbringing of Youth," *Sotsiologicheskie issledovaniia*, no. 2 (1978): 68. A different large-scale survey of working youth in 1972 also failed to demonstrate any correlation between Komsomol membership and participation in socialist competition: L. D. Alekseeva et al., *Sotsial'nyi oblik rabochei molodezhi* [The social temperament of working youth] (Moscow: Mysl', 1980), 190.

34. B. A. Grushin and L. A. Onikov, *Massovaia informatsiia v sovetskom promyshlennom gorode* [The mass media in a Soviet industrial city] (Moscow: Izdatelstvo polititicheskoi literatury, 1980) 393, 396.

35. The phrase is cited in Jim Riordan, "The Role of Youth Organizations in Communist Upbringing in the Soviet School," in *The Making of the Soviet Citizen: Character Formation and Civic Training in Soviet Education*, ed. George Avis (London: Croon Helm, 1987), 151. Similar labels—"outer cover" and "reddish dross"—were cited by Merle Fainsod in the late Stalin period (see *How Russia Is Ruled* [1953 edition] 259).

36. Lev Kassil in *Literaturnaia gazeta*, 25 May 1957. Cited in Kassof, *Soviet Youth Program*, 139. Kassof provides several examples of Khrushchev-era critiques of Komsomol, focusing on careerism of officials and formalism of meetings, 125–143.

37. TsK VLKSM, "Stenogram of July (3rd) Plenum (9–10 July 1963)," TsA VLKSM, f. 1, op. 2, d. 447, l. 76.

38. Central Committee stenograms were never published as part of any official record of proceedings. Only opening speeches and final resolutions were published after plenums. We can therefore assume that remarks made by speakers in the course of Central Committee "debates" were intended for internal consumption only. This practice changed only in the late 1980s, when comments made by most speakers were published.

39. Aryeh L. Unger, "Political Participation in the USSR: YCL and CPSU," *Soviet Studies* 33, no. 1 (1981): 123. A similar argument is made in Vladimir Shlapentokh, *Public and Private Life of the Soviet People* (New York: Oxford University Press, 1989). Even if one accepts this interpretation, however, there would be little support for hypothesis H1.1, since the regime would have been even less likely to rely on ideological controls *within* institutional hierarchies.

4. The Communist Youth League

1. See, for example, *Moscow News*, no. 19 (1989): 13, and *Argumenty i fakty*, no. 7 (1990): 6. In the *Moscow News* report, which featured two telephone polls of Muscovites taken in September 1988 and February 1989, only four of

twenty-three organizations received a lower "grade" than the Komsomol Central Committee, among them the reviled State Committee for Agricultural Industry (Gosagroprom) and ineffective Ministries of Trade and Public Health. Even the highly criticized Gosplan received higher rankings.

2. Several Western studies treat the early history of the Komsomol. Among the most detailed and insightful are: Peter Kenez, *The Birth of the Propaganda State* (Cambridge, England: Cambridge University Press, 1985), Chapters 4, 8; Merle Fainsod, *How Russia Is Ruled* (Cambridge, Mass.: Harvard University Press, 1963), Chapter 9; Ralph Talcott Fisher, *Pattern for Soviet Youth* (New York: Columbia University Press, 1959); Allen Kassof, *The Soviet Youth Program* (Cambridge, Mass.: Harvard University Press, 1965), Chapter 4; Peter Gooderham, "The Komsomol and Worker Youth: The Inculcation of 'Communist Values' in Leningrad During NEP," *Soviet Studies* 34, no. 4 (1982): 506–528; Jim Riordan, "The Komsomol," in *Soviet Youth Culture*, ed. Jim Riordan (Bloomington, Ind.: Indiana University Press, 1989), 16–44; Isabel Tirado, *Young Guard! The Communist Youth League, Petrograd, 1917–20* (New York: Greenwood Press, 1988); Ann Todd Baum, *Komsomol Participation in the Soviet First Five Year Plan* (New York: St. Martin's Press, 1987). The discussion of Komsomol history and structure that follows draws heavily from these sources, particularly Kenez, Fisher, Fainsod, and Riordan.

3. "On the Youth Leagues," Resolution of the 6th Congress of the RSDLP(b), July–August 1917, translated in *Youth and the Party* (Moscow: Progress, 1976), 38.

4. The name by which the league came to be known—Komsomol—is a contraction of this original Russian title: *Kommunisticheskii Soiuz Molodezhi.*

5. For a detailed discussion of these meetings, see Fisher, *Pattern*, 8–78.

6. Ibid., 11.

7. Ibid., 17.

8. Lenin, "Tasks of the Youth Leagues," in *Lenin on Youth* (Moscow: Progress, 1970), 242.

9. Kenez, *Birth*, 89.

10. Ibid., 176.

11. Merle Fainsod, *Smolensk under Soviet Rule* (Cambridge, Mass.: Harvard University Press, 1958; reprint, Boston: Unwin Hyman, 1989), 422–425.

12. Ibid., 426.

13. The importance of this distinction is elaborated in Joel J. Schwartz, "The Young Communist League, 1954–62: A Study in Group Cooperation and Conflict" (Ph.D. diss., Indiana University, 1965), 2–38.

14. Kassof, *Soviet Youth Program*, 183.

15. Graeme Gill, *Rules of the Communist Party of the Soviet Union* (Armonk, N.Y.:

M. E. Sharpe, 1988), 207, 226. This rule was in effect from 1966 to 1986. Prior to 1966, Komsomol had handled all Party admissions up to age twenty. In 1986, this age was raised from twenty-three to twenty-five.

16. *Komsomol'skaia pravda,* 14 January 1975, 2.

17. *Pravda,* 8 October 1971, 2.

18. *Pravda,* 25 October 1971, 1. The bonus stipends, and Komsomol's role in awarding them, was suggested a year earlier by an instructor at a Moscow institute; see L. Tulchinskii in *Izvestiia,* 22 October 1970, 2.

19. *Komsomol'skaia pravda,* 11 November 1960, 2.

20. V. Polianichko in *Molodoi kommunist,* no. 2 (1965): 42–48.

21. TsK VLKSM, "Stenogram of 3rd Plenum (26–27 December 1967)," TsA VLKSM, f. 1, op. 2, d. 505, l. 19.

22. *Pravda,* 25 February 1976, 1.

23. *Pravda,* 6 May 1979, 1

24. Vladimir Semichastnyi, "Unforgettable," *Komsomol'skaia zhizn',* no. 7 (1988): 5.

25. Ibid., 6.

26. Vladimir Semichastnyi, "Thank Me," in *Vokrug kremlia,* ed. Andrei Karaulov (Moscow: Novosti, 1990), 29–30.

27. Sergei Pavlov, "Others Will Take Our Place—Bolder and Better," *Komsomol'skaia zhizn',* no. 17 (1988): 3.

28. *Pravda,* 1 February 1961, 1.

29. Pavlov, "Others Will Take Our Place," 6.

30. Ibid., 7.

31. Petr Shelest, "Of Khrushchev, Brezhnev and Others," *Argumenty i fakty,* no. 2 (1989): 5–6.

32. TsK VLKSM, "Stenogram of 4th Plenum (12 June 1968)," TsA VLKSM, f. 1, op. 2, d. 522.

33. *Nezavisimaia gazeta,* 26 January 1991, 5.

34. *Pravda,* 4 April 1971, 4–5.

35. *Pravda,* 28 February 1976, 6–7.

36. *Pravda,* 30 March 1966, 1. Karen Collias discusses this speech, as well as Brezhnev's broader desire to emphasize patriotic upbringing that could *re-create* for youth the sacrifices of preceding generations, in Karen Collias, "Heroes and Patriots: The Ethnic Integration of Youth in the Soviet Union during the Brezhnev Era" (Ph.D. diss., Columbia University, 1987), Chapter 2.

37. *Pravda,* 18 May 1966, 1.

38. *Pravda,* 31 March 1971, 1.

39. *Pravda,* 24 April 1974, 1. In another measure of Tiazhel'nikov's sycophancy,

the state record company Melodia released Brezhnev's speech to this Komsomol Congress as a 2-LP set (*Pravda*, 14 June 1974). No sales records were available.

40. *Pravda*, 26 April 1978, 1

41. *Pravda*, 24 February 1981, 1.

42. *Pravda*, 16 June 1983, 1.

43. *Pravda*, 23 April 1983, 1.

44. In 1968, in the wake of a Party resolution commemorating the fiftieth anniversary of the Komsomol, two academics took great pains to note in *Pravda* that the "autonomy" of the Komsomol did not imply that it was "independent of" or "equal to" the Party, nor that it was politically "neutral." The authors dismissed these notions as "dangerous" products of "bourgeois ideology." (See Z. Apresian and V. Sulemov in *Pravda*, 18 October 1968, 2.)

45. Vladimir Shlapentokh, "Attitudes and Behavior of Soviet Youth in the 1970's and 1980's: The Mysterious Variable in Soviet Politics," in *Research in Political Sociology*, vol. 2, ed. Richard and Margaret Braungart (Greenwich, Conn.: JAI Press, 1986), 199–224.

46. The activities of this Institute are described in detail in Elizabeth Ann Weinberg, *The Development of Sociology in the Soviet Union* (London: Routledge and Kegan Paul, 1974), 82–107. Weinberg reproduces the Institute's questionnaires in Appendix 2.

47. The survey is described by Weinberg, *Development of Sociology*, 99, and is published in translation on 131–32.

48. Boris Grushin (sociologist), interview by author, Cambridge, Mass., 12 October 1989.

49. These articles appeared in 17 May and 13 September 1966 and are described in Weinberg, *Development of Sociology*, 99–100.

50. *Komsomol'skaia pravda*, 16 June 1965, 1–2.

51. Ia. Kapeliush in *Komsomol'skaia pravda*, 11 May 1967, 2

52. Ianaev was the first (and last) vice president of the Soviet Union; he was also a leader in the August 1991 coup against Gorbachev.

53. TsK VLKSM, "Stenogram of 3rd Plenum (26–27 December 1967)," TsA VLKSM, f. 1, op. 2, d. 507, l. 86.

54. Igor Kon (sociologist), interview by author, Moscow, 18 February 1990.

55. N. V. Trushchenko, "Certain Problems in the Scientific Analysis of the Annals of the VLKSM," in *Pozyvnye istorii* (Moscow: Molodaia gvardiia, 1976), 143.

56. TsK VLKSM, "Stenogram of 6th Plenum (25 December 1968)," TsA VLKSM, f. 1, op. 2, d. 571, l. 104.

57. Ibid., l. 8. Edits to Torusev's remarks appear in the archival copy as pencil

edits to the transcription of his spoken remarks. These edits, by either Torusev himself or another Central Committee official, were probably made a week or two after the actual plenum.

58. Ibid., l. 8.

59. These observations are the result of my personal examination of protocols, questionnaires, and results of youth-related surveys in the Data Bank *(Bank Dannykh)* of Soviet Institute of Sociology, February–April 1990. At that time, the Data Bank contained over 300 surveys, administered between 1971 and 1987.

60. Obshchii otdel TsK VLKSM, "Compilation of critical comments about Komsomol made at plenums of Party committees (14 July 1969)," TsA VLKSM, f. 1, op. 31, d. 426.

61. A. S. Kapto, "The Social Structure of Society and a Differentiated Approach to the Organization of Upbringing Activities," *Sotsiologicheskie issledovaniia* no. 4 (1981): 93–104.

62. *Sovetskaia kultura,* 10 March 1987, 1. In private, several years later, Mironenko tempered his criticism slightly. He asserted that his caution was rooted in the belief that sociology "can be extremely dangerous, because often sociologists find confirmation of whatever they want to confirm . . . I'm not criticizing sociology. I just want it to know its place" (Interview by author, Moscow, 20 March 1991).

63. Kon interview, 18 February 1990.

64. Igor Il'inskii (Director NITs VKsh), interview by author, Moscow, 27 April 1990. His exact Russian exclamation was, *"Znanie meshaet."*

65. V. Okpysh and Iu. Lavrinenko, "Review of letters to CC VLKSM on moral upbringing of youth (19 November 1976)," TsA VLKSM, f. 1, op. 2, d. 707. For a similar illustration of anecdotal and noncontextual use of apparently "scientific" data, see the discussion of the Komsomol biuro's consideration of a resolution on job assignments in Chapter 5.

66. Jerry F. Hough and Merle Fainsod, *How the Soviet Union Is Governed* (Cambridge, Mass.: Harvard University Press, 1979), 405.

67. TsK VLKSM, "Stenogram of 8th Plenum: Military/patriotic upbringing (28 December [evening session] 1965)," TsA VLKSM, f. 1, op. 2, d. 472, l. 115.

68. The plan for coverage in the period leading up to the Eighteenth Komsomol Congress began five months before the Congress convened (TsA VLKSM f. 6, op. 18, d. 439, ll. 1–115).

69. At the Eighteenth Congress in 1978, for instance, the section on "young specialists" was chaired by Academician E. P. Velikhov, Vice President of the Soviet Academy of Sciences. The meeting lasted four hours—the last devoted to greetings from foreign delegations and a vote on the final resolu-

tion—and was attended by 175 delegates and 145 guests. Section discussions were not published in the final Stenographic Report of the Congress (TsA VLKSM f. 6, op. 18, d. 47, 49).

70. Obshchii otdel TsK VLKSM, "Compilation of critical comments . . . (14 July 1969)," ll. 83–110. This comment, submitted to Komsomol Central Committee apparatchiks by Estonian Party Secretary I. G. Kebich, says as much about Party meetings as it does about the Komsomol.

71. TsK VLKSM, "Stenogram of 4th Plenum (28 October 1975)," TsA VLKSM, f. 1, op. 2, d. 694, l. 263. The offered clarification was not forthcoming.

72. *Komsomol'skaia pravda,* 29 April 1977, 1, emphasis added.

73. TsA VLKSM f. 6, op. 18, d. 446.

74. This appears to have been the practice at least before the Eighteenth, Nineteenth, and Twentieth Congresses, according to documents in the Komsomol archives. It appears to have been a standard part of pre-Congress preparation, though I was not able to examine documentation for earlier Congresses.

75. Letters and memoranda with suggestions for improving "Communist Upbringing" received prior to the Nineteenth Komsomol Congress, for instance, ran to thousands of pages (TsA VLKSM f. 6, op. 19, d. 296, 298–301, 304). Similar correspondence, in similar volume, was received prior to the 20th Congress, often repeating the same points made four years earlier (TsA VLKSM f. 6, op., 20, d. 202–206, 209–211, 264). A separate file was kept for the Twentieth Congress with comments on the new Komsomol Charter (TsA VLKSM f. 6, op. 20, d. 220, 221, 235, 243, 249–250).

76. TsA VLKSM f. 6, op. 19, d. 295.

77. TsK VLKSM, "Stenogram of June (7th) Plenum (10–11 June 1965)," TsA VLKSM, f. 1, op. 2, d. 464, l. 48.

78. Many of the responses to Pavlov's *doklad* at this plenum appear to have been spontaneous. This was, perhaps, a response to the vigor with which Pavlov pursued his attack. Though keynote addresses at plenums were generally interrupted by frequent outbursts of applause, Pavlov appears to have delivered his report to a silent hall. The stenogram of this plenum, which lasted two days, is one of the last prior to 1986 to contain anything approaching open debate among Central Committee members. Tiazhel'nikov held a plenum devoted to a similar topic in 1971. Though it featured some of the same speakers, the transcript reveals a mind-numbingly dull repetition of tired slogans and a self-satisfied invocation of "comradely, supportive Komsomol groups" and heroic Komsomol role models (TsK VLKSM, Stenogram of 3rd Plenum [20–21 January 1971], TsA VLKSM, f. 1, op. 2, d. 612, 614, 616).

79. TsK VLKSM, "Stenogram of June (7th) Plenum (10–11 June 1965)," d. 465, l. 42. Organization of Komsomol groups by common interests resurfaced in 1986 as a major avenue of attempted Komsomol reform.

80. Ibid., d. 465, l. 147.

81. Vladimir Bykov, *Sobesednik*, no. 3 (1986): 3.

82. According to *Ustav VLKSM* [Rules of the VLKSM](1962), 4.b, all decisions on enrollment into primary organizations required approval of the raikom (or gorkom) biuro.

83. If there was any confusion over control of organizational resources, it involved the Communist Party. Local Komsomol committees were effectively agents serving principals both at higher Komsomol levels and at parallel levels of the Party. Career advancement may have proceeded through levels of the youth league but it required Party approval. Since most Komsomol activists and staff aspired eventually to Party positions, keeping Party officials happy may occasionally have taken precedence over serving the interests of Komsomol superiors.

84. TsA VLKSM f. 6, op. 18, d. 453, 453a. Following the Eighteenth Congress, for instance, Komsomol files reveal the following among the (large) set of results: the Ministry of Culture provided musical instruments to the Komsomol musical theater of the Physical Chemistry Institute of the Academy of Sciences; the Mining Ministry responded to requests for more cultural and communal facilities in one Yakut city by promising to address the shortage once they'd built a few more thousand square meters of living quarters; and the Chief of the Soviet General Staff, Ogarkov, personally approved the assignment of a military transport plane to deliver a prefabricated library to a Komsomol work brigade assigned to the Siberian city of Urengoi.

85. TsK VLKSM, "Stenogram of June (7th) Plenum (10–11 June 1965)," d. 464, l. 48.

86. *Komsomol'skaia pravda*, 18 May 1966, 1.

87. Bronislav Lisin, "Problems in the formation and upbringing of Komsomol activists" (avtoreferat, Cand. Philos. Nauk, Academy of Social Sciences, USSR, 1973).

88. V. Ivanov and B. Lisin, *Kadry i aktiv: VLKSM* [Komsomol cadres and activists] (Moscow: Molodaia gvardia, 1980), 23–26.

89. This estimate is based on internal Komsomol statistics on turnover and category of next job for 1972, 1973, 1979, and 1985 (TsA VLKSM f.1, op. 71, d. 723, 747; op. 84, d. 987, 988, 990; op. 110, d. 703, 704, 709).

90. Through the 1970s, turnover rates appear to have been approximately 40–50 percent annually at the gorkom/raikom level and 30–40 percent at the obkom/kraikom level (TsA VLKSM f. 1, op. 84, d. 614, 987, 988, 990).

91. See Vladimir Azbel', *Radio Liberty Dispatch* 268/74, 23 August 1974.
92. TsK VLKSM, "Stenogram of June (7th) Plenum (10–11 June 1965)," d. 464, l. 48, 49.
93. Ibid, l. 26. The guilty official was Iurii Prokof'ev. Prokof'ev's career seems not to have suffered from the public rebuke: he went on to head the Moscow Party committee and was elected to the Politburo in 1990.
94. Fainsod, *Smolensk under Soviet Rule*, Chapter 21.
95. Obshchii otdel TsK VLKSM, "Questions raised during meetings with First Secretaries of Far East regions (7 January 1969)," TsA VLKSM, f. 1, op. 31, d. 426, ll. 12–13.
96. Obshchii otdel TsK VLKSM, "Compilation of critical comments . . . (14 July 1969)," l. 83.
97. Iurii Marshavin, "Party Supervision of Organizational-Political Strengthening of Primary Komsomol Organizations: Experiences and Problems (1970's and 80's)" (Cand. Hist. Sci. diss., Higher Komsomol School, 1989).
98. Egor Ligachev, "Address to 9th Komsomol Plenum (10 August 1984)," TsA VLKSM, f. 1, op. 100, d. 77c, l. 157.
99. Obshchii otdel TsK VLKSM, "Report on conference of Gagarinskii raikom Komsomol organization, Moscow (10 December 1969)," TsA VLKSM, f. 1, op. 31, d. 426, ll. 201–207.
100. TsK VLKSM, "Stenogram of 7th Plenum (28 April 1977)," TsA VLKSM, f. 1, op. 2, d. 710, l. 27.
101. TsK VLKSM, "Stenogram of 6th Plenum (25 November 1976)," TsA VLKSM, f. 1, op. 2, d. 704, l. 64.
102. Otdel sportivnoi i oboronno-massovoi raboty, "Notes to the TsK VLKSM (4 June 1981)," TsA VLKSM, f. 1, op. 116, d. 6, ll. 44–55.
103. TsK VLKSM, "Stenogram of July (3rd) Plenum (9–10 July 1963)," TsA VLKSM, f. 1, op. 2, d. 447.
104. Otdel sportivnoi i oboronno-massovoi raboty, "Information on preparation of youth for the draft and military schools (1967)," TsA VLKSM, f. 1, op. 38, d.101, l. 11.
105. *Krasnaia zvezda*, 22 August 1972, 2.
106. "Stenogram of a seminar of aktiv and secretaries of Komosmol organizations of Moscow VUZy (12–14 February 1971)," TsA VLKSM, f. 1, op. 39, d. 295. Apparently, not all the young activists exhibited the proper tone of somber disdain toward Peter Fonda's bourgeois decadence, since one Moscow City Committee member felt compelled to scold participants for not taking notes during the film and for heckling another speaker who had accused the audience of actually enjoying it.
107. In 1978, for instance, 87 percent of all members were reported to have some *porucheniia;* by 1985, this had fallen to 80 percent, presumably as

organizers included greater numbers of marginal members on the rolls. This was one consequence of the drive to sustain membership growth at all costs described below (TsA VLKSM f. 1, op. 84, d. 647, op. 110, d. 580a).

108. *Pravda,* 27 December 1968, 2.

109. For one obkom secretary's criticism that Komsomol officials were settling for high turnout even for events that may have offered little benefit, see R. Nikolaev in *Pravda,* 1968, 3.

110. Since the Komsomol was ostensibly a voluntary and selective organization, there was virtually no mention of these targets in the Soviet press or even at Central Committee plenums prior to 1986. An early hint of something resembling firm targets came in a 1968 *Izvestiia* article discussing the low prestige of factory Komsomol committees in Lugansk. In this article, an overworked secretary of a shop floor organization complained that once he finished distributing theater tickets and lottery tickets and arranging basketball games and amateur artistic activities, "the monthly schedule for Komsomol admissions is hanging over me." The authors of the article called the monthly admissions schedule "the height of bureaucratic wit" but did not express surprise at encountering it. (The original article and responses appeared in *Izvestiia,* 7, 10, and 12 March 1968.)

111. The waste of outside advice discussed in the previous section was particularly important, because utilizing information from outside the organization could have offered a partial solution to the problem of hidden information and ameliorated the ratchet effects.

112. TsK VLKSM, "Stenogram of June (7th) Plenum (10–11 June 1965)," d. 464, l. 54.

113. TsK VLKSM, "Stenogram of 7th Plenum (28 April 1977)," l. 21.

114. Otdel komsomol'skikh organov, "Report [Otchet] for the XIX Komsomol Congress (16 November 1981)," TsA VLKSM, f. 6, op. 19, d. 271, l. 5.

115. *Organizatsionno-ustavnye voprosy Komsomol'skoi raboty* [Organizational-statutory questions of Komsomol work] (Moscow: Molodaia gvardia, 1973), 59 (cited in Riordan, "The Komsomol," 21).

116. See, for instance, Otdel komsomol'skikh organov, "Report for the Nineteenth Komsomol Congress," l. 6.

117. Ibid., l. 5.

118. TsK VLKSM, "Stenogram of 4th Plenum (12 June 1968)," TsA VLKSM, f. 1, op. 2, d. 522, l. 39.

119. TsK VLKSM, "Stenogram of 7th Plenum (28 April 1977)," l. 21.

120. This trend was evident as early as the mid-1960s and was described by Kassof, *Soviet Youth Program,* 64.

121. As late as 1987, even as Komsomol membership levels were beginning to

fall around the country, only 161 Moscow University students of Komsomol age were not members of the organization (*Moskovskii universitet*, 1 February 1988, 2).

122. TsK VLKSM, "Stenogram of 7th Plenum (28 April 1977)," l. 21.

123. Marshavin, "Party Supervision."

124. TsK VLKSM, "Stenogram of June (7th) Plenum (10–11 June 1965)," TsA VLKSM, f. 1, op. 2, d. 464, l. 55.

125. *Komsomol'skaia pravda*, 19 May 1982, pp. 3–8.

126. Otdel komsomol'skikh organov, "Report [otchet] for the Nineteenth Komsomol Congress (16 November 1981)," TsA VLKSM, f. 6, op. 19, d. 271, l. 5.

127. TsK VLKSM, *Statisticheskii i spravochnyi material (delegatu XXI S"ezda VLKSM)* [Statistical Handbook Distributed to Delegates of the Twenty-first Komsomol Congress] (Moscow: VLKSM, 1990), 95.

128. Otdel komsomol'skikh organov, "Report for the Nineteenth Komsomol Congress, l. 6.

129. Otdel komsomol'skikh organov, "On Instances of the Violation of Komsomol Statutes in the Admission of New Members (May 1980)," TsA VLKSM, f. 1, op. 84, d. 1007, ll. 1–4.

130. Ibid.

131. Otdel komsomol'skikh organov, "Notes on Admissions in 1982," TsA VLKSM, f. 1, op. 110, d. 263, ll. 25–30. Accused were the Minsk, Buriat, Smolensk, Latvian, and Tambov organizations, among others.

132. Ibid. The practice apparently was condoned in Belgorod, Penza, Saratov, Tambov, and several Central Asian Komsomol organizations.

133. Otdel komsomol'skikh organov, "Report for the Nineteenth Komsomol Congress," l. 8. The exact figure for 1981 was 6.3 percent, or over two million individuals.

134. *Statisticheskii i spravochnyi material*, 96. The figure of members "vybyvshikh iz organizatsii bez sniatiia s komsomol'skogo ucheta" was 3.8 percent of the total membership in 1987 and rose to 5.9 percent in 1990.

135. Otdel komsomol'skikh organov, "Report for the Nineteenth Komsomol Congress," l. 12. The figure is for 1978–81. In some regions, this figure was as low as 20 percent.

136. *Pravda*, 7 July 1984, 1.

137. The idea was floated at least as early as 1980, in an internal memo from the Department of Komsomol Organs. The memo noted that, since four million students were admitted annually, many raikom and gorkom biuros were forced to deal with admissions of new student members at every meeting. The department proposed giving educational Komsomol committees the right to enroll new members directly without summoning them for

a listless interview at the raikom (Otdel komsomol'skikh organov, "On Instances of the Violation of Komsomol Statutes . . . [May 1980]," ll. 7–8).

138. See Resolution 44/13 of the Komsomol Biuro, dated 26 April 1985 (Otdel komsomol'skikh organov, "Notes on Admissions [1985]," TsA VLKSM, f. 1, op. 110, d. 579). Primary organizations in eight regions were given the authority to make final admissions decisions.

139. The proposal was raised in a late 1984 internal memo. See Otdel komsomol'skikh organov, "Notes on Admissions (1984)," TsA VLKSM, f. 1, op. 110, d. 481, ll. 19–20.

140. "On the Membership of the VLKSM on 1 January 1985," Resolution of the Biuro of the Central Committee of the VLKSM, 26 April 1985.

141. *Moskovskii komsomolets,* 4 February 1990, 2.

142. Ibid.

143. Egor Ligachev, "Address to 9th Plenum (10 August 1984)," TsA VLKSM, f. 1, op. 100, d. 77c, l. 155.

144. Iurii Poliakov, "ChP raionnogo masshtaba," *Iunost',* no. 1 (1985): 12–50. For background on the author, see *Sobesednik,* no. 49 (1986): 3.

145. Some of the more colorful of these accounts are reviewed in Riordan, "The Komsomol," 28–35. The citations in this paragraph are all from *Sobesednik* in late 1986 and early 1987 and are taken from Riordan's account.

146. Local Komsomol committees seem to have actively opposed distribution of the film (see, for instance, the discussion in *Sovetskii ekran,* no. 8 [1989]: 18–19). Viktor Mishin later expressed shock at the negativity of the film as compared to the original novel whose publication he had championed (*Moskovskii komsomolets,* 4 February 1990, 2). While it is true the cinematic character has fewer redeeming features than in the novel—one controversial scene came close to portraying him as a rapist—Mishin's recollection of the original character as a "disciplined" worker suggests he may have missed some of the author's irony.

147. A 1987 poll of Moscow youth reported that two-thirds had "negative attitudes" toward the Komsomol (reported in Nancy Traver, *Kife* [New York: St. Martin's Press, 1989], 120). Surveys comparing Komsomol to other organizations invariably ranked it near the bottom of the list. See Note 1 earlier in this chapter.

148. Mironenko interview, 20 March 1991.

149. Ibid.

150. *Argumenty i fakty,* no. 35 (1987): 1–2. Samples of these responses are bound in the Komsomol archives, sorted geographically. Many individual members apparently clipped "Open Tribune" coupons that appeared in Komsomol

newspapers and sent their comments on these; others wrote letters long-hand (TsA VLKSM f. 6, op. 20, d. 249–50).

151. TsA VLKSM f. 6, op. 20 (vrem.), d. 174 contains computer-generated tables produced to track suggestions and actions taken on them.

152. The quotes in these two paragraphs all come from *Sobesednik*, no. 38 (1986): 4–5.

153. Viktor Mironenko, *Pis'mo s"ezdu* (Moscow: VLKSM, 1987).

154. Ibid.

155. Mironenko interview, 20 March 1991. Riordan, in "The Komsomol," p. 23, suggests that Mironenko set 60 percent as the new target saturation level for the Komsomol in 1988. This assertion is not supported in the source cited by Riordan, and I can find no evidence for it. Mironenko's claim to have been fully prepared for the subsequent collapse of Komsomol membership might be a slight exaggeration, however, since it is at odds with the obvious alarm expressed at Central Committee meetings during 1989 and 1990.

156. Otdel komsomol'skikh organov, "Report for the Twentieth Komsomol Congress (no date, 1987)," TsA VLKSM, f. 6, op. 20, d. 178. The final quote was underlined in the report.

157. Ibid., l. 24.

158. Upravlenie delami TsK VLKSM, "Report for the Twentieth Komsomol Congress (no date 1987)," TsA VLKSM, f. 6, op. 20, d. 197, l. 11.

159. TsA VLKSM f. 6, op. 20, d. 235.

160. TsK VLKSM, [Booklet, April 1990], TsA VLKSM, f. 6, op. 20, d. 289.

161. VLKSM Twentieth Congress, "Stenogram (17–18 April 1987)," TsA VLKSM, f. 6, op. 18, d. 13. Perhaps in a confirmation of the perils of reform, Mironenko himself received the most votes against (54 of 4810).

162. *XX S"ezd VLKSM: Stenograficheskii Otchet* [Stenographic Report of the Twentieth Congress of the VLKSM] (Moscow: Molodaia gvardiia, 1987), 126–127.

163. TsK VLKSM, Booklet (April 1990), ll. 20–22; S. Liamin in *Argumenty i Fakty*, no. 44 (1988): 8; TsK VLKSM, *Komsomol i molodezh' Rossii (Delegatu s"ezda komsomol'skikh organizatsii RSFSR)* [Komsomol and the Youth of Russia; distributed to delegates at the first Conference of RSFSR Komsomol Organizations] (Moscow: 1990), 33–35.

164. Viktor Graivoronskii, "Where the Millions Are Flying," *Moskovskii komsomolets*, 24 April 1990, 2. This figure was confirmed to me by Mironenko. For purposes of comparison, the Komsomol's annual budget (composed mostly of dues income and spent mostly on salaries) was between 400 and 450 million rubles.

165. N. Kuchinskii, "Where Do Komsomol Dues Go?" *Argumenty i fakty,* no. 6 (1989): 5.

166. *Komsomol i molodezh' Rossii,* 35.

167. Graivoronskii, "Where the Millions Are Flying," 2. The author was Komsomol secretary of the Gagarin raikom in Moscow.

168. Bill Keller, "Soviet Youth League Falls on Difficult Times," *New York Times,* 7 February 1988, 1. Three years later, Mironenko admitted to me that his oldest son had, indeed, never joined.

169. *Statisticheskii i spravochnyi material,* 134–136. Nonconstruction industries were added in the 1970s; though they paid less than half what construction jobs offered, the work was far less arduous.

170. See *Izvestiia,* 1 July 1976, 5. For some discussion of the shortcomings of the brigades, see *Radio Liberty Research Bulletin* 206/79, 5 July 1979, and *Radio Liberty Research Bulletin* 316/74, 2 October 1974.

171. *Argumenty i Fakty,* no. 44 (1988): 8. On the activities of the "Moscow student brigade," reorganized in October 1989, see Moscow City Komsomol Committee, *Perekrestok* [Crossroads] (Moscow: MGK VLKSM, 1990), 71–77.

172. In particular, these regulations eased the strict separation between cash *(nalichnyi)* and credit *(beznalichnyi)* accounts for youth enterprises, permitting committees, for instance, to make capital expenditures using cash received as dues payments. They also enabled committees to pay salaries out of their credit accounts. These amendments were crucial in permitting primary organizations to control their own budgets, since most income at that level was from dues, and therefore was in cash. The same concerns also partly drove committees' desires to establish automatic dues payment systems, since such payments would go to credit accounts. These measures are described, in part, in *Komsomol i molodezh' Rossii,* 33, and TsK VLKSM [Booklet, April 1990], ll. 20–22. The right to transfer funds between *nalichnye* and *beznalichnye* accounts was extremely valuable and served as the basis for some of the earliest successes of Komsomol-founded financial enterprises like "Menatep."

173. S. Razin in *Komsomol'skaia pravda,* 25 April 1991, 1.

174. Many of these ventures initially operated under the guise of the "NTTM" program. As *perestroika* progressed and "cooperative" ventures became more commonplace, the initial Komsomol-inspired framework was often discarded. It is, therefore, difficult to give any estimate of the true scale of these commercial operations. For some examples, see I. Larin, "Komsomol on the Verge of Change," *Argumenty i fakty,* no. 12 (1987): 3, and David Remnick, "New Soviet Masters of the Universe," *Washington Post National Weekly Edition* 15–21 July 1991, 6–7.

175. Aleksandr Solomkin (Secretary for Student Affairs, Moscow City Komsomol Committee), interview by author, Moscow, 27 February 1990.
176. *Argumenty i fakty,* no. 16 (1988): 4–5.
177. To be more precise: the "Moscow City Committee" was reformed as the larger, more democratic "Moscow City Conference." Ingeniously, the new moniker produced the same acronym as the old, thus alleviating any need to change stationery, rubber stamps, or name plates on buildings or doors. The newly created Conference, with fifty-five members, was too large to meet continuously, and therefore nine separate Commissions were created, whose chairmen largely matched the roster of the disbanded Committee. The gorkom First Secretary, Viacheslav Kop'ev, was (re)elected as Chairman of the new Conference, unopposed. Two alternate candidates were proposed, but both withdrew because, as one delegate patiently explained to me, "It's always traumatic to lose." The only event at the two-day meeting that generated any sustained interest among the 350 or so delegates was the sale of Dale Carnegie's *Collected Works* under a stairwell. The sale was announced from the podium and drew an enormous queue.
178. *Komsomol'skaia pravda,* 1 December 1989, 2.
179. Tsentralnii komitet LKSM Estonii, *Ot s"ezda k s"ezdu* [From Congress to Congress] (Tallinn, 1987), 91.
180. Toivo Sikk (former Secretary, Estonian Komsomol Central Committee), interview by author, Tallinn, April 2 1990. Gorbachev's visit was so hastily arranged that speechwriters had no time to prepare an address to the Congress. Gorbachev simply recycled a speech he had just given in Riga, baffling his audience when he praised the efforts of "Latvian youth."
181. These and other regions combined to promote a "Surgut alternative," named after the Russian city where an initial platform was agreed upon in the summer of 1989. An early statement of the aims of this coalition was contained in a booklet published by several Moscow University Komsomol activists: S. Anokhin, V. Graivoronskii, V. Lepekhin, et al., *Ocherednoi krizis ili tupik?* [Routine Crisis or Dead End?] (Moscow, 1989).
182. *Komsomol i molodezh' Rossii,* 34. The initiative more than doubled Central Committee transfers to regional and local committees.
183. This was the case in Moscow, beginning in 1990. The measure presumably provided a great incentive for primary organizations to devise new means of raising profit margins in order to afford higher salaries (Moscow City Komsomol Committee, *Perekrestok,* 84).
184. Adverse selection is a manifestation of the broader problem of "hidden information," in which job applicants know better than prospective employers whether they are attracted to a job for the wrong reasons. Thus, police

departments are disproportionately likely to attract candidates drawn to violence and weaponry, even though they are trying to attract candidates devoted to the law.

185. TsK VLKSM, [Booklet, April 1990], l. 22.
186. Graivoronskii, "Where the Millions Are Flying," 2.
187. Mironenko interview, 20 March 1991.
188. Graivoronskii, "Where the Millions Are Flying," 2.
189. Joel Hellman, "Breaking the Bank: Building Market Institutions in the Former Soviet Union" (Ph.D. diss., Columbia University, 1993), 150. Menatep became one of the most successful financial concerns in the country, diversifying from banking services into trade, real estate, and stock transactions. Menatep began as a Komsomol Central Committee-sponsored "NTTM." In 1991, Mironenko told me, only half joking, "If I'm ever broke, I can sue them, because Menatep was originally my idea." For a more detailed discussion of the role of Komsomol banks in the new world of Soviet and post-Soviet commercial banking, see Chapter 4 in Hellman's study.
190. *Moskovskii komsomolets,* 30 May 1990, 1.
191. Mironenko interview, 20 March 1991.
192. In my interview with him, Mironenko was adamant on this point. He argued that the Estonian Komsomol, for instance, had never contributed to Central Committee coffers prior to 1980, being a net recipient of subsidies from the center (Gorbachev later used a similar argument to suggest that the Baltics should owe the Soviet government money if they chose to leave the Union). Though the Estonian or Georgian Komsomol might well have considered itself to be a part owner of the new banking concern whether or not it remained under the Komsomol umbrella, there was no framework of Soviet property law to resolve this question, and Mironenko's interpretation has apparently held.
193. The debate is published in *Verkhovnyi sovet SSSR, Tret'ia sessiia, Biulleten' No. 20,* 9 April 1990.
194. One former Komsomol official estimated that, by mid-1991, 20 percent of all private businesses in Moscow were somehow linked to the Komsomol (Margaret Shapiro, "Communist Youth Embrace Capitalism," *Washington Post,* 20 October 1991, A29).
195. "Vremia," news broadcast, 12 January 1990.
196. *Komsomol'skaia pravda,* 12 April 1990, 1.
197. *Moskovskii komsomolets,* 12 April 1990, 1.
198. The anthem was added to the agenda (and sung) after the first morning

break, and then only after a discussion and vote. A Soviet flag was placed beside the Komsomol flag only on the second day.

199. I was present for much of this debate at the Congress. Mironenko attempted to skirt the issue by arguing that the league could not afford to print new membership cards for its millions of members. The issue came back repeatedly to haunt him. On the final day, the exhausted delegates agreed to define the Komsomol as "a federation of youth leagues—uniting youth of Communist and Socialist orientations."

200. *Komsomol'skaia pravda*, 7 July 1990, 1.

201. In October 1992, secretaries of the final Moscow Komsomol gorkom gathered for a reunion to celebrate the 74th anniversary of the Komsomol's founding. According to Aleksandr Solomkin, former secretary for student affairs, all but one were successfully engaged in commercial enterprise. Many, including Solomkin, had used Komsomol contacts in the banking sector to attract startup capital at favorable interest rates and with little or no collateral. A 1995 study of elites in post-Soviet Russia found nearly 38 percent of the "business elite" had previously worked for the Komsomol— a much higher share than from Party or state agencies. See Olga Kryshtanovskaia, "Financial Oligarchy in Russia," *Izvestiia*, 10 January 1996, 5.

202. *Nezavisimaia gazeta*, 7 September 1991, 2.

203. *Kommersant*, no. 39 (1991): 13. The Komsomol was revived in 1992 as an ally of the Communist Party of the Russian Federation. It has no claim on its former wealth, however, and remains a marginal player in Russian political and economic life.

5. Job Assignments for University Graduates

1. Constitution of the USSR (1936), Article 118.

2. Ibid., Article 12.

3. Constitution of the USSR (1977), Article 14.

4. Ibid., Article 40.

5. The VUZ and SSUZ were but two of several options open to students completing secondary school in the Soviet Union.

6. Throughout this chapter, I employ the abbreviated Soviet designations of state offices and ministries wherever possible. For instance, I refer to the State Planning Committee as "Gosplan," the State Committee on Statistics as "Goskomstat," and the State Committee on Labor and Social Questions as "Goskomtrud." Though the Ministry for Higher and Specialized Secon-

dary Education of the USSR underwent several name changes in the post-Stalin period, for simplicity I refer to it simply as "MinVUZ," by which it was colloquially known. After 1988, when it was reorganized as the State Committee for Higher and Specialized Secondary Education, it was commonly referred to as "Gosobrazovaniia," and I use this moniker as well.

7. See Mervyn Matthews, *Education in the Soviet Union: Policies and Institutions Since Stalin* (London: George Allen & Unwin, 1982), 169–174, for a fuller description of this process. See also I. D. Alkin and M. S. Zeltyn', *Organizatsionnye formy raspredeleniia (pereraspredeleniia) rabochei sily v narodnom khoziaistve SSSR* [Organizational forms of the distribution (redistribution) of the workforce in the national economy of the USSR] (Moscow: MinVuz. RSFSR i Moskovskii Institut Narodnogo Khozaiastvo im. Plekhaniva, 1978); A. N. Konovalov et al., *Sovershenstvovaniie raspredeleniia i ispol'zovaniia spetsialistov kak faktor povysheniia effektivnosti vysshego obrazovaniia* [Refinement of the distribution and utilization of specialists as a factor in improving the effectiveness of higher education] (Moscow: Scientific-Research Institute on the Problems of Higher Schools of MinVUZ SSSR, 1982); K. P. Savichev, *Podgotovka i raspredeleniie molodykh spetsialistov v SSSR* [Preparation and distribution of young specialists in the USSR] (Moscow: Vysshaia Shkola, 1972).

8. *Pravda,* 17 March 1978, p. 3.

9. Universities and many institutes fell within the jurisdiction of republican ministries or committees of higher and specialized secondary education. A large number of institutes, however, and most specialized secondary schools were supervised by relevant branch ministries. For instance, the Urals Mining Institute was run by the Ministry of Mining and Metallurgy, not the Ministry for Higher Education. Overall guidelines and procedures for raspredeleniie were prepared and enforced by MinVUZ (later Gosobrazovaniia).

10. This chapter concentrates on assignments of graduates from VUZy, higher education institutions. Graduates of specialized secondary schools—hybrid institutions offering fairly narrow vocational education at an advanced secondary level but administered by the higher education bureaucracy— were also subject to raspredeleniie, but in the interest of simplification I shall not include them in this discussion. The assignment process for SSUZ graduates did not differ significantly from that for VUZ graduates, except that SSUZy were often closely affiliated with a few major local enterprises at which students received their *praktikum* training, and graduates often went on to work at one of these.

11. A student reporter describing the raspredelenie process at the Far East Politechnical Institute im. Kuibishev in Vladivostok noted that students with "excellent" or "good" grades (i.e., 4 or 5 on the Soviet grading scale) were

asked for their placement preferences, while the remaining graduates were summarily offered the "suggestion" of the committee. The author recounts an old joke, in which one of these relatively mediocre graduates replies to the committee: "You've been lying to me these last 5 years. You told me I'd never get anywhere with my brains, and now here you are sending me to Magadan!" Boris Iakovlev, *Politekhnik*, 29 December 1977, 2.

12. A. Kotliar, "The Employment System in the USSR," *Ekonomicheskie nauki*, no. 3 (1984): 56.

13. *Molodezh' SSSR* [Youth of the USSR] (Moscow: Finansy i statistika, 1990), 110, 143.

14. Some early references to no-shows are provided in Joel J. Schwartz, "The Young Communist League, 1954–62: A Study in Group Cooperation and Conflict" (Ph.D. diss., Indiana University, 1965), 93–94. According to Komsomol reports cited here, levels of compliance with raspredelenie assignments were less than 10 percent for Tbilisi Medical Institute in 1956.

15. TsK VLKSM, "Stenogram of July (3rd) Plenum (9–10 July 1963)," TsA VLKSM, f. 1, op. 2, d. 439, 447, ll. 14–15, 159.

16. G. A. Aliev in *Bakinskii rabochi*, 19 February 1974, 1–4. For a similar tale of no-shows from Erevan educational institutes, see *Pravda*, 25 May 1977, 3.

17. T. Matveeva, *Pravda*, 4 August 1973, 3.

18. Galina F. Gorbei (Deputy Chief, Department of Social Statistics, Goskomstat), interview by author, Moscow, 1 April 1991; Valeriia S. Lazareva and Igor V. Ivanov (respectively of the Directorate of Labor Resources and Employment, Goskomtrud, and Planovo-ekonomicheskoe upravlenie, Gosobrazovaniia), interview by author, Moscow, 27 February 1991.

19. G. Podgaev in *Izvestiia*, 19 November 1977, 2.

20. *Molodezh' SSSR*, 143.

21. The Georgian Press Agency, for instance, reported in 1983 that only one-third of VUZ graduates assigned to jobs that year were actually working in those jobs, while one-seventh were apparently not working at all (*Zaria vostoka*, 31 August 1983, 3).

22. A mimeograph of this report ("On the training and utilization of pedagogical cadres") was provided to me by Tatiana M. Goncharova, chief of the Division of Educational Statistics of Goskomstat. Cited figures appear on p. 3.

23. Matthews, *Education in the Soviet Union*, 172.

24. K. Savichev of the RSFSR Ministry of Higher Education in *Pravda*, 17 March 1978, 3.

25. *Pravda*, for instance, reported on the refusal of a Tadzhik planning agency to accept fourteen graduates assigned to it from a Leningrad technical

institute (14 May 1969). See also R. Ozerskaia in *Izvestiia,* 20 August 1968, for a comparable tale of a Leningrad agency refusing specialists from Kaliningrad. Behavior of this nature may derive from a belief on the part of managers that graduates of distant VUZy would have greater difficulty appealing to their home institutes for protection of their rights.

26. *Pravda,* 15 November 1971, 2. The letter writer drove the point home by noting that only 20 percent of the engineers were issued mops or brooms.
27. *Pravda,* 4 May 1978, 2.
28. Other examples are cited in *Radio Liberty Research Bulletin* 415/81, 20 October 1981.
29. *Izvestiia,* 20 July 1973, 2–3. The original draft was published on 5 April of the same year.
30. Goskomstat SSSR, *Sotsial'noe razvitie i uroven' zhizni naselenie SSSR* [Social development and standard of living of the population of the USSR] (Moscow, Gos. statisticheskoe izd-vo, 1989), 47, 214.
31. Ibid., 214.
32. For a discussion of the literature on Soviet enterprise management, see Chapter 2.
33. Iu. Shpakov, "On the Basis of Requests Pulled Out of Thin Air," *Pravda,* 9 June 1970, 3.
34. *Pravda,* 7 August 1981, 3.
35. *Pravda,* 14 November 1981, 3.
36. Savichev, *Podgotovka i raspredeleniie.* The author was head of the Department for the Placement of Young Specialists in the RSFSR Ministry of Higher Education.
37. Expressions of concern over the excessive pull of higher education include I. Ovchinnikova in *Izvestiia,* 28 May 1972, 4; Iu. Averichev in *Sovetskaia pedagogika,* no. 7 (1972): 12–19; L. Ponomarev in *Izvestiia,* 19 September 1975, 3; and V. P. Eliutin in *Komsomol'skaia pravda,* 25 May 1976, 2. These concerns are also reviewed within the context of Brezhnev's education policy in Voronitsyn, *Radio Liberty Research Bulletin,* 462/82, 19 November 1982. For a discussion of the roots of this debate, see Schwartz, "The Young Communist League, 1954–62," 95ff.
38. V. N. Turchenko, "The Scientific-Technical Revolution and the Problem of Education," *Voprosy filosofii,* no. 2 (1973): 18–29.
39. M. Prokof'ev, quoted in *Izvestiia,* 28 August 1980.
40. E. Shcherbanenko in *Komsomol'skaia pravda,* 10 August 1976, 4.
41. For studies linking job dissatisfaction to the lack of vocational training, see A. E. Kotliar, "Certain Aspects of Keeping Young Workers in their Production Jobs," *Planovoe khoziaistvo,* no. 6 (1973): 119–126, and A. E. Kotliar and

M. I. Talalai, "How to Keep Young Cadres in their Jobs," *Ekonomika i organizatsiia promyshlennogo proizvodstva (EKO)*, no. 4 (1977): 26–43.

42. Vladimir Shubkin, "The Bank of Dreams and the Balance of Fates," *Literaturnaia gazeta*, 8 January 1975, 11.

43. This is analogous to what economists describe as "extensive" growth: growth fueled simply by consuming more and more resources. Once resources are found to be limited, however, growth must increasingly become "intensive," relying on more efficient resource utilization.

44. For discussions of Khrushchev's education policies, which reached full expression in the 1958 Education Reforms, see Matthews, *Education in the Soviet Union*, 1–40, 97–141, and Joel Schwartz and William Keech, "Group Influence and Policy Process in the Soviet Union," *American Political Science Review* 62, no. 3 (1968): 840–851.

45. The provisions are contained in a Council of Ministers Resolution dated 9 May 1963. In place of a diploma, graduates were to receive temporary certificates noting the completion of their education *and* their assigned job. After a year at this job, the certificates were to be exchanged for formal diplomas. See MinVUZ Order *(prikaz)* No. 299 (30 September 1963), "On Temporary Certificates . . .," *Biulleten' vysshego i srednogo spetsialnogo obrazovaniia*, no. 11 (1963): 2–5.

46. Matthews, *Education in the Soviet Union*, 174.

47. This conflict over raspredelenie is thoroughly recounted in Schwartz, "The Young Communist League, 1954–62," 86–114. Komsomol's part in promoting this policy may have been one manifestation of their broader role under Khrushchev as ideological shock troops. It may also have been an element in a broader strategy to force *employers* to honor raspredelenie guarantees more scrupulously.

48. Matthews, *Education in the Soviet Union*, 174. Remembering the politics of the earlier initiative, Brezhnev's action may also have been linked with Komsomol's fall from grace under Brezhnev.

49. *Izvestiia*, 30 July 1972, 1. For Brezhnev's educational policy in general, see Matthews, *Education in the Soviet Union*, 40–66, 97–141, and Voronitsyn, *Radio Liberty Research Bulletin*, 462/82, 19 November 1982.

50. Beginning in 1974, the first year of the three-year assignment was designated as a "probationary period" *(stazhirovka)* during which the new specialists would follow "personalized" workplans aimed at developing specialized skills and would receive more personal attention from supervisors. The goal was apparently to ease adjustment of specialists to their new workplace and thus attempt to combat desertion of assignments. The terminology is somewhat disingenuous, however; neither the assignee nor the enterprise

seems truly on "probation." The only provisions for adjustment of assignments of the basis of this first year involved a review by a special commission at the workplace which could recommend promotions or transfers within the enterprise. The experiment seems to have been largely ignored or merely implemented by rote and was hardly mentioned after 1974. See MinVUZ Order No. 553 (25 June 1973), "Regulations for the Probation (Stazhirovka) of Young Specialists Graduating from VUZ," *Biulleten' Ministerstva vysshego i srednego spetsial'nogo obrazovaniia,* no. 8 (1973): 4–7, and N. Krasnov in *Izvestiia,* 30 August 1973, 5.

51. MinVUZ Order No. 870 (30 July 1980), "Regulations for the Inter-Republican, Inter-Departmental, and Individual Distribution of Young Specialists Completing Higher and Specialized Secondary Schools of the USSR," *Biulleten' Ministerstva vysshego i srednego spetsial'nogo obrazovaniia,* no. 10 (1980): 25–36.

52. Council of Ministers of the USSR Resolution No. 64 (27 January 1978), "On Improving the Planning of Specialists' Training and the Utilization in the National Economy of Graduates of Higher and Specialized Secondary Education Institutions," *Biulleten' Ministerstva vysshego i srednego spetsial'nogo obrazovaniia,* no. 5 (1978): 1.

53. CC CPSU and Council of Ministers USSR Resolution (29 June 1979), "On Further Developing the Higher Schools and Improving the Quality of Specialists' Training (excerpts)," in *Spravochnik partiinogo rabotnika* [Party worker's handbook], (Moscow: Izd-vo politicheskoi literatury, 1980).

54. Peter Hauslohner, "Managing the Soviet Labor Market: Politics and Policymaking Under Brezhnev" (Ph.D. diss., University of Michigan, 1984), 411–413.

55. Lazareva and Ivanov (Goskomtrud and Gosobrazovaniia), interview, 27 February 1991. Hauslohner considered only the 1978 government decree and was unable to examine the text of the new 1980 raspredelenie guidelines. Consequently, he overestimates the changes in the 1980 guidelines—which did little to make assignments more binding—and the role of Goskomtrud. See Hauslohner, "Soviet Labor Market," 473.

56. Ministry of Higher Education Order No. 834 (10 June 1948), "On Regulating the Distribution and Utilization of Specialists Graduating from Higher and Specialized Secondary Education Institutions," in *Vysshaia shkola: osnovnye postanovleniia, prikazy i instruktsii* [Higher schools: basic resolutions, orders and instructions], (Moscow: Ministry of Higher Education, 1957), 203–205.

57. These decrees were issued in August 1954 (joint with the Party Central

Committee), May 1960, May 1963, September 1966, July 1972, January 1978, and June 1979.

58. A thorough review of official criticisms of the raspredelenie system during the 1980s is offered in Georgii Iur'evich Vasil'ev, "Perfecting the Systems of Distributing and Utilizing Young Specialists under Conditions of Perestroika in the Higher Schools" (Cand. Philos. diss. Kharkov Law Institute, 1989), 76ff.

59. One exception to this generalization concerns an aborted initiative in 1964–65 to withhold diplomas from graduates until they appeared at their assigned job. This will be discussed further below.

60. Iu. Shpakov, "On the Basis of Requests."

61. *Pravda,* 7 March 1974, 1.

62. Gorbei (Goskomstat), interview, 1 April 1991.

63. Ibid.

64. After the 1978 Council of Ministers' resolution, data on one- and three-year attrition rates were collected by Goskomstat. These data were supplied by individual enterprises as aggregate figures and their veracity was not probed by central statisticians. Consequently, the figure reported by Goskomstat was the percentage of graduates assigned to jobs in a given year who "appeared on the workforce lists" on a specific subsequent date. (See *Molodezh' SSSR,* 143.)

65. Vladimir Nikolaevich Korolev (Chief, Sector of Labor Statistics, Div. of Social Statistics, Goskomstat), interview by author, Moscow, 17 April 1991.

66. Galina Gorbei (Goskomstat), interview by author, Moscow, 10 April 1991.

67. I had no access to Goskomstat archives, though officials did share with me documents which had been published "For Internal Use Only." There seems to have been no published summary of the supply-demand study, even for restricted circulation.

68. "Specialists" (VUZ and SSUZ graduates) were considered by planners as a different category of labor resources from "technicians" (vocational school graduates) or simply "workers" (lacking higher education or vocational training). The three categories of personnel were thus monitored separately. Each job at an enterprise was strictly classified by necessary skill and education level and placed on the appropriate nomenklatura list; the precise classifications were standardized across the country and were meant to specify both the selection criteria of the eventual employee and his or her salary and benefits. Employers routinely monitored the actual qualifications of employees holding jobs on different nomenklatura lists. Since formal selection criteria were often ignored by labor-hungry enterprises (particu-

larly to "stockpile" available skilled workers), many jobs were filled by employees whose qualifications appeared inappropriate.

69. *Narodnoe khoziaistvo SSSR v 1987* [USSR Economy in 1987] (Moscow: Goskomstat, 1987), 370.
70. Gorbei (Goskomstat), interview, 1 April 1991.
71. Korolev (Goskomstat), interview, 17 April 1991.
72. *Molodezh' SSSR*, 143.
73. Biuro TsK VLKSM Resolution B 4/13 (29 August 1978), "On the work of Komsomol committees on improving job assignments, employment services, and utilization of graduates of VUZy and SSUZy" in *Dokumenty TsK VLKSM 1978* [Documents of the Central Committee of the VLKSM], (Moscow: TsK VLKSM, 1978), 142–145. The language is copied verbatim from the 1979 joint party-State decree.
74. TsA VLKSM, f. 1, op. 88, d. 33c.
75. Ibid. The protocol of the meeting shows no evidence of any discussion accompanying approval of the resolution.
76. The most noteworthy innovation to the raspredelenie system from 1968 to 1988 was the order (in the 1978 Council of Ministers decree) to collect data on how graduates were being utilized by their new employers.
77. Some of the most influential and ambitious discussions of higher education and jobs include V. Shubkin, "The Beginning of the Road," *Novy mir*, no. 2 (1975): 188–219; *Vysshaia shkola kak faktor izmeneniia sotsial'noi struktury razvitogo sotsialisticheskogo obshchestva* [Higher education as a factor in the social structure of developed socialist society] ed. N. Rutkevich and F. R. Filippov (Moscow: Nauka, 1978); and M. N. Rutkevich and L. Ia. Rubina, *Obshchestvennye potrebnosti sistema obrazovaniia molodezh'* [Societal needs, educational system, youth] (Moscow: Izdatelstvo polit. literary, 1988). The following shorter articles describe other survey research which, while varying in quality and rigor, also provides interesting perspectives on career choice and job selection: I. N. Nazimov, "In Accordance with Man's Possibilities and Society's Requirements," *Ekonomika i orgnaizatsiia promyshlenogo proizvodstva (EKO)*, no. 3 (1977): 85–95; I. E. Zaslavskii, V. A. Kuz'min, and P. T. Ostrovskaia, "Social and Professional Placement of Moscow Schoolchildren," *Sotsiologicheskie issledovaniia*, no. 3 (1983): 132–34; V. Butov in *Pravda*, 18 September 1970, 3; A. Fomichev in *Izvestiia*, 22 February 1972, 5; and Kotliar, "The Employment System," 69. For an excellent discussion and extensive bibliography of Soviet sociology on choice of occupation, see Vladimir Shlapentokh, *Public and Private Life of the Soviet People* (New York: Oxford University Press, 1989), Chapter 2, especially 71–79. Another useful overview of academic research on educational issues through the early

1980s is Janusz Tomiak, "Soviet Sociologists and Soviet Economists on Soviet Education," in *Soviet Education in the 1980's,* ed. J. J. Tomiak (New York: St. Martin's Press, 1983), 240–277.

78. Shubkin, "The Beginning of the Road."

79. The Ministry of Light Industry, for instance, issued guidelines for changing "obsolete and ugly sounding" job names. The guidelines were implemented slowly, however. See *Sotsialisticheskaia industriia,* 28 September 1972, 2.

80. Filip Raf'elovich Filippov (Institute of Sociology, USSR Academy of Sciences), interview by author, Moscow, 9 February 1990.

81. When the study (Rutkevich and Filippov, ed., *Vysshaia shkola kak faktor*) was eventually published, some reviewers pointedly criticized the excessive publication delay. See *Molodoi kommunist,* no.3 (1979): 101–102.

82. F. R. Filippov, "What Sociology of Education Has Accomplished," *Vestnik vysshei shkoly,* no. 12 (1989): 13–19. In our interview, Filippov told me that officials at the Ministry of Higher Education dismissed requests to help expedite publication of the *Vysshaia shkola kak faktor* data by remarking, "Sociology makes mistakes."

83. F. P. Filippov, Letter to TsK VLKSM (1978), TsA VLKSM, f. 6, op. 18, d. 446, ll. 8–12.

84. Georgii Iur'evich Vasil'ev, "Perfecting the Systems of Distributing and Utilizing Young Specialists under Conditions of Perestroika in the Higher Schools" (Cand. Philos., diss., Kharkov Law Institute, 1989). Dissertation writers everywhere could probably sympathize with Vasil'ev's compulsion to support this statement with no fewer than six citations.

85. G. Kulagin in *Zvezda,* no. 1, 1974, 164–178.

86. The two strongest research centers were: the Central Scientific Research Laboratory on Labor Resources of the RSFSR Committee on Labor (known by its Russian acronym TsNILTR), founded in 1967 by the USSR State Committee on Science and Technology; and MinVUZ SSSR's Scientific Research Institute on the Problems of Higher Schools (NIIPVSh), which published several series of "research reviews" relevant to aspects of VUZ and SSUZ planning and management.

87. This conclusion is based on a review of TsNILTR's research monograph series *Trudovye resursy* and NIIPVSh's series of "research reviews" from the mid-1970s through the late 1980s. One exception to the rule is a survey of Moscow secondary-school graduates conducted by sociologists at the Scientific Research Institute on Labor of Goskomtrud SSSR, published as Zaslavskii, Kuz'min, and Ostrovskaia, "Social and Professional Placement."

88. Igor Ivanov (Gosobrazovaniia) interview by author, Moscow, 22 March 1991.

89. V. Savichev in *Molodoi kommunist*, no. 3 (1967): 78–81.

90. M. Anuchin, *Izvestiia*, 6 January 1973, 5; *Literaturnaia gazeta*, 14 November 1979, 11. In the latter reference, a conference participant reported that 35 percent of students at evening VUZ divisions in the RSFSR were failed applicants to daytime divisions who were not otherwise employed. Since workers could only enroll in specialties in which they already were employed, and often skilled workers were paid more than diploma-holding specialists, there was little incentive for workers to return to a student life most had rushed to be done with.

91. See *Uchitel'skaia gazeta*, 14 February 1978, 2, and 12 February 1981, 2.

92. Naturally, the chief entree into this "family circle" for individual students and graduates was through family influence or outright bribery. Both were, by all accounts, widespread in Soviet higher education, beginning with admissions and continuing through raspredelenie.

93. See, for instance, G. P. Revenko, "Questions of the Distribution and Rational Utilization of Young Specialists Graduating from Pedagogical Universities," in *Seminar-Meeting of Chiefs of Organizational Subdivisions of Ministries and Departments Responsible for Assignment and Utilization of Young Specialists (Sept. 1977)*, ed. V. A. Zhitenev (Moscow: TsK VLKSM & GoskomNauk, 1978), 78–84.

94. This pattern emerges clearly in working documents of Komsomol's Department of Students: TsA VLKSM, f. 1, op. 39, d. 236 (Main document dated 7 October 1970), TsA VLKSM, f. 1, op. 39, d. 288 (1971–72), TsA VLKSM, f. 6, op. 20, d. 186 (1987); TsA VLKSM, f. 6, op. 19, d. 278 (1 March 1982); TsA VLKSM, f. 6, op. 18, d. 429 (25 January 1978). A 1969 Komsomol Plenum devoted in part to the activity of VUZ Komsomol organizations proceeded without a single mention of raspredelenie: TsK VLKSM, "Stenogram of VIII Plenum (25–26 December 1969)," TsA VLKSM, f. 1, op. 2, d. 587.

95. MinVUZ Letter [Pis'mo] No. 96–16–19 (7 April 1981), "In the state inspection of VUZy," *Biulleten' Ministerstva vysshego i srednego spetsial'nogo obrazovaniia*, no. 6 (1981): 30–32.

96. V. A. Severtsev, "The Quality of the Preparation of Young Specialists: Fundamental Criteria," *Vestnik vysshei shkoly*, no. 4 (1986): 74–76.

97. *Literaturnaia gazeta*, 10 April 1968, 10.

98. *Literaturnaia gazeta*, 31 July 1968, 10. Birman's proposal was dropped after 1968, but may have influenced the designation, in 1974, of a "probationary" year at the start of job assignments. This so-called probationary, however, had no explicit provisions for rejecting graduates and was in no way linked to enterprise compensation of VUZy for specialist training.

99. The idea of delaying the awarding of diplomas until graduates arrived at

or even completed their assignments continued to surface amid calls for greater "discipline" overall. These proposals apparently never enjoyed much support, since there was never a serious effort to amend the Soviet Statutes on Higher Education, which mandated the immediate granting of diplomas to graduates (see, for instance, F. Panachin in *Uchitel'skaia gazeta*, 9 February 1980, 2). According to some reports, the Georgians, frustrated by a barely functioning placement system, may have unilaterally imposed such a delay in the early 1980s, in violation of state law. See Voronitsyn, *Radio Liberty Research Bulletin*, 154/83, 14 April 1983.

100. *Molodoi kommunist*, no. 3 (1967): 78–81.
101. Matthews, *Education in the Soviet Union*, 174, and V. V. Khorolets, "Pravovye osnovy raspredeleniia i ispol'zovaniia molodykh spetsialistov" (avtoreferat, Leningrad Shipbuilding Institute, 1988).
102. Ivanov (Gosobrazovaniia) interview, 22 March 1991.
103. Assignees, of course, could hardly be punished for wasting their educations sweeping floors if this was the only job offered to them by their assigned employers, or for not receiving promised housing. But, as indicated above, I have found no case of enterprise managers receiving punishment for violation of these raspredelenie guarantees.
104. *Argumenty i fakty*, no. 6 (1988): 1, 2.
105. Ibid.
106. Gennadi Iagodin (Chairman, Gosobrazovaniia), interview by author, Moscow, 27 February 1991. Reference is made to a *kvalifikatsionnii attestat* in the 1988 raspredelenie guidelines and in E. A. Motina and N. V. Udalova, "Young Specialists," in *Iuridicheskii spravochnik dlia naseleniia* (Moscow: Iuridicheskaia literatura, 1990), 133–137. Both sources suggest that certificates would be awarded on the basis of a certification test to be administered after three years. Gosobrazovaniia's Ivanov confirmed to me, however, that no details of this certification process were ever specified and the rule was essentially moribund.
107. Lazareva and Ivanov (Goskomtrud and Gosobrazovaniia), interview, 27 February 1991. This was the same "perception" eventually confirmed by the unpublished Goskomstat studies of the mid-1980s described earlier.
108. See, for instance, *Argumenty i fakty*, no. 14 (1988): 4, and *Sobesednik*, no. 14 (1986): 11.
109. *Izvestiia*, 30 January 1982, 3.
110. MinVUZ Order No. 831 (5 September 1975), "Confirming the List of USSR VUZ Specialties and Specializations," *Biulleten' Ministerstva vysshego i srednego spetsial'nogo obrazovaniia SSSR*, no. 12 (1975): 2–29. A new specializations list published in November 1987 reduced the number of possible majors to 299 (MinVUZ Order No. 790 [17 November 1987], "Confirming the List of

USSR VUZ Specializations," *Biulleten' Ministerstva vysshego i srednego spetsial'nogo obrazovaniia,* no. 1 [1988]: 8–15). This reduction was achieved primarily through consolidation of some of the narrowest specializations, like "Road construction" and "Airport construction," into slightly less narrow categories like "Road and airport construction." Other specializations mentioned here remained separate; many of these *kafedry* graduated fewer than 100 students nationwide annually.

111. V. P. Eliutin, Minister of Higher Education, complained in 1983 that some 70 ministries at the all-Union and republican levels had still taken no action to comply with state directives to limit their employment of VUZ graduates (*Pravda,* 22 February 1983).

112. Vasil'ev's dissertation examined raspredelenie in Kharkov for the 1987–88 academic year and found that the plan received by Kharkov State University, drawn up as much as three years earlier, called for 13 percent more placements than there were students graduating. Despite this apparent "shortage" of graduates, 237 still received permission for independent placement, as a result of which 155 placement slots went unfilled. Nevertheless, numerous graduates who were placed through raspredelenie that year were still turned away by their assigned employers (see Vasil'ev, "Perfecting the Systems").

113. *Molodoi kommunist,* no. 3 (1967): 78–81. These graduates were already exempt from regular placement committees, since it was assumed they would return to their earlier employers. Savichev argued that such an assumption neglected any changes which might have occurred in students' interests or skills during their time at the VUZ.

114. Savichev, *Podgotovka i raspredeleniie,* 97–102.

115. See *Pravda,* 17 March 1978, 3, and 22 March 1981, 3.

116. I. Prelovskaia (*Izvestiia,* 18 September 1971, 2) describes the Tomsk Polytechnic Institute's resort to direct contact with industry to place physical chemists after fourteen of twenty-two graduates were turned away by employers who no longer needed them. Similar cases are recounted in N. Zaitsev, *Pravda,* 7 August 1981, 3 (Kishiniev) and TsA VLKSM, f. 1, op. 88, d. 33c (29 August 1978) (Sverdlovsk and Rostov).

117. See, for instance *Pravda,* 6 January 1979, 3.

118. *Pravda,* 22 March 1981, 3

119. Anatolii Alekseevich Logunov in *Moskovskii universitet,* 25 February 1986, 3. Logunov, the rector of Moscow University, claimed that the plan for placements provided sufficient jobs for only eight of the University's faculties. Only 60–70 percent of graduates in the other faculties were placed according to plan.

120. *Materialy XXVII S"ezda Kommunisticheskoi Partii Sovetskogo Soiuza* [Materials from the Twenty-seventh Congress of the CPSU], (Moscow, 1986), 49.

121. Lazareva and Ivanov (Goskomtrud and Gosobrazovaniia), interview, 27 February 1991. According to Ivanov, the primary author of the reforms was the Ministry of Higher Education.

122. The reforms consisted of a Central Committee Resolution laying out basic principles and five joint Party-Council of Ministers decrees, all published in *Pravda* on March 21 and 25–28, 1987.

123. CC CPSU and Council of Ministers (SovMin) USSR Resolution No. 325 (13 March 1987), "On Measures for the Fundamental Improvement of the Quality of Training and Utilization of Specialists with Higher Education in the National Economy," in *Narodnaia obrazovanie v SSSR: sbornik normativnykh aktov* (Moscow: Finansy i statistika, 1987), 246–257. I refer to this hereafter as SovMin 325.

124. Ibid., 249.

125. Lazareva and Ivanov (Goskomtrud and Gosobrazovaniia), interview, 27 February 1991.

126. SovMin 325, 249–50. The 1987 reforms also dictated a greater role for contract research—based on direct orders from enterprises and ministries—in VUZ financing.

127. A. N. Konovalov, et al., *Sovershenstvovaniie raspredeleniia,* 33.

128. Gosobrazovaniia Order No. 286 (22 August 1988), "Regulations for the Distribution and Utilization in the National Economy of Graduates of Higher and Specialized Secondary Education," *Biulleten' Gosobrazovaniia: Seriia vysshee i srednee spetsial'noe obrazovanie,* no. 11 (1988): 12–24.

129. *Moskovskii universitet,* 25 May 1988, 3. Other faculties at Moscow University were already relying on long-term contracts. The geology faculty, for instance, signed an agreement in 1987 to supply 50 graduates annually to the USSR State Hydro-Meteorology Committee (*Moskovskii universitet,* 28 September 1987, 1).

130. V. A. Tverdislov, *Moskovskii universitet,* 30 May 1989, 4.

131. Council of Ministers USSR Resolution No. 708 (31 August 1989), "On the participation of state, cooperative and other social organizations and establishments in the restrengthening of higher and specialized secondary educational establishments and the training of specialists" (contained within Gosobrazovaniia Order No. 791 [13 October 1989], mimeo).

132. Ivanov, at Gosobrazovaniia, implied in the course of two interviews that he (hence, MinVUZ/Gosobrazovaniia) had taken a lead role in drafting the Council of Ministers resolutions of 1987 and 1990, but not the 1989 decree.

133. *Moskovskii komsomolets,* 8 April 1990, 2.

134. Gosobrazovaniia Order No. 791 (13 October 1989), mimeo, 11–12.
135. Gosobrazovaniia Order No. 466 (5 July 1990), "On the Procedure for Concluding Individual Agreements for the Training of Specialists with Higher and Specialized Secondary Education," *Biulleten' Gosobrazovaniia: Seriia professional'noe obrazovanie,* no. 10 (1990): 22–29.
136. Ivanov told me that Gosplan actually disbanded the department responsible for raspredelenie planning in 1990.
137. Council of Ministers USSR Resolution No. 1311 (19 December 1990), "On Measures for the Development of Contractual Relations for the Training of Specialists with Higher and Specialized Secondary Education," mimeo.
138. Ibid., emphasis added. The swiftness with which these new regulations take effect belies their novelty: it would be patently absurd for VUZy to learn in December that beginning in January they would need to define a system of job placements for that very spring, unless the VUZy were already doing so.
139. V. A. Sadovnichii in *Moskovskii universitet,* 30 May 1989, 3.
140. V. A. Tverdislov in *Moskovskii universitet,* 30 May 1989, 4.
141. *Moskovskii komsomolets,* 8 April 1990, 2.
142. Gennadii Iagodin, Address to meeting of VUZ rectors, *Biulleten' gosobrazovaniia,* no. 8 (1990): 2–7.
143. Ibid.
144. *Argumenty i fakty,* no. 44 (1988): 4.
145. In September 1990, I witnessed the consequences of this shift in power more intimately than I would ever have wished. Arriving in Moscow on an IREX fellowship arranged through Gosobrazovaniia, Moscow University (MGU) flatly refused to house me—or any other scholars from any Western country whose treaties were negotiated through Gosobrazovaniia rather than through MGU directly. "We don't take orders from them any longer," declared our chilly MGU contact. A similar reception awaited us at the hotel owned by Gosobrazovaniia, which also took advantage of our arrival to announce its independence from all ministerial control. After ten days of harried negotiations, extending to diplomatic threats of reciprocal expulsions, Iagodin was able to exert his personal authority over the hotel management to provide us with housing. MGU remained adamant for the duration of our research exchange, though it inexplicably handled our visa matters without any objections.
146. Lazareva and Ivanov (Goskomtrud and Gosobrazovaniia), interview, 27 February 1991.
147. "On the Status of Higher Educational Institutions," *Pravda,* 16 October 1990, 1.

148. I. Prelovskaia in *Izvestiia,* 22 July 1991, 3.

149. *Nezavisimaia gazeta,* 29 November 1992, 6.

150. *Izvestiia,* 2 February 1991, 3.

151. Alexander Massey, "Soviet Institutions' Plan to Charge Fees Is Declared Illegal," *Chronicle of Higher Education,* 24 July 1991; Alexander Massey, "In Break with Past, Many Soviet Institutions of Higher Education Plan to Impose Tuition," *Chronicle of Higher Education,* 17 July 1991. While the Parliament's move may have successfully halted the imposition of new fees on students, the chaotic state of Soviet lawmaking on the eve of the 1991 August coup—and the lack of alternatives for financing VUZ operations—made fee-based education inevitable. By 1992, private universities and academies were springing up around Russia, chiefly offering "business" training for fee-paying students. Meanwhile, enterprise subsidization of tuition costs for students still in the state-run system continued to be the norm. For two critical analyses of the post-1991 situation, see *Izvestiia,* 29 May 1992, 7, and *Nezavisimaia gazeta,* 14 December 1993, 6.

152. Ivanov (Gosobrazovaniia), interview, 22 March 1991.

153. Vladimir Lepekhin (former Moscow University and later Central Committee Komsomol official), interview by author, Moscow, 7 March 1991. Lepekhin's statement is especially striking since, in the mid-1980s, Moscow University students were being drafted for combat duty in Afghanistan. (See Chapter 6 for a detailed discussion of student draft deferments.)

154. *Moskovskii komsomolets,* 8 April 1990, 2. Iagodin, though still a supporter of the mandatory placement system, confessed it was "difficult to call it a privilege these days."

155. As the case of the Komsomol in Chapter 4 suggests, if these data *were* formalized as performance indicators, the result would have been a compounding of the problem of moral hazard, with the likely result of even poorer quality data being collected at the center.

6. Universal Military Service

1. Constitution of the USSR (1977), Article 63.

2. Extraterritorial basing also ensured that in the event of unrest in the non-Russian republics, nonindigenous troops would be available to restore order. See S. Enders Wimbush and Alex Alexiev, *The Ethnic Factor in the Soviet Armed Forces* (RAND Corporation Report R-2787/1), March 1982, 12.

3. Much of the information in this section is drawn from A. M. Dereviashchenko and K. O. Grushevoi, *Vash syn ukhodit v armiiu* [Your son goes off to the army] (Moscow: Voeniurist, 1990); Ellen Jones, *Red Army and Society: A*

Sociology of the Soviet Military (Boston: Allen & Unwin, 1985); Harriet Fast Scott and William F. Scott, *The Armed Forces of the USSR,* 3rd ed. (Boulder, Colo.: Westview, 1984); Richard A. Gabriel, *The New Red Legions* (Westport, Conn.: Greenwood Press, 1980), 36–38. The induction process was governed by the "Law on Universal Military Service," adopted by the USSR Supreme Soviet on 12 October 1967 (*Vedomosti Verkhovnogo Soveta SSSR,* no. 42, 1967).

4. Actually, according to Al'bert Sergeev, Chief of the Conscription Department for the Soviet General Staff, the voenkomaty themselves were "organs of Soviet power" at the local level, not Ministry of Defense organizations (Meeting of Defense Officials and Committee of Soldiers' Mothers, USSR Supreme Soviet, Moscow, 19 April 1991).

5. These terms of service were established in the 1967 Draft Law. Prior to its passage, under the terms of the 1939 Draft Law (amended), terms of service were three and four years, and youth were drafted at age nineteen.

6. See Chapter 5 for a broader discussion of this problem of oversupply of graduates with little interest in their chosen majors.

7. The regulations were issued as an attachment to a Ministry of Defense Order (Prikaz), which was never published or distributed. Basic guidelines were issued in 1973 and were amended several times during the 1980s. As I discuss later in this chapter, new guidelines were issued in 1987.

8. See, for instance, William Zimmerman and Michael L. Berbaum, "Soviet Military Manpower Policy in the Brezhnev Era: Regime Goals, Social Origins, and Working the System," *Europe-Asia Studies* 45, no. 2 (1993): 281–302. Examining results of an emigré survey, the authors found that 90 of 166 respondents who failed to serve in the army received medical deferments, even though elsewhere in the interview only eighteen reported being in poor health at age seventeen. See also Viktor Suvorov, *Inside the Soviet Army* (London: Granada, 1982), 334.

9. Jones, *Red Army and Society,* 86.

10. For a fascinating study of DOSAAF's predecessor organization, see William E. Odom, *The Soviet Volunteers: Modernization and Bureaucracy in a Public Mass Organization* (Princeton, N.J.: Princeton University Press, 1973).

11. Otdel sportivnoi i oboronno-massovoi raboty, "Results of the 1968 Draft" (10 June 1969), TsA VLKSM, f. 1, op. 38, d. 254, ll. 25–30.

12. Otdel sportivnoi i oboronno-massovoi raboty, "Report on Work Feb.–Nov. 1978," TsA VLKSM, f. 1, op. 66, d. 212, l. 25.

13. See, for instance, discussions of Seventh-Day Adventists in *Nauka i religiia,* no. 9 (1979): 32–35; and *Komsomol'skaia pravda,* 24 August 1973, 2. In 1984, a representative of the Army's Main Political Administration told a Komsomol plenum that the number of inductees with the "defect" of belonging

to religious sects was on the rise and that many of these individuals refused to bear arms (N. Koshelev, "Address to TsK VLKSM 9th Plenum [10 August 1984]," TsA VLKSM, f. 1, op. 100, d. 77c, ll. 132ff.).

14. Otdel sportivnoi i oboronno-massovoi raboty, "Results of the 1968 Draft."

15. Otdel sportivnoi i oboronno-massovoi raboty, "Information on preparation of youth for the draft in connection with new Draft Law (1968)," TsA VLKSM, f. 1, op. 38, d. 184.

16. According to the RSFSR Criminal Code, Article 198.1, as amended in 1969, the penalty for evading the draft was one year of prison and up to one hundred rubles; the penalty for evading registration was three months and twenty rubles.

17. Suvorov, *Inside the Soviet Army,* 334. Unfortunately, no date is given for these executions.

18. The RSFSR Criminal Code (Article 198.1) imposed an especially harsh penalty (three years' incarceration) for draft evasion "involving fraud, deception or self-mutilation." Apparently, though, successfully obtaining a certification of psychological incapacity resulted in "the fewest restrictions on future prospects for finding work" (Aleksandr Zapesotskii and Aleksandr Fain, *Eta neponiatnaia molodezh'* [These incomprehensible youth] [Moscow: Profizdat, 1990], 147).

19. *Nedelia,* no. 50 (1969): 23. The letter was written by a convicted murderer and was published to show the clear link between cynicism and homicidal depravity. The sentiments of the author, however, appear to have been widespread.

20. Otdel documentatsii [TsK VLKSM], "Notes on 25 May 1965 Meeting at General Staff Hq to discuss 1964 Draft," TsA VLKSM, f. 1, op. 31, d. 201; Otdel sportivnoi i oboronno-massovoi raboty, "Information on preparation of youth for the draft and military schools (1967)," TsA VLKSM, f. 1, op. 38, d. 101.

21. Otdel sportivnoi i oboronno-massovoi raboty, "Information on Qualitative Indicators of the 1973 Draft," TsA VLKSM, f. 1, op. 38, d. 585.

22. Otdel sportivnoi i oboronno-massovoi raboty, "Information on Qualitative Indicators of the 1971 Draft," TsA VLKSM, f. 1, op. 38, d. 460; and "Information on Qualitative Indicators of the Draft (1977)," TsA VLKSM, f. 1, op. 66, d. 20.

23. Otdel sportivnoi i oboronno-massovoi raboty, "Results of the 1968 Draft."

24. Otdel sportivnoi i oboronno-massovoi raboty, "Results of the 1968 Draft." In Estoniia, for instance, 20 percent of draftees received medical deferments; this figure was 15.7 percent in Tadzhikistan, 17 percent in Tatarstan, 15 percent in Armeniia, 18 percent in Tiumen' oblast, and 22 percent in Tuva.

25. TsK VLKSM, "Stenogram of 7th Plenum (21 August 1972)," TsA VLKSM, f. 1, op. 2, d. 643, l. 27.

26. Otdel sportivnoi i oboronno-massovoi raboty, "Qualitative Indicators of the 1971 Draft," "Qualitative Indicators of the 1973 Draft," and "Information on Qualitative Indicators of the Draft (1976)," TsA VLKSM f. 1, op. 38, d. 1132. Fitness *(godnost')* for service was reported sporadically at best in these Komsomol documents. This evidence, therefore, must be considered illustrative rather than systematic.

27. MIK: E. Nechaev (Head of Central Administration of Military Medicine, Ministry of Defense), Letter to V. Semukha, Deputy Chairman, Supreme Soviet Committee on Public Health (15 October 1990).

28. Nechaev, Letter to V. Semukha, p. 2. Youth were supposed to receive their first predraft checkup at age fifteen. The illness rate uncovered at these checkups rose from 7.5 percent in 1970 to 25.7 percent in 1988.

29. N. Koshelev, "Address to 9th Plenum (10 August 1984)."

30. Nechaev, Letter to V. Semukha. It must be noted, however, that the war in Afghanistan and the curtailing of student deferments was creating great pressure on draftees to find some way to qualify for medical exemptions.

31. I. Pavlovskii in TsK VLKSM, "Stenogram of 7th Plenum (21 August 1972)," ll. 134ff.

32. Otdel sportivnoi i oboronno-massovoi raboty, "Qualitative Indicators of the 1971 Draft," "Qualitative Indicators of the 1973 Draft," and "Report on Work Feb.–Nov. 1978," TsA VLKSM, f. 1, op. 66, d. 212.

33. TsK VLKSM, "Stenogram of 7th Plenum (21 August 1972)," ll. 134ff.

34. Ibid.

35. See, for instance, reports from the 7th DOSAAF Congress in *Pravda,* 21–24 December 1971, as well as A. Odintsov in *Krasnaia zvezda,* 28 April 1971, 2; N. Stepanishchev and I. Senetskaia in *Sovetskii patriot,* 16 July 1972, 3; and Jones, *Red Army and Society,* 65.

36. Jones, *Red Army and Society,* 192.

37. Otdel sportivnoi i oboronno-massovoi raboty, "Notes to the TsK VLKSM (1979)," TsA VLKSM, f. 1, op. 66, d. 304, ll. 184–186.

38. Ibid.

39. Otdel sportivnoi i oboronno-massovoi raboty, "Notes to the TsK VLKSM (4 June 1981)," TsA VLKSM, f. 1, op. 116, d. 6, ll. 44–55.

40. Jones, *Red Army and Society,* 192.

41. Otdel dokumentatsii, "Notes on 25 May 1965 Meeting."

42. N. Koshelev, "Address to TsK VLKSM 9th Plenum (10 August 1984)," l. 138.

43. Otdel sportivnoi i oboronno-massovoi raboty, "Notes to the TsK VLKSM (4 June 1981)."

44. N. N. Efimov and Iu. I. Deriugin, "Means of Improving the Effectiveness of Military-Patriotic Upbringing of Youth," *Sotsiologicheskie issledovaniia*, no. 1 (1980): 60–66.

45. See Jones, *Red Army and Society*, 138–140; and Natalie Gross, "Youth and the Army in the USSR in the 1980s," *Soviet Studies* 42, no. 3 (1990): 481–498.

46. A. I. Sorokin in *Voprosy filosofii*, no. 2 (1983): 3–17.

47. Iu. Deriugin in *Argumenty i fakty*, no. 41/42 (1987): 12.

48. For more on gruppovshchina, see Gross, "Youth and the Army in the 1980s," 482, 494 n.7.

49. "Sto dnei do prikaza," *Iunost'*, no. 11 (1987): 47–68. The novella was apparently written several years earlier. The title refers to the final hundred days of army service.

50. See *Argumenty i fakty*, no. 41/42 (1987): 12.

51. M. Melnik, "Incident in a Railway Carriage," *Komsomol'skaia pravda*, 20 July 1988. Actually, the victim of the incident recounted in this article—though identified in the article only as "Artur"—was Arturas Sakalauskas, a young Lithuanian soldier drafted into forces of the Ministry of Internal Affairs in 1986. Sakalauskas's beating and subsequent act of retaliatory violence occurred on 23 February 1987 and became a cause celebre throughout the Baltics.

52. See Stephen Foye, "'Non-Combat Deaths': Gorbachev Decree Reflects Army's Woes," *Report on the USSR* 2, no. 38 (1990).

53. Adyl Iakubov and Timur Pulatov, "Sons Go Off to the Army," *Ogonek*, no. 10 (1990): 20.

54. *Komsomol'skaia pravda*, 2 August 1990, 3.

55. Figures on the size of the pool of eighteen-year-olds are taken from Scott and Scott, *The Armed Forces of the USSR*, 321.

56. See, for instance, the Supreme Soviet debates on the adoption of the new law in *Izvestiia*, 13 October 1967 (suppl.), 7–8. This was also the chief focus of internal Komsomol discussions of the new Law, especially since Komsomol was to be expected to handle much of the "patriotic upbringing" work.

57. In Moscow, for instance, ten schools were exempted in 1989. Nine were engineering or technical institutes. Exemptions were also granted to students of selected Moscow University faculties (*Argumenty i fakty*, no. 7 [1989]: 8). Students at the Moscow Institute for International Relations, many of whom were sons of high-ranking officials, were also apparently exempt from service (see *Krasnaia zvezda*, 29 June 1985, 2).

58. The changes were made in a decree of the Presidium of the Supreme Soviet of the USSR signed 17 December 1980 (*Vedomosti Verkhovnogo Soveta*, no. 52 [1980]: art. 1121) and took effect 1 January 1982. For typically cursory

discussions of these changes, see *Krasnaia zvezda,* 15 May 1981, or *Na boevom postu,* no. 5 (1982): 49–51.

59. I. Tretiak, *Moscow News,* no. 8 (1988), quoted in Ellen Jones, "Social Change and Civil-Military Relations," in *Soldiers and the Soviet State: Civil-Military Relations from Brezhnev to Gorbachev,* ed. Thane Gustafson and Timothy J. Colton (Princeton, N.J.: Princeton University Press, 1990), 275.

60. See Jones, "Social Change and Civil-Military Relations," 275–276.

61. Aleksandr Savinkin, "What Kind of Armed Forces Do We Need?" *Moscow News,* no. 45 (1988). For some responses defending the status quo, see *Moscow News,* no. 4 (1989): 4 and *Krasnaia zvezda,* 4 February 1989, 1.

62. Mikhail Gorbachev, *Perestroika and Youth: Time for Action* (Moscow: Politizdat, 1988), 19. The publication is a booklet describing his meeting with Moscow-area youth, 29 October 1988.

63. Ia. Gungdodyev (First Secretary of the Turkmenistan Komsomol), Speech to Twentieth Komsomol Congress, 17 April 1987, *XX S"ezd VLKSM: Stenograficheskii otchet* [Twentieth Congress of the VLKSM: Stenographic record] (Moscow: Molodaia gvardiia, 1987).

64. *Znamenosets,* no. 2 (1989): 11.

65. Efimov and Deriugin, "Means of Improving the Effectiveness." Efimov was then at Moscow University, Deriugin was with the army.

66. Iu. Deriugin and N. Efimov, "Upbringing Role of the Soviet Armed Forces," *Sotsiologicheskie issledovaniia,* no. 4 (1981): 104–109. Though apparently based on survey data, the authors omit any description of their sample size or survey dates. This was a striking change from the thoroughness of their 1980 article. When I contacted Efimov (who had become prorector of Moscow University) by telephone in Moscow in March 1991 to ask about the original study and the military's reaction to it, he assured me that the response at the time was "positive." Though he said his work with Deriugin had generated "great interest," he claimed to be unable to remember any details of their collaboration or the response it generated. Deriugin spent several years writing platitudes about military upbringing work for DOSAAF and Komsomol (including a propaganda book about the American marines) before returning as a leading spokesman on social problems in the military in 1987. By 1990 he was writing extensively on dedovshchina and directing a new military sociological institute. Unfortunately, he suffered a heart attack in 1991 and was unavailable to give me his recollections of the 1980 research and its reception.

67. See Jones, "Social Change and Civil-Military Relations," 264–65; and Gross, "Youth and the Army in the USSR," 486–493.

68. Peter Kruzhin, *Radio Liberty Research Reports* 483/81 (4 December 1981).

69. Otdel sportivnoi i oboronno-massovoi raboty, "Notes to the TsK VLKSM (4 June 1981)," l. 51. The first combat divisions into Afghanistan were from the neighboring Turkmenistan Military District; many of these troops were drawn from the Central Asian republics. These divisions were later replaced by divisions with a greater share of Slavic soldiers.

70. According to Basile Kerblay, *Gorbachev's Russia* (New York: Pantheon, 1989), 158, n.8, just before his removal as Moscow Party boss, Boris Yeltsin claimed that a third of the letters received by the Moscow gorkom concerned the Afghan war.

71. The target of three applicants per slot was apparently established in Ministry of Defense order 270 (1969). It is referred to by the Vinnitsa Komsomol obkom in their 1973 report on the draft (Otdel sportivnoi i oboronno-massovoi raboty, "Qualitative Indicators of the 1973 Draft").

72. Otdel sportivnoi i oboronno-massovoi raboty, "Results of the 1968 Draft." Because of the desire to exercise some selectivity, not all applicants satisfying basic entrance requirements automatically enrolled. Candidates recommended by local Komsomol or DOSAAF committees, however, were expected at least to be able to meet basic entrance requirements such as passing the entrance examination.

73. Otdel sportivnoi i oboronno-massovoi raboty, "Qualitative Indicators of the 1971 Draft."

74. Otdel sportivnoi i oboronno-massovoi raboty, "Qualitative Indicators of the Draft (1976)."

75. Otdel sportivnoi i oboronno-massovoi raboty, "Notes to the TsK VLKSM (4 June 1981)."

76. Otdel dokumentatsii, "Notes on 25 May 1965 Meeting," ll. 51–54.

77. Otdel sportivnoi i oboronno-massovoi raboty, "Notes to the TsK VLKSM (4 June 1981)."

78. Komitet po molodezhnoi politike Verkhovnogo soveta SSSR, unpublished stenogram of Meeting, 4 April 1991. This would represent roughly 5 percent of the estimated draft contingent of one million.

79. MIK: D. Iazov (Minister of Defense), Letter to Peoples' Deputy L. T. Zhigunova, No. 315/4/2332 (5 October 1990).

80. These were contained in Ministry of Defense Order No. 260 of 9 September 1987. The order runs to over 340 pages and catalogues over 116 distinct medical conditions (personal archive of Maria Kirbasova). Parts of the order have since been published in *Ne prizvan po sostoianiu zdorov'ia* [Not drafted for reasons of health] and *Ne goden k voennoi sluzhbe* [Unfit for military service] (Moscow: Izdatelstvo Rossiiskaia gazeta, 1994), though there are some inconsistencies between this version and the earlier mimeo.

81. MIK: A. Vinogradov (Chief of Staff of Railway Troops), Letter to V. I. Semukha, Deputy Chairman, Supreme Soviet Committee on Public Health (231/1372) (12 October 1990).

82. MIK: L. M. Zaika (Office of the Chief Military Procurator), Letter to V. Semukha, Deputy Chairman, Supreme Soviet Committee on Public Health (No. 1-1741) (October 1990). Presumably, this constitutes only the small fraction whose incapacity was so severe that continued service proved impossible.

83. Ibid. Through an uncertain methodology, 49.6 percent of these cases were blamed on incomplete examinations and poor organization of medical certifications, while 34.7 percent were blamed on unqualified doctors and their disregard for outlined certification procedures. There would appear to be considerable overlap between these categories. The remaining 15.7 percent of cases were not explained.

84. For a discussion of this phenomenon that extends beyond the realm of military manpower policy, see Timothy Colton, *Commissars, Commanders and Civilian Authority: The Structure of Soviet Military Politics* (Cambridge, Mass.: Harvard University Press, 1979), 127–135.

85. *Moskovskii universitet,* 7 January 1988, p. 6. Steven W. Popper, "The Economic Cost of Soviet Military Manpower Requirements," *RAND Project AIR FORCE Report, R-3659-AF* (1989), 41, suggests that students from some other Moscow University faculties may have been called up as early as the fall of 1984.

86. Gosteleradio, "Ukhodit v armiiu student" [The student goes off to the army] (television Broadcast 17 November 1988). This documentary featured several Moscow University students discussing the draft.

87. *Moskovskii universitet,* 7 January 1988, 6.

88. "Why Do We Have So Few Genuinely Educated People?" *Literaturnaia gazeta,* 13 May 1987, 12.

89. *Krasnaia zvezda,* 22 May 1987, 2.

90. *Literaturnaia gazeta,* 3 June 1987, 11.

91. For summaries of this counterattack see Stephen Foye, "Students and the Soviet Military," *Report on the USSR,* 29 September 1989, and Popper, 40–42. I have also benefited from an untitled manuscript by Roth Herlinger, Dartmouth College, Summer 1989.

92. Iazov's speech to the groups was broadcast on the Central Television program "I Serve the Soviet Union," 16 January 1988; parts are cited in Jones, "Social Change and Civil-Military Relations," 276, and Herlinger, manuscript.

93. See, for instance, the article by B. Raushchenbakh in *Argumenty i fakty,* no. 30 (1988).

94. This is mentioned in MIK: "Committee of Soldiers' Mothers Appeal to Congress of Peoples' Deputies et als." (29 May 1989).

95. Kathleen Mihalisko, "Report from Kiev University on the Future of Student Military Obligations," *Report on the USSR,* no. 4 (1989). Actually, the main target of students' wrath was not the military per se, but the university's military kafedra and its Komsomol committee. The Kiev University Komsomol committee—which I had the pleasure of meeting in March 1989— was hardly in the forefront of perestroika, and their initial criticisms of boycott organizers (they were accused of "turning their backs on the memory of those who fell in Afghanistan") subjected them to considerable scorn in succeeding weeks.

96. Aleksandr Solomkin (Secretary for Student Affairs, Moscow city Komsomol committee), interview by author, Moscow, 27 February 1990. Mihalisko ("Report from Kiev University") notes evidence of protests against or boycotts of military preparedness classes in the Baltics, Irkutsk, Leningrad, Moscow, Voronezh, Tashkent, Odessa, Kiev, and other cities. The protests were not unlike the wave of opposition to ROTC programs that swept across U.S. college campuses, and, like those protests, were often appeased by concessions at the university level.

97. MIK: Markovskii (Deputy Chief of Main Administration of Ministry of Defense), Letter to Maria Kirbasova (315/4/1575), 31 October 1988.

98. Chapter 4 discussed how local Komsomol committees after 1987 began to transfer their assets to commercial activities. This is one example of how these assets, now under the control of local committees, were sometimes diverted to expressly political activities. Office space, telephones, meeting rooms, stationery, and printing capabilities—all of which Komsomol committees had in abundance—were extremely valuable to fledgling political organizations in the late Soviet period.

99. Gorbachev, *Perestroika and Youth,* 19.

100. M. A. Moiseev in *Argumenty i fakty,* no. 15 (1989): 1–2.

101. A Demidov in *Krasnaia zvezda,* 15 December 1988, 2. The assertion that the student draft was always considered to be temporary was actually made several years earlier by Gennadii Iagodin, the Minister of Higher Education. In an interview with the Moscow University newspaper *(Moskovskii universitet)* published 15 November 1986, he called the call-up of students "a temporary phenomenon, but one without which we cannot get by for now." No defense ministry official had conceded this point, however, during the year-long debate preceding Demidov's article; instead, the need for military service to be truly universal was a major assertion.

102. *Krasnaia zvezda,* 8 January 1989, 2.

103. *Izvestiia,* 12 April 1989, 1.

104. In addition to cited sources, this account of this March–July 1989 campaign draws on several interviews with Maria Kirbasova, Chair, Committee of Soldiers' Mothers, and Victor Minin, Deputy Chair, USSR Supreme Soviet Committee on Youth Affairs, in Moscow during March and April 1991. See also Kirbasova's interview in *Armiia i obshchestvo* (Moscow: Progress, 1990), 229–235.

105. MIK: "Committee of Soldiers' Mothers Appeal to Congress of Peoples' Deputies et als." (29 May 1989).

106. According to Kirbasova, this was Sovnarkom Decree No. 996, of 15 September 1943.

107. This was reported to me by several individuals in Moscow.

108. The poll of 263 student-soldiers was conducted 25 June. The results were tabulated and listed respondents' names, institutes and assignments.

109. The debate was published in the *Verkhovnyi sovet SSSR, Pervaia sessiia, Biulleten' No. 9*, 3 July 1989, 71–103.

110. Ibid., 72.

111. Ibid., 98. This particularly innovative idea, suggesting just how malleable medical deferments were perceived to be, came from Veniamin Iarin. Iarin later served briefly on Gorbachev's Presidential Council.

112. Ibid., 101.

113. *Verkhovnyi sovet SSSR, Pervaia sessiia, Biulleten' No. 22*, 11 July 1989, 125–126.

114. See Foye, "Students and the Soviet Military," 8–9.

115. Gosobrazovaniia Chairman Gennadi Iagodin was forced to sign a special order adjusting admissions targets for 1989 to relieve overcrowding and providing special budget supplements to cover stipends and other expenses associated with returning students (Gosobrazovaniia Order No. 593, of 18 July 1989). The impact on schools is also discussed in *Poisk*, no. 12 (1989).

116. G. Krivosheev, "O vseobshchnosti voinskoi sluzhby," *Krasnaia zvezda*, 31 August 1989, 2.

117. Ibid.

118. See Foye, "Students and the Soviet Military," 9–11, for a review of this class- and social equality–based campaign to preserve the principle of universal service.

119. See, for instance, *Argumenty i fakty*, no. 30 (1989).

120. Kirbasova interview, April 1991.

121. MIK: M. Moiseev (First Deputy Minister of Defense), Letter to Committee of Soldiers' Mothers (14 December 1989).

122. A. Vinogradov, letter to V. I. Semukha.

123. MIK: A. Zav'ialov (Deputy Chief, Construction and Troop Billeting, Ministry of Defense), letter to Iu. Borodin, Chmn., Supreme Soviet Committee on Public Health (231/1372) (17 October 1990).

124. Nechaev letter to Semukha. Nechaev was not saying that 97–98 percent of the *draft pool* was healthy, but rather that 2–3 percent of those who were *actually drafted* and sent to military units were not healthy.

125. The amendments were contained in Ministry of Defense Order 317 of 1 September 1989 and took effect with the fall 1989 draft. Among the changes made in this order was the reclassification of nine disorders, including asthma and dislocated retina, from "fit for noncombat duty" to "not fit for duty in peacetime; fit for noncombat duty in wartime." The category of "fit for noncombat duty" [in peacetime] was retained.

126. Zaika letter to Semukha.

127. *Verkhovnyi sovet SSSR, Biulleten' No. 9*, 73. Emphasis added. The 1988 figure, cited earlier in this chapter, was 55,000.

128. Ibid., p. 72.

129. MIK: V. Zolotukhin, "Report on the work of chairman of Subcommittee on Army Youth (of Supreme Soviet Committe on Youth Affairs), Maj. V. Zolotukhin, in Vologodskaia oblast' (September 1990)."

130. There were many accounts of this situation in the Soviet press of this time. For some examples, see Sergei Kaledin, "Stroibat," *Novyi mir*, no. 4 (1989); Karim Barkhiev, "Gruz 200," *Komsomol'skaia pravda*, 9 September 1990.

131. MIK: N. Shliaga (Chief, Main Political Administration of the Soviet Army and Navy), letter to M. I. Kirbasova, Chairman, Committee of Soldiers' Mothers (No. 172/5325) (6 September 1990).

132. Many of these protests ended up at the Supreme Soviet. The Smolensk and Ivanovo regional governments, for instance, protested to the newly elected Russian Parliament that the decision would force the suspension of post-Chernobyl cleanup activities (Smolensk) and the closing of a construction materials plant (Ivanovo) (MIK: A. V. Rutskoi, Memo from RSFSR Supreme Soviet Committee on Veterans' and War Invalids' Affairs to USSR Supreme Soviet Committee on Defense and State Security [No. 10-1] [10 August 1990]). The Chairman of a Housing Construction trust in Perm obl. complained that the 260 military builders working for him were irreplaceable because "Young people no longer aspire to the profession of builder, and experienced workers are all leaving for cooperatives" (MIK: A. Kerelov, letter to USSR Supreme Soviet Committee on Defense and State Security [No. 750] [27 June 1990]).

133. *Sovetskaia rossiia*, 16 November 1990, 1.

134. According to Kirbasova, a Lithuanian member of the KSM obtained copies of Ministry of Defense Orders 260 and 317, governing medical classifications, from a member of one Vilnius draft board in 1989 in return for a bottle of cognac. Since the orders were not classified "secret," it was not illegal to reproduce them. I obtained copies of these orders from Kirbasova.

135. V. A. Bespalov, Military Commissar (voenkom) for the city of Moscow, Komitet po molodezhnoi politike Verkhovnogo soveta SSSR, unpublished meeting stenogram, 4 April 1991. Though the trend indicated by these figures is clear, their exact meaning is more ambiguous. Bespalov suggested that 133,000 youth in Moscow were "subject to the draft" in 1990 but that only 22 percent were drafted. The rest received deferments, including 59 percent for attending VUZy. In the same testimony, however, he gave a figure of 82 percent to describe those "fit for military service" and suggested that 10,455 were unfit (versus 4,706 in 1988). The absolute total of 10,455, however, represents just 8 percent of the 133,000 draft contingent, leaving it unclear where he derived the 18 percent figure.

     Two weeks after giving this testimony, Bespalov repeated the 22 percent figure at a meeting I attended at the USSR Supreme Soviet (19 April 1991, organized by the Committee of Soldiers' Mothers). When I asked him to clarify it, he indicated that it did not include conscripts deemed unfit—that is, 78 percent of those *fit to serve* received educational or family hardship deferrals. It may also have included medical deferments granted at the time of call-up rather than at the time of registration, since that latter group was removed from the draftee rolls and therefore no longer "subject to call-up." This interpretation makes the 10,455 and 18 percent figures describing "unfit to serve" harder to reconcile, however, since the contingent of "registered" draft-age youth from which they were removed would therefore have been *larger* than 133,000. Perhaps the most important single moral to draw from this confusing set of figures is that the Ministry of Defense was eager to portray the status of manpower supply in the worst possible light, to support their claim that too many deferments were being granted.

136. See Stephen Foye, "Baltic Nationalism and the Soviet Military," *Report on the USSR* 1, no. 26 (1989): 22–27.

137. The Lithuanian law was passed 29 September 1989. The subsequent order, issued by the Presidium of the Supreme Soviet, was issued 23 October 1989.

138. On the background of this movement, see Elizabeth Fuller, "Georgians Win Concessions on Military Service," *Report on the USSR,* 9 July 1989, 20. The protests continued into the fall, as evidenced by a report in FBIS SOV-89-214, 7 November 1989.

139. This is taken from the testimony of Grigorii Krivosheev, Chief of the Organization-Mobilization Administration of the Soviet General Staff, before a committee of the Supreme Soviet (Komitet po molodezhnoi politike, Meeting stenogram, 4 April 1991). See also Stephen Foye, "Growing Antimilitary Sentiment in the Republics," *Report on the USSR* 1, no. 50 (1989): 22–27.

140. Krivosheev testimony, Komitet po molodezhnoi politike, meeting stenogram, 4 April 1991.

141. *Krasnaia zvezda,* 29 October 1989, 4; and *Leninskoe znamia,* 15 October 1989, 2.

142. Krivosheev testimony, Komitet po molodezhnoi politike, meeting stenogram, 4 April 1991.

143. Alternative draft laws were passed in 1990 by Latvia on 1 March, Estoniia on 11 April, and Armeniia on 3 May. Even Uzbekistan ordered voenkomaty to stop sending conscripts to military-construction units outside Central Asia. Ukraine on 16 July declared its right to have its own armed forces.

144. G. Krivosheev, "Draftees, Picketers, Refuseniks," *Pravitel'stvennyi vestnik,* no. 48 (1990): 12.

145. "Begletsy," *Krasnaia zvezda,* 4 January 1991, 1. As early as the fall of 1989, Moscow prosecutors had effectively halted the prosecution of draft dodgers. See I. Cherniak, *Komsomol'skaia pravda,* 28 November 1989, 1, 4.

146. I do not mean to assert here that the activities described in this subsection were wholly motivated by alarm over the state of the draft. The military's position was under attack in several areas, and the dismemberment of the country had more profound effects than simply disruption of the draft. Nevertheless, as I discuss here, draft noncompliance did serve as a catalyst for military moves in the Baltics, and they were a prominent theme in Iazov's June 1991 address to the Supreme Soviet, now recognized as a foreshadowing of the August 1991 coup. Military officials were certainly aware that any role the army wished to play in future politics would require a reliable conscript supply, if only to ensure the continued existence of the army as an institution.

147. *Molodezh' estonii,* 9 January 1991, 1. Furthermore, voenkomaty were unable to provide army officials with lists of youth in "alternative service" because ministries employing them had refused to share these data.

148. Kirbasova interview, 12 April 1991. This was confirmed to me by one Moskovskii komsomolets journalist who had helped organize the 1989 KSM event in Gorkii Park. As a result, many newspapers shifted military stories to female reporters.

149. *Komsomol'skaia pravda,* 7 March 1991, reported on one young city council deputy representing students in Ufa. He had defeated a Deputy Interior Minister for his seat and promptly found himself flunked out of the Aviation Institute and subject to immediate call-up.

150. See the letter from L. Belousova, *Argumenty i fakty,* no. 15 (1991): 5, and Iu. Mamchur, "Golos materi," *Krasnaia zvezda,* 24 November 1990, 2.

151. See Stephen Foye, "Student Deferments and Military Manpower Short-ages," *Report on the USSR,* 2 August 1991, 5–9. Iagodin's future remained

cloudy for several months, until he emerged as one of the few Cabinet members to vote against the emergency resolution that accompanied the August coup.

152. Both plans were published in *Pravitel'stvennyi vestnik*, no. 48 (1990): 5–12.

153. Krivosheev testimony, Komitet po molodezhnoi politike, meeting stenogram, 4 April 1991.

154. Ibid. The deputy was A. P. Viltsans.

155. Ibid., emphasis added.

156. Petr Korotich, Deputy Head of the Medical Service, Ministry of Defense, speech to meeting organized by Committee of Soldiers' Mothers, USSR Supreme Soviet, Moscow, 19 April 1991.

157. Iazov's speech was described in the 17 June issue of *Sovetskaia rossiia*, quoted in Serge Schmemann, "Soviet Rightists See a Nation Run Amok," *New York Times*, 28 June 1991. Iazov was giving figures before the conclusion of the spring draft season. Table 6.2 suggests either that the spring draft was not as bad as Iazov suggests or that republican military commissariats had found some way to "improve" the statistics.

158. This was first revealed by Ia. Zasurskii in *Komsomolskaia pravda*, 10 July 1991, 1.

159. See G. Krivosheev, "This Difficult Spring Draft," *Krasnaia zvezda*, 18 July 1991, 1; and V. Vyzhutovich, "The Trumpet Blows," *Izvestiia*, 15 July 1991, 1.

160. *Krasnaia zvezda*, 19 July 1991, 1.

161. *Rossiiskaia gazeta*, 1 August 1991.

162. *Izvestiia*, 2 September 1992.

163. *Moskovskii komsomolets*, 10 July 1992.

164. *RFE/RL Research Report* 1, no. 43, 63.

165. The law was passed on 11 February and published in *Krasnaia zvezda*, 27 February 1993.

166. In a speech at the Russian Defense Ministry on 14 November 1994, Yeltsin called contract-based service "ineffective" (RFE-RL Daily Digest, 15 November 1994). Nevertheless, during the 1996 Presidential election campaign, he promised to create an all-professional military by the end of the century, abolishing the draft altogether.

167. According to the Russian Ministry of Defense, in the winter 1995 draft only one in five men called up was actually being drafted. Most of the rest were taking advantage of one of twenty-one available exemptions. Given that call-up rate, the military warned, the draft would only induct 60 percent of the men it needed (OMRI Daily Digest, 21 February 1995). See also John W. R. Lepingwell, "Is the Military Disintegrating from Within?" *RFE/RL Research Report* 2, no. 25 (1993): 9–16.

168. Yeltsin restored some of these deferments (for some graduate students and graduates planning state service) when he signed new conscription legislation on 30 April 1995. How these exceptions to the law will work in practice remains unclear. The Defense Ministry proceeded with immediate plans to draft students graduating from college in 1995, including many who had thought their ROTC experience exempted them from the call-up (OMRI Daily Digest, 2 May 1995).

169. In January 1995, for instance, the President of Chuvashia ordered that no conscripts from his republic (an integral part of the Russian Federation) be used in the military action in Chechnya. It is unclear whether this order carried any weight.

170. There is presently little data available on progress of the draft in most non-Russian regions. Evidence from Ukraine and Belarus, however, suggests that desertion rates and evasion levels are comparable to those in Russia—unacceptably high (FBIS-SOV-93–034, 23 February 1993, 43; and FBIS-SOV-93–200, 19 October 1993, 61). For some preliminary analysis, see Stephen Foye, "Rebuilding the Russian Military," *RFE/RL Research Report* 1, no. 44 (1992): 51–56; "Military and Security Notes," *RFE/RL Research Report* 1, no. 45 (1992): 60; and the special section on "New States, New Armies" in *RFE/RL Research Report* 2, no. 25 (1993): 60–88.

171. Though this chapter focuses on the conscription system, the declining prestige of the Soviet army as a whole certainly contributed to its diminished reputation for punishing draft defiance. In addition to revelations about military failure in Afghanistan, 1989 saw the Soviet army standing on the sidelines as Communist regimes were toppled across Eastern Europe.

7. The Breakdown of Hierarchy: Comparative Perspectives

1. Chapter 4 did not examine in detail the control of local Party organizations over local Komsomol organizations. While there was certainly some "dual subordination," I found little evidence in Komsomol records of conflict as a result of this potentially divided loyalty. Most likely, this was because local Party officials made few demands on local Komsomol officials, besides providing warm bodies for occasional functions. Many Komsomol officials were laterally promoted to local Party work.

2. "On Designated Contract-Based Preparation of Specialists with Higher and Specialized Professional Education," *Biulleten' Gosudarstvennogo komiteta rossiiskoi federatsii po vysshemu obrazovaniiu*, no. 11 (1995): 1–5.

3. The question of defining bureaucrats' interests is most problematic for the case of conscription. The fundamental issue is whether they were "cap-

tured" by societal groups—draftees or their parents—or made preserving their jobs their top priority. If the former, then a purge of voenkomat officials should have accompanied the defense ministry's reassertion of its authority; if the latter, then turnover rates should have been much lower. Unfortunately, a study of turnover rates at the voenkomat level is beyond the scope of this study.

4. Phil Roeder, *Red Sunset* (Princeton, N.J.: Princeton University Press, 1993), 246.

5. This point is central to Terry Moe's discussion of how U.S. government agencies are sometimes "crippled" by design. See Terry M. Moe, "The Politics of Bureaucratic Structure," in *Can the Government Govern?* ed. John E. Chubb and Paul E. Peterson (Washington, D.C.: Brookings, 1989), 267–329.

6. For standard accounts of the early Gorbachev reforms, see Ed Hewett, *Reforming the Soviet Economy* (Washington, D.C.: Brookings, 1988), Anders Åslund, *Gorbachev's Struggle for Economic Reform* (Ithaca, N.Y.: Cornell University Press, 1989), and *Milestones in Glasnost and Perestroika. Volume 2: The Economy,* ed. Ed Hewett and Victor Winston (Washington, D.C.: Brookings, 1991). In moving to decentralize the economy, Gorbachev was essentially following the advice of most Western economists.

7. Simon Johnson and Heidi Kroll, "Managerial Strategies for Spontaneous Privatization," *Soviet Economy* 7, no. 2 (1991), 281–316. The process was also observed and documented in East Central Europe (particularly Poland and Hungary), where the obvious economic advantages it accorded the political ruling class earned it the label "nomenklatura privatization."

8. Johnson and Kroll, "Managerial Strategies." See also Stephen Fortescue, "The Restructuring of Soviet Industrial Ministries Since 1985," in *Market Socialism or the Restoration of Capitalism,* ed. Anders Åslund (New York: Cambridge University Press, 1992), 121–141.

9. Many of these banks were also created by Komsomol funds, as noted in Chapter 4. See Joel Hellman, "Breaking the Bank: Building Market Institutions in the Former Soviet Union" (Ph.D. diss., Columbia University, 1993); and Juliet Ellen Johnson, "The Russian Banking System: Institutional Responses to the Market Transition," *Europe-Asia Studies* 46, n. 6 (1994): 971–995.

10. These policy concessions by Russian policy makers, consisting chiefly of expanded opportunities for management buyouts of privatizing firms, are described in Michael McFaul, "State Power, Institutional Change, and the Politics of Privatization in Russia," *World Politics* 47, no. 2 (1995), and Maxim Boycko and Andrei Shleifer, "The Politics of Russian Privatization," in Olivier Blanchard, Maxim Boycko, et al., *Post-Communist Reform: Pain and Progress* (Cambridge, Mass.: MIT Press, 1993).

11. Such a purchase fund is a particularly concrete example of the "safety margin" sought by agents, as discussed in Chapter 2.

12. Louis Uchitelle, "How to Take Over the Store," *New York Times*, 2 August 1992, E7.

13. Donna Bahry, "The Union Republics and Contradictions in Gorbachev's Economic Reform," *Soviet Economy* 7, no. 3 (1991): 215–255. In this discussion, "republics" connotes the fifteen Union Republics of the USSR, while "regions" connotes territorial-administrative divisions like oblasts, krais, raions, and so forth.

14. Daniel Berkowitz and Beth Mitchneck, "Fiscal Decentralization in the Soviet Economy," *Comparative Economic Systems* 34 (Summer 1992): 1–18.

15. Bahry, "The Union Republics," 247; Berkowitz and Mitchneck, "Fiscal Decentralization," 2. A budget for 1991 was eventually approved but rendered moot after revenue projections proved meaningless (see John Tedstrom, "Soviet Fiscal Federalism in a Time of Crisis," *Report on the USSR* 3, no. 31 [1991]).

16. This practice was also introduced in the Komsomol, but only after the "bank run" had already been triggered by internal fiscal reforms. Since Komsomol officials faced a "natural" term limit in the form of age ceilings for most officials, the impact of elections on incentives was less severe.

17. These reforms—which involved allowing primary organizations to retain 50 percent of their income from membership dues but also mandated lower dues rates—are discussed in Graeme Gill, *The Collapse of a Single Party System: The Disintegration of the CPSU* (New York: Cambridge University Press, 1994), 155.

18. The budgetary problems of the Party are reviewed in *Izvestiia TsK KPSS*, no. 8 (1990): 91–98. On budgets and also membership, see Elizabeth Teague and Vera Tolz, "CPSU R.I.P." *Report on the USSR* 3, no. 47 (1991), and Gill, *Collapse of a Single Party System*, 154–160.

19. The story of the Party's massive "ruble launderette," based on documents from the Central Committee archives, is described in Chapter 6 of Stephen Handelman, *Comrade Criminal* (New Haven, Conn.: Yale University Press, 1995). Though these documents cover the Party's efforts to shield Central Committee funds, the fate of regional Party assets may never be known. The Party's treasurer, Nikolai Kruchina, committed suicide in the wake of the August 1991 coup.

20. On the KGB under Gorbachev and Yeltsin, see J. Michael Waller, *Secret Empire* (Boulder, Colo.: Westview, 1994); Amy Knight, *Spies without Cloaks* (Princeton, N.J.: Princeton University Press, 1996); Alexander Rahr, "The Revival of a Strong KGB," *RFE/RL Research Report* 2, no. 20 (1993); Jeremy Azrael, *The KGB in Kremlin Politics* (RAND/UCLA JRS-05, February 1989);

and Alexander J. Motyl, "Policing Perestroika: The Indispensable KGB," *Harriman Institute Forum* 2, no. 8 (1989).

21. See Handelman, *Comrade Criminal,* on the KGB's "entrepreneurial" activities.

22. The literature on Chinese reform is vast. In this account, I have drawn heavily on Susan L. Shirk, *The Political Logic of Economic Reform in China* (Berkeley, Calif.: University of California Press, 1993); Gordon White, *Riding the Tiger: The Politics of Economic Reform in Post-Mao China* (Stanford, Calif.: Stanford University Press, 1993); *Changing Central-Local Relations in China: Reform and State Capacity,* ed. Jia Hao and Lin Zhimin (Boulder, Colo.: Westview, 1994); and Victor Nee, "Organizational Dynamics of Market Transition: Hybrid Forms, Property Rights and Mixed Economy in China," *Administrative Science Quarterly* 37 (1992); as well as other works cited specifically below.

23. *The Economist,* 6 November 1993.

24. See, for instance, Shirk, *Political Logic,* 175, and *The Economist,* 6 November 1993, 32.

25. Dali L. Yang, "Reform and the Restructuring of Central-Local Relations," in *China Deconstructs,* ed. David S. G. Goodman and Gerald Segal, (New York: Routledge, 1994); see also *New York Times,* 23 November 1993, 1.

26. See White, *Riding the Tiger,* 170–197, on CCP reforms.

27. Nee defines hybrids as organizational forms that "use resources and/or governance structures from more than one existing organization." ("Organizational Dynamics," 2).

28. Ibid., 11.

29. Jean Oi, "Fiscal Reform and the Foundations of Local State Corporatism in China," *World Politics* 45 (1992): 100.

30. David Granick, *Chinese State Enterprises: A Regional Property Rights Analysis* (Chicago: University of Chicago Press, 1990), 48. Zhao Suisheng also traces the roots of local powers into the pre-Deng era, describing a pattern of decentralization and recentralization from 1957 through the 1970s ("China's Central Local Relationship: A Historical Perspective," in *Changing Central-Local Relations*).

31. Shirk, *Political Logic,* 150, fn. 2.

32. Prior to the November 1993 CCP Plenum, for instance, a significant number of provincial Party secretaries and governors were either rotated or retired, including the Party secretary of Jiangsu, China's richest province (see Yang, "Reform and the Restructuring").

33. Nee, "Organizational Dynamics," 13.

34. Shirk, *Political Logic,* 196. The term "quasi-ownership" is appropriate because the hybrid structure of the new rural enterprises assigned property rights

to different organizations rather than individuals. This position was advantageous to either a private businessman, who lacked the local officials' control over supply networks, interregional trade, and tax rates, or to purely governmental actors, who collected fewer rents.

35. A similar logic may explain why Soviet trade unions showed few signs of hierarchical breakdown. Officials in the trade unions had control over the distribution of benefits from the Pension Funds, which were (and still are) sizable. This begs the question, however, of why these Pension Funds were less susceptible to looting than, say, Komsomol accounts. I am not sufficiently familiar with trade union regulations to answer this, but I suspect the loopholes that permitted Komsomol committees to transfer funds to NTTMs and MZhKs—and thus convert "credit" rubles to "cash"— were not replicated for organizations like the unions.

36. See Christine P. Wong, "Fiscal Reform and Local Industrialization" *Modern China* 18, no. 2 (1992): 216ff.

37. This later came to be known as the Contract (or Enterprise) Responsibility System.

38. Barry Naughton, "Implications of the State Monopoly over Industry and Its Relaxation," *Modern China* 18, no. 1 (1992): 35. The point is reinforced by Christine P. W. Wong, "Central-Local Relations in an Era of Fiscal Decline: The Paradox of Fiscal Decentralization in Post-Mao China," *The China Quarterly* 128 (1991): 691–715.

39. Andrew Walder, "Corporate Organization and Local Government Property Rights in China," in *Changing Political Economies: Privatization in Post-Communist and Reforming States*, ed. Vedat Milor (Boulder, Colo.: Lynn Reiner, 1994). In the formulation advanced in Chapter 2, however, hierarchical authority is simply presented as a form of bilateral contracting that is, a chain of agency contracts. In either Walder's formulation or mine, however, the critical question is whether these "contracts" can be enforced by either actor.

40. Walder, "Corporate Organization," 64.

41. The center's share of tax revenues actually grew in the early 1980s and stabilized at about 30 percent (adjusted for borrowing) after the introduction of fiscal contracting in 1987. Though local governments tried various schemes to minimize their fiscal obligations to the center, they continued to "share up" revenues to Beijing. See Roy Bahl and Christine Wallich, "Intergovernmental Fiscal Relations in China," Policy Research Working Paper WPS 863, The World Bank (February 1992); Wong, "Central-Local Relations," esp. 700–706; and Jia Hao and Wang Mingxia, "Market and State," in *Changing Central-Local Relations*, esp. 49–50.

42. Dali L. Yang. "Policy Credibility and Macroeconomic Control in China,"

Paper presented at the American Political Science Association Annual Meetings, Washington, D.C., August–September 1993; and idem., "Reform and the Restructuring." In a review of Shirk's book *(Political Logic),* Yang criticizes Shirk for underestimating Beijing's capacity to reassert central controls in times of crisis; see "Governing China's Transition to the Market: Institutional Incentives, Politicians' Choices, and Unintended Consequences," *World Politics* 48, no. 3 (1996): 424–452. On episodes of recentralization, see also Yingyi Qian and Barry R. Weingast, "Beyond Decentralization: Preserving Federalism with Chinese Characteristics," manuscript, Stanford University, July 1994; and Jia Hao and Lin Zhimin, "Introduction," in *Changing Central-Local Relations.*

43. Nee and Lian make a similar point, arguing that political reform in the Soviet Union proceeded "too quickly, so that monitoring capacity weakened greatly"; this assessment is wholly consistent with the model presented here (Victor Nee and Peng Lian, "Sleeping with the Enemy: A Dynamic Model of Declining Political Commitment in State Socialism," *Theory and Society* 23 [1994]: 253–296).

44. In particular, Chinese authorities retained centralized control over heavy industry, which made up a far smaller share of the Chinese economy than the Soviet economy. Barry Naughton has called the Chinese approach "growing out of the Plan."

45. Kenneth Lieberthal, "Introduction: The 'Fragmented Authoritarianism Model' and Its Limitations," in *Bureaucracy, Politics and Decision Making in Post-Mao China,* ed. Kenneth Lieberthal and David Lampton (Berkeley, Calif.: University of California Press, 1992), 12.

46. On these new information-processing capacities, see Nina P. Halpern, "Information Flows and Policy Coordination in the Chinese Bureaucracy," in *Bureaucracy, Politics and Decision Making,* 125–150; and Yasheng Huang, "Information, Bureaucracy, and Economic Reforms in China and the Soviet Union," *World Politics* 47, no. 1 (1994).

47. See Oi, "Fiscal Reform," 114.

48. This point is based largely on Wong's analysis in "Central-Local Relations."

49. See, for example, Alan Gelb, Gary Jefferson, and Inderjit Singh, "Can Communist Economies Transform Gradually: The Experience of China," in *NBER Macroeconomics Annual 1993,* ed. Olivier Blanchard and Stanley Fischer (Cambridge, Mass.: MIT Press, 1993); John McMillan and Barry Naughton, "How to Reform a Planned Economy: Lessons from China," *Oxford Review of Economic Policy* 8, no. 1 (1992): 130–143; Ronald I. McKinnon, "Gradual versus Rapid Liberalization in Socialist Economies: The Problem of Macroeconomic Control" (including comments by Anders Åslund and Jacek Rostowski), *Proceedings of the World Bank Annual Conference on Development Eco-*

nomics, 1993, 63–107; Jeffrey Sachs and W. T. Woo, "Structural Factors in the Economic Reforms of China, Eastern Europe and the Former Soviet Union," *Economic Policy* 9 (April 1994): 101–145; Wing Thye Woo, "The Art of Reforming Centrally Planned Economies: Comparing China, Poland, and Russia," *Journal of Comparative Economies* 18 (June 1994): 276–308.

50. Gelb, Jefferson, and Singh, "Can Communist Economies Transform," 128. They refer to this, rather imprecisely, as "perestroika" before "glasnost'." Such a formulation implies that this separation and sequencing of political and economic reform is the result of explicit choices by central authorities.

51. An exception is Minxin Pei, who argues that "instead of reinvigorating [existing institutions of the communist party-state] through adaptation, reform sapped their vitality, reduced their power, corrupted their integrity, and accelerated their decay" (*From Reform to Revolution: The Demise of Communism in China and the Soviet Union* [Cambridge, Mass.: Harvard University Press, 1994], 205). Pei's dynamic of institutional decline is not endogenous, however, as he argues that in both China and Russia "the principal forces of change, whether economic or political, came from society." At least for the Russian case, the data presented in this study fail to support that conclusion.

52. Huang, "Information, Bureaucracy, and Economic Reforms," 134.

53. Wong, "Central-Local Relations," 711–713. Chinese reforms have also been criticized for unleashing massive corruption, but this was also characteristic of the Soviet reforms.

8. Conclusions and Extensions: Control and Collapse in Hierarchies

1. Max Weber, *Economy and Society*, vol. 2, ed. Guenther Roth and Claus Wittich (Berkeley, Calif.: University of California Press, 1978), 953, emphasis added.

2. Chester Barnard, *The Functions of the Executive* (Cambridge, Mass.: Harvard University Press, 1938; reprint, 1968), 5.

3. Edward Luttwak, *The Grand Strategy of the Roman Empire* (Baltimore: Johns Hopkins University Press, 1976), 49. I am grateful to Ron Rogowski for suggesting this example.

4. Ibid., 4.

5. Edward Gibbon, *The Decline and Fall of the Roman Empire*, Chapter 31.

6. Herbert Kaufman, "Collapse as an Organizational Problem," in *The Collapse of Ancient States and Civilizations*, ed. Norman Yoffee and George Cowgill (Tucson, Ariz.: University of Arizona Press, 1988), 228.

7. See, for instance, Shmuel Eisenstadt, *Political Systems of Empires* (London: Free Press of Glencoe, 1963).

8. Preparations for a transition would have both negative and positive elements. Negative measures include refraining from any actions (like suppressing unarmed demonstrators) that might be punished in a wave of posttransition retroactive justice. Positive measures include "nomenklatura privatization" and other attempts to seize the assets of the old regime while they are still within reach.

9. Joseph Tainter, *The Collapse of Complex Societies* (New York: Cambridge University Press, 1988).

10. See for instance Joel Migdal, *Strong Societies and Weak States* (Princeton, N.J.: Princeton University Press, 1988).

11. See ibid., and *Bringing the State Back In*, ed. Peter Evans, Dietrich Rueschemeyer, and Theda Skocpol (New York: Cambridge University Press, 1985).

12. For classic discussions, see Peter Evans, "The State as Problem and Solution: Predation, Embedded Autonomy and Structural Change," in *The Politics of Economic Adjustment*, ed. Stephan Haggard and Robert R. Kaufman, 139–181, as well as Alfred Stepan, *State and Society: Peru in Comparative Perspective* (Princeton, N.J.: Princeton University Press, 1978).

13. Peter Evans, in his discussion of "embedded autonomy," is careful to portray the relationship between state capacity and autonomy as complex and far from uniform. This is especially true if one contrasts predatory and developmental states; in the former, capacity and autonomy seem more loosely linked ("The State as Problem and Solution").

14. See, for instance, Stephan Haggard and Robert R. Kaufman, *The Political Economy of Democratic Transitions* (Princeton, N.J.: Princeton University Press, 1995); and Adam Przeworski, *Democracy and the Market* (New York: Cambridge University Press, 1991), especially Chapter 4.

15. On empirical versus juridical statehood, see Robert H. Jackson and Carl G. Rosberg, "Why Africa's Weak States Persist," *World Politics* 35, no. 1 (1982): 1–24.

16. Lisa Anderson, "The State in the Middle East and North Africa," *Comparative Politics* 20, no. 1 (1987): 12.

17. See for instance Robert Klitgaard, *Controlling Corruption* (Berkeley, Calif.: University of California Press, 1988).

18. For Chechen links to organized crime and the corruption of the republic's administration see Stephen Handelman, *Comrade Criminal* (New Haven, Conn.: Yale University Press, 1995), esp. Chapter 13. See also Jack Matlock, "The Chechen Tragedy," *New York Review of Books*, 16 February 1995.

19. See, for example, Mathew McCubbins, Roger Noll, and Barry Weingast, "Administrative Procedures as an Instrument of Political Control," *Journal of Law, Economics and Organization* 3 (1987): 243–77; idem., "Structure and Process, Politics and Policy: Administrative Arrangements and the Political Control of Agencies," *Virginia Law Review* 75 (1989): 431–82; Barry Weingast and Mark Moran, "Bureaucratic Discretion or Congressional Control: Regulatory Policymaking by the Federal Trade Commission," *Journal of Political Economy* 91 (1983): 765–800.

20. D. Roderick Kiewiet and Mathew D. McCubbins, *The Logic of Delegation* (Chicago: University of Chicago Press, 1991), 26ff. I discussed this problem as well in Chapter 2, in the context of reassessing the treatment of authority relations in agency models where the powers of the state are being delegated.

21. The NRO's egregious mismanagement was ultimately reported to Congress in May 1996 (see Tim Weiner, "A Spy Agency Admits Accumulating $4 Billion in Secret Money," *New York Times,* 16 May 1996, A17). The NRO gained notoriety in 1994 when it revealed it was constructing a $300 million "stealth building" on the outskirts of Washington, deceiving legislators and municipal officials about the true size and nature of the complex.

22. John E. Chubb and Terry M. Moe, *Politics, Markets and America's Schools* (Washington: Brookings, 1990). Michael Lipsky reaches similar conclusions about human services, including health and welfare provision, in *Street-Level Bureaucracy: Dilemmas of the Individual in Public Services* (New York: Russell Sage Foundation, 1980). Both studies focus on problems of defining performance goals and monitoring their achievement in public bureaucracies.

23. Lipsky describes similar behavior by health and welfare case workers in *Street-Level Bureaucracy.*

24. To be clear, robustness here implies the relatively unchallenged authority of principals over agents in the bureacratic order. It does not imply efficiency; indeed, Chubb and Moe *(Politics, Markets and America's Schools)* clearly find public schools to be less efficient than their private sector counterparts in the provision of educational goods.

25. Police and prison work are particularly susceptible to problems of "arbitrary rule" at the street level. See James Q. Wilson, *Bureaucracy: What Government Agencies Do and Why They Do It* (New York: Basic Books, 1989), 326–329.

26. The Sears case is well chronicled in Donald Katz, *The Big Store* (New York: Viking, 1987). It is also discussed in Gary Miller, *Managerial Dilemmas. The Political Economy of Hierarchy* (Cambridge, Mass.: Cambridge University Press, 1992), 90–93.

27. Katz, *The Big Store,* 85.

28. The story is told in Steven Bach, *Final Cut: Dreams and Disaster in the Making of Heaven's Gate* (New York: William Morrow, 1985). For a similar tale— of Sony's problems in overseeing its Hollywood investments—see Nancy Griffith and Kim Masters, *Hit and Run* (New York: Simon and Schuster, 1996).

29. For a discussion of these center-periphery agreements, see Steven Solnick, "Federal Bargaining in Russia," *East European Constitutional Review* 4, no. 4 (1995).

30. In addition, Russian leaders have been unable to build a reputation for retaliating against defiance by regional agents of the state. Corruption is rampant, and Ministry of Finance officials continue to complain of poor tax and regulatory compliance. The debacle in Chechnya may only make matters worse, in the manner of the Soviet army's failed operation in the Baltics in 1991.

31. Maxim Boycko, Andrei Schleifer, and Robert Vishny, *Privatizing Russia* (Cambridge, Mass.: MIT Press, 1995).

32. Even the Russian federal government encountered serious obstacles in exercising its shareholder rights over Gazprom, the giant natural gas monopoly. See, for example, *Financial Times,* 17 May 1997, 7.

33. As a step in this direction, many regional administrations within the Russian federation run their own banking operations.

Glossary and Abbreviations

CPSU   Communist Party of the Soviet Union

gorkom   city committee (Party or Komsomol)

Goskomstat   State Statistical Committee

Goskomtrud   State Committee on Labor

Gosobrazovaniia   State Committee on Higher Education (before 1988: MinVUZ)

KSM   Committee of Soldiers' Mothers

MinVUZ   Ministry of Higher Education (after 1988: Gosobrazovaniia)

MGU   Moscow State University

NITs   Scientific Research Center (e.g., at VKSh)

nomenklatura   personnel lists

NTTM   Centers for Scientific-Technical Creativity of Youth (Komsomol-created
        enterprises)

obkom   oblast-level committee (Party or Komsomol)

oblast   region

otdel   department (within bureaucracy)

raikom   raion-level committee (Party or Komsomol)

raion   district (subdivision of city or oblast)

raspredelenie   job-assignments process ("distribution")

RSFSR: Russian Soviet Federation of Socialist Republics

SovMin   Council of Ministers

SSUZ   Specialized Secondary Educational Institution (plural: SSUZy)

stroibat   military construction battalion

TsA VLKSM   Central Archives of the Komsomol

tselevaia podgotovka   directed training (of students selected outside normal
        admission channels)

TsK   Central Committee

VKSh   Higher Komsomol School

VLKSM   All-Union Leninist Communist Union of Youth (Komsomol)

voenkom   military commissar

voenkomat   military commissariat (draft board)

VUZ   Higher Education Institution (plural: VUZy)

zaiavki   planning requests

Index